THE ALLOTMENT MOVEMENT
IN ENGLAND, 1793–1873

THE ALLOTMENT MOVEMENT
IN ENGLAND, 1793–1873

Jeremy Burchardt

THE ROYAL HISTORICAL SOCIETY
THE BOYDELL PRESS

First published 2002
The Royal Historical Society, London
in association with
The Boydell Press, Woodbridge
Reprinted in paperback and transferred to digital printing 2011
The Boydell Press, Woodbridge

ISBN 97 0 86193 256 6 hardback
ISBN 978 1 84383 643 8 paperback

The Boydell Press is an imprint of Boydell & Brewer Ltd
PO Box 9, Woodbridge, Suffolk IP12 3DF, UK
and of Boydell & Brewer Inc,
668 Mt Hope Avenue, Rochester, NY 14620, USA
website: www.boydellandbrewer.com

A CIP catalogue record for this book is available
from the British Library

Library of Congress Catalog Card Number 2002003673

This publication is printed on acid-free paper

FOR ARNE

The Committee, having been furnished with the above lithographed Sketch, free of expence, by a zealous friend to the Society, have great pleasure in presenting it to the Subscribers.

Frontispiece to the 1835 volume of the *Labourer's Friend Magazine*.
Reproduced by permission of the British Library (ref. PP1090).

Allotments were rarely depicted in nineteenth-century Britain: plebeian and agrarian, they were the antithesis of the picturesque. This engraving highlights the centrality of family labour to allotments: they permitted the reconstitution of the household as a working unit, so mitigating the decline of employment for rural women and children. The house in the background symbolises the domesticity it was hoped that allotments would promote.

Contents

List of Tables

Acknowledgements

One of the greatest pleasures of writing this book has been the enthusiasm that so many people, chance acquaintances as well as friends, have shown for my subject. This has been a constant source of stimulation.

In more tangible respects, I have been assisted in my research by the generosity of the Marc Fitch Fund and the University of Reading in awarding me for three years the Marc Fitch Postgraduate Research Studentship. Subsequently, the Rural History Centre at the University of Reading has provided a congenial working environment, in large part because of the generosity and helpfulness of the other members of staff.

To many librarians and archivists I also owe a considerable debt. I would particularly like to mention the staff of the Bodleian Library, the University of Reading Library, and the British Library, where I have carried out most of my research, but I also owe much to the Greater London Record Office, the National Register of Archives, the Nottinghamshire Archives Office, the Gloucestershire Record Office, the Library of the Royal Agricultural Society of England, the Library of the Royal Horticultural Society, and Balliol College Library.

Part of the research for this book was undertaken whilst I was a postgraduate, and I benefited greatly from my supervisor Ross Wordie's encouragement, his experience, and his constructive criticism. His knowledge of both the most useful primary sources and of the secondary literature on the history of the nineteenth-century countryside was immensely valuable to me in the early stages of my research. It is also a pleasure to acknowledge my large debt to Balliol College, Oxford, where I was an undergraduate and where I undertook the first year of my postgraduate studies. I have been helped in many ways by Maurice Keen, Martin Conway, Jonathan Powis, and many others at the college. But of my Oxford debts the greatest is to my undergraduate tutor, John Prest. It was his deep knowledge and understanding of nineteenth- century England that developed my own initial interest in its history, and, after supervising my first year of postgraduate research, he continued to be a never-failing source of advice, guidance, friendship and academic inspiration.

Much of the research and writing for this book took place after I joined the staff of the Rural History Centre in 1997. I am particularly grateful to Professor E. J. T. Collins, then the director of the Centre, whose alert and critical mind and knowledge of nineteenth-century agricultural practices sharpened the questions guiding my research. Professor Collins also provided detailed comments on a draft version of chapter 6. Even more valuable, however, was his consistent encouragement and academic companionship.

Amongst the many other historians and academics whose suggestions and ideas have benefited me are David Eastwood, who gave valuable editorial advice in the later stages of the writing of this book, Bethanie Afton, John

Beckett, John Broad, Jamie Bronstein, Mark Casson, Malcolm Chase, Ros Faith, Charles Feinstein, Jane Humphries, Peter Mandler, John Martin, Avner Offer, Leigh Shaw Taylor, David Stead, Joan Thirsk, Michael Turner, Maria Twist and Roy Wolfe. I am also most grateful to those historians who have sent me photocopies of their work, or other information, in particular David Martin, Sylvia Seeliger, Eric Jones, Ewen Green and Gordon Mingay. Kenneth James very kindly read the first draft of this book, and made valuable and much-appreciated comments on it.

I would particularly like to mention two outstanding historians who are no longer alive. Angus Macintyre's Oxford Special Subject on 'The ministry of Peel, 1841–6' was a formative experience for a whole generation of historians; I benefited greatly from his brilliant gifts as a teacher of nineteenth-century English history. Raine Morgan was unstinting with her time in showing me how to use the Rural History Database; only after her death, through referring to her book and using some of her teaching notes, have I discovered that the uncompromisingly high standards she set herself as a bibliographer were also applied to her teaching and to her research.

Some of the most generous help I received in the early stages of my research came from fellow postgraduate students, particularly Betty Rieden. To many who are not professional historians I also owe a considerable debt. Ted Prince, of the Tetbury Local History Society, provided me with fascinating information about the Estcourt family of Shipton Moyne, who were pioneers of the allotment movement. I am also grateful to Clive Birch of the Birmingham and District Allotments Council, Len Parnell of the National Society of Allotment and Leisure Gardeners, and P. J. Molloy of the Lower Wolvercote Allotment Association. Viginia Moody, my Oxford landlady, provided an excellent working environment and always took an intelligent and friendly interest in my research. Isabel Dakyns and John and Nick Rieden gave valuable help with the technical aspects of producing this book.

For giving me the opportunity to test out my ideas on a critical but friendly audience, I owe thanks firstly to the British Agricultural History Society, and secondly to the Oxford University Department of Continuing Education, both of which invited me to give papers at conferences organised by them. The many useful comments made on these occasions have helped to make this book better than it otherwise would have been. I am also grateful in this respect for comments made after papers given to the Economic and Social History Research Seminar at Oxford, the University of Reading History Department Research Seminar, and the University of Reading History Department Postgraduate Seminar.

Finally I would like to thank Annie Jackson, an admirably meticulous subeditor, and Christine Linehan, who has been extremely helpful throughout the writing of this book and as a result of whose careful editing it is much more readable than it would otherwise have been.

Jeremy Burchardt
June 2002

Abbreviations

AEI   Agricultural Employment Institution
AgHR   *Agricultural History Review*
Annals *Annals of Agriculture*
EcHR   *Economic History Review*
F&I   *Facts and Illustrations*
GLRO   Greater London Record Office
JRASE   *Journal of the Royal Agricultural Society of England*
LF   *Labourer's Friend*
LFM   *Labourer's Friend Magazine*
LFS   Labourer's Friend Society
RC   Royal Commission
SBCP   Society for Bettering the Conditions and Increasing the Comforts
        of the Poor
SC   Select Committee
SICLC   Society for Improving the Condition of the Labouring Classes

Measurements

40 perches = 1 rood

4 roods = 1 acre

Introduction

In 1981 David Jones pointed out that '[t]he subject of allotments deserves a major study'.[1] This book, the first full-length account of the nineteenth-century allotment movement, aspires to fill that *lacuna*. As such it benefits from the advantages and pays the penalties that derive from working in a hitherto largely unexplored field. It is not, of course, the case that allotments have been entirely neglected, but much of what has been written is from an historiographical point of view unsatisfactory. Probably the best-known discussion of the subject is David Crouch and Colin Ward's *The allotment: its landscape and culture* (1988), this fine sociological text contains only two historical chapters, covering more than a century and a half.[2] These are largely based upon the brief historical introduction to the Thorpe Report, a government departmental paper on allotments published in 1969. Turning to works by professional historians, the situation was, until very recently, little better. When research for this book commenced, the only extended discussion of the nineteenth-century allotment movement by a modern historian was an article by D. C. Barnett which appeared in a *Festschrift* for J. D. Chambers, edited by Eric Jones and Gordon Mingay, in 1967.[3] But whilst Barnett's article is a pioneering (and widely-cited) study, it has several serious deficiencies. In the first place, it stops short in 1840, an unfortunate end-point since it obscures many of the most significant aspects of the allotment movement. Secondly, Barnett did not distinguish between allotments and other forms of land provision for labourers, notably cow pastures and potato grounds. Yet the relationship between allotments and cow pastures is central to any understanding of the early history of the allotment movement, while the existence of potato grounds had an important effect on the impact of allotment provision on rural society after 1830. Allotments, cow pastures and potato grounds were radically different in their social implications; lumping them together causes confusion. Finally, Barnett's influential map of the proportion of parishes with allotments in 1833, based on the poor law commissioners' 'Rural queries', not only conflates allotments and potato grounds but extrapolates in a statistically inappropriate manner from that report to produce results which seriously distort our understanding of the

---

[1] D. Jones, 'Rural crime and protest', in G. E. Mingay (ed.), *The Victorian countryside*, ii, London 1981, 578.
[2] D. Crouch and C. Ward, *The allotment: its landscape and culture*, London 1988.
[3] D. C. Barnett, 'Allotments and the problem of rural poverty, 1780–1840', in E. L. Jones and G. E. Mingay (eds), *Land, labour, and population in the industrial revolution: essays presented to J. D. Chambers*, London 1967, 162–83.

1

numbers and distribution of allotments in this period. It was therefore plain that not only was there a need for a major new study of allotments and the allotment movement in the nineteenth century, but that in view of the very underdeveloped secondary literature, such a study would have to start by establishing basic parameters such as the timing and scale of allotment provision. This book should therefore be seen as a preliminary attempt to map out largely unexplored territory. Further research will undoubtedly add to the evidence, modify some of the judgements and refine the concepts deployed.[4]

The initial problem standing in the way of a serious study of the allotment movement was that most of the basic quantitative information about allotments in the nineteenth century had yet to be established. In particular, the number and distribution of allotments and their average rents, plot sizes, yields and profits were almost completely unknown. To overcome this problem, a database of allotment sites was constructed, containing information on more than 1,600 different allotment sites between 1793 and 1873, gathered from as wide a range of primary sources as possible.[5] Information deriving from different sources was cross-checked for consistency and unreliable records removed. Estimates for the number and distribution of allotments prior to 1873 and the large-sample data on allotment landlords, plot size, rent, yields and profits constitute some of the most important findings of this study.

It soon became apparent that the original plan of writing a history of the allotment movement covering the whole of the nineteenth century would not fit within the bounds of a single book, so this study stops short at 1873, which is the year in which the first detailed national statistics about allotments became available. A date c. 1870 makes a convenient terminus for other reasons too. It marks the end of one phase of what this study has designated the second allotment movement and the beginning of a third movement. The third allotment movement developed in a quite different direction from the first and second and requires careful and extended treatment in its own right, not least because of the voluminous printed evidence it has left behind it. For the period prior to 1873, the sources available are still

---

4 Whilst this book was being written, two articles on nineteenth-century allotments appeared in the *Economic History Review*, the first by Boaz Moselle ('Allotments, enclosure, and proletarianization in early nineteenth-century southern England', *EcHR* 2nd ser. xlviii [1995], 482–500) and the second by John Archer ('The nineteenth-century allotment: half an acre and a row', *EcHR* 2nd ser. l [1997], 21–36). Both are concerned primarily with opposition to allotments rather than with allotments *per se*, although Archer in particular has some interesting points to make about reasons for the spread of allotments. *See* appendix 3.

5 Since the several forms in which land was provided to nineteenth-century rural labourers differed significantly from each other in their attributes and consequences, it is necessary to adopt a very precise definition of what constitutes an allotment (*see* appendix 2). Many sites which could have been included in the database had a more loosely-framed definition been acceptable have therefore been excluded. In addition, some allotment sites which do fall within the definition offered in appendix 2 have been excluded for technical reasons, as explained in appendix 1.

numerous and varied but less superabundant. For the early period, that before 1830, the *Reports* of the Society for Bettering the Conditions and Increasing the Comforts of the Poor, the county reports of the Board of Agriculture and Arthur Young's *Annals of Agriculture* were particularly useful. For each of these, the complete run of the series was scanned for information relating to land provision for labourers. For the post-1830 period, the publications of the Labourer's Friend Society were an invaluable source, in particular the society's journal, variously known as *Facts and Illustrations*, the *Labourer's Friend Magazine* and the *Labourer's Friend*. The unfortunately rather scanty archives of the LFS, catalogued under the heading of the 1830 Housing Society in the Greater London Record Office, were very helpful in elucidating the internal history of the LFS and its successor, the SICLC. Extensive use was also made of the parliamentary papers. Amongst those select committees, royal commissions and other inquiries which were especially useful were the 1830–1 House of Lords' Select Committee on the Poor Laws, the 1834 Royal Commission on the Poor Laws, the 1840 Royal Commission on the Handloom Weavers, the 1843 Select Committee on the Labouring Poor, the 1843 Report of the Special Assistant Poor Law Commissioners on the Employment of Women and Children in Agriculture, the 1845 Royal Commission on the Framework Knitters, the 1867–9 Royal Commission on the Employment of Children, Young Persons, and Women in Agriculture, the 1868–9 Select Committee on the Inclosure Act, the 1873 Agricultural Returns and the 1886 Return of Allotments. Extensive use was also made of the *Gardener's Chronicle* and the *Journal of the Royal Agricultural Society of England*. These major sources were supplemented by a wide range of publications (pamphlets, periodical articles and books) dating from the late eighteenth to late nineteenth century, in addition, of course, to the relevant secondary literature.

Some of the sources listed above, notably those emanating from the LFS, the *Reports* of the SBCP and the 1843 *Report of the Select Committee on the Labouring Poor*, are clearly potentially subject to bias. By drawing on a broad selection of material, however, most of it free of suspicion, it is hoped that this problem has been contained. Evidence from the SBCP, the LFS and the 1843 Select Committee was checked against evidence from other sources where possible and careful attention has been paid to the views of those who were hostile to allotments, although, for reasons which will become clear in the course of this book, such hostility became increasingly marginal within landed society after 1830. However, by comparing data from the pro-allotment sources with that from elsewhere, it became clear that whilst the importance attached to the allotment movement varied, the hard data on matters such as rents, plot sizes, yields and profits differed very little.[6]

There are four main arguments in the book. First, a new periodisation for the nineteenth-century allotment movement is proposed. It is argued that

6   See Jeremy Burchardt, 'The allotment movement in England, 1793–1873', unpubl. PhD diss. Reading 1997, 252–7, 298–306.

there were three allotment movements between the end of the eighteenth century and the beginning of the twentieth. The first commenced shortly after the outbreak of war with France in 1793 and lasted into the first years of the new century. The second, upon which this book concentrates, emerged quite suddenly in 1830 and was a much larger and more sustained affair, surviving into the early 1850s. It was also, unlike the first allotment movement, wholly dedicated to the promotion of allotments as opposed to other forms of plebeian landholding. The third allotment movement, which developed in the wake of the 'Revolt of the Field' of the 1870s, lies mostly beyond the ambit of this study, although harbingers of its very different characteristics were already apparent in the 1850s and 1860s.

The second main argument, which derives from the evidence provided by the database, is that allotment yields were quite remarkably high – perhaps even double those obtained by farmers. Even more important, these impressive yields translated into correspondingly high profits. Allotments therefore made a much larger contribution to living standards than has hitherto been recognised – far from being a marginal phenomenon, they played a crucial part in the family economies of those of the labouring poor who had them. Furthermore, since the number of allotments rose rapidly after the inception of the second allotment movement, and since these plots were concentrated in those parts of the country where living standards were lowest, allotments significantly affected the lives of many of those who most needed them.

The third major argument derives from an attempt to provide a fundamental explanation for allotment provision, proceeding from an outermost layer of explanation, framed in terms of precipitating events, down through successive layers to an economic core. The initial layer of explanation is that both the first and second allotment movements were responses to events which disrupted the order of landed society. In the 1790s this was a severe subsistence crisis in the context of war; in 1830 it was the Captain Swing riots. There follows an attempt to explain why, while the first allotment movement failed to establish an enduring presence, the second achieved impressive results. It is argued that perhaps the most important difference between the two was that the second allotment movement succeeded in establishing an active and highly effective national organisation, the LFS. This, and its vigorous local branches, played a crucial role in bringing allotments to the attention of landowners. But successful as the LFS was, since it did not let allotments itself it was in the last resort wholly dependent on the willingness of private landowners to provide allotments. The question then becomes: why did landowners decide to let land to labourers? The temptation to seek a mono-causal explanation should be resisted, for perhaps the most important feature of allotments from a landowner's point of view was precisely the diversity of goals that could be achieved by letting them. However, just as the LFS was ultimately dependent on the landowners to provide land, so landowners were dependent on labourers being prepared to take it. The success of the allotment movement, therefore, was ultimately a function of the strength of demand. Allotments were a major asset to labourers, both in material form and in less tangible ways. But many of the non-material benefits were consequent upon the large increment made by allotments to material living standards. The root cause of this, it is argued, was the negligible opportunity cost to labourers of cultivating an allotment. This in turn was a consequence of the massive scale of underemployment in rural England between 1815 and the early 1850s, affecting women and children even more than men.

Finally this book offers a critique of the traditional view of the allotment movement as an atavistic phenomenon, rooted in the production relations and social assumptions of a past era. The allotment movement, as presented in this book, is a very different entity: allotments, it is argued, were a vector for the modernisation of rural society. Not only were the behavioural and attitudinal changes which the allotment movement hoped to achieve forward-looking and liberal in character, but the effects of allotment provision were to bring rural labourers closer to, rather than further from, the mainstream of mid-Victorian urban Britain.

The structure of the book is as follows. Chapters 1 to 4 explore the pattern of development of the allotment movement between the 1790s and the 1840s. Chapter 1 focuses on the sharp increase in interest in the idea of land provision for labourers in the 1790s. What can explain the degree of public attention which the idea received at this time and why did interest die away in the early years of the nineteenth century? The chapter concludes with an attempt to assess how much the advocates of land provision for labourers actually achieved during this period and provides an estimate of the number of allotment sites created between 1793 and 1830. Chapter 2 investigates the great upsurge of interest in allotments which occurred in 1830 and demonstrates how this affected the number of allotment sites. Chapter 3 poses what is perhaps the central question raised by the nineteenth-century allotment movement – why interest was sustained after 1830. This chapter provides the first detailed account available in print of the history of the LFS and presents new evidence on the political complexion of the society, refuting previous suggestions that it was dominated by Tory influences. It argues that the main aim of the LFS in promoting allotments was to achieve a transformation in the moral character of the labouring poor, but that the direction of this transformation was towards values which were increasingly widely shared within 'respectable' society, rather than being the preserve of an unregenerate neo-feudal rearguard. Chapter 4 continues the attempt to explain why interest in and the provision of allotments was sustained so impressively after 1830 by gauging the contribution of the regional and local movements, including notable individuals.

Chapter 5, on the allotment landlord, assesses the diverse motives of landowners in providing allotments. It argues that the reason allotments were able to achieve so many different goals for landowners was because the eagerness of agricultural labourers to rent land gave landowners a point of purchase over labourers. The suggestion that labourers were eager to rent land contra-dicts a widely held assumption and the initial purpose of chapter 6, on the allotment tenant, is to demonstrate that labourers did indeed in general very much want to obtain allotments. This is easy to understand in view of the remarkably high yields and increase in family incomes which allotments could provide, and the equally important non-material benefits they offered. Furthermore, allotments were relevant not only to agricultural labourers but also to other groups of workers, in particular domestic outworkers.

Chapter 7, on the consequences of allotment provision, assesses the effects of allotments on rural social relations. It is argued that allotments improved relations between labourers and landowners but worsened those between labourers and farmers, and, more surprisingly, between landowners and farmers. Four major questions about the effects of allotments are then addressed in more detail: did allotments reduce rural crime, did they militate against riot and protest, did they affect political activism and, finally, what was their relationship to trade unionism? This chapter includes the first account of the ambivalent but highly-charged relationship between the allot-ment movement and Chartism and suggests that the success of the allotment movement in the east Midlands may have contributed to the genesis of the Chartist land plan. Contrary to the intentions of many of the landowners who let them, allotments appear to have had at least as much potential for encouraging as for dampening down radical political activity. This is particu-larly evident in the close relationship between agricultural trade unionism and allotments, which developed at the very end of the period of this study.

Chapter 8 considers the decline of the organised allotment movement in the period after 1845, and tries to explain the paradox that, despite this decline, the number of allotment sites continued to rise. The last part of the chapter draws attention to indications in the late 1860s and early 1870s that a fundamental change in the nature and priorities of the allotment move-ment was taking place, a change which would manifest itself fully only as the third allotment movement came to fruition in the 1880s.

The conclusion summarises the principal findings of the earlier chapters and offers an economic explanation for the pattern of growth of the allot-ment movement, focusing on the significance of persistent unemployment and underemployment in rural England in the first half of the nineteenth century. An assessment is offered of the likely impact of allotment provision on labourers' living standards and on other, less tangible, aspects of the life of the rural labouring poor. Finally, the consequences of allotment provision for rural social relations are considered. Throughout it is argued that the allot-ment movement cannot plausibly be seen as a backwards-looking phenom-enon, but that, on the contrary, its intentions and effects were to make rural labourers more, rather than less, like their urban counterparts. The allotment movement formed part of the process by which rural society became assimi-lated into a liberal, urban-dominated national culture and should therefore be seen as a modernising rather than a regressive influence on rural society.

PART I

THE FIRST ALLOTMENT MOVEMENT

1

The First Allotment Movement, c.1793–1830

The first phase of the allotment movement, between 1793 and 1830, occurred against a backdrop of severe pressure on rural living standards. Agricultural employment failed to keep pace with the rapid increase of the rural population, especially in the south, where most agricultural labourers lived and where the allotment movement initially developed, since in this region alternative employment in industry was rarely available. Low and almost certainly declining real wages were compounded by a rising dependency ratio.[1] The increasing specialisation of southern and eastern agriculture in cereal production may have raised aggregate demand for labour, but it entailed an exaggeration of the seasonal pattern of male unemployment and a reduction of female employment opportunities, in, for example, dairying, hay-making and even harvesting. It also reduced opportunities for family labour, which the evidence of emigrants' letters suggests was a high priority with the poor at this period. The labour surplus in the rural south, and the apparent tendency of male labour to force out female, further reduced female participation rates.[2]

Income from non-wage sources probably also declined during the late eighteenth and early nineteenth centuries. The effects of enclosure on the poor, particularly in respect to the keeping of animals and the gathering of fuel, food and materials have been much debated. However, recent analyses lend support to the Hammonds' view that enclosure had a serious effect on the income of the poor, mainly through the loss of the minor rights of common, whether exercised legally or otherwise.[3]

---

[1] David Chambers, *Population, economy and society in pre-industrial England*, London 1972, 118–21; Alan Armstrong, *Farmworkers: a social and economic history, 1770–1980*, London 1988, 37–43; Barry Reay, *The last rising of the agricultural labourers: rural life and protest in nineteenth-century England*, Oxford 1990, 79–80, 136–7.

[2] Armstrong, *Farmworkers*, 67–8; Keith Snell, *Annals of the labouring poor: social change and agrarian England, 1660–1900*, Cambridge 1985, 17–22, 46–51. See also idem, 'Agricultural seasonal unemployment, the standard of living, and women's work, 1690–1860', in Pamela Sharpe (ed.), *Women's work: the English experience, 1650–1914*, London 1998, 76–8, 90, 100–10.

[3] J. L. Hammond and Barbara Hammond, *The village labourer, 1760–1832*, London 1911 (4th edn 1927); Jeanette Neeson, *Commoners: common right, enclosure and social change in England, 1700–1820*, Cambridge 1993, passim; Snell, *Labouring poor*, 138–227. See, however, Leigh Shaw-Taylor, 'Labourers, cows, common rights and parliamentary enclosure: the evidence of contemporary comment, c. 1760–1810', *Past and Present* clxxi (2002), 95–126, for evidence that labourers were only rarely able to exercise the most valuable common right, that of keeping a cow.

Increasing unemployment and underemployment, the more severe seasonal imbalances in demand for labour, falling real wages and enclosure all led to increased dependence on poor relief, as contemporaries frequently pointed out.[4] The loss of independence attendant upon the removal of common rights, their reduction to the status of an agricultural proletariat and their sharply worsened economic position led to the progressive degradation of agricultural labourers. The 'Hodge' stereotype concealed more than it revealed but its prevalence indicated the deteriorating status of the rural labouring poor and the widening gulf that separated them from farmers and landowners.[5]

To some extent these unfavourable trends may have been alleviated between 1793 and 1815 by the impact of war on the agricultural labour market. It is true that Snell, whose work is based on a fuller and perhaps more accurate sample of wage data than has hitherto been available, has argued that the real wages of male agricultural labourers in the south of England fell from about 1780 right through to 1834 or beyond; and, moreover, that female real wages were falling in most of southern England from about 1760 to 1834 or afterwards, although in the west they may have risen slightly in response to growing regional specialisation in pastoral farming.[6] However, during this period the level of unemployment probably had more significance for rural living standards than that of real wages. Snell himself points out that his evidence, based on settlement examinations, can tell us nothing about the level (as opposed to the seasonality) of unemployment.[7] Yet, as Eric Jones argued, agricultural labour was probably in short supply during the war, partly because labour was siphoned off for military purposes and partly because the war stimulated the agricultural sector through high prices.[8] For this reason, it would be unwise to assume that real income from wages was lower at the end than at the beginning of the war.

But labourers may nevertheless have suffered as much between 1793 and 1815 as they did in the more obviously difficult post-war period. Armstrong emphasises that as many as fourteen of the twenty-two grain harvests

---

[4] See, for example, David Davies, *The case of labourers in husbandry stated and considered*, London 1795, 56–7, and Arthur Young, *An inquiry into the propriety of applying wastes to the better maintenance and support of the poor*, Bury St Edmunds 1801, 11–13.

[5] Mark Freeman, 'The agricultural labourer and the "Hodge" stereotype, c. 1850–1914', *AgHR*, xlix (2001), 172–86.

[6] Snell, *Labouring poor*, 23–66, 40–9.

[7] Ibid. 18.

[8] Eric Jones, 'The agricultural labour market in England, 1793–1872', *EcHR* 2nd ser. xvii (1964), 322–38. The validity of Snell's interpretation of the settlement examinations, on which his unemployment data is based, has been challenged by Norma Landau, 'The laws of settlement and the surveillance of immigration in eighteenth-century Kent', *Continuity and Change* iii (1988), 391–420. See also Keith Snell, 'Pauper settlement and the right to poor relief in England and Wales', *Continuity and Change* vi (1991), 375–415, and Norma Landau, 'Who was subjected to the laws of settlement? Procedure under the settlement laws in eighteenth-century England', *AgHR* xliii (1995), 139–59.

between 1793 and 1814 were deficient to some degree, and that 'poor men everywhere endured great hardships in the worst years'.[9] Wells has demonstrated that mortality increased in the wake of the harvest failures of 1794–5 and 1799–1800. Even if real wages maintained their value over the war years as a whole, this can have been of little comfort to labourers faced with intermittent food shortages so severe that Wells at least believes they should be described as a famine.[10]

Partly because of the extremity of these conditions and partly because the threat of invasion gave what would later be known as the 'home front' an enhanced political significance, a wide range of ideas aimed in whole or in part at tackling these problems was produced between 1793 and 1815. These ideas were astonishingly diverse, ranging from proposals that poor relief should be abolished altogether to the view that there should be a statutory minimum wage.[11] But one of the most commonly suggested and energetically pursued proposals was to provide the poor with land. This was not a new idea: in terms of English history it can be traced back at least as far as 1589, when an act required all cottages, with certain stated exceptions, to have at least four acres of land attached. This act was not enforced, but the fact that such a measure was proposed demonstrates that the idea of providing land for the poor was current even in the sixteenth century.[12] In times more immediately prior to the Napoleonic wars, Arthur Young made several appeals for land to be made available to the poor (whilst he continued, paradoxically, to advocate enclosure). In his *Observations on the present state of the waste lands of Great Britain* (1773), Young argued that the government should purchase all waste land offered for sale and resell it in lots of twenty or thirty acres, letting those purchasers with eight or ten children or more have their lots free of charge.[13] He repeated his argument in the first issue of his *Annals of Agriculture*, published in 1784.[14] Another writer of the pre-war period who advocated the provision of land for the poor was Nathaniel Kent. In his *Hints to gentlemen of landed property* (1775), he went out of his way to urge the division of waste land for the poor, or at the least the provision of good gardens.[15]

But apart from Young and Kent, there seem to have been no other prominent writers advocating the allocation of land to the poor in the pre-war period. Young was mounting something of a one-man crusade in his *Annals*; although he was able to cite Sir William Osborne and John Lord Sheffield as examples of landowners who favoured his proposal, he does not seem to have

9 Armstrong, *Farmworkers*, 56.

10 Roger Wells, *Wretched faces: famine in wartime England, 1793–1803*, Gloucester 1988, 55–70.

11 John R. Poynter, *Society and pauperism: English ideas on poor relief, 1795–1834*, London 1969, 39, 52.

12 Theodore H. Hall, *The law of allotments*, London 1886, 6–7.

13 Young, *An inquiry*, 44–5.

14 [Arthur Young], [Introduction], *Annals* i (1784), 51–71.

15 Nathaniel Kent, *Hints to gentlemen of landed property*, London 1775, 102, 228–39.

been able to obtain articles from other authors on this subject until after the outbreak of war.[16]

The war should be seen as marking a new beginning in the history of land provision not only because of a great increase in interest, but also because the terms of the argument shifted to become recognisably continuous with the impulses underlying the later allotment movement. After 1793 arguments for the provision of land, including those made by Arthur Young, stemmed from a concern with the problems of poverty, as did the arguments of the allotment movement in at least the first half of the nineteenth century. Before the war, Young had advocated the provision of land partly on the basis of his long-standing enthusiasm for agricultural improvement, in particular the cultivation of waste land, and partly from his desire to limit the rate of emigration to America, while Kent had placed his emphasis upon the duties of the rich rather than the needs of the poor.

Clearly the concept of providing land for the poor was very much a marginal one before 1793. It was the anxieties and tensions created by the war, and above all the fears engendered by the disastrous harvest of 1795 and the years of scarcity which followed, that converted the idea from something occasionally urged by the exceptionally cranky or exceptionally humane, into a topical and mainstream issue. Indeed, in his exhaustive survey of the intellectual background to the Poor Law Reform Act of 1834, Poynter identifies land provision as the principal measure urged for relief of the poverty of agricultural labourers in this period.[17]

A range of ways in which the poor might be given land was proposed during the war years. Although this book is primarily concerned with allotments rather than with other forms of landholding, it is important to consider the other proposals at this stage. This is partly because in this first phase the concept of an allotment in the modern sense had not emerged clearly – contemporaries tended to lump different forms of land provision together for most purposes – so that it makes little sense to discuss allotments in isolation; and partly because it is important to understand how it was that allotments emerged as overwhelmingly the dominant mode of providing agricultural labourers with land.

Proposals can be divided into two categories: those which sought to remove labourers from the need to labour by converting them into 'yeomen' or small farmers; and those which aimed to provide them with land without lifting them out of their condition. In the former group, most schemes involved what was called 'home colonisation'. This, as the name suggests, was conceived as an alternative to emigration. It was thought that waste land could be divided into what were in effect smallholdings and then occupied by the 'excess population' of rural southern England. Most proposals for 'home colonisation' were directed at common land, but crown land and

---

16 [Young], [Introduction], *Annals* i (1784), 53; i–xix (1784–93).
17 Poynter, *Society and pauperism*, p. xix.

uncultivated non-commonable land were also often considered suitable. Home colonisation was in a different league, in terms of its ambitions, from the other proposed methods of providing labourers with land. It was not only that it was meant to remove the agricultural labourer from dependence on employment altogether and make him a small farmer on his own account, but that it also aimed at a complete remodelling of English social structure, along the lines of restoring the fabled 'hardy peasantry' of the past. In keeping with these ambitions, home colonisation schemes almost invariably involved cottage-building as well as the division of land. A variant on home colonis- ation was the breaking up of large farms into small ones to be allocated to landless labourers.

Proposals which did not aim to transform the labourer into a small farmer can be divided into two further categories: those advocating the provision of pasture and those advocating arable. Although this classification is a good one, reflecting a major divergence of possibilities, the two forms were not always seen as incompatible; sometimes they were considered complemen- tary. Nevertheless, the idea of providing labourers with pasture had very different implications, and was to have a very different future, from the idea of providing them with some form of cultivable land.

Pasture usually meant 'cow pastures' – fields which could be used either individually or collectively by labourers for pasturing cows (or, more rarely, sheep and horses). Cow pastures must be thought of as a system of related practices rather than merely as specific plots of ground: the 'cow pasture system' required not only a summer pasture for the animals, but also a meadow for hay (or arable land for other fodder crops) and sheds to house the cows during the winter. A wide variety of practices existed. Sometimes stall feeding was used, in which case only arable land for fodder crops was needed. Cows might be kept for milk or for cheese, and the produce might be consumed at home, or sold. Often the milk would be used to help fatten one or sometimes two pigs. Many writers thought that cow pastures were desir- able, but there were also those who disagreed, and a heated debate ensued. A variant on the scheme, which nevertheless had the same aims and was often proposed as a more limited alternative to cow pastures was for farmers to 'let out' a cow to their labourers. All this meant was that in return for a small sum the labourer would receive the milk of one of the farmer's cows.

There were several methods of providing labourers with arable land without making them into small farmers. The first was simply to provide them with a field, or a few fields, of arable land – up to five acres or so, depending on the quality and location of the land. Another was to provide 'potato grounds'. This was a much more important category than the previous one, although generally offering little benefit to the labourer. Potato grounds were patches of land which would otherwise have gone uncultivated (either fallows or wastes), and which were offered to labourers, almost always on a temporary basis, to grow potatoes.

Potato grounds on fallows were small plots of a fallow field, let out either

13

free or at a rent to labourers. If the labourer was employed by the farmer who owned the field, he would not usually pay rent; otherwise he would usually do so. There is little evidence for this early period of the typical size of a potato ground on a fallow, but they were clearly small, one account recommending plots of ten poles.[18] Potato grounds on fallows were often ploughed by the farmer but manured by the labourer, although a great variety of formal and informal contractual arrangements existed.

Potato grounds on wastes were similar but did not form part of a farmer's cropping regime. They were often made temporarily available for cultivation by the poor for the duration of a subsistence crisis. Three types of waste land particularly often used were commons, the verges of roads and the corners of fields. In this context we need to remember that road verges, especially in the case of roads created by enclosure commissioners, were often much broader in the eighteenth and nineteenth centuries than they later became. In many parishes, road verges would have been the most obvious waste land available and perhaps also, because of their semi-public status, the most uncontroversially usable. In the case of potato grounds in the corners of fields, again we need to remember that the unused corners of fields were much larger in the days of horse-drawn ploughs than they became in the era of tractor cultivation.[19]

A third kind of arable provision for labourers was the familiar garden. Gardens varied enormously in size, but seem in the main to have been smaller than potato grounds. It was almost universally agreed that labourers should have adequately-sized gardens, although there was disagreement about what this meant. It was sometimes suggested that cottages with only small gardens should have them extended. Cottage-building, which was to become a favourite occupation of landlords with a strong conception of the 'duties of property' in the nineteenth century, normally entailed the provision of good gardens for the new cottages; this may in fact have been the main way in which the average size of agricultural labourers' gardens was increased during the nineteenth century. Although most labourers' gardens seem to have been used for traditional arable purposes, fruit-growing was also important in some areas.

The allotment could at one level be seen as a sub-category of the garden, although there were significant differences. Although of the forms outlined above allotments were to become by far the most significant in terms of attempts to provide labourers with land, it is worth reiterating that in the late eighteenth century allotments had not yet become clearly differentiated as a form in their own right – even the earl of Winchilsea's letter to the Board of

---

18 Anon., letter dated 17 Dec. 1795, Annals xxvi (1796), 215.
19 For further discussion of potato grounds, and of the relationship between them and allotments see Burchardt, 'The allotment movement', 556–620, and 'Land and the laborer: potato grounds and allotments in nineteenth-century southern England', Agricultural History lxxiv/2 (2000), 667–84.

Agriculture of 1796, which distinguished eight different ways of letting land to agricultural labourers, did not separate allotments from the general practice of letting agricultural land to labourers.[20]

Home colonisation, cow pastures, arable land, potato grounds, gardens and allotments were, then, the main forms of land provision for labourers proposed in the late eighteenth and early nineteenth centuries. What were the motives behind the movement to supply the labourer with land? And what were the arguments used for and against the different methods of doing so? It was only on the question of how far these different methods were likely to realise the hopes of their proponents that there were differences – there was almost complete agreement on what gains were desirable.

The alleged advantages of increasing access to land can be grouped together under four broad headings: increasing the material welfare of the labourer, improving his or her morals, saving money for those of higher social status and benefiting the country at large. Table 1, based on articles appearing in two contemporary periodicals, the *Annals of Agriculture* and the *Reports* of the SBCP, lists and quantifies the different reasons given in the two periodicals for providing labourers with land, and assigns them to the appropriate heading. The results cannot claim any kind of precision and need to be interpreted with caution. The main problem is that it is difficult to know how to weight the reasons offered. Equal weighting, given here in the absence of any information about their relative importance, will necessarily overstate the significance of subsidiary reasons and understate the significance of major ones. Another problem is categorisation: some reasons fall awkwardly between headings. Making labourers more independent could for example be classed under the heading of saving money for the wealthy, since one of the main aims was to make the labourers independent of poor relief; but it could also be categorised (as here) under improving labourers' morals. A different classification could of course have been used – in particular, the final category (benefits to the country at large) could have been split into separate subheadings – but the classification chosen seemed the best consistent with simplicity. A further difficulty concerns the relationship between the reasons given for allotting land in the periodicals and the motives of those who actually let land. Do the reasons given accurately reflect these motives? We cannot ultimately know. It is possible that in public writers advanced reasons which did not in fact weigh with them, or vice versa. The evidence from the *Annals* and the SBCP *Reports* is reassuring on this point in two respects. First, writers freely advanced reasons that reflected no particular credit on themselves, such as the desire to reduce poor rates; and secondly, it is difficult to imagine that there could have been many major reasons for letting allotments

---

[20] [The earl of Winchilsea], 'Letter from the earl of Winchilsea, to the president of the Board of Agriculture, on the advantages of cottagers renting land', in Board of Agriculture, *Communications to the Board of Agriculture on subjects relative to the husbandry and internal improvement of the country*, I/2: *Cottages*, London 1797, 1–8.

Table 1
Perceived advantages of letting land to labourers

Reason	Number of times cited		
	SBCP	*Annals*	Total
Increases wellbeing			
relief/comforts	9	12	21
happiness	2		2
condition		2	2
health/children's health	1	1	2
diet	1		1
demand for labour	1		1
social mobility		1	1
hope	1		1
			31
Improves morals			
industry	14	9	23
character/morals	5	3	8
sobriety	5	2	7
economy/thrift, etc.	4	1	5
lawfulness/honesty	1	2	3
independence	2	1	3
decency/neatness		2	2
stops tea drinking	1		1
			52
Saves money			
poor rate reduction	9	10	19
stable labour supply	2		2
keeps wages low	1		1
strength	1		1
children learn to work	1		1
creates good servants		1	1
			25
Benefits the country			
order/good conduct	4	2	6
attaches to country	3	2	5
contentment	2	2	4
raises national output	7	4	11
reduces emigration		2	2
creates 'improvers'		1	1
bread consumption falls	1		1
slow population growth	1		1
creates gratitude	1		1
enlarges tax yield	1		1
			33

Sources: SBCP, *Reports*, i–vii (1797–1818); *Annals* i–xlii (1784–1804).

that did not feature amongst the extensive variety put forward by the different writers. The latter seem in general to have been relatively unconstrained in what they wrote about land provision.

The information drawn from the *Annals* and from the SBCP *Reports* is less than ideal. But if we wish to answer the crucial question of the relative importance of the different motives that fuelled the movement to provide labourers with land, it is the best that is available.

As can be seen from table 1 the reasons given in the *Annals* and in the *Reports* are strikingly similar. The only noteworthy difference is that SBCP writers seem to have placed more emphasis on improving the morals of labourers. This is unsurprising in view of the strong evangelical influence on the SBCP.

To put some flesh on the bare bones of table 1 a more detailed examination of the perceived advantages of providing labourers with land is required. In what ways, then, was it thought that the welfare of the labourer would be measured by the possession (or occupation) of land? Primarily, it was believed that his or her standard of living would rise because of the additional income accruing from the land. Many writers thought that cottagers with land would be able to enjoy comforts such as milk, butter, cheese and bacon, which agricultural labourers could not usually afford.[21]

Closely connected with this view was the belief that providing labourers with land would improve their health and that of their children.[22] Dietary benefits were sometimes explicitly mentioned.[23] It was also sometimes suggested that providing labourers with land would increase the demand for labour and thus raise wages, but this was a controversial claim to make because the other side of the coin, that farmers would have to pay higher wages, was seen as a potential drawback – and indeed many proponents of land provision took trouble to deny that it would raise wages.[24] The suggestion that land provision might enable labourers to rise socially was an embarrassing one for similar reasons and was also rarely made.

The effects of land in giving labourers 'hope' (i.e. of improving their economic and social circumstances) were to generate great interest among campaigners for allotments in the 1830s and 1840s, but were rarely mentioned in the late eighteenth or the first three decades of the nineteenth century, perhaps because the rural poor had not yet sunk to the level of despondency of later years.

It would be a crude simplification to dismiss the genuine philanthropic interest that existed in land provision as a means of benefiting the poor. However, it is equally clear that considerably more interest was shown in

---

21 John Crutchley, 'Answers to queries', ibid. 18.
22 John Tuke, *General view of the agriculture of the North Riding of Yorkshire*, London 1794, 81; James Willis, 'On cows for cottagers', *Annals* xl (1803), 562.
23 SBCP, *Reports*, ii (1799–1800), 178.
24 Crutchley, 'Answers to queries', 18.

improving their moral character. The supreme virtue was industriousness, which was seen as the great merit of schemes to increase access to land by writer after writer. Indeed it could come to be almost synonymous with virtue. Winchilsea for example wrote of 'the great and primary object – of promoting virtue and industry'.[25] Why was it thought that labourers with land would be more industrious? Winchilsea implied that once a labourer had seen the advantages of, in this case, keeping a cow, the first thing he would think of would be working hard to save money to buy another one.[26] Sir Thomas Bernard, the moving spirit of the SBCP, thought that labourers would be encouraged to industry by having allotments because they could only gain from working hard on their land. Bernard referred to the allotments at Shipton Moyne (Gloucestershire) in the following terms: 'It is a prize lottery without blanks. It gives scope to the energy of the poor, and prospect of future advantage, without diminution in their existing means of life.'[27] The Revd R. A. Ingram saw the stimulus to industry as resulting from the convenient mode of accumulating savings provided by landownership.[28] Some writers – Thomas Stone, for example – suggested that varying amounts of land should be attached to cottages, and industrious labourers encouraged by being offered cottages with more land if they worked hard.[29] It was also thought that children would be taught to be industrious and learn appropriate skills of husbandry if their parents had land. This was a theme picked out by Bernard, Winchilsea, the bishop of Durham and William Morton Pitt, amongst others.

Many writers referred in frustratingly vague terms to the effects of land provision in improving the morals or the character of agricultural labourers. One might indeed expect this catch-all category to be the largest item under the heading of improving labourers' morals. That it is by no means so is testimony to the predominance of concern with industriousness.

Several writers saw the possession of land – particularly in the form of a garden or allotment – as a means of keeping the poor man from drunkenness. Generally the reasoning was that land would occupy leisure hours which would otherwise have been spent at the alehouse. However, the Revd R. A. Ingram thought that property in land would act as a kind of savings bank in which the labourer could invest money that he would otherwise have wasted on drink, while William Morton Pitt thought that a labourer could grow malt for home-brewing small beer, the want of which, he believed, drove the labourer to the alehouse.[30]

It was also thought that providing land, especially if it were close to the labourer's cottage, would positively encourage domesticity. As the writer of

---

[25] SBCP, *Reports*, iii (1801), 122.
[26] Ibid. i (1797–8), 93.
[27] Ibid. iii. 163.
[28] Ibid. iv (1802–5), 200–1.
[29] Thomas Stone, *A review of the corrected agricultural survey of Lincolnshire, by Arthur Young*, London 1800, 408.
[30] SBCP, *Reports*, iv. 200–1; ibid. i. 241.

an article for the SBCP entitled 'Of the comforts of the poor' wrote, 'if the labourer had pleasurable occupations at home he would find it more agreeable to spend his time there rather than at the alehouse'.[31]

Moreover, the possession of land would make labourers more thrifty. Joseph Scott, writing to the *Annals of Agriculture*, expressed this view as follows:

> In my humble opinion, if industrious labourers were only supplied with a rood of land each, even if they paid a fair rent for it, it would be of more real lasting advantage to them than anything that has been done for them this century; inasmuch as it would cause the labourer to lay out weekly his spare pence in garden seeds, instead of spending them in superfluities; attract him to labour in his garden mornings, evenings, and all leisure days.[32]

Another argument sometimes used in favour of providing labourers with land was that this could prevent crime. One of the rules of Thomas Estcourt's Long Newnton allotments, for example, was that any tenant convicted of an offence against the law making him liable to a fine or imprisonment was to forfeit his allotment. This rule apparently had considerable effect.[33]

Other prospective moral gains can be dealt with more briefly. 'Independence' was an ambiguous term, which could mean simply 'not dependent on poor relief' but in general encompassed a broader range of moral qualities. Landowners almost always wanted labourers to be more independent; farmers had more than a few doubts. Decency and neatness were thought desirable, and a good sign, but were not regarded as very important. Finally, in one instance at least, the hope was expressed that providing labourers with land would cure them of the pernicious habit of tea-drinking.

In what ways was it expected that providing labourers with land would save money for their social superiors? Overwhelmingly the greatest anticipated gain in this respect was the reduction of the poor rates. Bernard several times stressed the connection between the possession or occupation of land by labourers and low poor rates, as did Winchilsea and Estcourt. The case of the labourer Britton Abbot who, after settling on a rood of land, never again applied for poor relief seems to have impressed Bernard. He subsequently used the argument that landholding by the poor would reduce the poor rates as one of the chief grounds for providing land. Estcourt let his allotments at Long Newnton on the understanding that a tenant who accepted poor relief would be evicted. This scheme was very successful: none of the tenants required poor relief in the first four years of the scheme, whilst expenditure on poor relief fell from £212 16s. over six months in 1800/1 to £12 6s. over six months

---

31 Ibid. ii. 328–9. See also frontispiece.
32 Joseph Scott, 'Crops, markets, poor: Chatteris, 30 Dec. 1800', *Annals* xxxvi (1801), 377–8.
33 SBCP, *Reports*, v (1806–18), 71–83.
34 Ibid. v. 71–83.

in 1803/4. Estcourt admitted that 'This plan does not affect to be founded only on principles of benevolence to the poor or to give them anything; but to embrace the interests of the superior classes also.'[34] Other benefits to the landed classes were expected. First, it was hoped that if labourers had land they would become stronger, better workers. Thus Estcourt wrote of the allotments at Long Newnton that, since the plot-holders felt themselves obliged to provide for their own relief, they were more assiduous workers. 'The farmers of this parish allow they never had their work better done.'[35] Secondly, it was sometimes argued that if labourers had land a permanent supply of labour would be ensured. But this argument was infrequently advanced, perhaps suggesting that labour was not generally felt to be in short supply, and one of the two SBCP writers who did use it came from under-populated Lincolnshire. Third, it was sometimes suggested that providing labourers with land would reduce or control wages.[36] This, again, was an awkward argument to use since it detracted from the benefits labourers reaped from their land, but some certainly expected gains in this respect. William Morton Pitt, amongst others, believed, on the basis of a subsistence theory of wages, that if labourers had land they would live in more comfort and so the wages of labour would be kept within 'moderate bounds'.[37] Fourth it was sometimes thought that providing agricultural labourers with land would teach their children skill in husbandry from an early age. Finally, it was also occasionally suggested that labourers with land would themselves become 'better servants'.

The benefits expected for the country at large were first, greater social stability, and second, increased national production. The first of these was mentioned by a number of writers, perhaps most revealingly by Glasse and by Bernard. Glasse wrote that 'where the cottager has acquired at home a pleasurable object of industry, to which his hopes and wishes are directed, it has the effect of attaching him to his situation, of augmenting his energy, and of reconciling him to a life of labour and hardship'.[38] Bernard was equally forthright: a cottager with property, however small – a cow, pig, or even a garden – had an interest in his country and in the good order of society, whereas: 'He who has no property, is always ready for novelty and experiment.'[39] Increased national production took on particular importance in the war years because of the disruption of trade with continental Europe. Winchilsea expressed neatly what it was about giving land to labourers that many found exciting from this point of view:

---

[35] Ibid. v. 78–9.
[36] Crutchley, 'Answers to queries', 18.
[37] SBCP, *Reports*, i. 241.
[38] Ibid. i. 140–1.
[39] Ibid. ii. 181–2.

As land cultivated as a garden will produce a greater quantity of food for man than in any other way, and as four-fifths of the labour bestowed upon their gardens will be done by the labourers at extra hours, and when they and their children would otherwise be unemployed, it may not be too much to say, that 100,000 acres, allotted to cottagers as garden ground, will give a produce equal to what 150,000 acres cultivated in the ordinary way would give; and that, without occupying more of the time they would otherwise give to the farmers who employ them, than the cultivation of 20,000 acres would require.[40]

His view was echoed by William Morton Pitt, who argued that since well-managed garden ground was more productive than farm land, labourers should be given more of the latter.[41] He also argued that giving labourers land for potatoes would reduce the national consumption of bread.[42] Bernard declared that a 'vast increase' of national production would result from the extension of the allotment system, and calculated this at about 200,000 tons of potatoes.[43]

The references in table 1 to the effect of the provision of land on emigration should be read with caution. They are both from articles by Young written for the *Annals* before 1793 and reflect his earlier anxiety about the loss of population to America rather than the gains which he and others anticipated from the provision of land in the 1790s. In fact, by this time the tide was beginning to flow the other way: there was more anxiety about population being too high than too low. Either way, significant effects on population were not amongst the advantages most often anticipated from the provision of land.

Other gains to the country at large sometimes, but rarely, expected to follow from the provision of land were that it would stimulate labourers to become agricultural improvers, that it would increase the gratitude labourers felt to their superiors and that it would increase the tax yield.

Which of these motives were the most important? It seems clear that the desire to reform the moral character of labourers, in particular by making them more industrious, was the strongest. Benefiting the nation at large – accepting for the moment the happy assumption of the elite at this time that the preservation of the existing social order did that – seems to have been approximately on a par with material benefit to labourers. However, the desire to reduce the poor rates was also important. The situation is complicated because some of the gains listed above were clearly often desired as means to other ends. Thus many must have wanted labourers to be industrious primarily to reduce the poor rates, whilst some were concerned about high levels of poor relief because it undermined the moral character of the

---

40 Ibid. i. 100.
41 William Pitt, *General view of the agriculture of the county of Northampton*, London 1809, 140.
42 SBCP, *Reports*, i. 240–1.
43 Ibid. iii. 162–3.

labourer. Bernard wanted labourers to be industrious partly because he felt that only in this way could they become more prosperous. Glasse's concern with national stability probably had as much to do with the security of the property of the wealthy as with the good of the nation as a whole. Nevertheless, although it is always difficult to establish motives, the four categories outlined above probably do reflect the major aims of the proponents of land provision, even if sometimes one result was advocated as a means to another.

The arguments so far discussed derive partly from theoretical and partly from empirical sources. William Morton Pitt, for example, based his argument for home colonisation on the theoretical commonplace that the wealth and greatness of Britain were, in large part, due to 'the effect which the possession and security of property, enjoyed under our free and excellent constitution, have on the minds of men'. He reasoned further that 'If this effect has been so salutary among other classes, why may not similar encouragement create the same energy among the cultivators of the land?'[44] But Bernard seems to have drawn much more on empirical observation (not that his empiricism was, despite his scientific aspirations, of a very high order). Thus the proof he tended to give of the desirability of increasing access to land was that many instances given in the *Reports* had established this beyond doubt.

There were also arguments against providing labourers with land. It was often said that labourers did not cultivate land well. Even Arthur Young sometimes admitted that this could be a problem, as in his description of labourers' enclosure allotments at Glentworth, Lincolnshire, as 'most slovenly and wretched . . . run out and almost waste'.[45] There was particular concern about the ability of industrial labourers to manage land. They were, according to R. W. Dickson, author of the Board of Agriculture's revised survey of Lancashire, 'quite unfit for the management of land'.[46] Some writers feared that even agricultural labourers might have difficulties: they might be too exhausted after a hard day's work to cultivate their land.[47] A more common fear was that labourers with land would work less hard for their employers, either because they were exhausted by work on their own land, or because, no longer so dependent on wages, they would be less inclined to exert themselves for their employers.[48] It was probably this fear that prompted the very frequent reservation that, although labourers should have some land, it ought not to be very much. Taken to extremes, it was argued, the provision of land to labourers, by depriving farmers of labour, would put

[44] Ibid. i. 240.
[45] Arthur Young, *General view of the agriculture of the county of Lincoln*, London 1799, 411.
[46] R. W. Dickson, *General view of the agriculture of the county of Lancashire*, London 1815, 607.
[47] Stone, *Review*, 323.
[48] The fear that land provision would lead labourers to work less hard for their employers has been expressed in terms of economic theory by Boaz Moselle. Moselle argues that farmers employing labourers with land would have had to offer an 'efficiency wage' to compensate for this: 'Allotments, enclosure, and proletarianization', 495–8.

an entire stop to agricultural improvement.[49] Young's possibly loosely-worded suggestion that labourers should perhaps be given land aroused strong feelings, it being felt that this would set an unhealthy precedent – would indeed be the forerunner of an English *loi agraire*.[50] The idea of any publicly-administered provision of land for labourers was also opposed on the grounds that parochial officers were not fit to run such a scheme.[51]

In discussing the various arguments for and against specific modes of letting land to labourers, it should be borne in mind that many writers who favoured the provision of land to labourers did not distinguish between the different forms it took; and that of those who did, many had no strong preference but were willing to see which would work best or prove most acceptable to farmers and landowners. It was only a few who condemned one form of land provision whilst praising another.

Potato grounds were one of the most widespread forms of land allocation in the late eighteenth and early nineteenth centuries. Their most obvious advantage was that they were the quickest and least risky way of providing labourers with land, allowing landowners and farmers to respond quickly to subsistence crises such as occurred in 1795 and 1800 without involving themselves in a long-term commitment. Thus John Parkinson, in an article which argued principally for cow pastures, suggested that for immediate relief potato grounds should be preferred.[52] Some of the other major advantages of potato grounds were well described by George Wilbraham, in an article for Young's *Annals* on potatoes in Cheshire:

> The rent is very frequently paid by an equal division of the produce between the letter of the land and the cultivator. This arrangement obviates the difficulty the industrious labourer lies under, in many situations, to procure ground for this useful purpose; and moreover the rent being paid without the medium of money, the time necessary for bargaining and the expense of carrying the article to market are saved . . . and as no ready money passes, the temptation of spending a part of the profit in the alehouse is avoided: the farmer is also well repaid for his land by sharing the produce, together with the prospect of an abundant succeeding crop of grain.[53]

Whilst this form of sharecropping seems to have been common in Cheshire – Henry Holland comments upon it in his survey for the Board of Agriculture –

---

49 Stone, *Review*, 324.
50 Thomas Ruggles, 'Land for the poor: Clare, Suffolk, 15 Dec. 1800', *Annals* xxxvi (1801), 354.
51 Revd Dr Hinton, 'On land for cottages', ibid. xxxvi (1801), 266–7.
52 John Parkinson, 'Cottagers' land – crops in fallow open fields – Asgarby, Lincolnshire', ibid. xxxvi (1801), 362.
53 George Wilbraham, 'System in which potatoes are rendered beneficial to the poor in Cheshire', ibid. xxxv (1800), 11–12.

it may have been rare elsewhere, although not unknown.[54] Where temporary potato grounds on wastes were proposed, rent of any sort seems very rarely to have been expected; whilst potato grounds on fallows were very often in fact paid for by a money rent, even in Cheshire.[55] However, the advantages described by Wilbraham might still apply. In the case of rent-free potato grounds, there was also no money involved, whilst labourers were not of course under any 'difficulty', at least of a financial nature, in procuring land. But of the points mentioned by Wilbraham, the last, although the least obvious, was the most important. Potatoes were an excellent preparatory crop for wheat or barley.[56] It was often suggested that they were actually a better preparation than leaving the land entirely fallow.[57] Thus the farmer or landowner who offered potato grounds on fallows gained in most cases not only a rent in money or in kind, but also an improved crop of corn in the following year – even if no rent had been charged, the farmer or landowner would still often have been better off letting the land for potatoes than leaving it fallow.[58]

Gardens had one simpe advantage over all other forms of providing labourers with land: they adjoined the labourer's house. This was felt to be a good thing for two main reasons: it would be easier for the labourer and especially his family to cultivate it; and it would increase the attractions of domestic life, as against the beerhouse, for the labourer. The labourer would not have to exhaust himself further by trudging to a distant plot of land after work; he and his family could make use of any spare time, even if only a few minutes, in cultivating the garden, which obviously would not be possible if the labourer's plot was at any distance. Meanwhile the labourer, desiring to make the most of his land, would be drawn back home into his family circle rather than remaining out and about, constantly exposed to temptation.

Although there was never a consensus in favour of cow pastures in the way that there was for the idea that labourers should have at least a small garden, it was cow pastures that generated the most passionate support (often as a combined system with land for potatoes). They were, in practice, a more substantial boon to the labourer than potato grounds alone ever were and since providing arable land on a large scale to labourers was rarely considered realistic, cow pastures became the preferred solution of those who wanted a substantial increase in the labourer's access to land. Thus John Parkinson could write 'I know of no method which would ease the minds of cottagers so

---

54 Henry Holland, *General view of the agriculture of Cheshire*, London 1808, 146; Arthur Young, *General view of the agriculture of Oxfordshire*, London 1813, 185.

55 Holland, *Cheshire*, 145.

56 G. B. Worgan, *General view of the agriculture of the county of Cornwall*, London 1811, 72.

57 Young, *Oxfordshire*, 185; William Pulteney, 'Culture of potatoes', *Annals* xxxvii (1801), 80.

58 Another advantage of potato grounds, from the farmers' point of view, was that labourers were less likely to leave their jobs to seek higher wages during the harvest period: those who did so were liable to lose their potato grounds: Burchardt, 'Land and the laborer', 673–7.

much as allotting to each a moderate quantity of land to keep a cow and grow potatoes. Such has been my practice for many years where or whenever I had an opportunity.'[59]

Arthur Young became a near-fanatical apologist for cow pastures. In his *The question of scarcity* (1800) he proposed a scheme to provide cow pasture on waste land which he believed would 'raise thousands of families from a state of poverty, and dependence on rates, to a situation of ease and comfort; equally beneficial to landlords, farmers, and themselves'.[60] Young sent the youthful Robert Gourlay on a journey to Rutland and Lincolnshire to find out more about the 'Lincolnshire cow system', which resulted in a fiercely contested report in the *Annals* in 1801.[61] There were other enthusiastic and determined advocates of cow pasture, among them, for example, two influential members of the Board of Agriculture, the earl of Winchilsea and Lord Brownlow.

The main argument for cow pastures was that they were thought to be remarkably effective in lowering the poor rates. Gourlay's report was almost entirely devoted to establishing this proposition. In this, he was following the initial reports on Winchilsea's cow pastures in Rutland. One of the reasons there was thought to be so close an association between cow pastures and low poor rates was that where labourers had been deprived of their cows on enclosure, it was widely believed that rates had risen.[62] It was a natural extension of this to assume that providing cow pastures would lower the rates. A second argument for cow pastures was that they would provide labourers' children with milk, which was hard or impossible to come by in many villages, especially in arable areas.[63] It was sometimes argued that if labourers had a ready supply of milk, they would not be tempted to resort to more pernicious substances such as beer or the much-deplored tea.[64] Finally, cow pastures were thought by some to be preferable to other forms of landholding in that there was, so it was argued, less risk for the sponsor of the scheme. Labourers might find a substantial quantity of arable land more than they could manage, yet, developing a classic peasant mentality, be unwilling to relinquish their wasting assets, as was apparently the case on Abel Smith's estate in

---

59 Parkinson, 'Cottagers' land', 361.

60 Arthur Young, *The question of scarcity plainly stated, and remedies considered, with observations on permanent measures to keep wheat at a more regular price*, London 1800, 69.

61 Robert Gourlay, 'An inquiry into the state of the cottagers in the counties of Lincoln and Rutland', *Annals* xxxvii (1801), 514–49, 577–99.

62 Board of Agriculture, *General report on enclosures*, London 1808, 150–8. See also Neeson, *Commoners*, 315–19, and Jane Humphries, 'Enclosures, common rights, and women: the proletarianization of families in the late eighteenth and early nineteenth centuries', *Journal of Economic History* i (1990), 17–42.

63 Robert Barclay, 'On labourers in husbandry renting land', in Board of Agriculture, *Communications*, I/2: *Cottages*, 91–2; Tuke, *North Riding*, 81.

64 Willis, 'On cows for cottagers', 560–2.

Nottinghamshire.[65] Alternatively, labourers inexperienced in tillage might prove insufficiently skilled to manage arable land. Thus Arthur Young saw the failure of arable enclosure allotments for the poor at Glentworth in Lincolnshire as 'a strong instance to prove that their [i.e. the poor's] share ought always to be given in grass; they are unequal to any other tillage than that of a garden'.[66]

There were also strong arguments against cow pastures. Bentham, in an attack upon Pitt's 'cows clause' of 1796 made the point that 'attendance upon a *single* cow is a species of industry, if industry it can be called, which is, of anything that *can* bear that name, the nearest of kin to idleness'. He also pointed out that cows were expensive and perishable. This last point, that when a cow died labourers would find it very difficult to replace, was often made. But Bentham's main objection to cow pastures was that they would, if provided to every labourer, ultimately swallow up all available land.[67] Similar anxieties about the long-term tendency of the system were raised by John Boys, who saw cow pastures as leading to disaster:

> I will venture with great confidence to predict, that if every farming cottager, or in other words, every farmer's labourer in the kingdom, could be so accommodated, a famine would inevitably be the consequence in a short space of time; for experience has taught me to observe, that few men will labour hard any farther than necessity compel them to do so; and it is clear, that any cottager who has two or three acres of land, keeps a cow, and two or three hogs, and grows plenty of potatoes, is not much necessitated to labour for others.[68]

Thomas Stone, in his review of Young's survey of Lincolnshire, was nearly as pessimistic, seeing cow pastures as leading towards a total cessation of agricultural progress, again on the grounds that labourers with enough land to support their families in comfort would not be willing to work for farmers.[69] He also claimed that, as cows do not give milk all the year round, labourers would have to buy a 'fresh' cow every year, which would not be worth the capital expenditure.[70] Thomas Rudge, author of the Board of Agriculture's revised survey of Gloucestershire, also thought that cow pastures would get in the way of labour. He commented further that the system had so far only succeeded in areas of 'consolidated property' like the estates of Winchilsea in Rutland. Only in such areas would a benevolent landowner have the power to extend it widely. Whilst the system might be viable in other such areas, elsewhere it stood little chance of becoming general. Rudge also suggested that the commitments required for cow-keeping in terms of capital (notably

65 SBCP, *Reports*, ii. 136–7.
66 Young, *Lincolnshire*, 411.
67 Jeremy Bentham, quoted in Poynter, *Society and pauperism*, 72.
68 John Boys, *General view of the agriculture of the county of Kent*, London 1796, 31.
69 Stone, *Review*, 324.
70 Ibid. 314.

buildings) and time were beyond most labourers.[71] Further objections to cow pastures included the decay of pasture that would result from continuous grazing (as opposed to convertible husbandry); and that labourers would be so eager not to lose their cows that they would endure terrible privation for the sake of keeping them.[72]

Since allotments in the narrow sense were not clearly distinguished from the occupation of arable land by labourers, it is not surprising that arguments specifically in favour of allotments were not made. But it was agreed that in some situations cow pastures were not appropriate, such as in large towns or, more arguably, in entirely arable areas of the country.[73] This argument, of course, was one that worked as much in favour of gardens, or for that matter arable land in general, as it did in favour of allotments. The common view that any arable or 'garden' land should actually adjoin the labourer's house was, in effect, an argument against allotments.[74] But the main criticism of providing labourers with arable land in general was that any amount worth having would require too much of the labourer's time. Thus Lord Brownlow told the Board of Agriculture that he opposed the provision of arable land for labourers:

> I am a great advocate for grassland, with a comfortable house for a cottager, as the labourer then becomes attached to the spot, and interested in the welfare of the country; but to let plough land to a cottager, I think wrong; because the land is ill managed, they must hire their ploughing, and it takes up so much of their time, that they will not go to labourer's work at the times the farmers most want them.[75]

Those who argued for home colonisation as against other forms of land provision did so because they wanted a more systematic, perhaps government-sponsored approach; because they wanted to raise the labourer to the position of a small farmer; and because they wanted to see the very extensive wastes of Britain brought into cultivation. Home colonisation was at the extreme end of the spectrum of the methods proposed of providing labourers with land and only a few writers argued for it. We have already referred to some of Young's proposals on this subject (home colonisation, particularly with a view to waste land reclamation, was a pet scheme of his); another typical proposal was that published in 1797 by William Morton Pitt, who claimed that his scheme would give the home colonist permanency of property, the benefit of all improvements, higher social standing, lower expenses

---

[71] Thomas Rudge, *General view of the agriculture of the county of Gloucester*, London 1813, 48.
[72] Lord Brownlow, 'Answers to queries', in Board of Agriculture, *Communications*, I/2: *Cottages*, 86; Thomas Griffith, 'Support of the poor in South Wales', *Annals* xxxv (1800), 6.
[73] SBCP, *Reports*, i. 99–100, 141.
[74] Joseph Plymley, *General view of the agriculture of the county of Shropshire*, London 1803, 115; Rudge, *Gloucester*, 201.
[75] Brownlow, 'Answers to queries', 10.

and security of tenure.[76] All the usual arguments about taking the labourer away from agricultural employment applied to home colonisation with redoubled force; but in any event the proposal involved far too great a capital commitment and risk to stand a chance of being implemented on a large scale and was killed off by lack of serious interest more than by opposing argument.

The crisis of the war years threw up not only a plethora of ideas, but also some significant new institutions. In this context the most important of these were the Board of Agriculture and the SBCP, both of which came to have a strong concern with the provision of land for labourers. There were close links between the two organisations and between each of them and Young's *Annals*, which from 1793 began to take great interest in the question of land provision for labourers. Young was secretary to the Board of Agriculture and devoted much attention to it in his publication. Indeed, on one occasion he was forced to deny in print that the *Annals* were an official organ of the board. The SBCP had connections with the *Annals* too: many of its articles were written by writers who also published work in Young's journal. There was also a substantial overlap of personnel between contributors to the SBCP *Reports* and those active at the Board of Agriculture. Winchilsea, Estcourt and Sir William Pulteney were, for example, extensively involved in both. What we have here is therefore a single movement to provide labourers with land rather than several different groups of people working in isolation. However, it is convenient to examine the influence of each organisation in turn.

The Board of Agriculture was established in 1793 as a reward to Sir John Sinclair for his assistance to the government in the liquidity crisis of that year.[77] Its main aim was to increase the rate of diffusion of the best agricultural practice. It responded determinedly to the food scarcity of the mid-1790s. Its long-term policy was to encourage more enclosure, both by exhortation and by reducing the costs of parliamentary enclosure; its short-term policy was to promote cheaper alternatives to wheat (such as potatoes).[78] Both these policies, in the event, affected and stimulated the debate on providing land for the poor: the board's attempts to pass a general enclosure bill thrust into prominence its associated plan for home colonisation, whilst its advocacy of the potato led it to propose that the poor be allowed to cultivate temporary potato grounds on wastes. This positive attitude towards the provision of land to the poor can be traced to the enthusiasm of many of those most active in the board: Young, as secretary, was one of the major influences on the board's policy; Winchilsea, the great advocate of cow pastures, was an ordinary member and regularly attended meetings; Estcourt, who in 1795 established what may well have been the first allotments in the

76 SBCP, *Reports*, i. 243.
77 Rosalind Mitchison, *Agricultural Sir John: the life of Sir John Sinclair of Ulster, 1754–1835*, London 1962, 139.
78 Ibid. 156.

country, was also an ordinary member and correspondent;[79] Brownlow, second only to Winchilsea in his enthusiasm for cow pastures, although not at first a member, was an energetic correspondent. Other ordinary members with an active interest in the issue included the earl of Egremont and Sir William Pulteney.[80] We shall consider first the board's attempts to pass legislation through parliament, particularly in so far as this related to the provision of land for the poor, and then the effects of its public advocacy of such provision.

The board's attempts to pass a general enclosure bill met with little success. Not until 1801 was it able to pass any bill upon the subject, and even this was merely a bill facilitating enclosure by agreement, thus not addressing the great bulk of contested enclosures at all.[81] But long before this, the board's attempt to attach a home colonisation scheme to its bill had foundered. Its initial bill had included a provision whereby a portion of waste was to be set aside on any enclosure and vested in the lord of the manor, rector, vicar, churchwardens and overseers, for perpetual 'allotments' for the poor. Any labourer aged twenty-one years or more, and having a settlement in the parish, might claim a portion and hold it for fifty years, rent free, on condition of building a cottage on it and fencing it. Thereafter the land was to be let on twenty-one-year leases, at reasonable rents, half going to the owner of the soil and half to offset the poor rates.[82] But the bill was amended in committee to exclude these clauses, and in any case had not reached the Lords when Pitt dissolved parliament on 20 May 1796.[83] In subsequent years the board presented bills modelled upon this one, but not henceforth with any provision for land to be made available to the poor, other than those who were actually owners of cottages with common rights.

The board's attempts to persuade parliament to legislate on foodstuffs were more successful, in particular its measures to encourage the growing of potatoes. This ultimately resulted in the act of 1801, which permitted individual holders of common rights temporarily to enclose their share of land in order to cultivate potatoes. The act included a provision whereby land so enclosed could be let to the poor, also to be used to grow potatoes. The act, however, only applied to 1801, and not even to the entire year at that.

Whilst considering the role of the board in proposing legislation affecting the provision of land to labourers, the 'cows clause' of Pitt's abortive 1796 poor bill should be mentioned. This was the only other significant legislative attempt in this early period to extend the opportunities open to labourers to hold land, and because of the attention its sponsorship ensured, it was probably more important than the efforts of the Board of Agriculture. Pitt's

---

[79] See appendix 2.
[80] Board of Agriculture, list of members for 1796.
[81] 41 Geo III c 109.
[82] Hammond and Hammond, *Village labourer*, 51.
[83] Mitchison, *Agricultural Sir John*, 158.

original bill had, it seems, made no mention of cows, but the bill was amended in committee so that anyone in receipt of poor relief, who, if advanced the money, would be enabled to maintain their family by keeping a cow or other animal, was entitled to receive this advance.[84] It was this clause which aroused the mockery of Bentham; the bill as a whole, a hastily drafted one on a highly controversial subject, ran into a storm of protest and was dropped in the next session.[85] The whole episode appears to have done the cause of land provision, and in particular the idea of cow pastures, serious damage: both by being associated with so universally condemned a bill, and because of the prominent public criticism drawn down on the cows clause.

Thus the attempts of the board (and others) during the war years to pass legislation through parliament to help labourers gain access to land met with almost complete failure. The success achieved by the board through exhorting the public may have been a little greater. The board exercised an influence both through its members and through publications, whether its own – such as the county surveys or its various reports – or indirectly through the publications of others, notably Young's *Annals* which, unsurprisingly, kept a close watch on the affairs of the board. It is difficult to assess the influence of the board on its members: although many of them were enthusiasts for land provision, they may well have been so before becoming involved with the board. In some cases a conversion does seem to have taken place: thus Sinclair had shown very little interest in the subject before his conversation with his fellow member Winchilsea at the Farmers' Club on 12 December 1795. As regards the board's own publications, these probably had relatively little influence on the provision of land for labourers. Its 1795 report on potatoes warmly advocated potato grounds on wastes; similarly, the volume of *Communications* concerned with cottages was strongly in favour of cow pastures.[86] But the *Communications* only had a very limited circulation – probably no more than a few score copies – and it is unlikely that the report on potatoes was more widely circulated.[87] Whilst the county surveys probably reached a wider audience, the views expressed in them as regards the land issue were those of the authors rather than of the board. Some authors, such as Boys, who wrote the 1796 report on Kent, were in effect downright hostile.[88] Young's *Annals* did help to publicise the views of the board further, by reprinting reports such as that on potatoes, noting speeches made by the president calling for the cultivation of waste lands and so forth, but even the

---

84 Hammond and Hammond, *Village labourer*, 125–8.

85 Poynter, *Society and pauperism*, 62.

86 Board of Agriculture, *Report of the committee of the Board of Agriculture concerning the cultivation and use of potatoes*, n.d. [c. 1796]; idem, *Communications*, I/2: *Cottages*.

87 Nicholas Goddard, 'The development and influence of agricultural periodicals and newspapers, 1780–1870', *AgHR* xxxi (1983), 116–21.

88 Boys, *Kent*, 31.

Annals reached, at its maximum, only 3,000 or so readers which, as Goddard points out, was only 'a miniscule proportion of the farming community'.[89]

Another institution created during, and almost certainly as a result of, the post-1793 crisis, was the SBCP. This was founded in 1796 by a group of prominent evangelicals – William Wilberforce, Bishop Barrington of Durham, the Hon. Edward James Eliot and Thomas Bernard – with the aim of 'collect[ing] information respecting the circumstances and situation of the poor and the most effectual means of meliorating their condition'.[90] Unlike the Board of Agriculture, the SBCP had little or no intention of shaping government policy. It saw its role as purely educational and exhortatory. Nevertheless it was an influential organisation. Throughout its existence it was supported by some of the most prominent people in the country. Its patron was the king; in 1798 its committee included four bishops, eight noblemen and eight MPs, amongst whom was Addington, the speaker. The committee also included some of the most respected authorities on the poor, such as Patrick Colquhoun. There were 227 subscribers, all gentry, amongst them five bishops, seventeen noblemen and eighteen MPs.[91]

The SBCP seems to have had a considerable effect on its members. Many wrote to say that on reading an account in the *Reports* they had been encouraged to put similar measures into practice in their own parishes.[92] But the SBCP's influence is perhaps most strikingly seen in the number of other societies it formed or inspired. Most of these applied the SBCP's recommendations to a considerable extent in practice. Some were major national institutions in their own right. These included societies modelled on the SBCP in Cork, Dublin, Edinburgh, Liverpool, Sheffield and many lesser places. The Royal Institution, the Cancer Institution, the Fever Institution and the School for the Indigent Blind were also creations of the SBCP.[93] The SBCP was indeed at the forefront of the evangelical revival which affected upper-class opinion so powerfully in the last decade of the eighteenth century.[94] Patronised and endorsed by Wilberforce, it is not surprising that the SBCP was influential (almost certainly much more influential than the Board of Agriculture).

However, in considering its effect on the history of the provision of land for labourers, we should bear in mind that its influence probably declined with time. The later volumes of the *Reports* are just as bulky as the earlier ones, but cover a longer period: the first three volumes cover five years between them, whereas the last three cover thirteen years. Communications

[89] Goddard, 'Agricultural periodicals', 120–1.
[90] SBCP, *Reports*, i. 265.
[91] Ibid. i. 272.
[92] James Baker, *Life of Sir Thomas Bernard*, London 1819, 49; SBCP, *Reports*, ii. 165.
[93] Baker, *Life*, 44–7, 49, 69–70; SBCP, *Reports*, vi. 147, 209.
[94] Boyd Hilton, *The age of atonement: the influence of evangelicalism on social and economic thought, 1785–1865*, Oxford 1988, 98; *The Christian Observer* i (Jan. 1802), 51.

to the society were presumably becoming less frequent. The subscription lists were no longer published in the later years, suggesting that they had diminished embarrassingly. It is unclear whether the society continued to function after Bernard's death in 1818. The last *Report* was issued in 1817; Bernard had always in effect played the part of editor. There is a scrap of evidence which may indicate that the society did continue to exist: according to the *Dictionary of National Biography* Bishop Barrington was still president of the SBCP at the time of his death in 1826,[95] but if that is so it was clearly not very active.

Bernard was emphatically the dominant voice within the SBCP. Not only did he write lengthy introductions to each volume of the society's *Reports*, he also contributed a fair proportion of the 'communications' which formed the main body of each report. He was a vice-president of the society in every year from its foundation until his death in 1818, except for the year 1812 when he was in poor health. Bernard's views are the nearest we can get to the official voice of the society.

Bernard's basic premise was that only if the character of the poor was improved, and specifically if they became more industrious, could their condition be bettered. As he said in the introductory letter to the fifth volume, 'no plan for the improvement of the condition of the poor, will be of any avail . . . UNLESS THE FOUNDATION BE LAID IN THE MELIORA-TION OF THEIR MORAL AND RELIGIOUS CHARACTER'.[96] Similarly he declared that the poor's 'own industry, prudence, and domestic habits, far exceed in intrinsic value, MILLIONS which may be raised for their relief'.[97] The problem was, therefore, how to make the poor more industrious. Bernard argued that for two hundred years, the poor law had attempted to compel the poor to be industrious, with little success. It was now time to try to lead by kindness. In the introduction to the second volume he wrote that the only way to resolve the ever more unsatisfactory condition of the poor was to 'try encouraging that industry and prudence, which no act of parliament can compel'.[98] In the introductory letter to the fifth volume he explained that the failings of all previous schemes of poor relief had been that none of them proposed to operate as 'on free and rational agents, and on religious and accountable creatures'.[99] In the 'Preliminary address to the public' prefacing the first volume he had also declared that it was impossible to force people to improve their condition; it was necessary to make them want to improve it.[100]

In Bernard's view the best way of encouraging the poor was to hold out to the industrious the incentive of landholding. Thus in the introductory letter to volume three he wrote that 'The impressions which have been produced

---

95 *DNB* i. 1214.
96 SBCP, *Reports*, v. 47.
97 Ibid. v. 51.
98 Ibid. ii. 3.
99 Ibid. v. 32.
100 Ibid. i. iii.

upon the cottager's mind, by affording him the means of acquiring PROP-
ERTY, and of possessing objects of care and industry, are great . . . Experience
has yet to produce a single inconvenience, or a solitary variation of effect.'[101]

In the introduction to the second volume Bernard had also stressed the
advantages to labourers of possessing their own property, in this case explicitly a cottage, garden and cow.[102] This was also the subject of his famous
pamphlet, reprinted by the SBCP, on Britton Abbot, the industrious Yorkshire labourer who despite early misfortunes succeeded in raising six children
in comfort from the produce of a rood of land and occasional wage labour.[103]
Giving a labourer a better cottage or a garden tied in very well with another
of Bernard's concerns: that the labourer should be assisted in such a way as to
strengthen his attachment to his home. This would increase his happiness
and his patriotism and make him less likely to resort to the alehouse. Bernard
went so far as to declare, in his introduction to the fifth volume, that no
project was admissible if it tended to alienate the poor man from his
cottage.[104]

Bernard's enthusiasm for providing the poor with land is apparent in the
amount of space devoted to this subject in the *Reports*: the seven volumes
contain within them fifteen articles on the subject. These included pieces of
great significance for the nascent allotment movement. Winchilsea's cow
pastures, which became in subsequent years the most often cited example of
the benefits of letting land to labourers, were described in detail in three
reports by the bishop of Durham, Winchilsea himself and Bernard.[105] The
reports on the relief of the poor at Whelford and at Shipton Moyne were the
first detailed descriptions of allotments.[106] Vavasour's letter on stall-feeding a
cow was crucial in establishing that arable land could beneficially be let to
labourers.[107] Young, for example, noted in his *Annals* that Vavasour's letter
made Plymley's comments on the inadvisability of letting arable land to
labourers obsolete.[108] Estcourt's article on his allotments at Long Newnton
was the first to argue in detail what subsequently became the dominant
theme of the allotment movement, that allotments could have a
transformative effect on the moral character of the labourer, particularly with
regard to respect for the law.[109] In short, the SBCP was a pioneer of the allotment movement and did much both to establish the idea of providing

---

101 Ibid. iii. 30.
102 Ibid. ii. 6.
103 Ibid. ii. 293–308.
104 Ibid. v. 48.
105 Ibid. i. 83–5, 93–100; ii. 172–86.
106 Ibid. iii. 117–22, 153–63. A brief account of the Estcourt allotments had, however,
appeared in *Annals* xxvi (1796), 530–1.
107 SBCP, *Reports*, iii. 79–81.
108 Arthur Young, [Comment], *Annals* xlii (1804), 449.
109 SBCP, *Reports*, v. 71–83.

labourers with land (and even specifically allotments) in the public mind and to set out ideas that remained at the core of the project.

The strength of interest in the provision of land for labourers was, in this early period, at its greatest between 1795 and about 1805. After 1805 interest in land provision ebbed quickly and was not to regain its late 1790s' level until the early 1830s. It is true that there was a brief flurry of interest in parliamentary circles between 1817 and 1819. Several witnesses to the 1817 Select Committee on the Poor Laws mentioned allotments and in the committee's report it was suggested that legislation should be passed permitting parishes to let allotments.[110] This recommendation was embodied in some clauses tacked on to Sturges Bourne's Select Vestries Act (59 George III cap. xii), a major piece of legislation, the primary aim of which was to increase the efficiency (and exclusivity) of parochial government. The allotments clauses of the act gave parishes powers to take in hand parish land, or purchase or hire other land, in order to provide employment for the poor. This could be done either directly by the parish, or by dividing the land into allotments and letting them to the poor. But the provisions of the 1819 act with respect to allotments seem to have been little noticed at the time, and were evidently rarely acted on by parishes subsequently. For the next eleven years the paucity of references to allotments in parliamentary sources makes it plain that there was little political interest in them: the inclusion of allotments clauses in the 1819 act remained an isolated episode, little noted in the country at large in the years which followed and still less so in parliament.[111]

Why did interest in allotments decline after 1805, and why was it so long before it revived? Part of the reason for the decline was that the crisis which had brought the movement to provide labourers with land into existence was, in the main, a temporary one. After 1801 harvests were generally better and prices rose correspondingly less. Although there was another bad year in 1812–13, hardship was less than in 1794–6 or 1799–1801. The revolutionary tensions of the 1790s also eased. By 1798 English Jacobinism was a spent force.[112] It no longer seemed so urgently necessary to make sure that the rural labourer was content with his lot. But it was not simply a matter of altered external circumstances. To some extent the movement became dispirited because of its repeated failures. It became apparent that there was no prospect of passing an effective general enclosure bill; after the debacle over the cows clauses in Pitt's poor bill it was equally obvious that there was no chance of legislating on cow pastures either. These disappointments were compounded by personal difficulties for the leading figures of the movement. Bernard became an increasingly marginal figure as he devoted his energies ever more

---

110 *SC on the Poor Laws*, 1817, vi. 19.

111 Jeremy Burchardt, 'Land, labour, and politics: parliament and allotment provision, 1830–1870', in J. R. Wordie (ed.), *Agriculture and politics in England, 1815–1939*, London 2000, 99–100.

112 E. P. Thompson, *The making of the English working class*, London 1963, 1980 edn, 188.

to the repeal of the salt duties and the promotion of fisheries. In the second decade of the nineteenth century his health deteriorated and he died in 1818.[113] Young lapsed into reclusiveness after the death of his daughter Bobbin in 1797 and whilst he continued to write he made no further significant organisational contribution to the movement for land provision.[114]

In the last analysis, however, the personal and institutional vicissitudes of the movement matter less, at least from the point of view of the history of allotments, than the number of plots actually made available to labourers as a result of the efforts of the Board of Agriculture, the SBCP and their associates. The remainder of this chapter will trace the provision of allotments from the early 1790s through to 1830, and assess how widespread allotment-holding had become in England by the latter date.

Allotments were only just emerging as a separate and distinctive form of landholding in the 1790s. Perhaps the earliest that can be identified as lineal precursors of the modern allotment were at four sites in Wiltshire: Ashley, Long Newnton and Shipton Moyne (all let by the Estcourt family) and Little Cheverell. It seems probable, although it is not certain, that the Estcourt allotments preceded the Little Cheverell site. In the years that followed, several more allotments were created in the Wiltshire/Gloucestershire area, which emerged as the most significant cluster of allotments in the country. However, allotments were soon appearing in widely scattered locations across the south, the Midlands and East Anglia. Table 2 lists all allotment sites known to have been created before 1830.

Further research will undoubtedly uncover more pre-1830 allotment sites. But even with this proviso, table 2 gives an inadequate notion of the number and distribution of allotments over the period 1793–1830. From the individual instances of allotments created in this period which happen to be recorded in various sources, we cannot tell how many sites there were altogether. Nor, since we cannot be sure that what we have is by any means a random sample, are we able to say, on the basis of this information, how allotments were distributed across the country. Fortunately, contemporaries have left us with their own impressions, both in specific areas and nationally, for the years 1793–1830. By assessing this evidence on a county-by-county basis (from south-west to north-east), it is possible to build up an impression of the national picture on the eve of the 1830 Swing riots.

In Cornwall allotments seem to have been unknown before 1830, and indeed remained extremely scarce until the third quarter of the nineteenth century. Even in 1873 allotments were less common in Cornwall than in any other southern English county apart from Middlesex and Surrey, in both of which allotment provision had by this time been seriously affected by urbanisation.[115] Allotments made more headway in Devon, especially in those parts

---

113 Baker, *Life*, 106–7.
114 *DNB* lxiii. 361.
115 *Agricultural Returns of Great Britain for 1873*, 1873, lxix. 301–74.

Table 2
List of allotment sites before 1830

Parish	County	Date
Little Cheverell	Wilts.	between 1793 and 1803
Ashley	Wilts.	1795
Long Newnton	Wilts.	1795
Shipton Moyne	Glos.	1795
Wimpole	Cambs.	1800 or before
Whelford	Glos.	1800
Newton Ferrers	Devon	*c.* 1804
Great Somerford	Wilts.	1806
Willingham	Cambs.	1806
Orlingbury	Northants.	1809
Bishops Cannings	Wilts.	1811
Hambleton	Rutland	1813 or before
Kempsford	Glos.	1813 or before
South Broom	Wilts.	1813
Flamstead	Herts.	1817 or before
Nantwich	Cheshire	*c.* 1817
Barwell	Leics.	1817
Terrington St Clement	Norfolk	1817
Colerne	Wilts.	1818
Donnington	Lincs.	between 1819 and 1824
Fiddington	Wilts.	1819
Chesterford	Essex	*c.* 1820
Barton	Suffolk	early 1820s
Frome	Somerset	1820
Rodbourne	Wilts.	1820
Woodhouse	Leics.	1820
Crondall	Hants.	1821
Malmesbury	Wilts.	1821
Stroud	Glos.	1821
Spratton	Northants.	1822
Waterbeach	Cambs.	1823
Potterne	Wilts.	1824
Southam	Warks.	1824
Banwell	Somerset	1825
Byfield	Northants.	1825
Wells	Somerset	1825
West Lavington	Wilts.	1825
Holton	Suffolk	*c.* 1826
Farthinghoe	Northants.	1826
Weasinham Hall	Norfolk	1826
Bremhill	Wilts.	1827/8

Calne	Wilts.	1827/8
Sundridge	Wilts.	1827/8
Batheaston	Somerset	*c.* 1828
Caunton	Notts.	*c.* 1828
Cranfield	Beds.	1828
Barby	Northants.	1829
Littlebury	Essex	1829
Mauldon	Beds.	1829
Shepton Mallet	Somerset	1829
Worton	Wilts.	1829
Dauncey	Wilts.	1830 or before
Lambourne	Berks.	1830 or before
Market Lavington	Wilts.	1830 or before

Total number of sites known before 1830: fifty-four (of which twenty-five in Wiltshire or Wiltshire borders).

Sources: the table is based on an examination of all the sources listed in the bibliography.

of the county adjacent to Dorset and Somerset, but the rise in the number of plots seems to have taken place almost entirely after 1830, since there is no evidence of any sites in the county before that date other than that at Newton Ferrers listed in table 2. In Somerset allotments had been provided by the bishop of Bath and Wells at Banwell and at Wells itself in 1825. One or two other sites in the county (such as Batheaston, which should, however, probably be considered as part of the Wiltshire group) seem to have predated the Swing riots. But G. T. Scobell, whose familiarity with allotments in Somerset was unrivalled, knew of no allotments in the county before 1831, except those of the bishop of Bath and Wells and some 'not on a proper plan'.[116] Those so described could have been those at Frome and at Shepton Mallet, which were to go badly awry. They were let by the parish, and trades-men as well as labourers were allowed to rent plots, both features of which Scobell disapproved.[117] The Frome and Shepton Mallet sites are the only pre-1830 sites in Somerset discovered in the course of the research for this book, other than those mentioned above. However Scobell's comment could equally well refer to potato grounds, which were already widespread in Somerset in the early 1830s but were not yet always distinguished from allot-ments. Scobell had a strong dislike of potato grounds, which he frequently vented.[118] But however Scobell's comment is interpreted, it is clear that there were few allotments in Somerset before 1830. This is borne out by numerous assertions implying that the allotment system was first established in

116 *SC on the Labouring Poor,* 1843, vii. 16; *LF* cx (1853), 117.
117 *LFM* cxxxv (1842), 77.
118 Ibid. cxxxvi (1842), 99; (1834), 86.

Somerset in or around 1830 made by Scobell on other occasions, and by other authorities.[119]

The situation in Dorset is more complex. Temporary allotments were evidently provided on some estates in the crisis year 1800:

> There is another practice introduced by the earl of Dorchester, Mr Charles Sturt, and others, which will, I hope, be attended with very salutary effects, if followed up with spirit, that of setting out a quarter of an acre of land to each poor labourer with a family, or a proportion suitable to his wants, if he be not already provided with garden ground, in order to cultivate potatoes. . . . There are wastes at the sides of droves and other places in almost every parish proper for this purpose, on which the farmers have agreed for a few months not to turn any cattle, and to allow each labourer a small quantity of thorns or under-wood for a temporary fence. This will be attended with no serious expense; and the land being left naked after the potatoes are taken up, will soon revert to its pristine state.[120]

But these allotments, if such they deserve to be called, presumably reverted to the farmers after the subsistence crisis of 1800–1 was over, and in the research for this book no sites predating 1830 were discovered for Dorset. It is surprising, then, to find that D. O. P. Okeden, one of the 1832–4 assistant poor law commissioners, stated categorically in his report that there was 'scarcely a parish in Dorsetshire where there is not an allotment to the labourer'.[121] His subsequent comments, however, indicate that the 'allotments' he refers to were in fact potato grounds, while Stevenson's report for the Board of Agriculture of 1812, confirms that potato grounds were already widespread in Dorset before 1830.[122] There is also ample evidence that the allotment system was considered to be in its infancy in Dorset in the mid-1840s, and that the number of allotments in the county compared very unfavourably with the situation in Somerset at that time.[123] Captain Scobell went so far as to suggest that the bad reputation Dorset had for the miserable poverty of its agricultural labourers resulted from the failure of the county gentry to institute the allotment system:

> In my county (Somerset) I believe I may say that full one-half of the parishes have adopted the system of field-gardens, and in general it is progressing with the greatest success. I wish I could say (and I wish more had been said to good purpose) as much for the neighbouring county of Dorset. That county has obtained an unenviable celebrity; but I trust now that the landowners will address themselves to the work of ameliorating the condition of their labour-

119 Ibid. xcvii (1840), 20; cxviii (1841), 14; cxliii (1843), 18; (1835), 88; F&I, 366; SC on Agriculture, 1833, v. 246.
120 J. Wickens, 'Cottage gardens', Annals xxxv (1800), 206–7.
121 RC on the Poor Laws, 1834, xxviii. 15.
122 William Stevenson, General view of the agriculture of the county of Dorset, London 1812, 269–70, 429, 434, 454–5.
123 LF vi (1844), 120; xxix (1846), 182–7; xxx (1846), 195–203; xxxiii (1847), 23.

ers. I trust they will follow our example and allot to every man dependent upon them a piece of land on which he may raise vegetables for his family.[124]

So our conclusion must be that allotments were uncommon in Dorset before the 1840s and may indeed not have occurred there at all before 1830.

Wiltshire, on the other hand, had a substantial number of allotments before 1830. In addition to the eighteen sites known individually, it seems clear that there were several others and indeed that in some parts of the county allotments may have been the rule rather than the exception. Cobbett, riding from Devizes to Highworth in September 1826, tells us that:

> As I came along the road, for the first three or four miles, I saw great numbers of labourers either digging potatoes for their Sunday's dinner, or coming home with them, or going out to dig them. The landowners, or occupiers, let small pieces of land to the labourers, and these they then cultivate with the spade for their own use. They pay in all cases a high rent, and in most cases an enormous one. The practice prevails all the way from Warminster to Devizes, and from Devizes to nearly this place [i.e. Highworth].[125]

Cobbett's statement that some of these plots were let by occupiers, and that they were let in most cases at an enormous rent, does raise the possibility that what he had seen were potato grounds. However, Cobbett's remark suggests that some of these plots were let by landowners, and landowners did not in general let potato grounds. Furthermore, three allotment sites (Little Cheverell, Potterne and South Broom) that we know to have been established before 1826 did in fact lie along the route from Warminster via Devizes to Highworth, as well as several other sites that were probably established before 1830 (Coulston and Erlestoke, Great Cheverell, Littleton and Rowde and Bromham). Interestingly, Arthur Young in 'A farming tour in the south and west of England' (1796) had noted that there was 'much gardening and potatoes' around Warminster.[126] It is possible that allotments were already common in this part of Wiltshire as early as this. However, we know from Thomas Davis's account of Wiltshire, written for the board in 1811, that market gardening was extensively practised around Warminster, due to the sandy soil, which was particularly suitable for esculent vegetables, so too much should not be read into Young's comment.[127] Rather, it seems likely that Young's reference was to market gardens and that allotments only became common in the Warminster–Devizes area in the second and third decades of the nineteenth century, as is suggested by the dates of origin of those sites in this area for which we have the relevant information. The other

124 Ibid. xxv (1846), 110.
125 William Cobbett, *Rural rides*, [1830], Nelson Classics edn, n.d. n.p., 370.
126 Arthur Young, 'A farming tour to the south and west of England, 1796', *Annals* xxviii (1797), 460.
127 Thomas Davis, *General view of the agriculture of the county of Wiltshire*, London 1811, 82.

identifiable cluster of pre-1830 allotment sites in Wiltshire is around Malmesbury. This includes all three of the sites known to have been established before 1800 (the Estcourt sites at Ashley, Long Newton and, just across the Gloucestershire border, Shipton Moyne), and also another very early and well-known site, the Revd Stephen Demainbray's allotments at Great Somerford. Significantly, an allotment site between Malmesbury and Tetbury is the only one in the whole of England other than those between Warminster and Highworth that Cobbett mentions in *Rural rides*.[128] It seems almost certain that the site Cobbett is referring to here is that at Long Newnton, since Long Newnton is the only village on the road between Malmesbury and Tetbury.[129] Wiltshire seems indeed not only to have been the county in which the allotment system originated but also the county in which allotments were, by some way, the most numerous before 1830. In fact the areas around Devizes and Malmesbury respectively were the only ones in the country in which allotments could be said to be common before 1830.

There were allotments in Gloucestershire from the very beginning of the movement. Nearly as early as the Estcourt site at Shipton Moyne (1795) was Whelford in the Cotswolds, established in 1800, both sites sites clearly forming part of the Wiltshire concentration. Shipton Moyne is adjacent to Ashley and to Long Newnton (which itself borders Malmesbury), whilst Whelford is only two or three miles from Highworth. Interestingly, we know that there was a site in existence in the village of Kempsford, the next village to Whelford, before 1813. There is almost certainly a causal as well as a geographical connection between Whelford and Kempsford, in so far as the sites in both villages were administered, unusually and in fact possibly (at this time) illegally, by the parochial authorities. In view of these interrelations, it seems clear that we have here a compact district in which allotments were widespread. Since all the sites known in Gloucestershire were close to the Wiltshire border, with the arguable exception of Stroud, it is also probably safe to assume that apart from this spill-over effect the county had few if any sites before 1830, and that the total number of sites was correspondingly small.

One Oxfordshire site dating from before 1830 was discovered in the course of the research for this book. It may have been an outlier of the Wiltshire concentration, since there is nothing to suggest that there were any other sites in the county at that time.

There is no direct evidence of allotments in Worcestershire or Herefordshire before 1830. Arthur Lewis, reporting on Herefordshire, Shropshire and Monmouthshire to the poor law commissioners in 1833, stated that 'The custom of setting out or making allotments of land to labourers, either by proprietors of land, or their tenants, is of rare occurrence in these counties; I met with only three or four instances, and in those it was of very recent

---

[128] Cobbett, *Rural rides*, 387.
[129] My thanks for this point are due to Mr Ted Prince, of the Tetbury Local History Society.

introduction, and practised on a limited scale.'[130] Even as late as 1873 there were only 997 plots in all Herefordshire, although by this time Worcestershire was better provided for.[131]

There is little information on allotment provision in the south-east before 1830. In Hampshire in 1833 the poor law commissioners were informed that 'the practice is becoming general', which presumably implies that before this date it had not been so.[132] We do have evidence of one pre-1830 site, however: Crondall, established in 1821. Vaughan, the special assistant poor law commissioner, concluded in his 1843 report that whilst allotments had been tried in most parts of Sussex, Surrey and Kent, they were general in few parts of his district.[133] This is at least compatible with one of the few pieces of direct evidence that we have: a statement by Henry Martin, whose relationship to allotments in Kent parallels that of Captain Scobell to allotments in Somerset, to the effect that, with the exception of one or two early sites, allotments were first established in Kent in 1836.[134]

We have no evidence of any sites in Middlesex, Berkshire, Buckinghamshire or Bedfordshire until 1828–9 (*see* table 2). It was in 1829, according to Mr H. Trethewy, the agent of Earl de Grey, that the system was begun in Bedfordshire.[135] The first site known in Berkshire is Lambourne, probably dating from early 1830. But since this site is only two miles from the Wiltshire border, it probably belongs with that grouping. There is one pre-1830 record of what seems to be an allotment site in Hertfordshire. This is at Flamstead, dating to before 1817.[136]

It seems to have been Charles James Blomfield, later bishop of London but at that time merely rector of Chesterford, who began the allotment system in Essex. This was in about 1820, in his own village of Chesterford. However, allotments do not seem to have spread to any significant extent until the 1840s, except in the Saffron Walden area where they were introduced in many parishes in the early 1830s (and at Littlebury in 1829).[137] The Essex allotments were probably isolated from those in Cambridgeshire before 1830 and perhaps even after then; only thus is it possible to explain the claim made by an informed Essex witness that it was Blomfield who began the allotment system in 1820, when in fact George Law, later bishop of Bath and Wells, had instituted allotments at Willingham in 1806 (the Wiltshire allotments were,

---

130 *RC on the Poor Laws,* 1834, xxviii. 669.
131 *Agricultural Returns of Great Britain for 1873,* 301–74.
132 *RC on the Poor Laws,* 1834, xxxi. 437.
133 *Report of the Special Assistant Poor Law Commissioners on the Employment of Women and Children in Agriculture,* 1843, xii. 143.
134 *SC on the Labouring Poor,* 1843, vii. 1.
135 Paper entitled 'The allotment system', printed in the *Journal of the Central Farmers' Club,* Nov. 1858, and reprinted in *RC on the Employment of Children, Young Persons, and Women in Agriculture,* 1867–8, xvii. 199.
136 *SC on the Poor Laws,* 1817, vi. 73.
137 *SC on the Labouring Poor,* 1843, vii. 40; *LFM* (1834), 64; *F&I,* 202.

of course, even earlier).[138] There was, however, a relationship between the Willingham allotments and those instituted in 1823 at Waterbeach, just a few miles away. Alfred Power, the assistant poor law commissioner for Cambridgeshire in 1832–4, made the following comment about the Waterbeach site:

> The experiment has been tried here on a large scale for a longer period than elsewhere, I believe, in the county. The commissioners are well aware that an example had been set many years previously by the bishop of Bath and Wells, then Dr Law, at Willingham in this county. The practice, however, is not subsisting there at this time. It was owing to the humane consideration of Mr Fardell, the rector of Waterbeach, moved by the success of the experiment at Willingham, that in the year 1823, twenty acres of land conveniently adjoining the village were let in allotments of half an acre each to forty labourers, at rents equivalent to what could be obtained from the farmer.[139]

In addition to the sites at Willingham and Waterbeach, there was one at Wimpole. This was actually earlier than even the Willingham site, being recorded in one of the SBCP's reports in 1800. But it was on a small scale, with only six plots, and differed significantly from the later tradition of allotments in that the plots were divided from each other by internal hedges.[140] The Wimpole site seems not to have attracted the attention of later exponents of allotments (as Power's comment indicates) and it should probably be regarded as an isolated, *ad hoc* solution to a particular local problem and not as a part of the allotment movement as it subsequently developed in the nineteenth century. However, there is some reason to believe that the number of allotments provided in the county may have been rising in the late 1820s. The survey of all Cambridgeshire parishes carried out by magistrates in 1831, discussed more fully in chapter 2, implies that as many as a third of all Cambridgeshire parishes may have had allotments by that date, and it is difficult to believe that this level can have been reached in a mere two years.

There is no evidence of any allotments in Huntingdonshire before 1830. An incomplete survey of parishes in the county, carried out for the 1832–4 poor law commissioners, suggests that where allotments did exist in 1833, they had only recently been introduced.[141] In Suffolk, the particularly active Blything Hundred Labourer's Friend Society reported that, after several years of propagandising, far fewer than half the villages in their hundred had allotments as late as 1838.[142] The situation may well have been worse in parts of the county with a less well-organised local movement. Indeed, only two sites predating 1830, Sir Henry Bunbury's at Barton near Bury St Edmund's, and

---

138 *SC of the House of Lords on the Poor Laws*, 1830–1, viii. 170.
139 *RC on the Poor Laws*, 1834, xxviii. 254–5.
140 SBCP, *Reports*, iii. 92–7.
141 *RC on the Poor Laws*, 1834, xxviii. 702–9.
142 *LFM* xcv (1839), 21.

another at Holton, have been traced. Neighbouring Norfolk also seems to have had few allotments before 1830. We know only of sites at Terrington St Clement (1817) and at Weasinham Hall (1826), although it is also possible that allotments existed on Lord Suffield's estate at Gunton. One Mr Smith, a resident of Gunton, informed the 1843 *Report of the Special Assistant Poor Law Commissioners on the Employment of Women and Children in Agriculture* that:

> The system is general here. . . . It has been made general here in the last ten years. There were allotments before that, but only a few; we found that these worked so well, that they made the tenants so much more thrifty than those without them, that the late Lord Suffield made it general.[143]

Suffield was one of the foremost advocates of the provision of land to labourers, so it is particularly significant that even on his estate allotments were not widespread before 1830.[144] In 1833 it had been reported to the poor law commissioners that 'the system appears gradually spreading' in Norfolk, so it seems reasonable to conclude that, with only two or three isolated exceptions, allotments were probably first introduced into Norfolk in the 1830s.[145]

As regards the Midlands, the county where most allotments seem to have been established before 1830 was Northamptonshire. Research for this book has identified five Northamptonshire sites predating 1830. J. J. Richardson, the assistant poor law commissioner for the county, claimed in 1834 that the plan of letting land to the poor had become 'almost universal' in Northamptonshire.[146] But there are reasons for questioning this claim. Several of the relatively few Northamptonshire sites for which we have start dates were established in the 1840s or thereafter. J. R. Wartnaby, an owner-occupier of Clipston, told the Royal Commission on the Employment of Children, Young Persons and Women in Agriculture of 1867–9 that he could recollect wages being only 9s. per week about twenty years ago and 'there were very few allotments at that time'.[147] However, it is not entirely clear whether Wartnaby is referring to the situation in his own parish or to Northamptonshire more generally. More authoritative is the evidence of F. H. Norman, the special assistant poor law commissioner for Northamptonshire, that allotments were rare in the county 'thirty or thirty five years ago' (i.e. in the mid-1830s), since which time they had been 'enormously extended'.[148] Information about individual allotment sites supports Norman's assertion: the proportion of sites identified for Northamptonshire for which the first

---

[143] *Report on the Employment of Women and Children in Agriculture*, 1843, xii. 267.
[144] Hammond and Hammond, *Village labourer*, 296–8.
[145] *RC on the Poor Laws*, 1834, xxxi. 306.
[146] Ibid. xxxviii. 406.
[147] *RC on the Employment of Children, Young Persons, and Women in Agriculture*, 1867–8, xvii. 695.
[148] Ibid. 181.

evidence post-dates 1834 is very high in comparison to the figures for other counties (mainly due to the large number of records from the 1850s and 1860s). Thus it seems proper to conclude that Richardson's claim that allotments were almost universal in Northamptonshire in 1834 was exaggerated. This fits better with the lack of evidence for allotments on anything like this scale before 1830. The records we have, for five sites (as opposed to eighteen in Wiltshire), are not grouped in compact areas, as the Wiltshire sites were, but scattered across the county. This does not suggest any region or regions of dense allotment provision, but rather isolated individual cases. Furthermore, there is no contemporary evidence to suggest that allotments were common in Northamptonshire before 1830, in strong contrast to the considerable evidence to this effect for Wiltshire. Probably the best conclusion is that whilst there may well have been more allotment sites in Northamptonshire than in any other English county apart from Wiltshire before 1830, they were nevertheless only found in a few parishes and only became common after 1830. Had the number of sites grown rapidly after 1830 and continued to do so into the 1840s and 1850s, this would plausibly account for most of the evidence cited above.

It is difficult to know how common allotments were in the east Midlands before 1830. James Orange, the leading figure in the allotment movement in the area in the 1840s, thought that much of the resistance to his attempts to persuade the east Midlands artisans to take allotments was due to the novelty of the plan.[149] However, he qualified his remark by restricting it to the towns and manufacturing villages, which may account for the record of scattered allotment sites in Warwickshire, Leicestershire, Rutland, Nottinghamshire and Derbyshire. A letter from C. H. Bracebridge to the chairmen of Warwickshire poor law unions confirms that allotments were rare in that county before 1830.[150]

Evidence of allotments in the counties north of a line running from the Cambridgeshire/Lincolnshire border in the east, and then along the southern borders of Lincolnshire, Yorkshire, Cheshire, Staffordshire and Shropshire, is scanty. Only two sites predating 1830 have been identified in the whole of this vast region: at Nantwich in Cheshire and Donnington in Lincolnshire. However, there is also the statement by George Legard in his prize report to the Royal Agricultural Society on the agriculture of East Yorkshire:

> Cottage allotments, as a system, were first introduced into this Riding by the present Lord Wenlock, of Escrick Park, who, soon after he succeeded to the Escrick estate, viz. about the year 1823, among other plans for the amelioration of the agricultural labourer, established cottage allotments in each township on his property.[151]

---

149 *LFM* cxxxiii (1842), 55.
150 Ibid. clii (1843), 159.
151 George Legard, 'On the farming of the East Riding of Yorkshire', *JRASE* ix (1848–9), 127.

An earlier reference to allotments on the Escrick estate, however, suggests that they were in fact a development of the first years of the 1830s.[152] There seems to be no evidence for other sites in the north prior to 1830,[153] a state of affairs which seems to be confirmed by later sources which assert that allotments were still rare in various parts of the north even after 1830.[154]

The general picture, therefore, of allotments immediately before the Swing riots is that they were widespread only in Wiltshire and its immediate borders. A significant number of allotments may also have existed in Northamptonshire, but it seems more probable that the large increase referred to by several sources occurred almost entirely after 1830. Apart from this, allotments were well-established in a few places in Somerset and there were a few very scattered sites over most of the rest of the south, the Midlands and East Anglia. But they seem to have been entirely absent from the north, the Welsh borders and Cornwall. The total number of allotment sites before 1830 may not have exceeded one hundred. This picture fits with the more general evidence relating to the country as a whole: many of those who wrote or commented on allotments in the 1830s noted the rapid expansion that was taking place. The three parliamentary select committees on agriculture which sat during the 1830s are particularly interesting in this respect. Their concern with bread consumption and the price of corn, and to a certain extent with agricultural labourers, led them to ask frequent questions about allotments. Their questions often imply that the allotment system was of very recent introduction and many of the replies state this explicitly. The evidence from the select committees is consistent with the pattern outlined above, even to the extent of implying that in Wiltshire, and in Wiltshire alone, allotments had been introduced on a significant scale before 1830. It is also internally consistent: witnesses to the 1833 select committee referred variously to the allotment system as having been established for between one and three years, or in one case three to four years, whilst witnesses to the later select committees either gave a longer timescale or merely referred to the system as having been established recently.[155] The strong interest taken in allotments by all the select committees on agriculture, and even more so by

---

152 *LFM* (1834), 64.

153 However, an interesting article by K. J. Allison, which appeared too late to be incorporated into the text of this book, mentions allotments at Sproatley which 'may have existed by 1802' and at Cottingham, also in the East Riding, established in 1819. The latter subsequently had cottages built on them: 'The provision of allotment gardens in East Yorkshire', *Northern History* xxxvii (2000), 276.

154 *SC of the House of Lords on the Poor Laws*, 1830–1, viii. 201; *RC on the Poor Laws*, 1834, xxviii. 669–70, 739–40, 746–67; *LFM* cxxii (1841), 67; cxlvii (1843), 81–2; *SC on the Labouring Poor*, 1843, vii. 35, 71; *Report on the Employment of Women and Children in Agriculture*, 1843, xii. 343; *SC on Agriculture*, 1833, v. 44.

155 *SC on Agriculture*, 1833, v. 70, 246, 298, 493, 530–1, 574; *SC on the Causes and Extent of Agricultural Distress*, 1836, viii. 17, 171, 257; *SC of the House of Lords on Agriculture*, 1837, v. 37, 167, 304.

the 1830–1 Select Committee of the House of Lords on the Poor Laws and by the great poor law inquiry of 1832–4, is in itself strongly suggestive of a major upsurge in allotment provision in the early 1830s, especially when contrasted with the almost complete lack of interest shown by the corresponding pre-1830 inquiries.

For all the energetic proselytising of Sir Thomas Bernard, the earl of Winchilsea and the SBCP, therefore, the conclusion that the number of allotments established prior to 1830 was very low seems inescapable. Indeed, labourers may well actually have lost more land than they gained during this period, once the loss of gardens and other small patches of land to the farmers' ploughs during the war years is taken into account.[156] But it would be wrong to conclude that because the allotment movement of the late eighteenth and early nineteenth centuries had little immediate effect, it was entirely abortive. Two things, at least, were undeniably achieved: the idea of providing labourers with land was firmly established in the public mind, and the idea of allotments as a specific form of land provision had been worked out, made known and tried in practice.

That the idea of providing land to labourers was well established was important to the rapid success of the revived allotment movement after 1830, as was the fact that this revived movement could point to several examples of allotments already established that had been successful over a long period. Although almost a quarter of a century intervened between the decline of the first allotment movement after 1805 and the rise of the second in 1830, there were in fact many continuities between the two movements. There was at least some degree of continuity of personnel: thus Thomas Estcourt was to the fore in the 1790s whilst his son Thomas Grimston Bucknall Estcourt was a leading proponent of allotments in the 1830s. The *Labourer's Friend Magazine*, the chief organ of the second allotment movement, referred frequently to the work of the SBCP and often reprinted old SBCP articles.[157] Perhaps more important, many of the characteristic aims and forms of the later allotment movement were already emerging in this period. It is true that in the 1830s and 1840s there was more emphasis on the value of allotments in decreasing criminality and considerably less emphasis on their contribution to raising food production, But the major emphases on increasing well-being, industriousness and 'contentment', and on decreasing the poor rates, were just as characteristic of the second allotment movement as of the first.

In more detailed respects, too, the movement of the 1790s can be seen to foreshadow, and perhaps to set the pattern for, the larger movement of the 1830s. Estcourt's description of the conditions of tenure of his Long Newnton allotments, which appeared in the fifth volume of SBCP reports, does not differ in most respects from descriptions of conditions of tenure appearing in

---

[156] John Jacob, 'Crops in Kent', *Annals* xxiv (1800), 606.
[157] *LFM* lxxix (1837), 137–40; lxxx (1837), 153–6; lxxxi (1837), 169–72; lxxxv (1838), 49–51; xci (1838), 137–40; xcix (1839), 83–6; cxxv (1841), 112–13; *LF* xviii (1845), 330.

the *Labourer's Friend Magazine*. Restrictions on cropping and insistence on lawful behaviour on pain of eviction are cases in point.[158] Where the first and second allotment movements really differed was not so much with respect to their values as in their scope, ambition and commitment to allotments as opposed to other forms of land provision or even alternative, non-land-based methods of 'bettering the condition of the poor'. The second allotment movement represented a sustained and self-conscious attempt to reshape the character of the rural labouring poor. Whilst the SBCP and the Board of Agriculture hoped that land provision would have beneficial moral effects, they were less assured of its transformative powers than the LFS and did not associate these specifically and solely with allotments.

Given the many continuities between the first and second allotment movements, why, then, did the movement to provide labourers with land not 'take off' in the 1790s, as it did in the 1830s? An answer to this puzzling question requires an analysis of the events of 1830 and of the remarkable developments in the allotment movement in the wake of that dramatic year.

[158] SBCP, *Reports*, v. 71–83.

PART II

THE SECOND ALLOTMENT MOVEMENT

2

The Resurgence of Allotment Promotion and Provision after 1830

The progress of the allotment movement before 1830 was slow. However, in the 1830s there was a sudden and widespread upsurge of interest and activity, one of the first signs of which was the formation in 1830 of the LFS which was to play the leading role in the allotment movement for the next two decades. Two preliminary points about the society are appropriate at this stage. First, it was, unlike the SBCP, entirely dedicated to the promotion of allotments. Admittedly, its official title incorporated a reference to promoting loan societies, but neither the LFS nor its successor, the SICLC, made any progress in this area. Secondly, the LFS rapidly acquired influential support: within the first two years of its existence it had obtained the patronage of William IV, whilst on the platform at the society's first annual general meeting, held on 18 February 1832 at Exeter Hall, were four noblemen, two bishops and eight MPs.[1]

The LFS was not the only national society formed to promote allotments in the early 1830s. The Agricultural Employment Institution was in existence by 1832 and held its first public meeting at Freemasons' Hall on 23 March 1833.[2] Its aims were broader than those of the LFS, since it hoped not only to argue for but to let allotments to labourers. It too had influential patrons, including several lords, bishops and MPs, and there was some overlap of support with the LFS.[3] The AEI seems to have flourished rather briefly, and little is known of what it accomplished, but the fact that it attracted such prestigious connections is another indication of the remarkably high profile the allotments issue suddenly attained in the early 1830s.

It was not only in London that societies were being formed to promote allotments. Local societies, often affiliated to the LFS, were springing up in many counties. By 1833 there were at least seventeen of them.[4] County and regional agricultural associations were also taking an interest in allotments: in the course of 1832, for example, the Warwickshire, Devon and Bath and West of England societies all discussed and approved the allotment system, and it seems likely that many other agricultural societies did so too.[5] The

---

1 LFS, *Proceedings of the LFS 1832*, London 1832, 3, 8.
2 *Mark Lane Express*, 25 Jan. 1833, 3.
3 Ibid.
4 LFS, *Proceedings of the LFS 1833*, 6.
5 *Mark Lane Express*, 9 Jan. 1832, 2; 28 May 1832, 3; 31 Dec. 1832, 4.

local dimension of the allotment movement made a distinctive and pivotal contribution to its character and success, a contribution which will be assessed more fully in chapter 4.

Nor was all the activity confined to the sphere of voluntary organisations. A surprising amount of attention was paid to the allotment system by parliament. The first sign of awakened interest at Westminster came on 11 November 1830, when a speech by Lord Suffield in the House of Lords emphasised the effectiveness of allotments in holding down poor rates.[6] Eight days later J. I. Briscoe, a leading figure within the LFS, spoke in the House of Commons in favour of allotment provision.[7] Shortly afterwards, on 29 November, the marquis of Salisbury successfully moved in the House of Lords for a select committee on the poor laws.[8] The ensuing committee was dominated by members of the AEI, including the bishop of Bath and Wells, Earl Stanhope and Salisbury himself, and chose to take evidence from prominent advocates and exponents of the allotment system such as the Revd Stephen Demainbray, Richard Pollen, R. M. Bacon and T. G. B. Estcourt.[9] Although the extremely brief reports of the committee did not make any recommendations for legislative action on allotments, Salisbury took care to ensure that the evidence the committee had heard was brought to the attention of the upper house. Parliamentary interest diminished during the spring and early summer of 1831, but as thoughts turned to the likelihood of high levels of rural unemployment and of discontent during the coming winter, the government came under renewed pressure to take action to mitigate the hardships agricultural labourers would probably face.[10] The response was striking: three separate acts of parliament relating solely to allotments, and to the closely connected question of parochial employment by spade husbandry, were passed within the space of a year. The first of these amended the 1819 act to allow parishes to enclose up to fifty acres of waste, under certain conditions, for use as allotments or for spade husbandry.[11] The second allowed parishes to enclose up to fifty acres of crown land for the same purposes under similar conditions.[12] Both these acts were directly sponsored by the government. The third act, the most radical of the three, was a private member's bill, but appears to have had government backing. It concerned what were called fuel allotments. These had nothing to do with allotments in the ordinary sense of the word, but were portions of land made over in trust to the poor collectively under some enclosure awards to compensate for lost rights of fuel-gathering. They often yielded little revenue. The act required their

---

6 *Parliamentary debates*, 3rd ser. i, col. 375.
7 Ibid. i. 600.
8 Ibid. i. 687–91.
9 *SC of the House of Lords on the Poor Laws*, 1830–1, viii, passim.
10 Burchardt, 'Land, labour, and politics', 102–3.
11 1 and 2 Will IV c 42.
12 1 and 2 Will IV c 59.

trustees to let them as allotments in the ordinary sense of the word.[13] In addition to this unprecedented flurry of parliamentary activity (for never before had parliament passed an act which referred to allotments more than marginally: the 1819 act was the only previous public act to contain provisions relating to allotments at all) the famous Royal Commission on the Poor Laws gathered a large mass of information on allotments and reported favourably on them in 1834, although it did not recommend any immediate further legislative action.[14]

The number and distribution of allotments

Organisational activity, however, does not necessarily translate directly into practical results, as was demonstrated in the years before 1830. How far did the upsurge of interest in allotments in the early 1830s lead to an increase in the number of plots over the next fifteen years (i.e. during the period in which the second allotment movement was most active)? An obvious source of information is the 'Rural queries' section of the poor law report of 1834. One of the questions posed by the commissioners was whether any land was let to labourers, and if so, how much. The temptation to see this as a census of allotments is great. It is, indeed, upon the 'Rural queries' that Barnett based his map of the proportion of parishes in each county which had allotments. His procedure was quite simply to calculate for each county the proportion of 'yes' to 'no' answers. As the first serious discussion of the allotment movement by a modern social historian, Barnett's work deserves respect, but on this point his findings are misleading, for several reasons. First, only about a twelfth of parishes returned the questionnaire, and of these many did not fill in the question on allotments. Parishes with active magistrates or parochial officers may well have been more likely both to provide allotments, and to return and fill in the form. Second, in the case of many counties, the number of parishes answering the question on allotments is less than a dozen, an inadequate basis for generalisation. Third, Barnett does not distinguish between allotments and potato grounds, which for some counties such as Dorset grossly inflates the proportion of parishes taken to have allotments.

While it is often possible to tell whether the answers given to the poor law commissioners refer to allotments or to potato grounds, the remaining two problems remain insuperable: it is impossible to establish whether, and to what degree, the answers given to the 'Rural queries' are representative, and even if it were, the size of sample for many counties is far too small. This does not mean that the 'Rural queries' are useless as a source; but the indications they provide as to the county-by-county distribution of allotments are unreli-

13 2 Will IV c 42.
14 *RC on the Poor Laws*, 1834, xxvii. 100–8.

able. Unfortunately, no other single source provides comprehensive reliable data on allotment numbers, so estimates must be gathered from several different sources. In this way, by greatly extending the range of sources used, by critically evaluating the evidence they provide (including the 'Rural queries'), and by distinguishing between potato grounds and allotments, a considerably more accurate and informative estimate of the number of allotments existing in the 1830s and 1840s may be put forward.

Numerous sources agree on the general point that the number of allotments was growing in this period, and many of them suggest that it was growing rapidly. A few examples from the large number of references available illustrate what was happening in the years 1830–45. An article by Edward Edwards, for example, in *Blackwood's Magazine* of 1830 notes that the allotment system was attracting much attention and expresses gratification that it was spreading 'so rapidly' throughout the country.[15] Three years later, Captain Scobell was warning against complacency amongst the supporters of allotments:

> There is one misapprehension most necessary to be guarded against by the friends of the system; which is, not to be misled into a supposition from the zealous countenance which it has attracted in the newspapers and periodicals, that its establishment is further advanced than it really is, and therefore to slacken their efforts. The practice of allotments is yet, like distant and warning beacons – far and wide between – not one parish in fifty, perhaps, has yet participated in its benefits.[16]

Scobell was frustrated by the failure of the vast majority of landowners to adopt the system he so enthusiastically advocated, but to the historian the figure of one parish in fifty (i.e. perhaps about 300 sites nationally) seems reasonably impressive, bearing in mind that in 1830 there were probably fewer than 100 sites and that these had been established over a thirty-five-year period. Moving on a year, the 1834 poor law report, in its conclusion on the allotment system, informed its readers that the system was 'rapidly extending'.[17] This conclusion was borne out by the evidence on particular counties provided by assistant poor law commissioners. Two years later, in 1836, there is a statement from the committee of the LFS to the effect that they 'rejoice in the general extension of the allotment system and its adoption by public societies and private individuals'.[18] In 1840 the *Mark Lane Express* noted that the allotment system had extended widely in the preceding few years.[19] Finally, in 1844 the Revd S. Lane told the annual

---

[15] Edward Edwards, 'The influence of free trade upon the condition of the labouring classes', *Blackwood's Magazine* xxvii (1830), 567.
[16] *F&I*, 366.
[17] *RC on the Poor Laws*, 1834, xxvii. 108.
[18] *LFM* lviii (1836), 1.
[19] Ibid. cxi (1840), 82.

meeting of the Dorchester Agricultural Society that the allotment system was rapidly extending in Dorset and in other counties.[20]

Allowance must be made for the natural optimism of advocates of a new idea. For 'rapidly', 'fairly rapidly' might be more appropriate. The very fact that these comments are found over so great a span of years (similar statements can even be produced for the 1880s and 1890s) sets limits to how rapidly the system can have been growing. However, such statements were not found before 1830. Even though the precise tempo of growth cannot be gauged, the conclusion that the system was growing, and growing at a reasonably consistent and significant rate, seems unavoidable.

The evidence on the regional situation is seriously flawed in two respects: there is not enough of it, and what has survived is unlikely to be representative of the whole. The second problem deserves a little more discussion. The difficulty is that the sources provide much fuller information for some counties than for others. The most important source is the *Labourer's Friend Magazine*, which regularly included reports on the progress of allotments in Somerset, Kent and the east Midlands, sent in by the active local branches there. There was also frequent correspondence from Sussex, Essex, Suffolk and later from Middlesex. To some extent this probably reflects the actual distribution of allotments, in so far as areas where the movement was expanding rapidly would presumably have been more likely to establish contact with the society. However, it seems highly unlikely that every area where the system was significantly present sent reports to the LFS; since the coverage of sites for Somerset, Kent, Nottinghamshire, Leicestershire and, to a lesser extent, Warwickshire, seems relatively complete, it must be assumed that the other counties are to an unascertained extent underrepresented in the *Labourer's Friend Magazine*.

To some degree other sources compensate for this. For three counties there are useful surveys made in the early 1830s. Cambridgeshire is covered by the almost complete survey of land provision in the county made by the local magistrates in 1831. Wiltshire is in part covered by the survey conducted by the Devizes Labourer's Friend Society in 1833. Huntingdonshire and the Isle of Ely have a rather less satisfactory survey carried out by the 1832–4 poor law commissioners. The 'Rural queries' material, interpreted with appropriate caution, provides useful information about the situation in Hampshire, Sussex, Kent, Essex, Cambridgeshire, Suffolk, Norfolk, Cumberland and the West Riding. The three select committees on agriculture, whilst showing considerable interest in the effects of allotments, provide little detail about the distribution of sites, but various parliamentary reports of the early 1840s are more useful. The 1843 *Report of the Special Assistant Poor Law Commissioners on the Employment of Women and Children in Agriculture* is the most valuable of these. It covered Wiltshire, Dorset, Devon, Somerset, Kent, Surrey, Sussex, Suffolk, Norfolk, Lincolnshire, Yorkshire

---

[20] *LF* vi (1844), 115.

and Northumberland, and is particularly informative about the last five. But there is also useful information in the 1840 *Report of the Royal Commission on the Handloom Weavers*, particularly for the clothing districts of Wiltshire and Gloucestershire, in the 1843 *Report of the Select Committee on the Labouring Poor*, and, for the east Midlands, in the 1845 *Report of the Royal Commission on the Framework Knitters*. Numerous less significant sources provide patchy in-formation on other counties and there is no county for which there is a complete absence of information. The most serious gaps are for Devon and the south and west Midlands.

Taking the counties in groups, and starting with the south-west (which for present purposes consists of Cornwall, Devon, Dorset, Somerset, Wiltshire and Gloucestershire), the closest to a contemporary assessment of the extent of allotments generally in that region is a comment made by Austin, the special assistant poor law commissioner, in his 1843 report, to the effect that the allotment system 'has been rapidly on the increase of late years in Wiltshire, Dorsetshire, and Devonshire, but has not been adopted in Somersetshire to any considerable extent'.[21] This is a perplexing statement. Allotments were quite certainly common in Somerset and almost certainly rare in both Dorset and Devon at this time. Whilst it is true that they were common in Wiltshire, Austin's remark makes more sense if we assume that he was including potato grounds in his definition of allotments. These were clearly very common in both Dorset and Devon and seem to have had a significant presence in Wiltshire too. The statement that allotments had made no significant progress in Somerset can perhaps be explained by the constraints on Austin's inquiry. Since his commission was limited to thirty days he investigated only a few districts in his region and the district he chose in Somerset was the Bridgwater area, one which the lack of references in other sources suggests may have had few or no allotments.[22]

Turning to detailed evidence on the individual counties, the sources mention only three sites in Cornwall, significantly all on the coast – St Germans, Looe and Falmouth. It is known that the allotments at Looe were mainly intended for, and taken by, fishermen and it seems likely that this was also the case in the other two instances. This suggests that allotments had yet to make any impact on the purely agricultural parts of Cornwall.

Eleven definite sites in Devon in the 1830–45 period have been identified, mostly rural, and scattered across the county. Clearly evidence for this county is not adequate, but the small number of sites recorded and the almost complete absence of references in the sources on the subject suggest that whilst allotments were clearly not unknown, as was virtually the situation in Cornwall, they were nevertheless rare.

The number of sites recorded for Dorset, fourteen, is also low. The suprising comments of Okeden, the 1832–4 assistant poor law commissioner,

---

[21] *Report on the Employment of Women and Children in Agriculture*, 1843, xii. 15.
[22] Ibid. 1–3.

and of Austin, the 1843 assistant poor law commissioner, to the effect that allotments were numerous in Dorset, have been explained as referring to potato grounds. The well-informed George Bolls, a land agent who had worked for the tithe commissioners and who had formerly farmed in the county, offered a more discriminating opinion to the 1843 Select Committee on the Labouring Poor: 'the principal part [of the labourers in the county] have allotments; all Lord Portman's tenants, Mr Sturt's and Lord Russell's have allotments'. However he stated that the system was not universal in Dorset.[23] Other evidence points to a rapid growth in the number of sites, at least in some parts of Dorset, in the early and, especially, the mid-1840s. This includes, for example, Captain Scobell's statement in 1845 that the allotment system was as yet far less advanced in Dorset than in Somerset but was now beginning to be more widely practised in the former county and the Revd S. Lane's report to the Dorchester Agricultural Society's annual meeting that the system was rapidly extending in Dorset. There is much other evidence to the same effect. R. B. Sheridan, for example, informed the same meeting of the Dorchester Agricultural Society that allotments had been introduced in six or seven parishes in the Blandford area that year.[24]

This marked upturn in interest in allotments in the county in the early and mid-1840s can partly be attributed to external influences. The condition of Dorset's agricultural labourers had become a stick with which northern opponents of factory legislation could beat the leaders of the ten-hours movement, in particular Lord Ashley, who had extensive estates in Dorset.[25] These high-profile attacks led many, even of the country gentry, to regard Dorset as a disgrace, as can be seen from other comments made by Captain Scobell in 1846.[26] General opprobrium stimulated a defensive display of county solidarity and two large meetings of the county gentry, clergy and farmers were held in the autumn of 1846, at Beaminster on 10 September and at Dorchester on 26 October. Both were largely aimed at extending the allotment system within Dorset and each resulted in the formation of district labourer's friend societies.[27] Apart from the increased interest shown in the mid-1840s, it seems possible that there was an earlier, although much less considerable, flurry in the early 1830s, concentrated in the centre of the county around Blandford and Sturminster Newton. A meeting was held at Sturminster Newton on 9 June 1832 to promote allotments and several of the sites in this area are known to have originated in the early 1830s. However, it seems that this was but a brief episode. Only one record has been traced of a site created in Dorset between 1834 and 1844. It is furthermore suggestive

23 *SC on the Labouring Poor*, 1843, vii. 133.
24 *LF* vi (1844), 115, 120.
25 Edwin Hodder, *The life and works of the seventh earl of Shaftesbury*, KG, ii, London 1886, 27.
26 *LF* xxxiii (1847), 23.
27 Ibid. xxix (1846), 182–7; xxxii (1847), 3–10.

that at the Dorchester meeting in 1846 there were references to this earlier period of activity and even a proposal to reprint a pamphlet written in 1832, but no references to any subsequent initiatives.[28]

The situation in Somerset is more straightforward and much better documented. Austin's remark notwithstanding, there can be no doubt that allotments really were common in the county. Thus we have records of seventy-three sites in sixty-nine parishes. According to Captain Scobell there were no allotments in the twenty parishes of the Chewton division of Somerset in 1830, but by 1833 there were allotments in twelve of them.[29] In 1835 that number had risen to fifteen and there were also allotments in another eight parishes in adjoining divisions.[30] However, Scobell also estimated in that same year that taking the country as a whole only one parish in every fifty had an allotment site, and it seems likely that the Chewton district was well in advance of most of the rest of Somerset in terms of allotment provision. In 1839 Scobell stated that the number of sites in the county had grown slowly after its beginnings in 1830 until about 1836, after which it began to grow rapidly, so that 'soon there will not be a parish without it'.[31] The suggestion that allotments only became common in the county after 1836 receives support from evidence given to the 1837 House of Lords Select Committee on Agriculture. Bickham Escott, a Somerset witness, referred to the system of 'allotments in fields [as opposed to gardens], as lately introduced', and said that the last summer, being a very hot one and thus a bad one for potatoes, had not been a fair year to try the system out.[32] The LFS claimed that the system was 'general' in East Somerset in 1840.[33] In the late 1840s Scobell made a comprehensive attempt to assess the number of allotments in Somerset, the preliminary results of which he announced to the 1851 annual general meeting of the SICLC:

> I can ... tell you that the field-garden system in Somersetshire is making great progress. Wherever I travel it is spreading. I am now in the course of collecting from the clergymen of each parish in that county statements of the progress of the system; and I am happy to say that, so far as I can at present learn, I believe Somersetshire, for its acreage, will take the lead of all the counties of England.[34]

Scobell announced the result of his survey at the ninth annual meeting of the SICLC in 1853: it turned out that about 280 of the approximately 480 parishes in Somerset had allotment sites.[35] There is no doubt that these

[28] Ibid. xxxii (1847), 5.
[29] LFM (1834), 83.
[30] Ibid. (1835), 89.
[31] Ibid. xcviii (1839), 68.
[32] SC of the House of Lords on Agriculture, 1837, v. 303, 304.
[33] LFM cx (1840), 167.
[34] LF lxxxvi (1851), 112.
[35] Ibid. cx (1853), 117.

various references to the remarkable extent of allotments in the county do indeed refer exclusively to allotments rather than potato grounds, since Scobell was hostile to potato grounds and always distinguished sharply between the two forms of land provision.

For Wiltshire the evidence is rather more scanty. There is evidence for sites in fifty-three parishes but it seems clear that there were far more. In the area round Calne alone, Lansdowne let thirty-six separate fields, adding up to nearly 400 acres of allotments, whilst, according to the *Devizes Gazette*, the local landowner J. Neeld had let out more than 200 plots to labourers on his estates.[36] But the most useful evidence for Wiltshire in this period is a survey of allotments carried out in March 1833 by the Devizes Labourer's Friend Society. It is not comprehensive, and seems to cover only those parishes with which members of the Devizes Labourer's Friend Society were connected, i.e. principally the triangle of land between Pewsey, Westbury and Devizes, and the estate of the earl of Radnor immediately south of Salisbury. However, it indicates that in the Pewsey–Westbury–Devizes area there were already allotments in almost every village; the same was true of the much smaller area between Salisbury, Downton and West Grimstead. The survey identified a total of just under 904 acres let in allotments to 1,953 tenants in thirty-four parishes and hamlets.[37] The poor law report states that in Wiltshire there 'is hardly a parish in which potato ground or land is not let to the poor'. If we assume that in this context, contrasted as it is with potato ground, 'land' refers to allotments, this is further evidence that they were common in the county.[38]

Robert Hughes, a land agent and witness to the House of Lords 1837 Select Committee on Agriculture, was asked whether it was not the case that the allotment system had been carried to a greater extent in Wiltshire than in any other county, and replied that he believed that it had.[39] This is unsurprising bearing in mind that allotments clearly had a substantial presence in Wiltshire, and in Wiltshire alone, before 1830. Hughes's statement and that of Scobell, to the effect that Somerset was the county in which allotments were commonest at least in proportion to acreage, are not incompatible: Scobell's survey was carried out more than ten years after the 1837 select committee took its evidence, and the great expansion of the allotment system in Somerset took place only from 1836 onwards.

There is only one piece of evidence that runs counter to the otherwise uniform indications that allotments were very common in Wiltshire, and that is Austin's statement, in his capacity as assistant handloom weavers' commissioner, that the allotment system was 'not much in operation' in his

---

36 Earl Fortescue, 'Poor men's gardens', *Nineteenth Century* xxiii (1888), 395–6; *Report on the Employment of Women and Children in Agriculture*, 1843, xii. 56.

37 *F&I*, 413, 424–31.

38 *RC on the Poor Laws*, 1834. xxvii. 7.

39 *SC of the House of Lords on Agriculture*, 1837, v. 122.

district, i.e. Somerset, Wiltshire, Devon and Dorset.[40] Except perhaps as regards Devon and Dorset, this is clearly an outstandingly misleading statement. It is best explained by the geographical distribution of handloom weaving in the south-west, concentrated as it was in a few small towns: Shepton Mallet, Frome, Trowbridge and Bradford-on-Avon. Interestingly Chapman, one of the 1832–4 assistant poor law commissioners, provides evidence in his report that the allotment system had been tried unsuccessfully in all four of these towns, and in all four of them the system had been given up or was probably about to be given up.[41] It seems likely, then, that when Austin visited the handloom-weaving towns, allotments no longer existed in any of them and that this led him to believe that allotments were uncommon in his four counties. Nevertheless, the apparent absence of allotments in these towns by 1840 should not be given undue emphasis: the important point in the present context is that allotments were, in general, common in Wiltshire and in some parts of the county were indeed found in almost every village. It seems clear that, in the 1830s, there were more allotments in Wiltshire than in any other county; subsequently, during the 1840s, it is possible that the county was overtaken by Somerset and perhaps also by Northamptonshire.

For Gloucestershire there are records of forty sites in thirty-five parishes for the period 1830–45. All but three of the sites were in the Cotswolds, across which they were widely distributed, although with concentrations in the clothing district around Stroud, along the Wiltshire, and along the Oxfordshire border. However, there are few references to the county in the sources, other than in connection with handloom weaving, and it seems unlikely that allotments were anywhere near as common in Gloucestershire as in the neighbouring counties of Somerset and Wiltshire. In particular, the organised allotment movement seems to have been very weak, with not a single auxiliary labourer's friend society recorded. The impression given by the distribution of known sites – sites on the Cotswolds, but very few indeed in the Vale of Gloucester – accords with an observation made by Samuel Lysons in 1842. According to Lysons, who established the allotment site at Hempsted, near Gloucester, there had been little attempt to promote the system in the Gloucester neighbourhood prior to that date.[42]

For the south-east (i.e. Hampshire, Berkshire, Sussex, Kent, Surrey and Middlesex), the nearest to a general assessment again comes from the 1843 *Report on the Employment of Women and Children in Agriculture*. Vaughan, speaking of allotments in Kent, Surrey and Sussex, states that there were 'few districts in which they have not been tried to some extent, and few in which they can be said to be general'.[43]

---

40 *RC on the Handloom Weavers*, 1840, xxiii. 2.
41 *RC on the Poor Laws*, 1834, xxviii. 441–2.
42 *LFM* clvii (1844), 51.
43 *Report on the Employment of Women and Children in Agriculture*, 1843, xii. 143.

For Hampshire there is definite evidence of allotments in thirty-eight parishes. This accords well with evidence given to the 1832–4 commissioners that allotments had been adopted in 'many parishes' in Hampshire.[44] However, as with Gloucestershire, the organised allotment movement does not seem to have had any presence and in none of the sources is the county ever particularly singled out as being one in which allotments were very common (unlike, for example, Somerset, Wiltshire and Northamptonshire). So it seems reasonable to conclude that whilst allotments were well established in Hampshire, the county was not in the first rank in terms of numbers of sites.

For Berkshire there are records of twenty-one sites in fourteen parishes. A correspondent told the LFS that for many miles around Abingdon it appeared that almost every landowner was acting on the allotment system.[45] A letter written to the LFS claiming that the system was rapidly gaining ground in the county in 1838 interestingly cited examples almost exclusively from the Vale of the White Horse (i.e. near Abingdon), and it seems possible that allotments were relatively numerous in this small area of Berkshire, whilst being uncommon in other parts of the county.[46] Certainly by 1868, when the Royal Commission on the Employment of Children, Young Persons, and Women in Agriculture investigated the county, allotments seem to have been far commoner in the Vale of the White Horse than elsewhere, and since numbers of allotments seem to have peaked in Berkshire some years before this, the fact that there were so many in the Vale adds to the probability that numbers had been significant in this one area of Berkshire even before 1845.[47]

In Sussex we know of thirty-two parishes in which there were allotment sites at some point in this period. A high proportion of them date from the early 1830s, which may relate to the energetic efforts of several major Sussex landowners – notably the earls of Egremont and Chichester and the duke of Richmond – to promote the system in these years. The low figures for Sussex in 1873 suggest that allotment numbers may not have increased very much after the early 1830s and it seems unlikely that Sussex was one of the counties in which allotments were commonest in 1845. What additional evidence the sources offer tends to support this conclusion. Thus Stephen Wileman, a farmer from Cuckfield, told Vaughan that there were 'but few allotments in this neighbourhood: they are not much approved by the poor, as they have in many instances given their allotments up'.[48] Sussex was not mentioned by any of the sources as being remarkable for allotment provision, and the prevalence of potato grounds – an alternative rather than a complement to allot-

---

44 RC on the Poor Laws, 1834, xxvii. 298; xxxi. 437.
45 F&I, 449.
46 LF xcvi (1839), 36.
47 RC on the Employment of Children, Young Persons, and Women in Agriculture, 1868–9, xiii. 616–33; J. B. Spearing, 'On the agriculture of Berkshire', JRASE xxi (1860), 44.
48 Report on the Employment of Women and Children in Agriculture, 1843, xii. 203.

ments – in the county also suggests that allotments may have been the exception rather than the rule in Sussex in this period.[49]

For Kent we know of forty-eight sites in forty-five parishes. According to Henry Martin, the system was first effectively established in Kent in 1836 (interestingly this was the same year in which it apparently 'took off' in Somerset).[50] The West Kent Labourer's Friend Society reported in 1839 that there were sites in more than forty parishes in the county, and in 1840 in more than fifty.[51] Richard Summerfield, honorary secretary to the Maidstone Agricultural Association, stated in 1843 that 'allotments to agricultural labourers are common in this county'.[52] This is perhaps an overstatement; virtually all our references to allotments in Kent in this period come from a compact area in west Kent (within which Maidstone lies). The LFS frequently repeated the claim that by the early 1840s more than 3,000 plots were available to labourers in Kent, which is impressive in comparison with most other counties, but does suggest that, on the basis of an average of about fifty plots per site, there were in the county as a whole only a few more than the fifty-odd sites that we know of from the Maidstone area.[53] Evidently allotments were a substantial presence in a part of west Kent, but taking the county as a whole they were considerably less numerous than they were in some other counties.

For Surrey we know of twenty sites in eighteen parishes and have the word of Christopher Baxter, bailiff, that allotments were not common in the county in 1843.[54] Relative to other counties in the south of England this was also the case in 1873 and there are no indications anywhere in the sources that anyone ever suggested that allotments were common in Surrey.[55] But to be set against this is the unfortunately incomplete evidence from a survey of allotments in west Surrey compiled by the West Surrey Labourer's Friend Society in 1846. The report of the survey, which is all that appears to survive, was written to highlight the need for further efforts to extend the allotment system and so presumably does not overstate the adequacy of existing provision. Nevertheless, of the sixteen parishes mentioned, thirteen clearly had allotment sites, with one doubtful case.[56] It is difficult to reconcile this conflicting evidence. The balance of probability seems to lie with the conclusion that the West Surrey Labourer's Friend Society's evidence is misleading, at least for the county as a whole, and that in this period allotments were relatively uncommon in Surrey.

49 *LFM* cix (1840), 53–6.
50 *SC on the Labouring Poor*, 1843, vii. 1.
51 *LFM* ciii (1839), 146; cxiii (1840), 109.
52 *Report on the Employment of Women and Children in Agriculture*, 1843, xii. 189–90.
53 *LFM*, 'Thirteenth annual report of the LFS', 1844, 3. The figure for average plot size was calculated from the database.
54 *Report on the Employment of Women and Children in Agriculture*, 1843, xii. 195.
55 *Agricultural Returns of Great Britain for 1873*, 1873, lxix. 301–74.
56 *LF* xxii (1846), 45–7.

For Middlesex seven sites in six parishes are known, many dating from the very end of this period, when the newly-established SICLC was involved in extending allotment provision considerably in the county in an attempt to provide highly visible models which would then be followed in other parts of the country. Allotments were very uncommon in Middlesex in 1873 and, bearing in mind that we know that several sites were created in the county in the post-1845 period, it seems reasonable to conclude that the very low number of pre-1845 allotments known for the county is representative of the real position.[57]

In East Anglia (Essex, Cambridgeshire, Huntingdonshire, Suffolk, Norfolk and also Lincolnshire), there is evidence for forty-one sites in Essex in thirty-three parishes. In 1832 Lord Braybrooke expressed regret that allotments had not been adopted 'on anything like an extended scale' in the Saffron Walden area, with the exception of the parishes of Littlebury and of Saffron Walden itself.[58] However, in 1843 it was noted that allotments were numerous around Saffron Walden and also around Chelmsford, although they were still rare in other parts of the county.[59] But the system had apparently come to a standstill due to opposition from farmers.[60]

For Cambridgeshire there are records of fifty-three sites in fifty-two parishes. There is an interesting comparison between the evidence from the 1834 'Rural queries' and that from the 1831 survey. Answers to the 'Rural queries' provide evidence that twenty parishes definitely had allotments, and eleven definitely did not. The 1831 survey was almost comprehensive in its coverage of parishes – of the 128 parishes in Cambridgeshire it obtained answers to its survey from 120. Of these, ninety-six provided definite information about allotments: thirty-six parishes definitely had allotments and sixty did not. The survey was quite carefully completed, certainly by comparison with the 'Rural queries'. It is likely, of course, that there was some increase in the number of parishes with allotments in the years between the two surveys, but since the 'Rural queries' were answered in 1833 this was only a period of two to three years and it would be surprising if the number of sites were to double in so short a time. The number of parishes with allotments in Cambridgeshire in the early 1830s was probably closer to the figure of a little more than a third suggested by the 1831 survey than to the two-thirds one would obtain were one to extrapolate the figures from the 'Rural queries'. This gives some indication of the degree of over-representation of parishes with allotments in the answers to the 'Rural queries': however, there is no reason to assume that Cambridgeshire was a typical county in this respect so

---

57 *Agricultural Returns of Great Britain for 1873*, 1873, lxix. 301–74.
58 *F&I*, 225.
59 *LFM* cxxv (1841), 112; *SC on the Labouring Poor*, 1843, vii. 40; *RC on the Poor Laws*, 1834, xxvii. 234; xxxi, 178.
60 *SC on the Labouring Poor*, 1843, vii. 39.

that the figures for other counties cannot simply be adjusted proportionally along the same lines.

The conclusion that rather more than a third of Cambridgeshire parishes had allotments in the early 1830s is supported, or at least not undermined, by the other evidence we have for Cambridgeshire in this period. The 1832–4 poor law commissioners compiled detailed information on allotment provision and other matters relevant to parochial relief for Huntingdonshire and the Isle of Ely, which was included in the evidence appended to the report; this showed that of fourteen parishes in the Isle of Ely for which information about allotments was recorded, allotments were provided in four. This figure is roughly in line with the estimate that something like a third of all Cambridgeshire parishes may have had allotments in the early 1830s. Other information is also compatible with this conclusion. It is known, for example, that allotments were particularly numerous in Ely itself, and that the duke of Rutland had between 300 and 400 allotments in the county by 1845.[61] Alfred Power, the 1832–4 assistant poor law commissioner, reported that the allotment system was beginning 'to be very generally adopted' in the county in 1833.[62]

For Huntingdonshire there are records of sites in thirteen parishes; and also a statement that the duke of Manchester had adopted the system on his estates in the county by 1844.[63] For a small county the figure of thirteen sites may seem relatively large, but information for Huntingdonshire is unusually good because of the 1832–4 poor law commission survey. This records eight parishes as having allotments out of a total of twenty-seven for which information on the question was provided.[64] If the survey is in any way representative – and there are no means of establishing this – it would imply that allotments were present in rather fewer than a third of Huntingdonshire parishes and that, whilst the system was quite well established by 1833, allotments were probably a little less common than in Cambridgeshire.

In Suffolk records provide the names of forty-six sites in forty parishes where there were allotments. The 1838 report of the Blything Labourer's Friend Society stated that 'many more than half' the parishes within the poor law union were still 'deprived' of allotments.[65] However, by 1843 things had evidently improved in the district: one Mr R. Appleton, a resident of the parish of Thorington in the hundred of Blything, told the commissioners that there were allotments of about a rood 'in almost every parish'.[66] The evidence taken by the 1843 commission reveals that allotments were exciting a considerable degree of interest in Suffolk (and other East Anglian counties) at this

61 LFM lxxxiv (1838), 37; RC on the Framework Knitters, 1845, xv. 140.
62 RC on the Poor Laws, 1834, xxviii. 254.
63 LF clvii (1844), 64.
64 RC on the Poor Laws, 1834, xxviii. 702–9.
65 LFM xcv (1839), 21.
66 Report on the Employment of Women and Children in Agriculture, 1843, xii. 266.

period and that many parishes in the county had them.[67] A survey of parishes in west Suffolk, carried out by Sir Henry Bunbury for the newly-formed Suffolk Labourers' Improvement Society in 1845, discovered that of sixty-seven parishes replying, there were sites in thirty-six.[68] There were 'a great many' sites around Stowmarket by 1842 and several around Glenham by 1843, although allotments were not general in the latter district at this time.[69] Since there were several active proponents of allotments in other parts of the county, including L. F. Page at Woolpit, Sir Edward Kerrison at Oakley Park and Walton Kent at Walsham-le-Willows, and since the presence of such proponents often seems to have led to a considerable extension of allotments in the area around them, it seems reasonable to assume that by 1845 allotments were numerous in Suffolk, although probably more on a par with the situation in Hampshire than with that in Somerset.

For Norfolk thirty-four sites are known. Thomas Brettingham, churchwarden, responding to the 'Rural queries', states that 'letting land is becoming much more common' and that 'the system appears gradually spreading'.[70]

Lincolnshire has twenty-seven known sites in twenty-six parishes for the period; apparently in Lindsey in 1831 it was unusual to let land to cottagers.[71]

For the south Midlands – Oxfordshire, Buckinghamshire, Hertfordshire, Bedfordshire and Northamptonshire – there is little information. In Oxfordshire twelve sites are known, likewise in Buckinghamshire, in Hertfordshire sixteen in fifteen parishes, in Bedfordshire twenty-eight in twenty-seven parishes and in Northamptonshire eighteen in sixteen parishes. The low figure for Oxfordshire is compatible with Arthur Ashby's estimates of allotment numbers in the county: using a slightly different periodisation, Ashby suggested that almost all the 9,088 plots recorded for the county in 1873 were established after 1840.[72] For Bedfordshire, there is evidence that allotments were first provided in the late 1820s, promoted initially by the duke of Bedford and Earl de Grey, and that other proprietors followed their lead.[73] It is also known that by 1873 Northamptonshire had become the county with the second highest number of allotments (over 16,000 plots); this growth would seem to have taken place almost entirely after 1830 (see chapter 1) but we do not know what proportion of it occurred before 1845.[74]

For the west Midlands – Worcestershire, Warwickshire and Staffordshire –

---

67 Ibid. 259–60, 262–6.

68 LF ix (1845), 172.

69 LFM cxxv (1841), 112; Report on the Employment of Women and Children in Agriculture, 1843, xii. 259.

70 RC on the Poor Laws, 1834, xxi. 306.

71 SC of the House of Lords on the Poor Laws, 1830–1, viii. 201.

72 Arthur Ashby, Allotments and small holdings in Oxfordshire, Oxford 1917, 3–4, 31.

73 Paper entitled 'The allotment system', originally printed in the Journal of the Central Farmers' Club, Nov. 1858 and reprinted in RC on the Employment of Children, Young Persons, and Women in Agriculture, 1867–8, xvii. 199.

74 RC on the Employment of Children, Young Persons, and Women in Agriculture, 1867–8, xvii. 179.

there is more information. The number of sites identified in Worcestershire is seven, in Warwickshire twenty-five in twenty-two parishes, and in Staffordshire two. The Stewponey (Worcestershire) branch of the LFS had let out 190 acres, 1 rood, 35 perches of allotments in twenty-five parishes by 1847.[75] In Warwickshire, there is testimony from C. H. Bracebridge, chair of one of the local poor law unions, to the effect that allotments existed in 'less than' a quarter of the county's 291 parishes in 1843.[76] This seems quite impressive in comparison with the putative totals for some other counties, perhaps putting Warwickshire on a par with Kent or even higher. Staffordshire seems to have had far fewer allotment sites. Indeed, the only one for which there is a positive reference, at Lichfield, can be explained by the parish's connection with chancellor Law, a close relative of that ardent allotments enthusiast George Law, bishop of Bath and Wells.[77]

For the east Midlands, there are references to four sites in Derbyshire, thirty-six in thirty-four parishes in Nottinghamshire, thirty-two in twenty-seven parishes in Leicestershire and four in Rutland. For the entire region, sixty-three land allotment societies (more or less corresponding to parishes with allotments) had let about 800 acres to several thousand individuals by 1843.[78] The duke of Newcastle had let 2,000 plots in Nottinghamshire, also by 1843 (some of which may be included in that 800 acres).[79] The situation in the town of Nottingham is complex. Briefly, the town had, from early in the nineteenth century, an extraordinary number of small gardens let out to artisans and labourers. There is evidence that by 1842 there were an astonishing 8,000 or more of these plots in the town. However, it is unclear whether these were really allotments or whether they were more like the 'guinea gardens' found in Birmingham. These differed so much from the allotments provided to rural labourers that they should probably be considered a distinct form of landholding rather than a sub-category of allotments. Guinea gardens were let at very high rents on a commercial basis to well-paid artisans and tradesmen. They were private gardens, individually hedged, and primarily served leisure rather than economic purposes.[80] If the Nottingham plots were allotments rather than guinea gardens, the town appears to have been unique amongst large towns in having a significant number of allotments at this early date; in general, urban allotments seem only to have developed on an extensive scale in the last quarter of the nineteenth century or later.[81]

In Leicestershire, the system is said to have been adopted 'on a large scale'

75 *LF* xlvi (1848), 45.
76 Ibid. clii (1843), 159.
77 *RC on the Poor Laws*, 1834, xxvii. 268.
78 *SC on the Labouring Poor*, 1843, vii. 90.
79 Ibid. 137.
80 Jane Rowton, 'Rented gardens in Birmingham 1823–1837', unpubl. undergraduate diss. Birmingham 1975.
81 *LFM* cxliii (1843), 30–1.

by 1843.[82] For Rutland, the tiny figure of four allotment sites is belied by a statement made by R. W. Baker at the December 1836 meeting of the Rutland Agricultural Society, to the effect that over 700 people in the county had benefited from the system.[83]

On the Welsh borders – Monmouthshire, Herefordshire, Shropshire and Cheshire – there are scant traces of the allotment system: twelve sites recorded for Herefordshire, two for Shropshire and two for Cheshire. Significantly, respondents from these counties to the question on land in the 'Rural queries' failed even to realise that the question referred to the allotment system – evidently they were unaware of the existence of any such thing. Their answers refer either to gardens or to individual small fields rented by labourers.

In the north-west, allotments were similarly little known. One site is recorded for Lancashire, none for Westmorland and none for Cumberland. As many as thirty-five parishes or townships responded to the 'Rural queries' question in Cumberland, so the absence of any reference to allotments is striking. The answers again show a lack of understanding of the question. Evidence for the near-total absence of the allotment system from the north-west is therefore compelling.

In the final area, the three ridings of Yorkshire, Durham and Northumberland, the East Riding is known to have had eighteen sites during this period; the West Riding, fourteen sites in twelve parishes; the North Riding, nine sites. There are no records of sites in Durham and only two in Northumberland. Almost all the sites in Yorkshire seem to date from the 1840s; this may partly reflect source bias (the 1843 Royal Commission on the Employment of Women and Children in Agriculture chose Yorkshire as one of its counties for study, whereas the *Labourer's Friend Magazine*, so useful for the 1830s, devoted little attention to the north). However, source bias is not the only factor at work. There is evidence, for example, that there were no allotments in Holderness before 1843 except those at Sigglesthorne.[84] Allotments were only found in two parishes in the whole of the Beverley Union, according to the union's clerk, Mr J. Boyes, and were 'not general' in the Howden neighbourhood, also in 1843.[85] As regards the West Riding, the *Labourer's Friend Magazine* seems to imply that the system was all-but-unknown there before J. G. Marshall established his sites at Holbeck and Headingley in 1843.[86] There is independent evidence that allotments were unknown in the Huddersfield area in 1843 and that there were 'very few' in the Bingley area.[87] For the two parishes in west Yorkshire mentioned in the 'Rural queries' as definitely having sites, there were forty-seven which defi-

82 Ibid. cxl (1843), 52.
83 Ibid. lxxiii (1837), 56.
84 *Report on the Employment of Women and Children in Agriculture*, 1843, xii. 345.
85 Ibid. 312, 338.
86 LFM cxlvii (1843), 82.
87 *SC on the Labouring Poor*, 1843, vii. 71, 35.

nitely did not. Likewise for the North Riding, it was reported in 1843, that allotments were a 'rare sight'.[88] It is clear, however, that unlike the other northern counties, Yorkshire was beginning to have a significant, if still small, number of allotments.

Respondents to the 'Rural queries' from Durham, like those from Cheshire and Cumberland, failed to understand the reference of the question. With respect to Northumberland, according to the *Labourer's Friend Magazine*, a gentleman started the allotment system there in about 1840 or 1841.[89] There is, indeed, no evidence of any allotment in the county before this time.

Any estimate of the number of allotment sites nationally by 1845, formed on the basis of this county-by-county survey, must be tentative in the extreme, although it is possible to be slightly more confident about the geographical distribution. Thus counties may be ranked in terms of the proportion of parishes with allotments, from highest to lowest, thus:

1. Somerset, Wiltshire, Northamptonshire
2. Cambridgeshire, Suffolk, Nottinghamshire, Leicestershire, Rutland, Huntingdonshire, Warwickshire
3. Kent, Essex, Hampshire, Gloucestershire, Sussex, Surrey, Dorset, Norfolk, Hertfordshire, Bedfordshire, Berkshire, Oxfordshire, Buckinghamshire, Yorkshire, Middlesex, Devon, Worcestershire, Derbyshire
4. Herefordshire, Cornwall, Shropshire, Staffordshire, Cheshire, Lancashire, Westmorland, Cumberland, Durham, Northumberland

These four groups represent: (1): counties where more than half of all parishes seem to have had allotments; (2): counties where between a half and a quarter of all parishes seem to have had allotments; (3): counties where some, but fewer than a quarter, of parishes had allotments; (4): counties where allotments did not exist or were a negligible presence. Within each group the counties are arranged in approximate descending rank order.

It is clear that fewer than a quarter of English parishes had allotments in 1845; less clear is how far short of this level they fell. In lowland southern England at least, however, the proportion would almost certainly have been more than a quarter.

There are a few 'global' contemporary estimates. Lord Ashley told the 1848 annual general meeting of what had, by this time, become the SICLC, that the allotment system had been introduced in nearly 2,000 parishes.[90] That amounts to about a sixth of English parishes, a figure which accords well with the estimates already provided. The *Labourer's Friend Magazine* informed its readers in 1842 that the LFS committee had tried but failed to obtain accurate statistics about the number of allotments, but that it had been ascer-

---

88 *Report on the Employment of Women and Children in Agriculture*, 1843, xii, 343.
89 LFM cxxii (1841), 67.
90 LF xlix (1848), 90.

tained that the system had been introduced into thirty-three English counties (almost exactly the same number as that suggested above).[91] Moreover, despite the failure of the LFS committee, John Ilderton Burn felt able to assert in 1842 that more than 100,000 allotments had been created since the foundation of the LFS twelve years previously, an estimate which was congruent with his earlier claim that there were about 100,000 allotments in England in 1840.[92] This figure, or more than that by 1842, may be something of an exaggeration, since Burn was inclined to optimism. However, it is unlikely to be wildly wrong: there were certainly tens of thousands of allotment tenants by 1845. If allotments were still the exception rather than the rule in the mid-1840s, there had nevertheless been quite a remarkable growth in their numbers since the revival of the movement in 1830.

---

[91] *LFM* cxxxiv (1842), 66.
[92] Ibid. cxxxvii (1842), 107; cxvii (1840), 170.

3

The National Movement and the
Labourer's Friend Society

There is little doubt that the immediate cause of the dramatic upsurge in the number of allotments described in the last chapter was the Captain Swing riots of 1830. The evidence for this is, firstly, contemporary statements; second, the very close chronological fit between the riots and the revived interest in allotments; third, the geographical fit between the riots and revived interest; and last, the absence of any other event in 1830 of sufficient magnitude to provide a plausible alternative explanation.

Landowners often cited the riots as the initial prompt to letting land in allotments. Some typical examples, a small proportion of the many that might be given, are as follows. Samuel Lysons told the Worcestershire Labourer's Friend Society with respect to his allotments at Rodmarton, Gloucestershire, in 1844, that 'The attention of my late father and myself was drawn to the subject of the allotment system at the period of the agricultural riots in 1830–1.'[1] Another landowner who stated explicitly that she had adopted the allotment system as a direct result of the 1830 riots was Mrs Davies Gilbert, a well-known figure in allotment circles, who let over 400 plots in Eastbourne.[2] Mr W. Gray told a meeting of the London Central Farmers' Club in 1858 that the allotments in Alconbury, Huntingdonshire, were begun as a response to the Captain Swing riots.[3] Similarly the Revd W. F. Chilcott decided to try to get the allotment system adopted in his parish in the 'bad, riotous winter' of 1830.[4]

The closeness of the chronological fit is evident in that the foundation of the Labourers Friend Society, the beginning of renewed parliamentary interest in allotments, and the decisive increase in the rate at which new allotment sites were created can all be dated precisely to 1830; and in the case of renewed parliamentary interest in allotments, to the months immediately following the riots. As regards the number of allotments, the total number of sites recorded as being created in all years before 1830 is less than the total number of sites recorded as being created in the single year 1830.

1 *LFM* clvii (1844), 50.
2 Letter from Mrs Davies Gilbert, read by Mr Fardon at the 1844 annual meeting of the Worcestershire Labourer's Friend Society, printed in *LFM* clix (1844), 81.
3 Mr W. Gray, speech at meeting of London Central Farmers' Club, 1858, reprinted in *RC on the Employment of Children, Young Persons, and Women in Agriculture*, 1867–8, xvii. 264.
4 *Taunton Courier*, 24 Oct. 1833, repr. in *F&I*, 331.

There seems also to be a geographical fit between the riots and the renewed interest in allotments. Thus of the four chief Swing counties, Hampshire, Wiltshire, Kent and Berkshire, the first three are prominent in the allotment movement in the 1830s. However, the fit is by no means perfect: it was in Somerset, for example, a county apparently little affected by the riots, that the allotment movement was at its most vigorous in the 1830s and 1840s. It is worth noting in this context that Swing was not merely a local but a national phenomenon (or at the very least a regional one), in the sense that it made a deep impression on landed society in general as opposed to only having an effect on those living in villages where there were disturbances.

The last consideration is that in order to explain so sharp a discontinuity, it seems necessary to invoke a major event, rather than any gradual process. The only relevant event significant enough to explain the change is the Swing riots. Other historians have noted the connection too, although often (in the influential article by Barnett for example) insufficient emphasis is placed upon its significance.[5]

A comparison of the Swing riots and the tensions of 1795–1800

That a period of high social tension in the countryside, such as that of the 1830–1 riots, should lead to increased interest in allotments is not in itself surprising. The poor harvests, high prices and disturbances of 1795–1800 had similarly led to an upsurge of interest in allotments. However, no sooner is the comparison made than it is clear that there were two very significant differences between 1795–1800 and 1830–1, both of which require explanation: first, the much greater scale of the response in 1830–1, and second, and above all, the fact that the interest in allotments generated in 1830–1 was sustained. To borrow a phrase from the historiography of the industrial revolution, 1830–1 marks the take-off of the allotment movement into sustained growth; 1795–1800 can, by contrast, be seen as an abortive attempt to achieve this. Before investigating this crucial issue, however, it is necessary to consider why the initial interest in allotments provoked by the Captain Swing riots was so much greater than that stimulated by the tensions of the last five years of the eighteenth century.

Two principal reasons can be advanced: first, that allotments were no longer a new idea in 1830 but rather a tried and tested one – at least to a certain extent; and second, the threat to social stability posed by the Swing riots, and what they revealed about the underlying mood of the labourers, was felt by the rural ruling class to be substantially greater than that posed by the tensions of 1795–1800.

By 1830 the oldest allotments had been in existence for thirty-five years; and

---

5 Barnett, 'Allotments and the problem of rural poverty', 179; Archer, 'The nineteenth-century allotment', 23.

twenty sites are known to have been in existence for more than ten (*see* chapter 1). Of fifty-four sites (including the twenty just mentioned) known to have existed before the Swing riots broke out, at least eighteen were considered highly satisfactory by those who had let them. Only in four cases were any problems reported, but in two of these (Bishop's Cannings, Wiltshire, where two of the thirty-two tenants had been dismissed for breaking the rules and Whelford, Gloucestershire, where some of the tenants had not cultivated their plots well) the overall verdict of those letting the allotments was nevertheless enthusiastic.[6] In a third case, Shepton Mallet, it was acknowledged that the labourers had benefited from the allotments; the 'problem' was simply that the poor rates had not fallen.[7] Since the information for many of these sites comes from the *Labourer's Friend Magazine* it might be argued that it is not surprising that so many of the reports were favourable; however, whilst the problems associated with allotments may have been a little greater, and the advantages a little less, than suggested by the *Labourer's Friend Magazine*, extreme scepticism is not warranted. The *Labourer's Friend Magazine* proved to be willing – indeed, in its efforts to explain failures and dispel misconceptions, almost anxious – to record and consider instances in which allotments had not proved successful. There are other reasons too for thinking that the early allotments were probably in general regarded as successful. Many of them had, as we have seen, been in existence for several decades, which is in itself evidence that they were at least viable. Further-more, several of those who were to be the most enthusiastic promoters of allot-ments in the 1830s were those who had been letting plots for longest. Thus the Estcourt family had been letting allotments since 1795, the Revd Stephen Demainbray since 1806 and the bishop of Bath and Wells since 1807.

It seems reasonable, then, to conclude that the early allotments were in general considered successful and would have provided a kind of reassurance to prospective allotment letters which was not available in 1795–1800. It seems highly likely that this was an important factor in 1830–1, but direct evidence on the point is scanty. One point which does tell strongly in this direction is that allotments seem to have spread most rapidly after 1830 in those areas – notably Wiltshire, Somerset and Cambridgeshire – where they were well-established before 1830. The very small numbers of allotments in existence altogether must have meant that other than in those areas the vast majority of landowners had no experience of them.

In this context it is worth emphasising the importance of the emergence of the allotment as by far the most highly-regarded way of providing labourers with land. In the days of the SBCP and the Board of Agriculture, there were several rival methods. The most favoured of these, cow pastures, was not a solution which could ever have been widely adopted, since the costs, in terms of quantity of land and numbers of cows required, were prohibitive. There is reason to believe that the energy expended in the 1790s in promoting this unrealistic form

6 SC on the Poor Laws, 1817, vi. 165; SBCP, *Reports*, iii. 120.
7 RC on the Poor Laws, 1834, xxvii. 504.

of landholding diverted attention from the viable one, i.e. allotments. But because in the intervening years allotments had emerged as a well-recognised, distinctive form, and because they had conclusively won the battle with cow pastures, there were no distracting alternatives to stand in their way when the favourable moment for the expansion of the movement came.

So it seems reasonable to suppose that the fact that allotments were, by 1830, a proven and fully-developed means of benefiting the poor was one major factor in the much greater interest in them evident in 1830–1 as against 1795–1800. But a second and equally significant factor was the far deeper alarm that the rural ruling class seems to have felt in consequence of the Swing riots when compared to its reaction to the problems of 1795–1800. Thus in 1830 the duke of Buckingham was talking of the country being in the hands of rebels.[8] Whilst the period 1795 to 1800 did witness riots, these were localised and never on the scale of what happened in 1830–1.[9] Moreover, the Swing riots coincided with widespread political unrest at home and revolution abroad.

So much for the question of why the 1830–1 riots stimulated so much more interest in allotments than the tensions of 1795–1800. But the more interesting, important and difficult question is to explain why this interest was sustained.

Why was interest in allotments sustained after the 1830–1 crisis?

One preliminary qualification is needed. Whilst the general interest in allotments, as evident in the activity of the LFS and of the local societies, and in the ever-rising number of sites, was sustained at a high level throughout the 1830s and for most of the 1840s, the same is not true of the parliamentary interest. After the immediate social and political crisis of 1830–2 was over, there was no further legislation on allotments until 1845 and indeed virtually no parliamentary interest at all until 1843 (the parliamentary events of 1843–5 will be considered subsequently; the point being made here is that they represent a second wave of parliamentary interest rather than a continuing concern). However, the fact that parliament's interest in allotments did recede after 1832 should not distract from the main point, which is that, unlike after 1795–1800, the movement as a whole continued to make progress despite the relaxation of social tension. Why was this?

To answer this question adequately it will be necessary to consider the contribution made to the movement by the 1831–2 legislation and the LFS (to which the remainder of this chapter will be devoted); by local allotment societies and individual activists (chapter 4); and by non-activist allotment landlords (chapter 5).

8   Hammond and Hammond, *Village labourer,* 219.
9   Andrew Charlesworth (ed.), *An atlas of rural protest in Britain, 1548–1900,* London 1983, 151–4.

The legislation of 1831–2

The existence of legislation permitting and encouraging parishes to let allotments was in many ways the most impressive achievement of the initial burst
of post-1830 interest and it might have been expected to have had substantial
results. Unfortunately this seems not to have been the case. Admittedly, the
acts were sometimes applied by parishes to let allotments, as for example in
the 1830s at Uffculm (Devon) and Walton-on-Thames (Surrey).[10] There
were other instances too, but overall they were rare.[11] The great defect of the
acts was that they made the provision of allotments dependent on action by
the parish vestry and in most rural parishes it was the farmers, often bitter
opponents of allotments, who were the effective power in the vestry. Whatever slim prospects there were of extending the provision of allotments by
means of the acts seem to have been finally destroyed by the 1835 Union and
Parish Property Act. This transferred the powers given to parochial authorities under the acts of 1831–2 to the boards of guardians of the poor. Sir
William Miles MP, one of the witnesses to the 1843 Select Committee on the
Labouring Poor, explained that 'the whole of this [i.e. the 1831–2 acts] is now
put under the guardians of the poor, the parochial management is taken away,
the consequence is, it has become a perfectly dead letter'. He went on to say
that the problem was that the upper limit on the quantity of land that could
be taken for allotment purposes, fifty acres, was now applied to a whole
union, not just to a parish.[12] Clearly fifty acres fairly divided between the
parishes of a union would result in ludicrously – indeed unviably – small allotment sites. Hall, the legal authority on allotments, agreed in 1886 that the
practical effect of the 1835 act had been to render the earlier acts useless.[13]

It is clear, therefore, that the legislation of 1831–2 did not contribute
significantly to the continued vigour of the allotment movement in the
1830–45 period.

The Labourer's Friend Society

The LFS was much the most significant single element within the allotment
movement in the 1830s and 1840s and requires extended treatment. the
central figure in its formation was Benjamin Wills, a London surgeon and
therefore, significantly, a member of the urban middle class rather than the
rural upper class, although by 1827 he had become a minor landed proprietor.
According to his own account, Wills first began to meet with a group of
friends to discuss ways of improving the living standards of the poor shortly

---

10 *LFM* xlvi (1835), 13; *SC on the Labouring Poor*, 1843, vii. 118–19.
11 Hall, *Law of allotments*, 19–22.
12 *SC on the Labouring Poor*, 1843, vii. 108, 116.
13 Hall, *Law of allotments*, 23–4.

after the end of the Napoleonic wars. The group appears also to have maintained an irregular correspondence with like-minded individuals in other parts of the country. It is not clear whether the activities of Wills and his friends at this earlier stage amounted to anything more than a convivial exchange of opinions, but on 19 February 1827 they put their meetings on a more formal basis, constituting themselves the General Association for the Purpose of Bettering the Condition of the Manufacturing and Agricultural Labourers. Wills was the honorary secretary and one of the five directors of the new association; there was also a central committee consisting of 'eight or nine' more people. Discussion meetings took place at the Golden Lion, West Smithfield, and the resolutions made were subsequently published and sent to other societies with which the association corresponded. Appeals were also issued to landowners and to the middle class for assistance in bringing the views of the association before parliament.[14]

It seems possible that the General Association was at least initially more active than Wills and his friends had previously been. Certainly their efforts to obtain parliamentary attention were successful: the Select Committee on Emigration of 1827 took evidence from Wills and subsequently published as appendixes to its report copies of a circular and resolutions issued by the association. The evidence gathered by the select committee provides valuable information about the aims and ideology of the General Association. The fundamental principle guiding it seems to have been that labour was the source of all value, and that it therefore had an equal if not prior claim to legislative protection as compared to other interests. However, the introduction of machinery threatened to displace manual labour. So the burden of taxation should be shifted away from 'commodities of subsistence and comfort' and placed on steam power and machinery, which, it was pointed out, produced without consuming. A further proposal was to pass a law making agreements between meetings of masters and journeymen binding, due to the 'prevailing disposition of unprincipled or mistaken employers speculating against labour'. A general association of employers and employees was necessary: rightly understood, their interests were not in conflict. The acts empowering JPs to regulate wages should be reinstated and a minimum wage introduced. Instead of emigration, home colonisation should be undertaken, including 'the allotment of small portions to cottagers and labourers'. In his evidence to the select committee, Wills amplified the last suggestion. He proposed a general enclosure bill, permitting a certain proportion of the land enclosed to be taken 'for the nation'. A hundred acres of this land would be divided into small farms, which would be let, rent-free, for the first thirty years. The enclosure commissioners would also add some land to every existing cottage, so that all agricultural cottages would have two acres of land

14 SC on Emigration, 1826–7, v. 590, qq. 3770–83.

attached to them; and some of the land would also be divided into five-acre lots.[15]

The proposal for the division of waste land outlined by Wills to the select committee, and described also in the General Association's circular and resolutions, is the earliest sign of a specific interest in the provision of land to labourers on the part of Wills and his associates. We do not know for certain whence it derived, but in his evidence to the select committee Wills described the deep impression that the enclosure of Croydon common had made on him:

> I would not wish to speak to the expense; but I can speak to the effect it has had upon the circumstances of Croydon; the effect of taking away the rights of those poor people has been that I have seen 900 people summoned for the poor's rates. These are the facts that I want to substantiate today. By the destruction of the common rights, and giving no remuneration to the poor man, a gentleman has taken an immense tract of it and converted it into a park; a person in the middling walk of life has bought an acre or two; and though this common in its original state was not so valuable as it has been made, yet the poor man should have been consulted in it; and the good that it was originally to him was of such a nature, that destroying that has had an immense effect.[16]

It seems reasonable to suggest that Wills's interest in providing land for the poor, which eventually bore fruit in the LFS policy of promoting allotments, arose directly from his revulsion against enclosure.

One of the most striking features of the General Association is the extent of its affinity with political radicalism. The plan to recreate small farms and attach two acres of land to every rural cottage, the introduction of a minimum wage and the suggestion that taxation should be shifted from consumption to machinery were all characteristic features of radical programmes. Similarly, one of the association's circulars invoked the language of radicalism by denouncing Britain as 'a country surrounded by monopolies and exclusions'. The same circular repeatedly emphasised that labour was the source of all value, declared that 'property, not labour' was the most legitimate object of taxation, and followed this by demanding a tax on property invested in machinery, 'which creates goods and destroys customers at one and the same time'. The 'doctrine of redundant population' was brusquely rejected, as was the 'influence of a ruinous system of individual competition, in reducing the wages of labour'. As a corresponding society, the General Association was, of course, cast in a well-established radical political form. Even the class-integrating concept of a 'general association, not only of manufacturers and workmen, but of all classes who feel an interest in and are favourably disposed towards the objects sought' has echoes of the similarly

---

[15] Ibid. v. 590, qq. 3785–6; 592–4, qq. 3812–26; 800–1.
[16] Ibid. v. 592, qq. 3803–11.

trans-class radical belief in the notion of 'the people', defined as much by their commitment to the common good as by their social position or economic role.[17]

The close parallels between the language used by the General Association and that characteristic of radicalism, and still more the position taken by Wills on enclosure, raise the question of whether there was any direct connection between the association and radicalism, especially the agrarian strand within radicalism which remained active in London throughout the 1820s. Although Wills was clearly no socialist, some of the features of his proposal are reminiscent of Thomas Spence, especially the suggestion that parishes should take possession of land and let it out in small farms of varying sizes. However, the precise nature of the link between Wills and agrarian radicalism, if there was one, remains to be established.[18]

Wills was, perhaps unsurprisingly, regarded as a dangerous and deluded crank by the predominantly Malthusian 1827 select committee, whose final report embraced the General Association in a sweeping denunciation of economic heresies:

> It is from an entire ignorance of the universal operation of the principle of supply and demand regulating the rate of wages that all these extravagant positions are advanced, and recommendations spread over the country which are calculated to excite false hopes and consequently discontent in the minds of the labouring classes. Among the most extravagant are those brought forward before your committee by a society professing to be established for the purpose of bettering the condition of the manufacturing and agricultural labourers of Great Britain. The extent of misconception which appears to pervade the opinions of this society can only be fully understood by an examination of its doctrines, as explained in the Evidence and Appendix.[19]

It is remarkable that Wills, extremist and outsider as he appeared to be in 1827, should within four years establish an organisation (the LFS) which by the time of its first public meeting on 18 February 1832 had already obtained royal patronage and an elite membership of between 400 and 500, including

---

17 [The Directors and Central Committee of the General Association for Bettering the Condition of the Manufacturing and Agricultural Labourers], 'An appeal to the nation, from the directors and central committee of the General Association, established in London, for the purpose of bettering the condition of the manufacturing and agricultural labourers, to secure the property and promote the welfare of all classes of society, by the encouragement of industry and reduction of poor rates', reprinted as appendix v to *SC on Emigration*, 1826–7, v. 798–801.

18 Bronstein also notes parallels between the ideas of the LFS and those of agrarian radicalism: *Land reform and working-class experience in Britain and the United States, 1800–1862*, Stanford, CA 1999, 45–8. On Spence's plan for the parochial ownership of land see Malcolm Chase, *The people's farm: English radical agrarianism, 1775–1840*, Oxford 1988, 29–37.

19 *SC on Emigration*, 1826–7, v. 237–8.

several bishops, noblemen and MPs.[20] Part of the explanation is that Wills moderated his tone with time, as did many of his associates. The journals of the LFS contain no references to the desirability of a minimum wage or to a shift in taxation from consumption to machinery, and the society soft-pedalled its continuing interest in home colonisation. However, it is also quite clear that in 1830, when Wills decided to relaunch the General Association as the new Labourer's Friend Society, he had seized an opportune moment. The Swing riots had thrown landed society into dismay and many were casting about for a way forward; Wills offered it. This demonstrates vividly how surprisingly abrupt the change in the trajectory of the allotment movement was in 1830: during the ten years in which he had been actively promoting measures on behalf of the poor prior to 1830, for three of which we know that he had been advocating land provision, Wills had, to the best of our knowledge, failed to get even a single allotment site established.

The LFS initially continued the same pattern of activities as the General Association, but with one major difference: it published a monthly magazine or journal with the cumbersome title *Facts and Illustrations Demonstrating the Important Benefits which have been, and still may be Derived by Labourers from Possessing Small Portions of Land: Proving the Low Amount of Poor's Rates, where such Holdings have been Granted or Continued to the Labouring Population, and its Advantages to the Farmer, the Landowner and the Country*. This was based on the correspondence of Wills and his society with landowners about the benefits of land provision. It may have been the success of the new publication that put the LFS in a position to hold so impressive a first public meeting.

After 1832 the LFS held public meetings annually and continued to publish *Facts and Illustrations* (renamed the *Labourer's Friend Magazine* in 1834). A 'general' (executive) committee was established, which met at least once every month. These meetings continued regularly until 1844, when the LFS was reformed as the SICLC (*see* chapter 8). The primary aim of the LFS was, from the outset, to encourage the provision of small allotments of land to the labouring poor. The society argued that the labourer's condition was miserable and deteriorating, due above all to enclosure and the ensuing separation from the land: 'as a matter of justice to the poor, nothing can be more evident than that their having been deprived of the common rights . . . tended very much to depress their condition'.[21] Secondary causes included the consolidation of small farms into large ones. The LFS argued that this was an important source of rural unemployment, since large farms employed fewer workers per acre. Furthermore, the elimination of small farms had important consequences for social mobility as well as for employment. Where there were no small farms, a vital rung of the ladder by which a labourer might hope to rise out of his condition was missing. This destroyed the labourer's hope of social advance-

---

[20] Ibid.
[21] *F&I*, 89.

ment.[22] However, desirable as the restoration of small farms was, this would necessarily be a major, long-term undertaking, fraught with many difficulties. The immediate priority was to alleviate the problems of rural unemployment and low incomes and to restore some connection between the labourer and the land, which could best be done by the provision of allotments. This would

> place the labourer in a situation in which he can employ himself during his spare days and hours; he will then feel that he has an interest in the soil and that he is indeed a member of, and not an outcast from, society; he will then become attached to the land of his forefathers, and be once more reinstated in that just standing in the social system, to which as a British-born subject he is so fully entitled.[23]

The LFS and its followers believed that allotments would promote a whole panoply of virtues. Perhaps the most important of these was self-respect. Those who argued for allotments repeatedly expressed the belief that allotments would raise the self-respect of labourers. A typical example, taken from the annual report of the Blything Labourer's Friend Society in 1838, states that: '[the allotment system] is creating self-respect, which will increase the labourer's feeling of moral responsibility for his family, employer and society'.[24]

Another of the virtues which it was widely thought allotments would produce was independence. In the context of the effects of allotments something more than merely 'independence' from poor relief was meant, although this of course was included within the sense of the term. Roughly speaking, 'independence' was closely related to self-respect, but also implied a certain individualism, initiative and financial security. Frederick Thynne put the concept into words for the 1843 Select Committee on the Labouring Poor in the following way:

> I think it will raise the character of the labourer the moment he is put into a situation by which he can earn his own livelihood; you raise him to a respectable man when you enable him by his own industry to get 'a stake in the hedge'.[25]

---

[22] Lovelace Bigg Wither, a regular correspondent of the LFS, believed that by the provision of allotments and a 'gradation of farms, rising from the one acre of the day labourer, by successive steps, to the four hundred or five hundred acres of the wealthy yeoman . . . would be filled up that impassable chasm that is now fixed between the labourer and the class next above him. He would again recover his long lost energy and almost-forgotten manliness of character. Hope restored would become the parent of many virtues': F&I, 190. See also the editorial introduction: F&I, 3–4.

[23] Editorial comment, F&I, 176.

[24] LFM xcv (1839), 20.

[25] SC on the Labouring Poor, 1843, vii. 45.

Self-respect and independence were both near relatives of a third important virtue which those who argued for allotment provision believed would
be promoted as a result of it – self-help. A good example is the first annual
report of the Labourer's Friend Society, written in 1832, which began by
stating that the basis of the Labourer's Friend Society's appeal was that the
most useful service it was possible to give was to help others to help themselves.[26] The emphasis on self-help was one frequently made by advocates of
allotments. One other of many examples must suffice. Francis Pym, at a
meeting of the Bedfordshire Agricultural Association at Bedford in 1847
declared that the 'great object to be attained [by allotment provision] was
putting the labourer in a condition to help himself, and eat the bread of independence'.[27]

The importance of the concept of self-help was reflected in the attitude of
supporters of allotments to the question of whether allotment provision
should be seen as a form of charity. Most advocates of allotments were
adamant that the allotment system should not be seen thus. The reason that
this point was considered as of such fundamental importance was that if the
labourer felt that he was in receipt of charity, the effectiveness of allotment
provision in inculcating the desired sentiments of self-respect, independence
and self-help would be imperilled. So, for example, the Taunton and West
Somerset Labourer's Friend Society carefully explained that they

> wish it to be kept in mind that this [i.e. the letting of allotments] is not to be
> considered in the light of *charity*, but simply for the promotion of industrious
> habits among the labouring classes, and affording them assistance in procuring
> land, which they might not be otherwise able to effect by their own unassisted
> efforts.[28]

The anxiety to avoid any appearance of charity accounts for the frequent
insistence amongst advocates of allotments that the rents charged for allotments should be 'fair', i.e. whilst they should not be more than that which a
farmer would pay for the same land, they emphatically should not be less.
Captain Scobell, wrote to the Hadlow Labourer's Friend Society in 1841 to
the effect that the rent charged for an allotment 'should of course never be
more than the wholesale rent paid by the farmer . . . a just amount is charged
so that the allotment tenant may feel the plan to be enduring, and unmixed
with debasing charity'.[29]

Of the other virtues which contributors to the *Labourer's Friend Magazine*
frequently adduced as reasons for letting land to labourers, the most important
were industriousness, thrift, prudence, sobriety and respect for the law.

[26] LFS, *Proceedings of the LFS*, 1832, 7.
[27] LF xl (1847), 173.
[28] F&I, 504.
[29] LFM cxxvii (1841), 144.

As is evident from the comprehensive scope of these virtues, what the society was attempting to do in promoting allotment provision amounted to a complete restructuring of the character of the rural labouring population.[30] The motives that inspired the leading figures within the LFS in this grand undertaking were in the first place humanitarian, moral and religious. A characteristic note was struck by Captain Scobell at a meeting of the East Somerset Labourer's Friend Society in 1835:

> The wants of the poor were little understood; what the poor wanted was an opportunity of maintaining themselves by honest industry, and whoever begrudged this opportunity to the poor man had either a bad heart or a weak head. The legislature had made laws, and judges and magistrates might administer them, but laws after all were to repress or to punish; there was a better avenue to the human heart which had not been so frequently tried – the avenue of sympathy.[31]

The Revd Stephen Demainbray spoke in similar terms of his response to a 'very liberal' offer made to him as rector of Great Somerford (Wiltshire) for a commutation of tithes on enclosure:

> considering it my duty to attend to the interest of my poorer parishioners, I did not consent, till I obtained for them the following conditions, namely, that every poor man whose cottage was situated on the commons or waste lands should have his garden, orchard or little enclosure taken from the waste within the last twenty years confirmed to him; and that in case the same did not amount to the half-acre, it should be increased to that in quantity.[32]

The same insistence on religious duty and moral sympathy pervades the words of the Revd W. B. Whitehead at the founding meeting of the West Dorset Labourer's Friend Society in 1846:

> They who possessed the better things of this life might go on revelling in their luxuries – they might continue in the enjoyment of their worldly possessions, careless of the starving population around them, but such a state of apathy was little in accordance with the sentiments of a man who loved his country and his fellow creatures – totally inconsistent with the obligations of Christianity.[33]

---

30 Compare E. P. Thompson, 'Time, work-discipline and industrial capitalism', reprinted in his *Customs in common*, London 1991, 352–403. Thompson's factory-owners had direct and obvious economic interests in creating a new kind of worker. It is less easy to see how such a remaking of the character of agricultural labourers served the economic interests of landowners. But technological, organisational and institutional changes, notably enclosure, high farming and the shift to annual tenancies at rack rents, were also changing the character of agricultural production in the late eighteenth and nineteenth centuries.

31 *LFM* lxvii (1835), 88.

32 S. Demainbray, *The poor man's best friend, or land to cultivate for his own benefit*, London 1831, 16.

33 *LF* xxx (1846), 201.

However, moral and religious values invariably have ideological and political connotations. What was the dominant ideological emphasis within the LFS? David Roberts has argued that the mid nineteenth-century allotment movement should be seen as a manifestation of a reinvigorated rural paternalism.[34] But what is striking about the virtues which those who promoted allotments seem to have been trying to inculcate is that, far from being backward-looking or feudalistic, they were, in general, quite the opposite. They were, in fact, the archetypal 'Victorian' values of liberal mid nineteenth-century Britain: self-respect, independence, self-help, industry, prudence, thrift, sobriety and honesty. The insistence that allotment provision should be untainted by charity indicates particularly clearly how far the allotment movement was from being an atavistic attempt to restore any form of feudal dependency. The hope was, in fact, almost precisely the opposite: that allotments would make their tenants more self-reliant, rather than more dependent on landowners.

The suggestion that the allotment movement was associated with a regressive High Toryism is further undermined by the political connections of the LFS. The organisation out of which the LFS developed – the General Association – had strong radical overtones, an awkward posture for a society dependent on landowners' goodwill for the realisation of its projects, and with the formation of the LFS and the acquisition of influential landed support, Wills and the other leading members of the society moderated their stance. Nevertheless, an analysis of LFS subscription lists, which include a considerable number of MPs, demonstrates how far the society was from being dominated by High-Tory influences. In 1833, for example, all but two of the twenty-six MPs subscribing to the LFS described themselves as Whigs or Reformers and J. I. Briscoe and W. F. Cowper, the two MPs who were most energetic in promoting allotments in parliament in the early 1830s, were both Whigs. In the course of the next two decades, the political balance of the LFS moved towards Conservatism but in this it was only reflecting a broader shift within the political nation as a whole. In 1850, of the forty MPs on the subscription list, fifteen were Whigs or Liberals, thirteen were Protectionists and eight were Peelites. This was quite a close approximation to the relative parliamentary strengths of the different political groups. Since the Gladstonian Liberal Party was formed from a coming together of Whigs, Liberals and Peelites, it is fair to suggest that, even in 1850, a majority of the MPs subscribing to the SICLC were of a liberal persuasion.[35] But it would be misleading to argue that the LFS and the SICLC should be bracketed politically together with the Liberal Party (although not as misleading as to suggest that they were orientated towards High-Tory paternalism). The important

---

[34] David Roberts, Paternalism in early Victorian England, London 1979, 132–3; cf. Bronstein, Land reform and working-class experience, 45–50.
[35] LFS subscription list for 1833, bound into LFS, Proceedings of the LFS, 1833; SICLC subscription list for 1850, bound into 1850 volume of LF.

point is that in its breadth of support the allotment movement reflected the mainstream of contemporary political opinion, which itself was increasingly informed by a liberal hegemony.

In its religious character, too, the LFS spanned the contemporary spectrum. While it is true that the society was quite heavily Anglican, thus reflecting the bias within the landed and political elite from which it drew its strength, the LFS cannot be associated with any one particular religious grouping. In fact it was not without nonconformist involvement, a prominent example being the independent minister James Orange, the leading figure in the allotment movement in the east Midlands. A number of Quaker landowners were also associated with the LFS, including Samuel Gurney (West Ham, Essex), Edward Neave (Gillingham, Dorset), William Matravers (Westbury, Wiltshire) and W. Lockwood (Woodbridge, Suffolk).[36] Within the Church of England, the LFS counted amongst its adherents both moderate evangelicals like Viscount Sandon and Viscount Ebrington, and Recordites like Lord Ashley, J. I. Briscoe and R. B. Seeley. There was even a Catholic presence within the upper ranks of the society: Thomas Wyse MP spoke at both the first and third public meetings in 1832 and 1834 respectively.[37]

What united those who gave their support to the second allotment movement was perhaps less a matter of political tradition or religious adherence than of temperament: the outlook of the LFS was distinguished by an optimistic confidence that social problems could be solved using benign methods.[38] Indeed, many of the articles which appear in the *Labourer's Friend Magazine* evince an almost unbounded faith in the capacity of allotments to transform not only the labouring poor but rural society *tout court*. Montagu Burgoyne, for example, one of the regular correspondents of *Facts and Illustrations* was convinced that 'the best, and I believe the only method of bettering the condition, and indeed the morals of the labouring poor, is to provide them with small allotments of land'.[39] An account of Edward Berkeley Portman's allotments at Pylle, Somerset, which appeared in the *Labourer's Friend Magazine* in 1834, referred to allotment provision as 'this great system of national regeneration'. Similarly, an article describing Sir Alexander Coke's allotments at Studley and Horton in Oxfordshire expressed 'an opinion, formed after much inquiry and some personal observation, that if anything is likely to restore the agricultural population of the kingdom to a healthy (that is, to a more moral and industrious) state it will be the general adoption of the allotment system'.[40] George Curtis

---

36 *F&I*, 78, 411; *LFM* lxvii (1835), 187; lviii (1836), 4.

37 LFS, *Proceedings of the LFS*, 1832, 1833, 1834.

38 The involvement of a number of Quakers in the LFS, marking the beginning of a long association between the Society of Friends and allotment provision, may be significant in this respect, although of course Quakers formed a small minority within the LFS.

39 *F&I*, 87.

40 *LFM* (1835), 192.

Rawlence, honorary secretary of the Fordingbridge Labouring Man's Friend Society, wrote to Benjamin Wills that he was

> fully convinced from what I have seen of the allotment system that it is the *best* plan yet devised for improving the condition of the labourer, and for lessening pauperism; and that if it were more generally adopted, poaching and crimes of various descriptions would decrease; and we should have the satisfaction of finding that it would make the labourers *more honest, more industrious*, and therefore cause them to become *better servants, better men* and *better Christians*.[41]

John Ilderton Burn, one of the most active members of the general committee of the LFS, was tireless in pointing to the immensely beneficial consequences which he was convinced would flow from the extension of the allotment system. Burn claimed that in every instance where the allotment system had been tried its advantages had been proved. In an article for the *Labourer's Friend Magazine* about a bill promoting allotments introduced into the House of Commons by Lord Lincoln in 1845, Burn quoted *Bell's Weekly Messenger* with glee:

> It will be seen that this is the commencement of the field allotment system by the government itself, and we hail it as such, as a new era for the comfort of the labouring poor. This system has worked well wherever it has been introduced. . . . It has converted some of the most rough and uncomely villages in the kingdom into so many rural Auburns – into scenes of comfort, cleanliness, and picturesque beauty – into cottage gardens, breathing the scent of flowers around, and the bees humming in the summer sun.[42]

The confidence of the LFS in the transformative powers of allotments was not limited to their role in rural society: many within the LFS regarded allotments as the best hope for resolving the social problems of English industry as well as agriculture. If rural England was troubled by machine-breaking, rick-burning and animal-maiming in the 1830s and 1840s, urban England manifested even clearer symptoms of discontent. Mass protests in favour of parliamentary reform in the early 1830s were succeeded by the prolonged struggle against the new poor law, by the ten hours movement and, above all, by Chartism. But if the rural crisis peaked in 1830, the urban crisis probably did not reach its high-water mark until 1842, a year of grave economic dislocation and political ferment. Many supporters of allotments believed that they would be just as effective in restoring economic stability and social harmony in urban and industrial as in rural areas. These concerns are particularly evident in the early 1840s (for example in the minutes of evidence of the 1843 Select Committee on the Labouring Poor). Industrial work was seen by many landed supporters of the allotment movement as intrinsically unnatural, impermanent and socially dangerous. It was natural for landowners

---

41 *F&I*, 396.
42 *LFM* cxxvii (1841), 137; *LF* xiii (1845), 227.

(and, as the work of Malcolm Chase and Jamie Bronstein has demonstrated, not only landowners) to look to the land for a solution to economic problems, including trade-cycle unemployment.[43] This is striking testimony that, even as late as the 1840s, many contemporaries remained unconvinced that the future was industrial rather than agrarian, and still regarded industrialism as reversible. Nor were they necessarily as wrong as the 'condescension of posterity' might lead us to suppose. During the last two decades, in large part due to the work of Nick Crafts and other 'new economic historians', we have become aware that industrial growth during the classic period of the 'industrial revolution' (1760 to 1850) was far less impressive and pervasive than had previously been believed. Labour productivity grew only slowly and living standards rose little, so a shift back towards agriculture would have required a less drastic adjustment than an earlier generation of historians believed. So the interest of the LFS in the relevance of land to industrial instability should not be dismissed out-of-hand as unrealistic. Nevertheless, it should be emphasised that, enthusiastic about the possibility of extending the allotment system to industrial workers as the *Labourer's Friend Magazine* was, the central and over-riding preoccupation of the society was with the potential offered by allotments to remould rural society.[44]

Another dimension of the optimism of the LFS was the unyielding hostility of most of those connected with the society to emigration, and to the Malthusian premises which underlay the assertion that emigration was necessary. To the LFS, it was impossible to accept a view of the world which implied that people should have to leave their homeland in order to be able to enjoy an acceptable standard of living. Allotments were, amongst other things, a way in which national food output could be raised sufficiently to make emigration superfluous. In this respect, the LFS was in sympathy with those who, in the late eighteenth century, had argued for 'home colonisation'. But partly for pragmatic, tactical reasons the LFS avoided the pitfalls of committing itself to home colonisation, preferring to concentrate on the single issue of promoting allotments, a policy which was much less controversial and open to attack. Typical of the LFS attitude to emigration was the title of one of J. I. Burn's articles: 'Emigration injurious and not beneficial to the country'.[45] Wills, too, was a fierce critic of emigration, which did him little good with the 1827 select committee.[46]

The LFS's temperamental optimism was perhaps the most important respect in which it differed from the SBCP. Although the predominant view within the SBCP, and certainly that of Sir Thomas Bernard, was also that it was desirable where possible to 'lead by kindness', the SBCP *Reports* show a

---

43 Chase, *The people's farm*; Bronstein, *Land reform and working-class experience*, esp. pp. 53–63.
44 N. F. R. Crafts, *British economic growth during the industrial revolution*, London 1985.
45 *LFM* ci (1839), 117.
46 *SC on Emigration*, 1826–7, v. 594–5, qq. 3823, 3830.

more intense, and typically evangelical, consciousness of 'our corrupt and fallen nature', which Bernard was convinced would 'sooner or later break forth' unless redeemed by the awakening of Christian faith.[47] Correspondingly, the SBCP *Reports* tend to be less confident of the likelihood of any change in the character of the labouring poor occurring as a direct result of material improvements in their living standards than the LFS, which was in little doubt that 'when the poor are prosperous, they are prudent'.[48] Indeed, for all its continuities with the SBCP, in some respects the ideological discontinuity between the two movements is more striking. As we have seen, the SBCP was closely identified with evangelicalism. In the years between 1800 and 1830, evangelicalism, especially of the moderate or 'Clapham sect' variety which had characterised the SBCP, became ever more thoroughly imbued with political economy, mainly through the works of Christian political economists like Malthus and Whately. Moderate evangelicals like Edward Copleston and Thomas Chalmers preached the 'laws' of political economy and believed that people (especially the poor) had to be exposed to the disciplines of the market if they were to be purged of their sinful idleness and folly. Boyd Hilton quotes a comment made by Peel with respect to the financial crisis of 1825, which he takes to exemplify the moderate evangelical understanding of market processes as a form of educative chastisement: Peel declared that 'ultimate good, after some severe suffering, will result'.[49] The suffering was integral to, indeed was causative of, the good.

The LFS took a very different view. It looked upon what its predecessor, the General Association, had described as the 'ruinous system of individual competition' with doubt or disfavour.[50] It was bitterly critical of Malthus, publishing one of its articles attacking the 'principle of population' under the gleeful heading 'Malthus in contradiction to Malthus'.[51] Far from believing that the way to make the poor virtuous was to restrict their entitlements and drive them into industriousness, the LFS argued that what the poor needed to become more industrious and independent was additional resources and encouragement. The differences between the LFS and Christian political economy crystallised over attitudes to the new poor law. Whilst the poor law report and the ensuing act of parliament exemplified the moderate evangelical view of the divine corrective engine, many within the LFS regarded the new law as anathema and even the more circumspect official line adopted by the *Labourer's Friend Magazine* was that the new poor law could only be made to work in conjunction with the allotment system.

What the second allotment movement and the new poor law were trying to

---

[47] SBCP, *Reports*, v. 20.
[48] LFS, *Proceedings of the LFS*, 1834, 9.
[49] Sir Robert Peel to E. J. Littlejohn, 23 Dec. 1825, quoted in Hilton, *Age of atonement*, 224.
[50] [Directors and Central Committee of the General Association for Bettering the Condition of the Manufacturing and Agricultural Labourers], 'An appeal to the nation', 798.
[51] *LF* cvii (1840), 27–8.

do was essentially similar: to remake the character of the rural labouring poor, and in a similar direction. Where the two differed was in their analysis of motive. Whilst the new poor law followed the 'gloomy science' of political economy in supposing that only fear ('less eligibility') would drive the poor into self-reliance, the allotment movement took a diametrically opposed view, arguing that unless it was made possible for the poor to support themselves, they would fail to do so. It was necessary to increase their resources if they were to become 'independent'. One of the speakers at the 1839 annual meeting of the East Somerset Labourer's Friend Society, a Dr Parry, expressed this particularly clearly. Parry explained that when the East Somerset society was founded, it had merely been assumed that allotments would be beneficial, on the basis of a 'knowledge of the constitution of man'. 'They knew that an entire dependence on contingencies . . . such as the demand for labour, the scale of wages etc., only produced improvidence or despair . . . They knew that a grand improvement could be effected by increasing in each individual his own self-respect and esteem, by raising in him the principle of a virtuous independence.' Parry then averred that the necessity for allotments had arisen from the effects of enclosure during the Napoleonic wars, which had made the poor dependent on relief. By providing allotments, the East Somerset Labourer's Friend Society had 'swept away this degradation'.[52]

The second allotment movement can therefore be seen as an ambitious attempt to reshape the character of the labouring poor, and especially of the rural labouring poor. The means by which the LFS hoped to achieve this goal were very simple and remained constant throughout the period between the society's formation in 1830 and its conversion into the SICLC in 1844: by distributing to as wide an audience as possible information about the advantages of allotments. This was not, of course, the only – nor the most adventurous – strategy that could have been followed. The AEI, for example, adopted the direct method of hiring land and letting it to labourers themselves – the method the SICLC was to adopt after 1844. A letter written by Lord Kenyon to Benjamin Wills, dated 6 October 1832, suggests that the LFS, or at least Wills, may in the early days have considered departing from their indirect methods. The letter was mainly concerned with Kenyon's experience of letting land to labourers, but ended with this postscript: 'On looking again at your letter I find I have not quite hit the point of it, but I do not think any association could purchase land to accommodate local difficulties or meet local desires.'[53]

The dangers of becoming involved in potentially complex local situations, and the undesirability of 'interfering' between landlord and tenant, were frequently cited by the LFS as reasons for not becoming involved in letting allotments directly. Mr Caldwell, one of the travelling agents of the LFS, explained in 1836 that 'The society does not itself procure land to allot to

---

[52] LFM cviii (1840), 38–9.
[53] Lord Kenyon to Benjamin Wills, 6 Oct. 1832, in a bundle of miscellaneous letters, 1831–67, GLRO, 7/6/734.

labourers, for two reasons: first, they do not pretend to be acquainted with local exigencies . . . secondly, if they were, they are not disposed to interfere between landlord and servant, or between master and servant.'[54]

These protestations must be treated with a degree of scepticism, since not only did the LFS seek to form subsidiary local societies which it fully intended to let allotments, thus 'interfering' between landlord and tenant, but, when it acquired greater financial resources on the formation of the SICLC, it promptly set about doing what it had hitherto so roundly condemned. Even allowing for the shades of ideological difference between the LFS and the SICLC, we must suspect that the financial constraints so frequently bemoaned by the LFS had at least as much to do with the society's passive role as did any conviction that such a role was ill-advised.

The principal vehicle of the LFS's educative campaign was intended to be the society's monthly magazine, known first as *Facts and Illustrations* and later as the *Labourer's Friend Magazine*. This was directed at landowners and clergymen and contained, month after month, an astonishing quantity of information about allotments, strongly tending in their favour but giving prominence to the arguments of those who opposed allotments too, if only in order to combat them. Each issue consisted of contributions from subscribers, usually detailing experiences of letting allotments, together with extracts from the national and provincial press, reports from local allotment societies, and details of the recent activities of the LFS itself. Almost every item directly concerned allotments. A typical issue might run to fifteen pages. The LFS also published various occasional papers, principally extracts from the magazine, and a regular didactic pamphlet directed at labourers entitled *Useful Hints*.

However, the LFS did not confine itself to publishing: it also sent out 'travelling agents'. The principal agent of the LFS during the 1830s was G. W. Perry, who travelled very extensively on behalf of the society. Other agents included Mr Caldwell, who took the society's message to Ireland, Mr Christian, and a farmer from Waterbeach named Sanxter, who unfortunately absconded whilst on the society's business, compelling the LFS to advertise in the Sussex press for news of his whereabouts.[55] These agents worked on the basis of contact lists of potential supporters and their function was, firstly, to lecture on the benefits of allotments, secondly, to form local auxiliary societies, and thirdly, to gain new subscriptions for the LFS. Most of the agents, especially Perry and Caldwell, seem to have been very active, and their itineraries make impressive reading. The first report of the LFS stated that Perry had recently visited Surrey, Sussex, Hampshire and Wiltshire, and praised his ability, energy, perseverance and tact.[56] In 1833 he visited Hampshire, Dorset, Somerset, Wiltshire, Middlesex and Berkshire, attended twenty-seven public meetings, helped to form seventeen auxiliary local societies and was again commended

[54] *LFM* lxi (1836), 71–2.
[55] LFS, general committee minute book, 1832–9, GLRO, 7/1/617, passim.
[56] LFS, *Proceedings*, 1832, 11.

by the annual report.[57] The 1834 report stated that Perry had visited Berkshire, Oxfordshire, Gloucestershire, Buckinghamshire, Essex, Suffolk, Norfolk, Northamptonshire, Surrey and Sussex in the past year.[58] In an era before journeys like these could be made by railway, Perry's energy is all the more impressive.

The effectiveness of agents in extending the allotment system was widely acknowledged. A note in the minute book of the society, dated 15 July 1832, records that the initial results, in terms of the formation of new local societies and increased subscriptions, of employing Perry were such that it had been agreed that the society would consider sending out another agent.[59] Another note, dated 22 September 1832, records that Mr Sanxter had been employed in this capacity.[60] The society did encounter various difficulties with agents, most spectacularly with Sanxter's disappearance, but more persistently with respect to the difficulty of persuading agents to submit regular reports of their activities.[61] But in the early 1840s, after ten years' experience of agents, both the LFS and its supporters remained committed to their use. Thus Samuel Catton, at the end of a letter enthusing about the advantages of allotments, printed in the Labourer's Friend Magazine in 1841, urged that agents be employed to spread the system.[62] The LFS had not changed its views on the advantages of travelling agents, as its report for the annual meeting in April 1841 makes clear.[63] It appears to have been lack of resources alone that prevented the society employing agents on a wider and more consistent basis in this period: the 1843 annual report announced that, although a financial appeal to consolidate the society's position had succeeded, the society still regretted not having the wherewithal to spread the allotment system more widely by the further employment of agents.[64] However, the inability of the society to afford agents itself did not stop it recommending them to its offshoots. In 1842, for example, the LFS had urged the recently formed Exeter St Thomas Labourer's Friend Society to employ an agent, commenting that it was 'by living agency alone that so much has been done in Somerset, west Kent and recently in Nottingham and the surrounding villages'.[65]

The LFS's agents travelled assiduously and, if one adds to this the circulation of the Labourer's Friend Magazine, it is clear that the LFS had a widely distributed presence. But it would be misleading to imply that the society was active in all areas of the country. Some parts were much more strongly represented than others. London was obviously a major centre, but in this period the

[57] Ibid. 1833, 6.
[58] Ibid. 1834, 7.
[59] LFS, general committee minute, 1832–9, GLRO, 7/1/617, 272.
[60] Ibid. 239.
[61] Ibid. passim.
[62] LFM cxxv (1841), 112.
[63] Ibid. cxxii (1841), 66.
[64] Ibid. cxlvii (1843), 88.
[65] Ibid. cxxxiii (1842), 60.

centripetal effect of basing the society in the capital was balanced by the energy of some of the local societies, in particular those in Somerset and, later, in Kent and the east Midlands. The society was not, as it was later to become, a London society masquerading as a national one. Nevertheless, its geographical coverage was uneven. There were, for example, only the most infrequent contacts with Scotland and Wales, although Ireland was regularly reported on and Caldwell travelled extensively there on the society's behalf. The potential for allotments in the West Indies was much discussed, but, apart from Lancashire and Yorkshire, the needs of the northern counties were quite neglected. In general most attention was paid to the southern counties, excluding Cornwall which was rarely mentioned. East Anglia, the home counties and the east Midlands received some attention, but the west Midlands and the Welsh borders rather less. This seems to have reflected the pattern of subscriptions to the society, although it also reflected the areas in which allotments had the most obvious potential.

We are now in a position to assess how much the LFS actually achieved. First we should consider its direct influence upon those members of the elite who came within its ambit: the various political, social and religious leaders who attended its annual meetings or who subscribed to the *Labourer's Friend Magazine*. The impressive array of noblemen, churchmen and politicians attending the first annual meeting has already been mentioned. Most subsequent meetings were not so well attended, but throughout this period the LFS continued to attract the patronage and support of powerful figures. Even if these men did not all put the allotment system into practice (and many did), their support conferred respectability and prestige on the LFS and on the allotment movement more generally.

However, possibly even more important was the influence of the LFS on the mass of its subscribers and those who, by one means or another, came into contact with the *Labourer's Friend Magazine*. As usual, it is well-nigh impossible to demonstrate that what people read influenced their thoughts and actions. However, in a few cases we do have direct testimony. Thus L. F. Page, landlord of the Woolpit (Suffolk) allotments, established in 1834, wrote to the *Labourer's Friend Magazine* that 'I had long been of opinion, that the letting of land to the labouring classes would add to their comforts and improve their morals, and when I had read the valuable book published by your society, I determined to begin at once.'[66] A similar tale is told by the landlord of the High Ongar allotments (Essex): in this case the creation of the allotment site in 1836 followed from a conversation with an unnamed member of the LFS.[67]

Clearly an organisation counting so many active and influential members of society among its supporters, with so extensive a correspondence and with a magazine having so significant a circulation is likely to have been directly instrumental in the creation of many more than just these two allotment

---

[66] Ibid. lxi (1836), 59.
[67] Ibid. lxxiv (1837), 69.

sites. But, beyond general statements to the effect that the LFS had been immensely useful, and so forth, there is no direct proof. However, it is possible to outline some of the ways in which it can be safely assumed that the LFS was influential.

In the first place, then, the LFS must have made a very large number of people who had not hitherto even heard of allotments aware of their exis-tence. Although the idea of providing labourers with land had attracted much attention in the late eighteenth century, it was not alive as an issue again until 1830, so the LFS had a vital role to play in terms of basic familiari-sation with the idea of allotments. Secondly, the society had not just to make people aware but to bring allotments to the forefront of the minds of contem-poraries. How far did the LFS succeed in this? We must acknowledge, of course, that the allotments issue never came to figure more than marginally on the political agenda, at least not for most of the 1830s and 1840s. But whilst this provoked frustration in the more impatient LFS adherents, such as John Ilderton Burn, it should not blind us to the fact that the profile of allot-ments was very much higher in the twenty years after 1830 than it had been in the twenty years before. Much of the credit for this must go to the LFS.

The LFS had, of course, to do more than make people aware of allotments and raise the profile of the issue. It had also to persuade people of their merits. In this it was remarkably successful. The press, both national and provincial, came to be almost unanimous in its support for allotments. Even the farmers' journals, the *Mark Lane Express* and the *Farmer's Magazine* were advocates of allotments. As we have seen, the county agricultural societies were also generally in favour of the idea. It is often suggested in the secondary literature that the arguments for and against allotments were evenly balanced, neither side having the upper hand. This is misleading: it seems fairly clear that by the early 1840s at the latest there was a consensus in upper-class circles that labourers ought to have allotments.[68] There were many who urged that plots should be limited in size, governed by tight regulations and so forth, but outright opposition was rare. Indeed, it would not be going too far to suggest that to speak out against the idea of labourers having allotments had become a little scandalous by this time.

An incident at the seventh annual meeting of the Banbury Agricultural Society in 1841 is revealing in this respect. The young Sir Henry Dryden spoke out strongly against the allotment system, asserting that it made labourers into thieves. Dryden's reasoning was that labourers with allotments were able to claim that corn which they had in fact stolen from their employers had been grown on their land. But Dryden's remarks raised a storm

68 Three main groups stood outside this consensus: some political economists, such as J. R. McCulloch; some radical politicians, such as John Bright; and most farmers. For the first and third groups see Jeremy Burchardt, 'Rural social relations, 1830–50: opposition to allotments for labourers', *AgHR* xlv/2 (1997), 165–75. On farmers see also Moselle, 'Allot-ments, enclosure and proletarianization', 493–500, and Archer, 'The nineteenth-century allotment', 32–6. On radical politicians see Burchardt, 'Land, labour, and politics', 120–1.

of protest: he was immediately rebuked by the chair of the meeting, W. R. Cartwright MP, and three other speakers then in turn put on record their dissent from Dryden's views and their support for the allotment system. Apparently no one was prepared to second Dryden openly. The *Northampton Herald*, which reported the meeting, put its own gloss on the matter: Dryden's speech displayed 'the ingenuousness of youth' and – it was implied – his egregious error could therefore be excused. The newspaper then went on to mount its own not insubstantial defence of the allotment system. The *Labourer's Friend Magazine* was evidently astonished by the whole episode and gave considerable prominence to it under the heading 'An attack on the allotment system'. It described Dryden's charge that allotments made labourers dishonest as 'extraordinary', noted that it had been 'temperately but satisfactorily' refuted by several gentlemen present at the meeting 'who spoke from experience' and concluded that 'we shall not despair of seeing Sir Henry a subscriber to the allotment system'.[69]

The most important point to note about this episode is that Dryden's attack on allotments was found shocking by his peers, by the local press, and – if we are to credit the LFS with sincerity – even by the *Labourer's Friend Magazine*. If public attacks on allotments had been at all common, one might have expected the journal to have been inured to them. It seems clear that to attack the allotment system in public, at least if one belonged to the landed elite, was regarded as 'not the done thing', and indeed as rather embarrassing. Class solidarity had nevertheless to be maintained, of course, and it is instructive to note, not only how quickly Dryden's peers moved to counter his assertions, but also that Cartwright, the *Northampton Herald*, and the *Labourer's Friend Magazine* all sought to explain away Dryden's remarks on the grounds of his youth and inexperience, thus minimising the damage done to the unity of local landed society.

The hegemony achieved by the allotment movement in the public sphere was partly a result of the flood of written and spoken propaganda issued by the LFS. But the rhetorical strategy deployed by the allotment movement was also important. One of the great strengths of the society's case was its insistence that the British agricultural labourer was at bottom a 'heart of oak' who would prove his solid worth if only he were given a chance to do so. Opponents of allotments often found themselves forced to assert that the labourer was irredeemably idle, or, even worse, dishonest. The trouble with this was that one of the most powerful political shibboleths of the time was the view that when not led astray by unscrupulous demagogues, the mischievous operation of a degenerated poor law etc., the British working man was upright, manly and independent. Perhaps this view was a legacy of Pittite patriotism, but whatever its ultimate source it seems in the early nineteenth century to have been crucial to the way in which the aristocracy made sense of the world it lived in and ruled. Thus Peel, speaking in the Commons debate on the People's Charter in 1842, furiously denounced

---

[69] *LFM* cxxviii (1841), 157–61.

Feargus O'Connor as 'a man who has perverted to his own evil purposes the minds of the respectable, intelligent, industrious, honest labouring classes of this country'.[70] We can see an example of the way in which the same phenomenon could undermine opposition to the allotment movement by looking again at the Dryden incident. It was Dryden's charge that the labourers were dishonest that provoked the strongest reactions. The *Northampton Herald's* report of the Revd J. R. Rushton's reply to Dryden runs as follows: 'He differed from Dryden (hear, hear). If the labourers were ignorant, educate them; if immoral, improve them; but above all do not show distrust (hear). Do not estimate the use of a thing by its abuse (cheers).'[71]

One subscriber to the *Labourer's Friend Magazine* was so outraged by Dryden's comments that he wrote in to deny Dryden's 'slur' categorically:

For a person to accuse another of so serious and disgraceful a crime as dishonesty, and that without the least provocation, merely because he (the accused) by the excellent manner in which he tills his ground, grows more on his allotment than the farmer does on his land, is, in my humble opinion, extremely unjust and unchristianlike.[72]

Winning the public argument about allotments was a victory which, in the absence of any other organised body of support for allotments, we must assume was essentially the achievement of the LFS. It is hard to overstate the significance of this victory, especially in the long term, since it placed the burden of proof on those who objected to allotments and made it more difficult to resist efforts to extend the allotment system. It was, nevertheless, only a first step for the movement: it was still necessary to motivate those who had been converted to take action. To what degree did the LFS succeed in doing this? It was not simply a matter of keeping up spirits but also of helping to solve practical problems and of 'networking'. As regards keeping up spirits, the *Labourer's Friend Magazine* must have been quite effective. Certainly it could not be accused of lacking enthusiasm. Numerous articles testified to the remarkable benefits which were found to result from letting allotments and some of its writers believed that if allotments were made universal, all the country's most serious problems would be resolved. Thus Samuel Lysons wrote to say that the general adoption of allotments would result in a doubling of food output, independence of foreign supplies of food and the raising of the general character of the labourers.[73]

Whatever the truth of such statements, their optimism, confidence and frequent appearance in the *Labourer's Friend Magazine* must have done much to

---

70 *Parliamentary debates*, 3rd ser. lxii, cols 1373–81.
71 LFM cxxviii (1841), 159.
72 Ibid. cxxix (1841), 177. An important contribution to the moral ascendancy which the LFS was able to establish over its opponents was the support of the great majority of the clergy for allotments: Burchardt, 'The allotment movement', 356–8.
73 LFM clvii (1844), 52.

keep the enthusiasm of the magazine's subscribers alive. Given that many supporters of allotments were isolated, this was an important function. But probably more important was the role of the *Labourer's Friend Magazine* in providing those who supported allotments with useful practical information about how to set out allotments, draw up rules and tenancy agreements, encourage tenants to cultivate their plots well and so forth. The magazine provided literally hundreds of models for such problems, with accompanying commentary highlighting the important points or, on occasion, suggesting amendments. This was a ready resource to draw on and must have helped many who were well-disposed towards allotments but anxious about the practicalities of implementing the system. The widespread exchange of experiences, information and ideas in the magazine must also have contributed effectively towards the diffusion of best practice. A similar function was performed by the travelling agents, who, as the minute books of the LFS make clear, spent a considerable amount of their time giving advice about the 'setting out' of new allotment sites.[74]

It is perhaps appropriate to note at this point that it is unlikely that the LFS had much effect on the attitude of labourers themselves towards allotments. The only direct contact between the society and the labourers was the magazine *Useful Hints*. This paid relatively little attention to allotments, being in fact replete with 'improving' stories, anecdotes and information of the crudest kind. It is unlikely that it would have made any impression – certainly not a favourable one – on any labourer unlucky enough to find a copy in his hands; its circulation was in any case small.

It is necessary to assess the society's political as well as its social influence. The high standing of many LFS supporters has already been noted. Of the most senior, those who played the most active roles within the society did not in general wield the maximum political influence, but there were a few men who were both prominent within the LFS and in national politics. The most important example in the early years was Lord Morpeth, and in later years Lord Ashley and William Cowper. It is difficult to know – if indeed it makes sense to ask – to what extent the activity of these men to promote allotments in parliament was the result of an independent conviction of their value, and to what extent it was the result of the organising and motivating influence of the LFS. In Ashley's case, however, his most substantial measure in favour of allotments was taken before he became actively involved with the LFS.

To what effect did the LFS exert political leverage? We have already discussed the legislation of 1831–2 and the possible influence of the society on it. We will now turn to the developments of the early 1840s. These seem to have had their origin in the renewed social and economic crisis culminating in 1842.[75]

Political action follows from social events with a time lag, and, just as in 1830–1, the turbulent events which seem to have prompted political action

---

[74] LFS, general committee minute book, 1832–9, GLRO, 7/1/617, passim.
[75] For a more detailed account of the parliamentary politics of allotment provision in the 1830s and 1840s see Burchardt, 'Land, labour and politics', 98–127.

on allotments were already past their peak by the time the action was under way. The *Labourer's Friend Magazine* tells us that the allotments issue was brought before parliament on 14 March 1843, when Mr Stanton moved a resolution on the subject. On 30 March W. B. Ferrand moved to bring in a bill which would have required one-twentieth of the uncultivated land in every parish to be allotted to the poor, on twenty-one year leases, with provision for building cottages. The bill was thrown out after its first reading on the grounds that it, in effect, proposed the compulsory creation of smallholdings.[76] On 6 April Mr Buller brought in a motion on home colonisation but this too was rejected. None of these MPs seems to have had a close connection with the LFS. But then on 11 April W. F. Cowper successfully moved that a select committee on allotments be appointed.[77]

The membership of the 1843 Select Committee on the Labouring Poor (Allotments of Land) included several people who had some connection with the LFS: W. F. Cowper (the committee's chair), Lord Robert Grosvenor and Lord Ashley. The witnesses called reflected an even stronger LFS influence. They included one of the society's travelling agents, Henry Martin, and also such LFS stalwarts as the Revd Stephen Demainbray, Captain Scobell and James Orange. Other witnesses with a long record of involvement with the LFS were Sir George Strickland MP and William Miles MP. Little attempt was made to hide the enthusiasm of the committee for allotments, as the questions asked of the witnesses reveal, and its final report predictably endorsed the allotment system: 'the tenancy of land under the garden allotment system is a powerful means of bettering the condition of those classes who depend for their livelihood upon their manual labour'.[78]

The committee recommended that allotments should be of a quarter of an acre, that they should be as near the labourers' houses as possible, and that rents should be no higher than those a farmer would pay. All rates, taxes and other charges should be included in the rent and discharged by the landlord. The system was, the committee suggested, most beneficial of all when carried out by individual landowners, but since it had not been adopted by these to a sufficient extent, the committee recommended that all future enclosure bills should include a permissive clause allowing allotments for the poor to be set out. The other legislative recommendations it made were, firstly, that the parochial authorities be relieved of their responsibilities under the allotment acts and that some sort of national body of trustees replace them, and secondly that provision be made to permit charity lands to be let as allotments.[79]

The committee's report seems to have been influential in high places. At a meeting of the Lichfield Agricultural Association in late 1843, the prime

---

[76] *LFM* cxlvi (1843), 70–9; Hall, *Law of allotments*, 28.
[77] *LFM* cxlvi (1843), 70–9.
[78] *SC on the Labouring Poor*, 1843, vii, p. iii.
[79] Ibid. pp. iii–vii.

minister, Peel, not hitherto noted for his support for allotments, spoke as follows: 'it is of immense importance to property owners that the farm labourer should have a deep interest in the soil. Important evidence on allotments was heard at the Select Committee on the Labouring Poor . . . having read the evidence I favour giving small allotments for leisure hours. I do not know a better leisure occupation for him'.[80]

Peel then apparently read the conclusion of the report, urging landlords to provide allotments and said that he thought a system of allotments would have 'a great tendency to raise the moral character and increase the happiness of the class of farm labourers'. The *Labourer's Friend Magazine* justifiably attached considerable importance to Peel's words, noting that they were particularly remarkable bearing in mind Peel's characteristic caution and official reserve.[81]

Shortly after the report of the committee had been issued, Ashley, one of its (albeit less active) members, introduced another allotments bill, supported by Mr Stanton and the earl of Surrey. This would have created a national body of trustees in line with the committee's second legislative recommendation. The proposed National Allotments and Loan Superintendence Society would have been given the power to obtain leases of waste without the consent of the commoners. The bill gained support from the *Morning Herald*, but was attacked by *The Times* for its centralising tendencies. Rather surprisingly, Ashley then withdrew his bill and, despite his stated intention to introduce a similar measure in the next session, did not do so.[82]

The next significant development was in early 1844, when Cowper indicated that he was considering moving an amendment to Worsley's general enclosure bill with respect to allotments. In the event Cowper decided to bring forward a bill of his own,[83] which was more moderate than Ashley's of the previous year. Under its provisions any parish might appoint non-poor law officers to act as intermediaries between the allotment tenants and their landlord, the rent to be secured on the rates. The bill, which did not feature any form of compulsory taking of land, fell through, as it did when reintroduced in 1845.[84] However, all this activity had not been entirely in vain, since the government's General Enclosure Act, passed in 1845, contained clauses requiring as a condition of the use of the act that on the enclosure of any waste, allotments be provided, unless the commissioners provided a written statement explaining why this was not desirable.[85] The specific clauses of this act may have had their genesis in a resolution moved by

---

[80] *LFM* clii (1843), 155–6.
[81] Ibid.
[82] Hall, *Law of allotments*, 28; *LFM* cl (1843), 128–32.
[83] *Parliamentary debates*, 3rd ser. lxxiii, cols 423–32, 965–79.
[84] *RC on the Employment of Children, Young Persons, and Women in Agriculture*, 1867–8, xvii. 39–40.
[85] Hall, *Law of allotments*, 29–31.

George Pryme in 1833, which proposed exactly this.[86] The LFS expressed its pleasure at the inclusion of the allotments clauses, although the defeat of the series of bills of the last two years must have been a disappointment to the society.[87] But the act was to prove, if not a dead letter, a far cry from the effective legislative facilitation of the spread of allotments that the LFS had hoped: although there were, at least initially, some cases of its being adopted, as at Great Missenden in 1850, by 1886 a mere 2,113 acres of allotment land (out of a total of 370,848 enclosed) had been provided under it.[88] This seems to have been largely because of the unsympathetic attitude of local and national enclosure commissioners, although we should also note that much of the waste remaining to be enclosed after 1845 was in sparsely populated districts where allotments might have been of limited value. In any case, admirable as the anxiety of the LFS and its supporters to ensure that the poor were treated fairly under any future enclosure awards was, it was hardly realistic to base hopes for a national extension of the system on provisions which would only affect the small number of as yet unenclosed parishes.

Whilst it seems reasonable to accept that the LFS was the dominant force promoting the allotments legislation of the 1840s, it must be concluded that the direct effects of this legislation on the numbers of allotments were negligible. The indirect effects, particularly through the evidence and report of the 1843 select committee, but also through the public seal of approval given to the allotment system through the various acts passed in its favour, and indeed the airing given to the case for allotments by prolonged discussion in parliament, were almost certainly very much more substantial, although again this is well-nigh impossible to prove.

What conclusions can be drawn about the overall contribution made by the LFS to sustaining the allotment movement? There can be no doubt that it was of immense importance. It is, indeed, tempting to see the difference between what happened after 1795–1800 and what happened after 1830 as being explicable solely in terms of there being an effective national organisation dedicated to the promotion of allotments in the second period. But, as we shall see, there were other agencies and forces, some of them powerful, which also contributed to the continued growth of the movement after 1830.

[86] *SC on the Labouring Poor*, 1843, vii. 141.
[87] *LFM* xvi (1845), 305.
[88] Hall, *Law of allotments*, 37–8.

4

The Local Movement and Individual Activists

The role of the local societies in sustaining the allotment movement in the years 1830–45 needs considerably more research. National sources, on which this study heavily relies, provide sound information on the national movement and about the characteristics of allotments, but only patchy information on the local movement. County studies based on local newspapers would undoubtedly much increase knowledge. Particularly interesting questions include what the regional distribution of local allotment societies was, what proportion of them bought or rented land rather than confining themselves to less ambitious support functions, what, if any, was the nature of their connection with the LFS, and from when and for how long they were active.

Although, in the present state of knowledge, any conclusions on what was happening in the localities can only be regarded as provisional, it can safely be asserted that the number of local allotment societies rose during the 1830s and early 1840s. Some societies, for example the Chard, Crewkerne and Ilminster Labourer's Friend Society, were founded very early, in this case in 1832.[1] By the early 1840s there were dozens of local societies, perhaps as many as a hundred. However, the vast majority of these were village societies, not the much larger district societies like the Chard, Crewkerne and Ilminster. Most village societies had no aspirations beyond running their local site as well as possible and, in a few cases, perhaps enlarging it. This was, admittedly, a vital function. It is evident from the *Labourer's Friend Magazine* that where active village societies existed more attention was given to the needs of plot-holders, rules were better framed and enforced, prizes were often awarded for good cultivation, tools, seed and manure might well be subsidised and, often, there was an annual rent supper – occasions, to judge by reports, of much conviviality. All these things were easier to afford because a village society could draw on its subscriptions – from the leading inhabitants – to fund them. It is easy to see that a site administered in this active way would be likely to prove far more successful and enduring than one where no such society existed and the entire administration was in the hands of a single individual. However, important as the village societies were, they did nothing directly to foster the extension of the allotment system to other parishes. It was of course possible that a neighbouring parish would imitate the example set, especially if, as will be argued, allotments did to a great extent possess the visible advantages their supporters claimed. But such a result would be purely

---

1   *LFM* xcv (1839), 2.

incidental. Of the local societies, it was only the district societies which played a major part in extending the system.

Most of the district societies were in many ways smaller (although some-times not very much smaller) versions of the LFS. Although they did not publish magazines nor, in general, send out travelling agents, they neverthe-less aimed to fulfil the same informational and advisory role. Their main method – that used not only by the LFS but by almost all other nine-teenth-century voluntary organisations – was the annual general meeting. This drew together as many worthies of the society as possible, ideally from the whole of the geographical area covered. There would be the usual long self-congratulatory speeches, resolutions, possibly a dinner and occasionally a distribution of prizes to allotment tenants. These meetings, very much on the model of the county agricultural associations, to which indeed many of the members of the society often belonged, were well reported in the local press and served a useful function not only in drawing attention to the allotment system and its advantages but also in giving it the stamp of approval of the local elite.

However, the district societies were not merely a lower tier of the LFS. They also, in most cases, took on a direct role in the management of allot-ments, although they did not usually let them. This was a role the LFS loudly eschewed, at least until 1844. Some of the district societies came to have large commitments in this respect – the Chard, Crewkerne and Ilminster had, by 1846, more than 800 allotment tenants in thirty parishes under its rules.[2] It was here, to a large extent, that their importance in extending the allot-ment system lay: the societies regarded it as part of their remit to enter into discussions with local landowners in parishes in their areas which were inade-quately supplied with allotments.

Almost all the societies, both village and district, appear to have been connected with the LFS (often referred to by members of local societies as the 'parent society'); many, indeed, were founded as a result of a visit by an LFS travelling agent. G. W. Perry seems to have been particularly active in this respect. Many of the local societies he founded must have had a short life-span, but others flourished for years. Thus the Chard, Crewkerne and Ilminster, one of the best documented because it issued a printed annual report, was still active as late as 1880.[3] This, however, may well have been the only district society to survive into the era of the third allotment movement.

The distribution of active societies was very uneven. The main areas were Somerset, Kent and the Midlands. Somerset had three large and active district societies, the Chard, Crewkerne and Ilminster Labourer's Friend Society, the East Somerset Labourer's Friend Society and the Taunton and

2   Ibid. xxvi (1846), 119.
3   LF (1880), 86–7.

West Somerset Labourer's Friend Society. Kent's only district society was the West Kent Labourer's Friend Society, but this was an impressive affair with at least forty village societies affiliated to it. The Midlands had, from the early 1840s, the Northern and Midland Counties Artisan's and Labourer's Friend Society, a remarkable institution which will be considered more carefully in the context of the activities of its leading figure, James Orange. A second district society in the Midlands was the Northampton Artisan's and Labourer's Friend Society, but this confined its attention largely to the town of Northampton, unlike the Northern and Midland Counties Artisan's and Labourer's Friend Society which covered Nottinghamshire, Leicestershire, Derbyshire and even a few villages in Warwickshire. From the mid-1840s there was also a cluster of three active district societies in Worcestershire and Hereford.

Of the remaining, more scattered, district societies, the most active seems to have been the Blything Labourer's Friend Society in Suffolk. District societies of sorts also covered parts of Devon, Wiltshire and Bedfordshire. Sussex had a district society, the rather obscure Sussex Association for Improving the Condition of the Labouring Classes, which appears, however, to have had little contact with the county's numerous village allotment societies. Yorkshire, by the mid-1840s, possessed three urban-based societies which fell mid-way between the village and the district societies in terms of scale and ambition.

What did these district societies achieve? The West Kent Labourer's Friend Society seems to have had some success. The allotment system was greatly extended in West Kent in the late 1830s and 1840s and it is clear that the society's travelling agent, Henry Martin, was the major force in this. But the society's work was confined to a relatively small area of Kent around Maidstone. In the case of Somerset, where the allotment system attained a much greater extent in this period, we can fairly give the three main local societies credit for much of the success. The societies, particularly the Chard, Crewkerne and Ilminster and the East Somerset, showed great energy. Typical of their exuberant confidence at this time was the 1841 report of the Chard, Crewkerne and Ilminster which, in its ninth year, noted that instead of the usual onset of lukewarmness about a new idea, the society grew annually more popular, that the allotment system was spreading in all directions, that all the letters the society received were approving and that not one practical farmer who had joined the society had left it.[4]

The Northern and Midland Counties Artisan's and Labourer's Friend Society had by the early 1840s become, on paper at least, a very extensive body. But on closer inspection its central organisation, as opposed to its numerous village affiliates, turns out to have consisted essentially of a single individual, the remarkable James Orange.

4   LFM cxxix (1841), 172.

The individual activists

No history of the allotment movement in the first half of the nineteenth century could afford to neglect the crucial role played by individual activists. Indeed, their prominence and achievements are one of the main reasons why the growth of the movement in this period cannot simply be attributed to the development of organisation. Of course the relationship between individual activists and the organised movement was reciprocal, the activists being enabled to operate more successfully because of the support offered by the LFS and its district offshoots, as well as the societies being – in many cases – sustained and invigorated by the activists. However, individual activists deserve more credit than such a purely reciprocal model would allow. In the first place, they often began their work before any local society existed, and indeed in several cases either before the LFS had been founded or before they became aware of its existence. Secondly, they were often themselves the founders of the local societies in their areas. Thirdly, the support they received from the LFS was not always as generous and effective as perhaps it could have been. Finally, in several cases single individuals seem to have acted as the motors of their local societies. At the eighth annual meeting of the East Somerset Labourer's Friend Society in 1840, for example, the honorary secretary of the society, Captain Leigh Lye, apologised for the lack of an annual report and attributed it largely to the illness of Captain Scobell.[5]

Individual activists were a varied group; there is space to consider only the most important. The Estcourt family of Shipton Moyne in Gloucestershire falls into this category. Thomas Estcourt, more than anyone, deserves to be remembered as the inventor of the idea of allotments and as the first practitioner of the movement. Whilst it was Thomas Estcourt who took the most prominent public role in advocating allotments – his articles appeared in both the SBCP *Reports* and in the *Annals* – his family retained an interest in the subject for the rest of the nineteenth century. His son, the evangelical Thomas Grimston Bucknall Estcourt, was a member of the 1843 Select Committee on the Labouring Poor, although not a major figure in the LFS.

The Revd Stephen Demainbray lived within ten miles of Shipton Moyne, at Great Somerford in Wiltshire. He was aware of what the Estcourts had done, citing their example several times in his numerous statements in favour of allotments, and may have been personally acquainted with the family (he certainly had plenty of time to become so, since he died in 1854 at the age of ninety-four, having been rector of Great Somerford for fifty-five years).[6] Demainbray first became involved with the provision of allotments in 1806, when on the enclosure of the parish and commutation of tithes he stipulated that allotments be provided for the poor. These, eight acres in total, were

5   Ibid. cxviii (1841), 12.
6   *SC on the Labouring Poor*, 1843, vii. 11; inscription on tombstone in Great Somerford church.

unusual in that they were to be let to poor families free of charge.[7] They are still in use today. Demainbray became an enthusiast for allotments, to an almost obsessive degree. (This intense commitment also characterised several of the other leading figures in the allotment movement during the 1830s and 1840s, notably Captain Scobell, James Orange and John Ilderton Burn.) Demainbray played a more prominent role in the second allotment move-ment than the Estcourts. He appeared as a witness before both the 1830–1 House of Lords Select Committee on the State of the Poor Laws and the 1843 Select Committee on the Labouring Poor. He was actively involved with the LFS, speaking occasionally at its annual meetings in London and contrib-uting to the *Labourer's Friend Magazine*. He was also an author on his own account, publishing in 1831 a work entitled *The poor man's best friend*, which set out his experience of allotments.[8]

Demainbray's influence was undoubtedly substantial. Whilst his manner of speaking was often obscure, the evidence he provided to the two select committees was impressive, spanning as it did so long a period of years. His unabated enthusiasm for allotments, evidently as great or even greater after forty years than it had been initially, was – and is – even more impressive. The early spread of allotments in Wiltshire, and the continued strength of the movement there, may well have been, in part, a consequence of his example (*see* chapter 2).

The great strength of the second allotment movement in Somerset cannot be attributed wholly to the influence of one or two activists. But the move-ment there did owe much to two figures: George Law, bishop of Bath and Wells, and Captain George Treweeke Scobell, RN. Law's initial experience of allotments dated back almost as far as Demainbray's, to 1807, when he had introduced allotments in the Cambridgeshire parish of Willingham of which he was then rector. On his appointment to the bishopric of Bath and Wells in 1824 he soon established sites at Wells and at nearby Banwell. The site at Wells occupied 100 acres (more than six times the national average), making it amongst the largest in the country at this time.[9] It was regarded as highly successful by both landlord and tenants and made a deep impression on many visitors. Two examples are worth quoting to give an indication of the surpris-ingly intense response a visit to the bishop's allotments could provoke. The first is taken from a letter written by one Matthew Phillips to the bishop in 1838:

> I . . . beg to offer a few observations, which have fallen under my notice, in many walks round your terrestrial paradise. The three hundred and sixty tenants with their wives and children, averaging at least four in a family, are benefited much by the great assistance, comfort, and employment in the culti-

---

7   *SC of the House of Lords on the Poor Laws*, 1830–1, viii. 27.
8   Demainbray, *The poor man's best friend*.
9   Calculated from the allotments database. See appendix 1.

vation of their several allotments of land . . . the grateful expressions of the people do them much credit; indeed, they say that hundreds of men, women and children would be almost in a state of starvation without the land.[10]

Similarly strong sentiments were expressed in a letter written by Joseph Emery, an apothecary in Wells, to the *Farmer's Magazine*. Emery declared that if the industrious poor were provided with allotments 'such a beneficial change will be effected for the better in twenty years in this country, as has never entered the mind of man to conceive'. He offered as proof of this:

> the beautiful splendid sight, now blooming, of a kitchen garden full of the bounties of Providence, of one hundred acres subdivided, from four to five hundred industrious, I will not say poor, but happy allotment tenants just now gathering in the profits of their own and their children's labour.

Emery's letter was signed by six other men as well and included the following postscript: 'N.B. We humbly call upon all who have time and means to come and see us. They shall find a John Bull hearty welcome. The garden is half a mile, a delightful walk, from the residence of the bishop and the town hall of Wells.'[11]

The bishop's allotments were much visited, and several other favourable accounts could be cited. Law clearly regarded his allotments with special interest and affection: we are informed, for example, that he rode down to inspect them every morning.[12] He seems to have regarded them as one of the sights of Wells, and regularly to have taken his visitors to see them. It seems likely that his example was widely influential; it was certainly often cited. Law's allotments seem to have had a powerful influence on the clergy in his diocese; by 1832, as he explained to the first annual meeting of the LFS, very few of the clergy with glebes in his diocese had not let some land in allotments.[13] This was in sharp contrast to the position in other dioceses. Law was also active in both local and national allotment societies, in particular the East Somerset Labourer's Friend Society, the AEI and the LFS. He sat on the 1830–1 Select Committee of the House of Lords on the Poor Laws. In short, he was active in most of the major areas of work in the allotment movement. Nationally, his political influence and prestige lent weight to the allotment movement although since the movement had other powerful supporters within the elite, his role here was probably not indispensable. Locally, there can be little doubt that his enthusiasm, and the prominent success of his allotments at Wells, were major factors in the leading role played by Somerset during the second allotment movement.

---

[10] Matthew Phillips to G. H. Law, 19 Nov. 1838, printed in *LFM* xciv (1839), 12–13.
[11] Letter dated 19 Sept. 1836 'at Mr Emery's cottage in the middle of the hundred acre garden', to the *Farmer's Magazine*, reprinted in *LFM* lxx (1837), 8–9.
[12] Augustus Bozzi Granville, *The spas of England, and principal sea-bathing places*, II: *Midland and southern spas*, London 1841, quoted in *LFM* cxxvii (1841), 145.
[13] LFS, *Proceedings*, 1832, 14.

Another Somerset figure, however, contributed even more to the local movement, whilst also being active, if to a lesser extent, on the national level. This was George Treweeke Scobell of High Littleton. Scobell was the founder of the East Somerset Labourer's Friend Society and one of the first landowners to let allotments in this part of Somerset. Scobell's energy was remarkable even by the high standards of the early Victorians; contemporaries often attached the adjective 'indefatigable' to his name, almost as a sobriquet. At the seventh annual meeting of the East Somerset Labourer's Friend Society, for example, the honorary secretary expressed his regret at the absence due to illness of 'the humane, intelligent, and indefatigable founder of their institution'.[14] Other than through illness, Scobell did not miss an annual meeting of the East Somerset Labourer's Friend Society during this period. He also attended national LFS meetings regularly and was one of the few regional activists to try to bring his experience to benefit another area, when in 1841 he wrote a long letter to the Hadlow (Kent) Labourer's Friend Society.[15] He gave evidence to the 1843 Select Committee on the Labouring Poor and was still urging his contemporaries to adopt the allotment system in the 1850s, twenty years after he had first taken it up, but now in his capacity as a member of the national committee of the SICLC. He spoke and wrote voluminously on the advantages of allotments at every possible opportunity and persistently badgered neighbouring landowners to provide plots for the local labourers. He claimed that allotments had been introduced into all the parishes within many miles' radius of High Littleton; this was presumably largely as a result of his efforts.[16] Scobell was a man of admirable qualities, although he must have been a thorn in the side of those local gentry who simply wanted to lead a quiet life. His motivation seems to have been purely to improve the lives of the labourers. He wrote in 1840 that of all the things he had done in the course of his life 'this disinterested and independent alliance with my neighbours [i.e. the labourers in his village] has yielded me the most gratifying and the most enduring inward satisfaction'.[17]

How much did Scobell's indefatigability achieve? Although a very different figure, the extent and character of his influence were probably similar to those of the bishop of Bath and Wells. In the bishop's case it seems reasonable to suppose that far fewer of his clergy would have created allotments on their glebes but for his influence. In Scobell's case, it is the fifty-odd parishes within a radius of a dozen miles from High Littleton which would almost certainly not have adopted the allotment system to such an extent but for him. It is also true that Scobell's role in creating and sustaining the East Somerset Labourer's Friend Society was vital: although the society might have survived without him, it would not have been as energetic nor as effec-

14 *LFM* cix (1840), 49.
15 Ibid. cxxvii (1841), 141–4.
16 Ibid. cxix (1841), 13.
17 Ibid. cxix (1841), 14.

tive. On a national level, again like G. H. Law, Scobell was useful but not individually essential. One respect in which his influence nationally may have been particularly important, however, was in its humane tenor. There were always those who favoured a restrictive, disciplinarian approach to letting allotments. But Scobell raised his voice loud and clear on behalf of the labourers: as he told the Select Committee in 1843, 'I think you must place confidence in them.'[18]

Kent owed much of its prominence in the allotment movement in this period to the activity of Henry Martin. However, whilst Demainbray, Law and Scobell (and, as we shall see, Orange) were personally committed to the allotment cause and only became involved with the various institutional expressions of the allotment movement because of this pre-existing commitment, Martin falls into a different category. He was the travelling agent of the West Kent Labourer's Friend Society and as such had been appointed by the society, was paid by them and acted, at least in theory, under their direction. To a certain extent we can assume that had the West Kent Labourer's Friend Society not found Martin, they would have found someone else to do his work. But Martin deserves notice here for two reasons: first, because the energy with which he entered into his work was beyond the call of duty; and second, because, unlike the travelling agents of the LFS, he can be shown to have had a substantial impact on the development of the allotment system in a particular region.

Martin worked for the West Kent Labourer's Friend Society from 1836 onwards and had, so he told the 1843 select committee, been instrumental 'to a very great extent for the last seven or eight years' in providing allotments in Kent.[19] This may not have been the most modest of statements, but the annual reports of the West Kent Labourer's Friend Society bear it out, with the reservation that the activities of Martin – and the west Kent society – did not extend to east Kent, where allotments seem to have been almost unknown at this time (see chapter 2). However, in west Kent Martin's efforts were impressive. The 1839 report of the west Kent society records that in the previous year Martin had formed fourteen new village societies and extended three of those already in existence.[20] At the annual meeting in 1841 the chair, Sir John Croft, stated publicly that the report showed the great zeal of the society's agent.[21] In subsequent years Martin continued to visit parishes where allotments were not yet in existence, to form village societies, to arrange or facilitate the extension of allotment sites already in existence and to attend the annual festivities of the various village societies. On the formation of the SICLC in 1844, he was appointed agent for the national society, an appointment which, whilst it may have reflected a prejudice against the

---

18 SC on the Labouring Poor, 1843, vii. 24.
19 Ibid. 1.
20 LFM ciii (1839), 144.
21 Ibid. cxxi (1841), 57.

other leading candidate (the Nonconformist James Orange), would presumably not have been made had Martin not proven himself with the West Kent Labourer's Friend Society. To a greater degree than in most counties, the extension of the allotment system in Kent in the 1830s and 1840s was the work of one man.

There were many other individuals who contributed much to the allotment movement in this period. Benjamin Wills, John Ilderton Burn, W. F. Cowper, Lord Ashley, the various travelling agents of the LFS and James Orange spring to mind. If the LFS is seen as being, as it essentially was, the creation of Benjamin Wills, acting on his own initiative, then of course his contribution was momentous (*see* chapter 2). With regard to the others, however, their contribution was with one exception general and less direct, and, again with the one exception, the allotment movement and the number of allotment sites would probably not have looked very different in this period had any one of them not been involved. The exception is James Orange.

Little is known about Orange's early life, or about what happened to him after 1853, but we do know that in the early 1830s he was the joint pastor of Barker Gate Chapel, Nottingham, an Independent meeting house. He helped set up the New Charity School for the poor, adjacent to the chapel, in 1831. But sadly the Barker Gate Chapel was saddled with debt incurred under the preceding ministry and both it and the school were forced to close. In his *History of Nottingham*, from which this information is taken, Orange wrote that 'it was the heaviest affliction of our lives, to many of us, to be deprived of the school and chapel'.[22]

Orange seems to have felt a strong desire to benefit his fellow men: we next hear of him energetically, and without any remuneration, promoting the allotment system in the east Midlands. How he came to see allotments as of such central importance is not known, but it was not through the LFS, since he was unaware of the society's existence at this time. In any event, in 1840 he wrote a series of articles in the Nottingham press advocating allotments and in December of the same year published a pamphlet entitled *A plea on behalf of the poor*, which again urged allotments as the answer to poverty.[23] In March 1841 the Northern and Midland Counties Artisan's and Labourer's Friend Society was established, with the principal aim of letting cottages and gardens or allotments to labourers.[24] It is unclear whether the society ever attempted to let cottages, but it – or rather, since he seems to have borne almost the whole burden of the society's affairs, James Orange – accomplished a great deal in a short space of time in the matter of letting allotments.

Orange's chief activities were lecturing on the benefits of allotments at public meetings, forming societies, assisting in negotiations with landowners

---

[22] James Orange, *History and antiquities of Nottingham*, ii, London 1840, 947–8.
[23] *LFM* cxxx (1842), 5.
[24] Ibid. cxxix (1841), 179.

to provide land for allotments and writing to the local press.[25] His work was not confined to Nottingham, but extended across the east Midlands. It was principally concentrated on the framework-knitting villages between Nottingham, Leicester and Derby (as well as taking in the first two of these cities), but he also formed societies in Warwickshire at Nuneaton, Coventry, Leamington Spa and Warwick.[26] He described his typical procedure to the Select Committee on the Labouring Poor. First he would book a place for his lecture in a village or town where the allotment system was not yet in full operation. Then he would give his lecture. If the local clergyman was sympathetic Orange would visit him. Then he would ask the villagers which of the local gentry would be suitable members of a committee to promote allotments in the village. He would then, sometimes after further lectures, attempt to form a local society, which would take responsibility for the difficult and protracted business of finding suitable available land. Where no land could initially be obtained, Orange would revisit the village, often several times, in order to keep up the spirits of those who wanted allotments.[27]

Orange worked prodigiously hard on behalf of the Northern and Midland Counties Artisan's and Labourer's Friend Society for at least the next three years. The LFS, which Orange had contacted by this time, praised his 'unwearied exertions' and noted that he was working 'most ably and zealously' for the allotment system. It granted him £20 for expenses and regretted that it lacked the resources to pay him a permanent salary (which he richly deserved).[28] Perhaps the LFS really could not have done more for Orange than it did, but nevertheless one cannot help feeling that his efforts did not receive the reward they deserved. He certainly had great difficulties to contend with. The main one was finding land – often local societies had to wait for several years before land became available, and it is not suprising that some did not survive. Orange noted in his journal that it was only by frequent lecturing that it was possible to sustain interest in the allotment system in villages which experienced such long delays.

Orange did indeed lecture most assiduously. He must have given hundreds of lectures in the east Midlands in 1842–3, revisiting some villages where land was not quickly forthcoming again and again.[29] His schedule was crowded, even though all his activities were entirely voluntary, and he often gave several lectures in a single week. The lectures were substantial affairs and could last as long as two hours.[30] He had to contend not only with bad weather and transport difficulties (he made much use of the recently opened local railway network), but also with opposition from some elements of local

---

25 *SC on the Labouring Poor*, 1843, vii. 90.
26 *LFM* cxl (1842), 167–9.
27 *SC on the Labouring Poor*, 1843, vii. 94.
28 *LFM* cxxxiv (1842), 68.
29 Ibid. cxxxiii (1842), 55.
30 Ibid. cxxxii (1842), 44.

society. Perhaps his previous occupation as Nonconformist preacher brought more opposition down on his head than would otherwise have been the case. Clergymen sometimes denied him the use of the local schoolroom and farmers the use of their barns. In the face of all this he remained undaunted, resorting on at least one occasion to lecturing in the open air in a manner reminiscent of Joseph Arch at Wellesbourne.[31]

Orange's experience of lecturing to the east Midlands framework knitters was a mixed one. But his dedicated work bore practical fruit. By 1843, only two years after he began his campaign, sixty-three local societies had affiliated to the Northern and Midland Counties Artisan's and Labourer's Friend Society and about 800 acres had been let out in allotments.[32] Nor is this all: since the allotment movement in the east Midlands was to a large extent Orange's creation, he should have at least part of the credit for its continued expansion in subsequent years. By 1873 Leicestershire and Nottinghamshire were respectively third and fourth in the county table of allotment numbers with a combined total of 34,809 plots.[33] More strikingly, perhaps, than for any other area, the history of the allotment movement in the east Midlands bears witness to the vital role which a dedicated individual could play in extending allotment provision in a local context.

[31] Ibid. cliii (1843), 179. Orange also encountered serious difficulties on account of the ambivalent relationship between allotments and Chartism in the east Midlands. This is discussed more fully in chapter 7.

[32] SC on the Labouring Poor, 1843, vii. 90.

[33] Return of Allotments Detached from and Attached to Cottages, in England and Wales, and Scotland, 1887, lxxxviii. 689–719.

PART III

ALLOTMENTS AND RURAL SOCIETY

5

The Allotment Landlord

The central relationship at the heart of allotment provision was that between allotment landlords and allotment tenants. In view of the failure of public provision of allotments in early and mid nineteenth-century England, the fate of the movement hung on the response of private and institutional landowners. An impressively large number of allotment sites had been established in the countryside by the third quarter of the nineteenth century, so it is clear that landowners did respond to the publicity of the LFS. The primary aim of this chapter is to explain why they did so. But before entering into this question, the identity of allotment landlords needs to be clarified.

Who let allotments?

Theodore Hall, the leading nineteenth-century legal authority on allotments, specified five different kinds of allotment landlord in his *Law of allotments* of 1886: landowners, glebe owners, parish officers, allotment wardens and trustees of charities.[1] This list is a useful starting point, but two further categories should be added: tenant farmers and allotment societies. It is also useful to subdivide the category 'landowner' into peers and other landowners.

The most useful source of information about the characteristics of allotment landlords between 1793 and 1873 is the allotments database.[2] For each of the 1,641 sites in the database, the name and status of the landlord is given, if this is known. The database distinguishes between peers, other landowners, tenant farmers, parish officers, allotment societies, allotment wardens and trustees. However, in many instances insufficient information was given in the original source to classify the landlord reliably: a common problem is that the name of the landlord is given but no indication of social status (for example whether landowner or a tenant farmer). The database can be supplemented by two contemporary local surveys yielding statistical information about the characteristics of mid nineteenth-century allotment landlords. The first of these was carried out by the Devizes Labourer's Friend Society in 1833, and relates entirely to Wiltshire. The second is the putatively comprehensive list of allotment sites in the three east Midland counties of Derbyshire, Nottinghamshire and Leicestershire reproduced in the 1845 *Report of the*

---

1   Hall, *Law of allotments*, p. v.
2   The allotments database is described in more detail in appendix 1.

Royal Commission on the Framework Knitters.[3] Both sources have limitations: between them they cover only a very small part of the country and both are imprecise in their categorisation of landlords, whilst the 1833 survey may be additionally unrepresentative because it relates primarily to the estates of landowners who were associated with the Devizes Labourer's Friend Society. Nevertheless, they provide an interesting comparison with the evidence from the allotments database.

Peers feature prominently as allotment landlords in many of the major primary sources, including the *Labourer's Friend Magazine* and most of the relevant parliamentary inquiries. Some peers let out large acreages in allotments. The Lansdowne estate was one of the most notable providers from the early years of the nineteenth century onwards. Ten fields on the estate had already been let by 1818 and the quantity was increased to thirty-six fields between 1831 and 1836.[4] In 1834 it was stated that there were over 700 allotment tenants on the estate and in 1843 that a total of 400 acres was thus employed.[5] By 1868 the estate had 580 acres let out to 882 labourers.[6] Other peers who had large acreages of allotments were the duke of Bedford (about 600 plots in Bedfordshire by 1832), the duke of Richmond (1,500 plots on his estates in the 1830s) and the duke of Newcastle (nearly 2,000 allotments in Nottinghamshire by 1843).[7] Peers were not, however, the main source of allotment provision. Of 533 sites in the allotments database for which it is possible to identify whether the landlord was a peer or not, only 100 (19 per cent) were let by peers.[8]

However, even if the aristocracy were not necessarily essential to the allotment movement as providers of land, they do seem to have made a distinctive contribution in three other respects. First, the fact that several peers took up allotments on a very large scale, and gave conspicuous public support to the movement, contributed significantly to its impetus. The impressive number of plots established by the dukes of Lansdowne, Bedford, Richmond and Newcastle in the 1830s and 1840s was frequently referred to in contemporary literature on allotments, and it seems likely that the local impact of such initiatives in prompting other landowners to let allotments was even greater. Secondly, peers and other great landowners often played the leading role in introducing allotments into counties that had been slow to adopt them. As

---

3 *F&I*, 424–64; *RC on the Framework Knitters*, 1845, xv. 138–9.

4 Fortescue, 'Poor men's gardens', 395–6.

5 LFS, *Proceedings*, 1834, 10; *Report on the Employment of Women and Children in Agriculture*, 1843, xii. 56.

6 *RC on the Employment of Children, Young Persons, and Women in Agriculture*, 1868–9, xiii. 144.

7 *F&I*, 479; Roberts, *Paternalism*, 108; *SC on the Labouring Poor*, 1843, vii. 137.

8 Peers remained a minority among allotment landlords later in the nineteenth century. Lady Verney, writing in 1886, noted that whilst individual landowners sometimes let whole districts in allotments, taken nationally most plots were not let by great landowners: 'Allotments', *Nineteenth Century* xix (1886), 912.

we have seen, in most counties in the south of England significant numbers of allotments were introduced in the 1830s, and here the aristocracy did not stand out for their contribution, except in the case of Sussex. But in the north the progress of allotments was much slower and great landowners seem to have played a major role as pathbreakers. Sir Rowland Hill and Lord Kenyon appear to have been responsible for the introduction of allotments into Cheshire and great landowners seem to have been almost alone in providing allotments in the 1830s in Shropshire, the East and West Ridings and Northumberland.[9] Thirdly, because they typically owned very large acreages, peers were often able to experiment with different kinds of allotment provision in a way that others generally could not. The great landowners had incomes of a size sufficient to absorb any losses that might result from an unsuccessful experiment and often they were in a better position to force their tenants to surrender land on a large scale, usually a prerequisite for any major experiment. For these reasons, great landowners were responsible for many of the more ambitious and comprehensive allotment schemes. On the Lansdowne estate, for example, not only were allotments made available to virtually the entire labouring population of the district, but by the late 1860s a gradation of plot sizes from forty perches to two and a half acres had been established.[10] This had obvious advantages for labourers, whose changing family circumstances altered both the quantity of land they could manage and the quantity they needed, but to let such a complex mix of large plots required more land and greater administrative resources than were available to less extensive landowners.[11]

Since great landowners provided only a minority of allotments, and since the number of allotments let by clergymen was relatively limited, it seems likely that lesser landowners provided more allotment plots than any other single group. This assumption is supported by the database, which identifies 180 of 565 relevant sites (32 per cent) as being let by 'other landowners' (i.e. private landowners who were neither peers nor clergymen). However, this amorphous group did not attract much contemporary notice for their role in letting allotments, and it is difficult to isolate any respect, other than sheer

---

9   *SC on Agriculture*, 1833, v. 297–8; *SC on Agriculture*, 1836, viii. 286; *RC on the Poor Laws*, 1834, xxviii. 739–40.

10   *RC on the Employment of Children, Young Persons, and Women in Agriculture*, 1868–9, xiii. 474–5.

11   As well as initiating some of the most ambitious allotment schemes, aristocrats were the major providers of cow pasture to labourers. Cow pastures had a different chronology and geography from allotments, and required a different mix of capital and labour inputs, but their history relates to that of allotments at many points. A full-scale study of cow-keeping by nineteenth-century labourers is needed. *SC on the Poor Laws*, 1817, vi. 166; *SC of the House of Lords on the Poor Laws*, 1830–1, viii. 204; *F&I*, 78; *SC on Agriculture*, 1833, v. 590–1; *Report on the Employment of Women and Children in Agriculture*, 1843, xii. 341; *RC on the Employment of Children, Young Persons, and Women in Agriculture*, 1868–9, xiii. 182, 300, 309, 320.

numbers of plots let, in which it made a distinctive contribution to the allotment movement.

The third group to be considered is the clergy. Rectors were often able to let out their glebe in allotments and in some counties, in particular Northamptonshire, glebe seems to have provided a high proportion of allotment land.[12] However, the role of the clergy in lending their moral support to the allotment movement was more significant than the number of sites they let, which has sometimes been exaggerated.[13] The evidence from the database can be summarised as follows. Of 1,096 records for the entire period, 194 records (18 per cent) were of sites let by clergymen. Of the thirty records for the 1793–1829 period, eight (27 per cent) were let by clergymen, whilst for the 1830–49 and 1850–73 periods, clergymen let 128 of 748 sites (17 per cent) and 58 of 318 sites (18 per cent) respectively. The percentage figures for the 1830–49 and for the 1850–73 period are almost identical, presumably because of the large number of sites in both samples (although it also suggests that there was little change in the proportion of sites let by clergymen over the 1830–73 period). The higher proportion of sites let by clergymen in the pre-1830 sample may reflect the relatively small number of sites in the sample rather than any real change; but several of the most prominent early allotment landlords were clergymen, notably the Revd Stephen Demainbray and the bishop of Bath and Wells, so it is possible that clergymen did form a slightly higher proportion of allotment landlords before 1830 than afterwards.[14]

The important point to emerge from these figures is that whilst clergymen were indeed significant in terms of the proportion of sites let by them, they were not of overwhelming importance. Even if no clergymen had let allotments, the number of sites let over the 1793–1873 period as a whole would have been only about 18 per cent lower than it actually was.

Tenant farmers rarely let allotments to labourers. Only 23 of 565 relevant sites in the allotments database were let by private tenants and of these five were definitely not farmers and only two certainly were. This suggests that no more than 3 per cent and perhaps as few as 0.4 per cent of allotment sites were let by farmers. The picture is confused, especially for the early period, by the fact that farmers very often let potato grounds to labourers. While potato grounds should not be confused with allotments, it remains true that, particularly in the early 1830s, when allotments were still a relatively unfamiliar phenomenon, not all commentators distinguished clearly between the two. So we have a reference to allotments in Dorset being let mainly by the farmers, which on closer investigation turns out to mean that there were

12 William Bearn, 'On the farming of Northamptonshire', *JRASE* xiii (1852–3), 91.
13 G. E. Mingay, *Rural life in Victorian England*, London 1977, 104, 155; Crouch and Ward, *The allotment*, 58.
14 For a more extensive discussion of the contribution of clergymen to the allotment movement see Burchardt, 'The allotment movement', 347–68.

many potato grounds in Dorset.[15] However, there are a number of clear cases of farmers letting allotments in the proper sense of the word, as for instance at Whelford in 1800 (*see* chapter 1).[16] There were other cases subsequently; but taken as a whole it is clear that very few allotments were let by farmers.[17] Even those few farmers who looked favourably upon allotments were often unable to provide them, since their own tenancy agreements often specifically forbade underletting.

Parish vestries were permitted to let land in allotments, the land to be vested in the churchwardens and overseers, under the legislation of 1819, 1831 and 1832. However, it was generally agreed that the Union and Parish Property Act of 1835 had put an end to the effectiveness of this legislation.[18] Even before 1835, few parishes had taken advantage of the legislation, and of the 565 sites with identified landlords in the allotments database only 42 were let by parishes (7.4 per cent). The explanation is an interesting one. Churchwardens and overseers were in the main farmers, and, hence, *ceteris paribus*, unlikely to favour allotments. Parliament – which was in this period still overwhelmingly a landowners' parliament – was aware of this. However, those MPs who wanted to see the allotment system extended were by and large hostile to any form of centralisation, and in the absence of any genuinely local alternative public body, were forced to fall back on the parish. The institution of allotment wardens to administer allotment sites created under the 1845 General Enclosure Act was a less than wholly successful attempt to circumvent the parochial officers whilst retaining local (parish-level) control; only twenty of 565 relevant sites in the database (4 per cent) were let under its provisions.[19]

Charities – that is to say local (mainly village) charities – were involved in the letting of allotments, although only to a limited extent (4 per cent of relevant sites in the database). Many charities had their endowment in the form of land. By the mid-nineteenth century this had, in many cases, been allowed to degenerate until it was almost valueless. It was sometimes suggested that if the land were let out in allotments, not only would labourers benefit in the usual way from the cultivation and produce of the allotments, but a higher rent could be charged and a greater sum could thus be applied to the original purposes of the charity. However the trustees of charities were again often farmers and partly for this reason charity land was rarely let as allotments. This caused much discontent amongst labourers, particularly in the 1870s and thereafter.[20]

---

15 *RC on the Poor Laws*, 1834, xxviii. 15.
16 SBCP, *Reports*, iii. 117–22.
17 *SC of the House of Lords on Agriculture*, 1837, v. 33–4; *RC on the Employment of Children, Young Persons, and Women in Agriculture*, 1868–9, xiii. 477–8.
18 Hall, *Law of allotments*, 23–4.
19 See 8 and 9 Vict c 118, s 108. The 1845 act and its consequences are considered in more detail in chapter 8.
20 M. K. Ashby, *Joseph Ashby of Tysoe, 1859–1919*, Cambridge 1961, 50, 122–34.

Societies specifically dedicated to allotment provision were responsible for letting out some allotment sites, although in this case too the acreage involved was small (10 per cent of all sites in the database). It seems that the first society to do this was the AEI, which took a substantial quantity of land at Cholesbury and let it out to labourers in large portions.[21] However, the AEI did not last long and it is not clear that it let allotments except at Cholesbury. The district allotment societies – the East Somerset, the West Kent, the Chard, Crewkerne and Ilminster and so forth – played an important role in co-ordinating the allotment movement and in awarding prizes but few of them became involved in letting allotments directly themselves. In some instances, however, local (village-level) societies did so. This was quite common in the east Midlands, as James Orange's private journal, extracts of which were printed in the *Labourer's Friend Magazine* between 1841 and 1843, makes clear.[22] The function of these east Midlands village societies was in effect to act as guarantors of rent, standing between a landlord who did not wish to go to the trouble of collecting a large number of small rents himself, and the allotment tenants. In terms of national prominence, the most significant instance of a dedicated allotment society providing allotments was the decision of the SICLC to do so in 1844. Even in this case, the quantity of land let seems to have peaked at a few hundred acres in the early 1850s, with just over 1,000 allotment tenants.[23] In short, the contribution of societies to the number and total acreage of allotment plots was, in terms at least of direct letting as opposed to influence, slight.

The database statistics so far cited can be compared with the evidence provided by the Devizes Labourer's Friend Society and by the Royal Commission on Framework Knitters. The distinctive feature of these two surveys is that they specify the names of the landlords of the allotment sites they list. The Wiltshire survey, dating from 1833, suggests that of fifty-four sites, sixteen were let by peers, thirty by other landowners, two by clergymen, two by farmers and four by parishes. However, the figures need to be interpreted with some caution. The two sites let out by farmers appear to have been potato grounds, suggesting that in the areas of Wiltshire covered by the survey (*see* chapter 2), allotments were rarely or never let by farmers. On the other hand some of the sites attributed to landowners could actually have been let by farmers, since in some instances the survey does not make clear to which category the individuals cited belonged. Since in all the doubtful cases the context makes it more likely that landowners rather than farmers are being referred to, it has been assumed that this is indeed the case. It should also be noted that the figure for peers may be inflated by the significant pres-

---

[21] F&I, 470.
[22] LFM (1841–3), passim.
[23] LF xcviii (1852), 102.

ence of the earl of Radnor, who accounted for fifteen of the sixteen sites let by peers.[24]

The east Midlands evidence for 1845 suggests a slightly different balance. Of the sixty-eight sites recorded for Leicestershire, thirty-six were let by clergymen, ten by peers and twenty-two by other landowners. For Nottinghamshire, of the eighteen sites recorded, three were let by clergymen, seven by peers, and eight by other landowners. Of Derbyshire's five recorded sites, three were let by clergymen and two by peers. For the region as a whole, therefore, out of ninety-one sites, forty-two were let by clergymen, nineteen by peers and thirty by other landowners. The most striking feature of the comparison with the Wiltshire evidence is the much greater significance of clergymen in the east Midlands (although not typical of the country as a whole), and a complete absence of allotments let by parishes. As regards farmers, similar difficulties apply to the interpretation of the east Midlands evidence as to the Wiltshire evidence. The significance of peers in the east Midlands as well as in Wiltshire is impressive, but fits with the interpretation offered above that whilst the great landowners were sometimes actively involved with allotments, and certainly contributed their full share to the movement, they let only a minority of plots.[25]

Why did landowners let allotments?

Perhaps the most obvious reason landowners might have had for letting allotments was that it was profitable. The first step towards resolving the question of whether this was indeed the case is to identify the average rent at which plots were let. Table 3 presents results from the database, rents being given in shillings per acre. The other side of the equation is the cost to landowners of letting, which initially at least could be quite significant. The land was sometimes in a foul condition and had to be cleared. It would probably have to be thoroughly dug, perhaps several times, and possibly drained and fenced as well. The plots had to be measured out and in some way marked off, and paths laid out. Occasionally these initial costs were avoided by offering the land to the new tenants as it was and getting them to undertake the necessary work themselves. In such a case the land was usually let free or at a reduced rent for the first year or sometimes the first several years.[26] However, labourers were often unwilling to undertake all this drudgery, and in many cases either refused to take the land under these conditions or, after a few weeks or months, abandoned its cultivation. This was especially true in the early days of the allotment movement, when allotments were an innovation of which

24 F&I, 424–64.
25 RC on the Framework Knitters, 1845, xv. 138–9.
26 Ibid. 503; LF xi (1845), 203.

Table 3
Mean rent, 1795–1873

1795–1829: 36s.   (14 records)
1830–49:   44.42s. (355 records)
1850–73:   51.13s. (193 records)

Source: Database.

labourers were often suspicious.[27] So a more common way of passing on the initial costs of providing allotments to labourers was to add a sum to the rent for this purpose, again normally only for the first year or so. It seems to have been rare for landlords to bear the entire initial costs of providing allotments themselves, although this did sometimes happen.[28]

Once provided, fences, gates, paths and drainage ditches all had to be maintained. This was usually the responsibility of the allotment tenants themselves, although sometimes landlords preferred to keep these matters under their own control and would simply add a permanent surcharge to the rent. This avoided the difficulties which could result if some tenants failed to attend to the fences and other features which were their responsibility, and was fairer since otherwise tenants with plots on the edge of the site had a greater burden of costs and work than tenants of plots without an external border.[29]

Thus, in one way or another, the initial costs of providing allotments and the costs of maintaining them were normally passed on to the tenants. However, allotment landlords also incurred ongoing costs. One of the arguments often used against allotments was that it would be difficult to collect the rents of so many tenants. It is not clear that this proved to be the case, at least generally. In the period covered by this study, allotments, once established, seem to have been greatly in demand from labourers, who were, it appears, normally eager to keep them.[30] There is a large amount of contemporary testimony to the impressive regularity with which allotment rents were paid.[31] It was often stated that allotment rents were better paid than those of the farmers.[32] Arrears rarely mounted up and rents were usually paid on the day they were due or, at worst, very shortly afterwards.[33] It seems less often to

---

[27] LF xxx (1846), 203. The suspicion with which labourers unfamiliar with allotments sometimes regarded the offer of land is discussed in chapter 6.
[28] LF lxxxv (1851), 96.
[29] F&I, 170–3.
[30] There is extensive evidence of the strong attachment labourers had to their plots. Some of the most telling is in the *Report on the Employment of Women and Children in Agriculture*, 1843, xii, appendixes vii, viii, x, xi, xii, and pp. 66–71, and in the *RC on the Employment of Children, Young Persons, and Women in Agriculture*, 1867–8, xvii. 32, 119, 133. See also chapter 7.
[31] *SC on the Labouring Poor*, 1843, vii. 12; LF lviii (1849), 34; T. E. Kebbel, *The agricultural labourer: a short summary of his position*, London 1887, 106.
[32] *SC of the House of Lords on the Poor Laws*, 1830–1, viii. 204.
[33] LFM (1835), 84.

have been necessary to grant rebates to allotment tenants than to farmers.[34] There were some cases of rents poorly paid, but this seems to have occurred only under special circumstances, for example where the allotments were let by the parish rather than by an individual.[35] But even though allotment rents were almost certainly better paid than farm rents, it probably did cost landlords somewhat more to collect them, simply because there were so many more tenants per acre.

A major cost to the landlord of letting land in allotments was the various taxes (primarily tithes, poor rates and other local rates) which the land had to bear. These would have been paid by the farmer if the land had been let as farmland. But in fact a sum set to cover tithe and rates was almost invariably added to the rent paid by allotment tenants and charged to them either separately, or more commonly in a lump sum with the rent. Thus this cost was in fact almost always borne by the tenant rather than the landlord.[36] It should be noted, moreover, that when contemporaries cited figures for allotment rent, these almost invariably included the charge for tithe and rates.

There were certain costs commonly associated with letting allotments which might best be described as 'optional'. The two most important were rent-suppers and prizes. Rent-suppers were offered mainly by large landowners who wished to foster good relationships with the labourers living in their villages. Almost invariably, roast beef and plum pudding were offered. A subordinate function of rent-suppers was to collect all the tenants together to pay their rents; tenants who were late with their rent were not eligible to attend the supper. The cost of rent-suppers could be considerable and sometimes absorbed a significant proportion of the rent. Prizes were often distributed. These too could be quite substantial, with prizes of a pound or even more going to the tenant judged to have cultivated his plot best, and often numerous subsidiary prizes, sometimes given in the form of tools. However, prizes seem normally only to have been given when there was a large number of tenants on a particular site, or where a number of sites had grouped together to form a district society. It seems clear that only a minority of sites offered prizes, although they were rather more widely offered than rent-suppers. So even if the cost of rent-suppers and prizes is discounted the level of profit to the landlord is probably not significantly affected.[37]

Occasionally landlords provided other benefits to allotment tenants in addition to those cited above.[38] Sometimes manure was provided, or more

---

34 Other than in 1845–7, when potato blight affected allotments very badly (see ch. 6), only one instance of rent being remitted was discovered in the course of the research for this book; see also *LF* xv (1845), 288.

35 *SC on the Labouring Poor*, 1843, vii. 119–22.

36 Hall, *Law of allotments*, 76–7.

37 Much the best source of information about rent suppers and prizes is the publications of the LFS. Examples include *LFM* lxxxi (1837), 180–1; lxix (1836), 227; cvi (1840), 3–4; cxxxii (1842), 47; *LF* xxiv (1846), 71–2; xxx (1846), 206; cxxviii (1854), 7–8.

38 See chapter 6.

commonly merely carted, free of charge by the landlord. But where manure was supplied or carted – and this seems to have been rare – it was normally charged for.[39] Seed was also occasionally provided free, although normally only in the first year of a site, or in exceptional circumstances.[40] Tools were also very occasionally provided at a subsidised rate to allotment tenants.[41] But none of these benefits seems to have been commonly enough offered to affect the general level of profits from offering allotments.

Always acknowledging that they include a sum to cover tithe and rates and that the costs of rent collection may have been rather higher for allotment than for farm landlords, it would therefore seem that the rents given in table 3 are free of hidden costs which might invalidate a comparison with rents paid by farmers. Indeed, now that the Turner–Beckett–Afton rent index is available, it is possible to make a direct comparison between allotment and agricultural rent. The mean rent for rural allotment sites for the 1830–49 period was 37.9s. per acre *per annum*.[42] The mean assessed rent of agricultural land between the same years was 19.8s. per acre *per annum*.[43] Allotment rent therefore appears to have been a little less than double that of agricultural rent in the 1830s and 1840s.

However, in its raw form this comparison is misleading. In the first place, we need to make a deduction from the allotment rents to take account of tithes and taxes. This is problematic in that the level of tithes and local taxes varied from parish to parish. In his survey of agricultural taxation in volume vii of the *Agrarian history of England and Wales*, Gordon Mingay concludes that tithes in England and Wales amounted to at least 10 per cent of rent. Other local taxes were negligible, with the exception of poor rates.[44] Some indication of the incidence of poor rates can be derived from the Cambridgeshire magistrates survey of 1831. For seventy-two parishes with usable data on land provision, total parochial acreage and total poor relief expenditure, the average level of the poor rate was 3.7s. per acre.[45] Taking this as an order-of-magnitude proxy for the national average and subtracting it from the average rent of allotments reduces the latter figure from 37.9s. to 34.2s. per acre. Reducing this by a further 10 per cent to allow for tithes, leaves a sum of 30.8s. per acre. A further deduction should probably be made to cover the putatively higher costs of collecting allotment rent, but no figures are available for this. The deduction would in any case be a very small sum when expressed on a per acre basis.

---

39 *F&I*, 170–3.

40 *LF* xxxiii (1847), 22–4.

41 Pamela Horn, *The rural world, 1780–1850*, London 1980, 142.

42 Calculated from the allotments database.

43 Calculated from M. E. Turner, J. V. Beckett and B. Afton, *Agricultural rent in England, 1690–1914*, Cambridge 1997, 316–17.

44 G. E. Mingay, 'Agricultural taxation', in E. J. T. Collins (ed.), *The agrarian history of England and Wales*, VII/1: *1850–1914*, Cambridge 2000, 936–44.

45 *SC of the House of Lords on the Poor Laws*, 1830–1, viii. 316–33.

There is, however, a further complication: average rents for small plots of land were much higher than the average rent for farmland as a whole. This was probably because small farmers could not afford to include any marginal land in their holdings, relying on intensive cultivation of good-quality land.[46] It is unclear whether allotment land was also typically of higher intrinsic value than ordinary farm land. But, *pace* Moselle, it seems likely that it was.[47] Whilst commentators noted a few instances in which allotment land was of unusually poor quality, the received wisdom of the LFS was that it was better to provide labourers with good-quality, easily worked land. More important, however, than the nature of the soil in determining the value of allotment land was its location. It was almost universally accepted that allotments should be located as close to the homes of their tenants as possible. This necessarily meant that they should be located close to villages. Land close to villages was usually more highly rented than other land, precisely because it was more convenient for a wide variety of purposes.

Moreover, the intensive cultivation and manuring characteristic of allotments tended within a few years to produce a fine tilth, the value of which might bear little relation to that of the soil on which an allotment site was originally established. It is, therefore, probably more appropriate to compare allotment rents with the average rent at which small plots of land were let than with farm land in general. Turner, Beckett and Afton provide data from the 1894 Royal Commission on Agriculture which suggest that at that time the average rent of land let in plots of between one and five acres (the smallest unit given) was 2.3 times as high as the average rent of all farm-land.[48] Assuming that the proportion between the rents of plots of between one and five acres and the average rent of farmland had not changed between 1830–49 and 1894, this implies that the average rent per acre of small plots of land would have been 45.5s. in 1830–49. Since the rent at which allotments were actually let, after having made deductions for tithes and poor rates, was only 30.8s. per acre, we can see that the average rent of allotments in the 1830s and 1840s was substantially below that at which we would expect plots of between one and five acres to have been let. Presumably the average rent of farmland let in plots of below an acre would have been even higher.[49]

The suggestion that allotment rents were set at a level below that which

46 Turner, Beckett and Afton, *Agricultural rent*, 117. See also D. R. Denman and V. F. Stewart, *Farm rents: a comparison of current and past farm rents in England and Wales*, London 1959, 64–74.

47 Moselle, 'Allotments, enclosure and proletarianization', 493.

48 Turner, Beckett and Afton, *Agricultural rent*, 117.

49 At this point it is important to reiterate the distinction between allotments (usually let by landowners) and potato grounds (usually let by farmers). The rents of the latter were normally much higher than those of the former – typically £8 an acre in the case of potato grounds and £2 pounds an acre for allotments. Where contemporaries use vague terms such as 'land' or 'potato land', it cannot without more specific evidence be assumed that the land in question consisted of allotments.

landowners could have obtained is supported by the rate of return on allotment-holders' capital, which was far higher than economic theory would predict. For the four sites for which we have complete balance sheets (Great Missenden in Buckinghamshire and Avington, Easton and Itchin in Hampshire), it is possible to calculate what the rate of return on the allotment-holder's capital was.[50] The combined outlay by the allotment tenants on the four sites was £149 5s. 3d., whilst total profits were £358 5s. 6d.[51] However, the figure for profits does not include an allowance for labour. As will be argued in chapter 6, this is appropriate when calculating the increment of allotments to living standards, but it is misleading if we are trying to compare the rate of return on allotment-holders' capital with that of farmers. We do not know how many days' labour was expended on the four sites in question, but it was usually reckoned that it took the equivalent of twenty days' labour to cultivate a forty-perch allotment.[52] Wage rates in Buckinghamshire in 1831–2 appear to have been about 9s. per week for an adult male agricultural labourer and in Hampshire in 1846 (the nearest available date) between 8s. and 10s.[53] The imputed cost of twenty days' labour at 9s. a week for the eighty-four allotment tenants on the four sites is £126. Subtracting this from the figure for profits leaves us with a return of £224.28 on an outlay of £149.26, or a rate of return of 150 per cent.[54] Hueckel's study of farm accounts for the 1793–1815 period suggests that even in the favourable circumstances of the war years farmers were rarely able to achieve rates of return on capital of more than between nine and fourteen per cent.[55] This confirms that allotment landlords were setting rents at a level well below that which would have reduced labourers' profits to normal levels.

It seems, then, that most mid nineteenth-century allotment landlords did not charge the most that they might have been able to get for their allotments, but something closer to what the LFS described as a 'fair' rent: in other words, the rent the landowner would have obtained if he had let the land to a farmer.[56] It was important to landowners not to let land at less than this rate,

---

[50] Allotment profits are considered in more detail in chapter 7.

[51] Profits on these four sites were below average, so this calculation tends to understate the rate of return on capital obtained by allotment holders: see chapter 7.

[52] LFM (1835), 89.

[53] A. H. John, 'Statistical appendix', in G. E. Mingay (ed.), The agrarian history of England and Wales, VI: 1750–1850, Cambridge 1989, 1089, 1092.

[54] F&I, 455–69; LFM (1834), 134–6.

[55] G. Hueckel, 'English farming profits during the Napoleonic wars, 1793–1815', Explorations in Economic History xiii (1976), 342–3.

[56] Interestingly, Samuel Lysons believed that 'the allotment system would be more extended if it were less insisted on that the rent should be the same as that of the neighbouring farmers'. This suggests that the moral suasion of the LFS was sufficient to deter some landowners from letting allotments at rents above the 'fair' level. The consequence may have been that allotments were more advantageous for those who had them but less widely distributed than they might otherwise have been: LFM clvii (1844), 53.

both because they did not want to suffer a fall in income themselves, and because some of them at least accepted the LFS insistence that labourers should not feel that they were getting the land as a form of charity. But it is clear that labourers would often have been willing to pay very much more than the 'fair' rent. Farmers, whose attitude to letting land to labourers was far more genuinely market-based, let potato ground at a rent of about £8 an acre. The contention that many landowners let allotments at what they considered to be a 'fair' price, rather than at rack rent, is further supported by the fact that waiting lists, often consisting of hundreds of labourers, existed at many (perhaps most) sites in this period.[57] Waiting lists are an indication that prices have not been raised to the level where the number of buyers has been reduced to the same as the number of items on sale. In short, the relatively low level of allotment rents in relation to comparable agricultural rents, the abnormally high rate of return on capital obtained by allotment tenants and the existence of waiting lists at many sites should be seen as evidence that few mid nineteenth-century allotment landlords let allotments with a view to making a profit.[58]

Public authorities, our limited evidence suggests, were even less concerned with profiting from allotments, and, interestingly, paid no heed to the concept of fair rents. Allotments provided by public authorities (i.e. parish vestries, in this period) were let at much lower rents than those let by landowners (see appendix 6, table 25). Farmer-dominated parish vestries were very rarely prepared to let allotments to labourers. When they did so, they may have had different motives from landowners, perhaps being more concerned about the material aspects of allotment provision (i.e. prevention of poverty and hence reduction of the poor rates) than about its broader social and moral aspects. A cheap rather than a 'fair' rent might be the more sensible one in this situation.

Some landowners did, of course, attempt to make a profit from letting allotments. Hard-up clergymen may have been particularly likely to succumb to the temptation to maximize the return on their glebe by dividing part of it into allotments. Plots let by the clergy were typically slightly more expensive to rent than those let by other landowners; between 1830 and 1849, for example, the average rent per acre of sites let by non-clergymen was 45.1s. (192 records) as compared to 49.5s. (55 records) for sites let by clergymen. It is also possible that as rural society became more settled and the acute problems of poverty and social discontent of the 1830s and 1840s waned into a

---

[57] See chapter 6.

[58] One of the most remarkable features of British allotments let by public authorities has been that their rents have consistently been set at levels well below that indicated by the value of the land, even though they are not a public service (like health or education) but a private source of income. It seems likely that the anomalous assumption that allotments should be treated as if they were a public service can be traced to the expectation that rents would be set at 'fair' levels established by the LFS.

bitter memory, some allotment landlords began to value the income-generating possibilities of letting allotments more highly in comparison to their social virtues. Certainly F. H. Norman, the assistant commissioner responsible for Northamptonshire to the 1867–9 Royal Commission on the Employment of Children, Young Persons, and Women in Agriculture, reported many cases of highly-rented allotments.[59] The average rent of allotments was higher in the 1850s and 1860s than it had been in the 1830s and 1840s, which perhaps suggests that some landowners were attempting to extract more income from them.

In addition to allowing landowners to raise rental income, allotment cultivation could enhance the capital value of land through its effects on soil fertility. Allotment cultivation was, and is, highly intensive. Plots were frequently dug over, whilst weeding was performed to a much higher standard and manuring was, acre-for-acre, heavier than on farmland. It was often noted (as it still is today) that sites which had been cultivated for a long period of time were much more fertile than those which were of recent origin, and that land which had once been poor was, if put to use as allotments, normally much improved in quality after some years had gone by.[60] Indeed some landowners took advantage of this effect and let waste or degenerated land to allotment tenants for a few years, usually at a low rent, before taking it back to let to a farmer at a much enhanced rent (as compared to the rent taken before the land had been let in allotments).[61] So it seems likely that the value of land rose over the years through being let in allotments. However, it is not clear that the increased value of allotment land was often tapped by landlords. There was a strong feeling against raising rents because the land had become more fertile – just as it was felt that the value of improvements made by farmers to their farms ought to be secured to them. Allotment tenants usually paid at least as good a rent as farmers so there was normally little point in reletting improved allotment land to farmers. It is true that allotment sites were quite often converted to other uses, but these uses were almost always non-agricultural (mainly building) and it can be assumed that the price paid for the site was determined by its value as 'accommodation land' rather than by its agricultural value.[62] So although 'on paper' letting land in allotments probably tended to increase its value, this increase was in practice rarely captured by landlords.

If most landlords let allotments at fair, rather than rack rents, and did not seek to capitalise on the higher land values created by allotment cultivation,

---

[59] RC on the Employment of Children, Young Persons, and Women in Agriculture, 1867–8, xvii. 659–700.

[60] D. M. Moran, 'The origin and status of the allotment movement in Britain, with particular reference to Swindon, Wiltshire', unpubl. PhD diss. Oregon 1976, 138.

[61] RC on the Employment of Children, Young Persons, and Women in Agriculture, 1867–8, xvii. 545.

[62] LF cxxvii (1854), 186.

why did they let land to labourers? In effect, the gap between the price at which landowners supplied allotments and the price which rural labourers would have been willing to pay for them left landowners with a choice. Either they could pass this benefit on to their allotment tenants in its entirety, or they could extract some or all of it in the form of conditions imposed on allotment tenants. In the first instance, the landlord would maximise benefits to the allotment-holder and hence any benefits to himself which depended directly on the tenant's wellbeing (such as reducing discontent). In the second, the landlord would be able to impose restrictions on the tenant that he or she might otherwise have been unwilling to accept (such as attending church on Sundays or refraining from poaching), up to the point where these restrictions became sufficiently irksome to outweigh the benefits to the tenant. Some goals could be achieved through either or both of these strategies. These included the LFS project of reshaping the moral character of the rural population, which could operate both internally through the inherent effects of allotments on character and externally through behavioural changes exacted by means of conditions of tenure; and also gaining or maintaining peer approval, which depended more on the fact of allotment provision than on the conditions attached to it. Goals which could be achieved primarily through the first strategy (but which might be undermined by the imposition of oppressive restrictions on tenants) included improving social relations with labourers, gaining political adherents, mitigating rural unrest and raising labour productivity. The second strategy was best suited to enforcing behavioural changes which were highly visible and easily checked, such as not committing criminal offences, abstaining from poor relief and attending church.

The second allotment movement, it was argued in chapter 3, constituted an attempt to reshape the character of the rural labouring population. Some of the landowners and clergymen who let allotments in the years after the Swing riots shared fully in these hopes and were motivated by them in letting land. An example is the Revd Philip Gurdon of Cranworth, Norfolk. In a letter to Stephen Denison, one of the special assistant poor law commissioners who gathered evidence for the 1843 Report on the Employment of Women and Children in Agriculture, Gurdon expressed his view that 'there cannot, I think, exist a doubt of the general benefit arising from the allotment system', that he was convinced that there was 'an ostensible difference in the moral condition, as well as in the general comfort, of those families which have them' and that he knew of 'no plan that I could have adopted that could possibly have so materially improved the welfare and respectability of my parishioners'.[63] But most allotments were probably provided by landlords whose enthusiasm for the grand project of the LFS, if indeed they entered

---

63 *Report on the Employment of Women and Children in Agriculture*, 1843, xii. 270–1.

into it at all, was to a greater or lesser degree subsidiary to more pragmatic considerations.

One of the most important reasons why landowners let allotments was to maintain or achieve social approval. Surprisingly quickly it became accepted within landowning society that letting allotments was one of the things which a responsible landowner did. As early as 1846, for example, Benjamin Disraeli incorporated a reference to allotment provision which depended on this assumption in one of his novels, *Sybil*. The obnoxious Whig Lord Marney was damned by Disraeli for being 'tremendously fierce against allotments'.[64] Disraeli was not alone among leading politicians in his support for allotment provision: Peel and Sir James Graham intervened in support of allotments legislation during the debates on Cowper's bill in 1845, whilst Russell chaired the 1848 annual general meeting of the SICLC.[65] By the mid-1840s allotments therefore enjoyed a consensus of support among the leaders of all three of the main political factions. The role of the clergy in promoting a climate in which allotment provision became part of what defined a 'good landowner' was also very important.[66] Thus many landowners may have let allotments because other people – 'public opinion', other local landowners, the incumbent of the parish, or for that matter the poor – expected it of them.[67] As allotments became more and more widespread, this influence became increasingly important, to the point where the provision of allotments could be numbered, in the words of F. M. L. Thompson, among 'the more usual incidents of benevolence in discharge of the social responsibilities of landowners towards their parishes'.[68]

Amongst the goals which allotment landlords could more easily achieve by passing as much as possible of the benefit of 'fair rents' on to allotment-holders, perhaps the most important was improving social relations with labourers on their estates. In letting allotments landowners were trying to reconnect themselves with the rural poor. But this response was not specific to landowners: rather it was part of a more general reaction to the social chasm revealed by the political turbulence of the 1830s and 1840s, a reaction often summarised in the phrase 'the Condition of England question'. The social polarisation of the second quarter of the nineteenth century was more obvious and on a larger scale in the towns than in the countryside, and the conscious decision of English landowners to reach out a hand across the gulf which separated the 'two nations' replicated a similar, and at the time more noticed, attempt on the part of the educated elite of the urban middle class. The most important effect of the political upheavals of the 1830s and

---

64 B. Disraeli, *Sybil, or the two nations*, Harmondsworth 1985, 73.

65 *Parliamentary debates*, 3rd ser. lxxxi, House of Commons, 2 July 1845, 1426.

66 Burchardt, 'The allotment movement', 356–8.

67 See the discussion of the role of the LFS in achieving this result in chapter 3.

68 F. M. L. Thompson, *English landed society in the nineteenth century*, London 1963, 1971, 209.

1840s (especially Chartism) on the wealthy was an indirect one. Chartism did not so much frighten the elite as awaken them, with a shock, to the profound alienation between a large part of the population and themselves, in terms both of sympathies and of cultural values and life experiences. A seminal response was that of Carlyle. In *Chartism* he argued that whilst the particular demands made by the Chartists might be inappropriate and impractical, it was vital to recognise that so great a movement of men implied a real source of discontent, which required investigation. Similarly, many of the mid nineteenth-century novelists, notably Mrs Gaskell in *Mary Barton*, Charles Dickens in *Hard Times* and Disraeli in *Sybil*, drew attention to the gulf of experience and sentiment which existed between rich and poor. Nor was this anxiety to re-establish broken social connections confined to the literary establishment. As Patrick Joyce has shown, factory-owners showed themselves every bit as concerned as landowners to find ways of bridging the affective gap between themselves and their employees.[69]

The impulse to seek closer and more genial social contact with the labouring population was therefore one which was common to urban as well as rural England, and which elicited a strong response from liberal, progressive writers and industrialists. Despite the tenurial aspect of allotment provision (which, it should be noted, was shared by industrialists who built housing for their workers), the temptation to interpret it as a regression to an earlier, organic model of society should be resisted. David Roberts's argument that the allotment movement formed part of a backwards-looking revival of paternalism, and his implication that this was the main reason for landowners providing allotments fails to do justice either to the diversity of motivation on the part of landowners or to the modernising values they in the main sought to inculcate.[70] In truth, only a minor and eccentric strand within the allotment movement can accurately be described as paternalistic, if by this is meant a systematic attempt to revert to a society based on deference and hierarchy: notably Disraeli's 'Young England', several of whose members saw allotments in this light.[71] The attitudinal changes which those who argued for allotment provision expected to result from it were in fact far from tending towards a new feudalism. On the contrary, contemporaries anticipated that allotments would encourage independence and self-help. An anachronistic attempt to revert to 'feudalism' was not an important component of the allotment movement in the mid-nineteenth century.

A specific aspect of improving social relations with labourers was to gain political support. Some landowners do appear to have let land for this reason in the period of this study. Sir Cullen Eardley Smith, prospective MP for

---

[69] Patrick Joyce, *Work, society and politics: the culture of the factory in later Victorian England*, Hassocks 1980.

[70] Roberts, *Paternalism*, 132–3.

[71] Notably Disraeli's friends, W. B. Ferrand, who established allotments at Bingley and Methwold in West Yorkshire, and Lord John Manners: *LF* cxxviii (1855), 13–16.

North Lincolnshire, was, for example, reported to have gained great popularity in Caistor by opening allotments to artisans and tradesmen as well as to the poor, whilst the competing Yarborough interest apparently responded by letting allotments at a low rent.[72] But it is significant that Caistor was a small town rather than a village, and one in which there appears to have been an unusual degree of interest in allotments from enfranchised tradesmen. In general the opportunities of benefiting politically through letting allotments were slight before 1884. A negligible proportion of those who might be expected to benefit from allotments were voters and, worse still, many or even most of those who did have the vote were tenant farmers, who were more likely to be hostile than favourable to allotment provision.

Closely allied to improving social relations with labourers was a concern to mitigate rural unrest and social discontent. Indeed, Archer argues that this was the primary basis for allotment provision and that it largely explains the way the movement developed. According to Archer, '[t]he real catalyst for the introduction and the eventual spread . . . of allotments was endemic rural unrest'.[73] His claim deserves careful consideration. Bearing in mind the speed with which interest in allotments, and actual allotment provision, manifested itself in 1830, it does indeed seem difficult to imagine what other catalyst than the Captain Swing riots there could have been for the onset of the movement.[74] But is fear of rural unrest really a sufficient explanation for continuing allotment provision after the early 1830s? The more we reflect on this question, the less convincing does such an explanation seem. In the first place, the Captain Swing riots were the last major outbreak of agricultural rioting in the nineteenth century; and whilst the period between the end of the Napoleonic wars and 1830 had been studded with major instances of rural rioting, the period after 1830 saw little more than what, from the point of view of the landed elite, was the almost risible 'Battle of Bosenden Wood' in 1838. Bearing in mind the contrast in this respect between the pre-1830 and post-1830 periods, it is hard to believe that landowners remained deeply anxious about a further major outbreak of agricultural rioting for long; and in this respect the almost complete political quiescence of the rural proletariat during the Chartist years must have been extremely reassuring. The Hammonds' view, that after 1830 agricultural labourers were too cowed to provide a major threat on the scale of the Swing riots, is surely correct.[75]

However, whilst landowners may have had little reason to fear a renewed outbreak of major rioting after the early 1830s, they did have more grounds for anxiety about more covert and private acts of hostility and revenge such as rick burning, animal maiming and poaching. In using the term 'endemic rural

[72] LFM (1834), 154. See also J. A. Perkins, 'Allotments in nineteenth-century Lincolnshire', Lincolnshire History and Archaeology xviii (1983), 24.
[73] Archer, 'The nineteenth-century allotment', 23.
[74] See chapter 3.
[75] Hammond and Hammond, Village labourer, 248–300.

unrest', indeed, Archer seems to be pointing towards these smaller scale but undoubtedly alarming manifestations of hatred, which he himself has explored in depth in his work on rural crime and protest in East Anglia.[76] But whilst this interpretation extends Archer's explanation for the provision of allotments through into the 1840s, it can scarcely account for the continuing strong growth in allotment numbers after 1850, since Archer himself argues that in the 1850s and 1860s rural crime became increasingly a matter of isolated acts by those outside the village community (notably, it would seem, vagrants passing through the village) rather than something committed by the village labourers themselves.[77] Clearly, allotment provision would have been of little value in reducing crime committed by vagrants, since they would have been quite outside the reach of whatever beneficial effects allotment provision might have.

A consideration of the geography of the growth of allotment provision adds to the difficulties of interpreting it primarily in terms of rural unrest. In many counties it was not, in fact, in 1830 that allotment provision began, but several years after this. In Dorset, for example, it seems to have been from about the mid-1840s that allotments began to be provided extensively, although there had been some small-scale growth earlier, whilst the leading authority on allotments in Kent at this time stated that they had only begun to spread in that county from 1836 onwards.[78] Similarly, it was in the early 1840s that allotments began to be provided in the east Midlands on a large scale.[79] In Somerset, one of the counties where the allotment movement was most active, allotment provision nevertheless apparently grew only slowly until 1836, after which growth was much more rapid.[80] In many other counties it is also clear that the rise in the number of allotments did not begin until the late 1830s, the 1840s, or even later. In particular, allotments seem to have been virtually unknown in the three ridings of Yorkshire before the 1840s. Similarly, it seems likely that it was only after 1850 that allotments began to appear in significant numbers in the Welsh border counties, in Cornwall and in the north as a whole outside Yorkshire. In the south Midlands, whilst allotment sites were certainly being established in the 1830s and 1840s, it was again only in the 1850s and 1860s that numbers seem to have begun to rise substantially.[81]

Furthermore, in many counties where allotments came to be common there was no tradition of discontent among agricultural labourers, and

76 J. E. Archer, *By a flash and a scare: incendiarism, animal maiming, and poaching in East Anglia, 1815–70*, Oxford 1990.

77 Ibid. 120–2, 161–2, 187.

78 *LF* vi (1844), 115, 120; xxix (1846), 182–7; xxxii (1847), 3–10; xxxiii (1847), 23; *SC on the Labouring Poor*, 1843, vii. 1.

79 *LFM* cxxxiii (1842), 55.

80 Ibid. xcviii (1839), 68.

81 See chapter 2.

'endemic rural unrest' was of much less significance than it was in Norfolk and Suffolk. Somerset, for example, was not a county noted for unrest, and was only slightly affected by Swing, yet allotments were probably more common here than in any other county by the early 1840s.[82] Leicestershire, Warwickshire and Nottinghamshire were, according to Hobsbawm and Rudé, only marginally affected by Swing, yet were by 1873 first, fourth, and sixth amongst English counties for the number of allotment plots they had; many of the other counties in which allotments had become quite common by this date had also been virtually untouched by the riots of 1830.[83] Clearly, then, mitigation of unrest is not the sole explanation of the pattern of allotment provision after 1830. But it was nevertheless an important motive for much of the 1830s and 1840s and had indeed clearly been the dominant reason during the very early 1830s. Interestingly, there was a sharp decrease in the average size of allotment plots in the mid 1830s from 76 perches in 1830–4 (248 records) to 50 perches in 1835–9 (39 records). This is paralleled by a corresponding fall in the average recommended plot size. One possible interpretation is that the best plot size, from the point of view of a landowner wanting to buy off an angry labourer, was a generous one, but once it was clear that the danger of another labourers' uprising had receded, a smaller size of plot was preferred, large enough to fill the labourer's leisure hours but not so large as to enable him to dispense with paid work.[84]

Another reason some landowners had for providing allotments was to improve labour productivity. This benefited landowners both directly as employers and indirectly through increasing efficiency in agriculture (part of the reward for which landowners could extract in the form of raised rents). It might seem unlikely that allotments could significantly raise labour productivity, but in fact they may well have done so. In the first place, the large increases to living standards which allotments provided almost certainly meant that allotment-holders were better fed than those labourers without land.[85] Especially significant was the fact that it was vegetables, rich in a variety of vitamins and nutrients, that were most often grown on allotments. Contemporaries were well aware of the beneficial effects allotments could have on the health of their tenants.[86] Secondly allotments may also have stimulated labour productivity through their effects on character, and it was to this that contemporaries attached most importance. It was argued that a man who had an allotment had something to work for in life, and acquired a general habit of hard work and 'wanting to get on'. Advocates of allotments

---

[82] E. J. Hobsbawm and G. Rudé, *Captain Swing*, London 1970, 129–30, 305; *LF* lxxxvi (1851), 112.
[83] Hobsbawm and Rudé, *Captain Swing*, 304–5; *Agricultural Returns of Great Britain for 1873*, 1873, lxix. 301–74.
[84] Burchardt, 'The allotment movement', 268–84.
[85] See chapter 6.
[86] *SC on the Labouring Poor*, 1843, vii. 81, 131; *LFM* cix (1840), 50; cxvii (1840), 177.

often claimed that labourers with allotments were better workers: at Hadlow, for example, the three labourers with the best allotments were thought to be the three best workmen in the parish, whilst at Colerne in Wiltshire it was reported that the allotment-holders had confounded the farmers' fears by turning out to be the most industrious labourers in the parish.[87] A closely related concern was with sobriety. This was a growing problem in the countryside in the mid-nineteenth century. Apart from diminishing the reliability and effectiveness of rural labour, it also had implications for expenditure on poor relief. Landowners believed, probably correctly, that labourers with allotments would be less likely to go to the beerhouse in the evening after work since they would go to their plots instead.

Perhaps the most important of the goals which allotment landlords could, at least on the face of it, more easily achieve by imposing restrictive conditions on allotment tenants was reducing the poor rates. Contemporary advocates of allotments often claimed that they reduced the burden of poor relief. Some evidence to support this can be derived from the survey of parishes undertaken by the Cambridgeshire magistrates in the winter of 1830–1. This survey, reprinted in the minutes of evidence of the House of Lords Select Committee on the State of the Poor Laws, records a range of socio-economic information, including some information on allotment provision and on the level of poor relief expenditure. Parishes with allotments had higher poor relief bills (averaging £495 1s. 1d.) than those in which no land was let to labourers (averaging £400 16s. 5d.). This should not of course lead us to conclude that allotments raised rather than lowered the poor rates, because it is quite probable that allotments were more likely to be introduced in parishes where expenditure on poor relief was high.[88] More interesting is the information that can be derived from the survey about parishes in which relief expenditure had increased over the preceding three years. A clear difference is apparent between parishes in which labourers had allotments and those in which they had no land. Of the thirty-two parishes where labourers had allotments, relief expenditure had increased in fourteen (44 per cent), remained the same in five (16 per cent) and fallen in thirteen (41 per cent). These figures are markedly better than for parishes where labourers had no land, for which expenditure increased in 61 per cent of cases, remained the same in 16 per cent and fell in only 23 per cent.[89]

---

87 *SC on the Labouring Poor*, 1843, vii. 2; *F&I*, 33. See also *SC on the Labouring Poor*, 1843, vii. 22, for Captain Scobell's view that allotments improved the quality of agricultural labour.

88 It may well have been that allotments were more likely to be introduced into parishes where poor rates were high because high poor rates probably correlated with low labouring incomes, high unemployment, higher criminality and a greater incidence of drunkenness – in short with most of the problems that landowners were trying to redress through providing allotments (another of which was also, of course, high poor rates in themselves).

89 *SC of the House of Lords on the Poor Laws*, 1830–1, viii. 316–33.

However, whilst the Cambridgeshire magistrates survey is interesting, it cannot satisfactorily resolve the question of the effect of allotments on poor relief expenditure. The main difficulty is the date. Allotments were scarce before 1830, so many or even perhaps most of the sites listed in the survey were probably very recently established. The long-term effects of land provision on poor relief expenditure, which are of more interest than the immediate effects, cannot therefore be deduced from the survey. Further grounds for caution in assuming that allotments reduced poor rates derive from contemporary opinion. Whilst pro-allotment tracts frequently cited this as a major advantage of letting allotments, reports by those who had actually put the system into practice were more ambivalent. Usually allotments do not seem to have made an impact on the poor rates appreciable enough to be apparent to those who let them.[90] Perhaps the safest conclusion in the present state of knowledge is that if allotments did have an effect on poor relief expenditure it was probably a minor one, insufficient to make much difference to rate-paying allotment landlords. There is clearly a need for further research into the relationship between the availability of allotments and poor relief expenditure.

Nevertheless, in view of the intensity of concern with the level of the poor rates in the years between 1830 and 1834, it seems likely that a significant number of allotment sites established in these years were created primarily with a view to reducing the rates. Surprisingly, this is not reflected in the rules of allotment sites. Of the thirty-three sites for which complete rule sheets survive, not a single one makes tenancy conditional on abstention from poor relief (see appendix 8). Some earlier, pre-1830 sites did, however, stipulate this, including the original Estcourt site at Long Newnton.[91] Understandably labourers appear to have been reluctant to take land under such conditions.[92] This was probably the main reason why virtually no sites required labourers to forgo their right to poor relief after 1830. Another reason was the determination, characteristic of the second allotment movement, to make a complete separation between allotment provision and poor relief. Since allotments were supposed to encourage independence and to be sharply differentiated from charity, it was essential that they should not perceived as an alternative form of poor relief.

After 1834, a diminishing proportion of sites was probably created in order to reduce the poor rates. Not only were landowners generally much less concerned about the relief bill after 1834, but in any case the continuing failure of attempts to prove that allotments did reduce poor expenditure must have done much to reduce the attractiveness of allotment provision from this point of view.

[90] RC on the Poor Laws, 1834, xxvii. 103–6.
[91] SBCP, Reports, v. 72–3.
[92] RC on the Poor Laws, 1834, xxvii. 128, 592.

Another goal landlords could attempt to achieve by letting allotments was a reduction in the level of rural crime. Advocates of allotments frequently referred to their effectiveness in preventing crime, especially in the 1830s and 1840s (there was less concern with rural criminality in the 1790s). The rules under which allotments were let confirm that many landowners hoped that allotments would be an effective means of crime reduction. Of thirty-three sites for which complete sets of rules survive, as many as seventeen (52 per cent) specified that a criminal conviction would result in the termination of the plot-holder's tenancy.[93] This seems to demonstrate that reducing crime was an important but not overwhelming motivation in providing allotments: many but by no means all landowners chose to make crime avoidance a condition of tenancy. One of the crimes that landowners were most uneasy about was poaching. But although landowners would have liked allotments to reduce poaching, this was not one of the advantages most often anticipated from allotment provision. Only seven of thirty-three surviving complete allotment site rule sheets specify that tenants must refrain from poaching. Perhaps the reason that landowners doubted whether allotments would have very much effect on poaching was that it was a difficult crime to detect, so a clause prohibiting it in an allotment tenancy agreement would be unlikely to achieve very much. It was also pointed out by one contributor to the *Labourer's Friend Magazine* that allotments created a new opportunity for poaching: it would be easy for tenants to set snares on their own plots.[94]

It is important to remember that nearly a fifth of mid nineteenth-century rural allotments were let by Anglican clergymen. Intricately linked with the aristocracy and gentry through shared education, family ties, social interchange, political values and economic interests, the clergy in most respects formed a part of the landed elite rather than a separate element in rural society, above all perhaps after the commutation of tithes had made rectors substantial landowners in most parishes. Clerical allotment landlords had very similar reasons for providing allotments to non-clerical landowners (although perhaps with a slightly greater propensity to use allotments to generate income), except in one respect. This was the promotion of church attendance. Whilst non-clerical landowners sometimes aimed to promote this too, it was naturally of special concern to clergymen. It has indeed been suggested, first by Alexander Somerville in a letter to *The Times* written in 1844, and latterly by J. A. Perkins in an article in the 1983 volume of *Lincolnshire History and Archaeology*, that competition with Nonconformity for congregations is a significant part of the explanation for allotment provision.[95] An analysis of the rules of allotment sites, however, raises doubts about

---

[93] This includes one site where the tenancy was terminated only if the plot-holder was convicted of a felony.
[94] *RC on the Framework Knitters*, 1845, xv. 466.
[95] Letter from Alexander Somerville to *The Times*, cited in *LF* ii (1844), 42; Perkins, 'Allotments in nineteenth-century Lincolnshire', 24.

this. Only eight of thirty-three sites for which full sets of rules survive from the 1793–1873 period required Sunday worship as a condition of tenancy. Furthermore, where it was required, allotment rule sheets usually made it very clear that attendance at a Nonconformist chapel was as acceptable as at an Anglican church. Only one of the thirty-three sites with full sets of rules specifically required attendance at an Anglican place of worship. No doubt many clergymen did hope that by letting allotments they would improve attendance at their services. But the lack of emphasis on this in allotment rule sheets suggests that this was not a goal which allotment landlords (whether clerical or otherwise) pursued with great vigour.

One of the most important reasons why landowners provided allotments in the last quarter of the nineteenth century seems to have been to reduce out-migration.[96] But in the first half of the century the rural population was in almost all parts of the country still growing. The influence of Malthus was pronounced in the 1830s and 1840s and landowners were far more concerned to prevent population increase than to hinder out-migration. Indeed one of the main arguments put forward by opponents of allotments was that they might have a tendency to increase population and cause people who would otherwise have migrated to remain in the countryside.[97] It seems unlikely, then, that a wish to prevent out-migration can have been a motivation for more than a handful of landowners in providing allotments in the first half of the nineteenth century.

Landowners therefore provided allotments for many reasons. Some believed with the LFS that allotments were a powerful and indispensable means of reconstructing the values and behaviour of the rural poor. Others, although possessed of no such grand vision, nevertheless thought that allotments would have important practical benefits. They might help to reduce the burden of poor relief, by supplementing the family incomes of labouring families. They could lead to a reduction in theft and poaching, either through an insistence that those who had been convicted of a crime would lose their allotments, or through their effects on attitudes to property. Land provision might serve as a bulwark against further outbreaks of rural rioting and could attach labourers more closely to the owners of the estates on which they lived. Some landowners, especially clergymen in the 1850s and 1860s, sought to improve their rental incomes (or even the value of their land) by letting allotments, whilst better attendance at church was another potential benefit. The ideas of 'Young England' probably had little practical effect on most allotment landlords, and electoral politics and concern about depopulation, although very important in the genesis of the third allotment movement of

---

[96] S. R. Haresign, 'Small farms and allotments as a cure for rural depopulation on the Lincolnshire fenland, 1870–1914', *Lincolnshire History and Archaeology* xviii (1983), 27–36.
[97] Burchardt, 'Rural social relations', 167–8.

the 1880s, were of small significance before 1873. However, an increasingly important stimulus towards allotment provision from the early 1840s onwards was the growing presumption that letting allotments was one of the fundamental attributes of a responsible landowner. The pressure of social expectations helped to maintain the impetus of allotment provision after the period of social disarray which had brought the allotment movement into being had long receded. But even in the early 1870s it remained one amongst several other persuasive reasons landowners had for letting allotments. It was not least because allotments offered such diverse and flexible benefits to landowners that they became so common and persistent a feature of the social landscape of rural England after 1830.

6

The Allotment Tenant

Many historians of nineteenth-century rural society appear to have believed that English agricultural labourers had little interest in any form of land-holding, including allotments. Dunbabin, for example, wrote sceptically about the level of demand for allotments amongst late nineteenth-century labourers.[1] Hobsbawm and Rudé's *Captain Swing* reinforced this position by stating that 'there were virtually no examples of anyone connected with these movements [i.e. the agricultural protests of the first half of the nineteenth century] demanding land'.[2] The most recent standard work on the history of agricultural labourers, Alan Armstrong's careful and scholarly *Farmworkers*, perpetuates the view that allotments were far from universally popular with agricultural labourers.[3]

The underlying assumption was that by the early nineteenth century, English agricultural labourers were thoroughly proletarianised and that, as proletarians, their concern was with wages rather than land. This in turn was part of a model of English rural society that emphasised its difference from other, less 'advanced' European societies.[4] In this model, English agriculture was portrayed as being essentially capitalist, consisting of a three-tier structure of landowners, farmers and labourers. As modern proletarians rather than traditional peasants, English farm labourers were expected to have foregone atavistic, peasant-like land hunger, and be on the road towards the same cultural values and social institutions (notably trade unionism) thought to be characteristic of urban proletarians. It was therefore axiomatic that the movement for allotments and smallholdings must have been an alien, middle-class, urban phenomenon, which was of little real interest or importance to the rural proletariat. As Hobsbawm and Rudé saw it, 'land reform was then [i.e. in 1830] as later a nostalgic dream of townsmen, not a serious concern of rural proletarians'.[5]

Captain Swing, published in 1969, was a pioneering work of rural social history. Since that time there has been an explosion of research into nineteenth-century society, and the archives have been trawled far more

[1] J. P. D. Dunbabin, 'Labourers and farmers in the late nineteenth century', *Bulletin of the Society for the Study of Labour History* xi (1965), 6–9.
[2] Hobsbawm and Rudé, *Captain Swing*, 66.
[3] Armstrong, *Farmworkers*, 68.
[4] The belief that England followed a fundamentally different trajectory to other European societies owed much to A. Macfarlane, *The origins of English individualism*, Oxford 1978.
[5] Hobsbawm and Rudé, *Captain Swing*, 16.

thoroughly than thirty years ago. As a result we now know much more about both the rural and the urban working class in the nineteenth century. Recent work has begun to show that the traditional three-tier model of English rural society is extremely oversimplified. Not only did traders and artisans consti- tute an important presence in most villages, but labourers were by no means always proletarianised; nor can any sharp distinction be maintained between labourers and small farmers. The contrast between 'peasant' continental agri- culture and 'capitalist' English agriculture has been overdrawn. Many labourers continued to be paid partly in kind, giving them a direct interest in the land and its produce. Where, as in many parts of the country, small farms continued to exist, the possibility of social mobility was a real one. Common pasture rights may or may not have been broadly enough dispersed to act as a significant bulwark between labourers and proletarianisation, but even if they were not, the lesser rights of common (especially fuel gathering) were far from negligible in value. Land was therefore more relevant to the experience of nineteenth-century agricultural labourers than has been supposed.[6]

In view of this, it is not surprising that the painstaking and thorough investigation of archival sources which has taken place since the 1960s should have uncovered evidence that rural labourers were, after all, not so indifferent to land. Barry Reay's detailed reconstruction of the social and mental world of the labourers of Hernhill and Dunkirk in Kent, for example, suggests that the aspiration to land was one of the most significant underpin- nings of the labourers' uprising which culminated in the 'Battle in Bosenden Wood'.[7]

Demand for land in general does not imply demand for a particular form of land provision. When the conditions under which land was offered were sufficiently unattractive, labourers were of course less enthusiastic about accepting it. This seems to have been the case with respect to potato grounds.[8] So we now need to assess to what extent the interest of labourers in land in general applied specifically to allotment provision as well.

Allotments were so rare before 1830 that very little information about the

---

[6] M. Reed, 'The peasantry of nineteenth-century rural England: a neglected class?', *History Workshop* xviii (1984), 53–76, and 'Nineteenth-century rural England: a case for "peasant studies"?', *Journal of Peasant Studies* xiv/1 (1986), 78–99; D. Mills, 'Peasants and conflict in nineteenth-century rural England: a comment on recent articles', *Journal of Peasant Studies* xv/3 (1980), 395–400; A. P. Donajgrodzki, 'Twentieth-century rural England: a case for "peasant studies"?', *Journal of Peasant Studies*, xvi/3 (1989), 425–42; A. Hall, 'Fenland worker-peasants: the economy of smallholders at Rippingale, Lincolnshire, 1791–1871', *AgHR* supplement ser. i (1992), 1–61; A. Howkins, 'Peasants, servants and labourers: the marginal workforce in British agriculture, c. 1870–1914', *AgHR* xlii/1 (1994), 57–60; A. Mutch, 'The "farming ladder" in north Lancashire, 1840–1914: myth or reality?', *Northern History* xxvii (1991), 162–83; Humphries, 'Enclosures, common rights, and women', 17–42.

[7] Reay, *The last rising of the agricultural labourers*, 105–6, 109, 176.

[8] Burchardt, 'Land and laborer', 667–84.

extent of demand can be identified. It is therefore necessary to begin by considering evidence from the second allotment movement (i.e. from the 1830s and 1840s). Statements about landholding by labourers themselves rarely survive from this period, but those which do often indicate an intense desire for land, as in the case of the three reproduced below:

> My husband has forty lugs of land, for which he pays ten shillings a year . . . we should like to have forty lugs more.

> We have . . . two small pieces of ground, together sixty-five perches . . . upon which we grow potatoes. We would like to have an acre more, for then we could raise a little corn.

> My husband hired fifty-four lugs of land, and I continued it after his death; without it I could not get on.[9]

The level of rent labourers were, when necessary, prepared to pay for land points to the same conclusion. Although most allotments were probably not let at rack rents, labourers were often prepared to pay rents far higher than the average. Richard Pollen informed the 1831 Select Committee of the House of Lords on the Poor Laws that 'from the avidity of those persons [i.e. labourers] to try the [allotment] system, they will give anything which is asked'.[10] Sir George Strickland told the 1843 Select Committee on the Labouring Poor that he had 'heard of £8 an acre, in consequence of the great desire of labourers to take land at any value, even far beyond its worth'.[11] Similarly, Captain Scobell stated that labourers 'would be glad to take any land, for land is like air; the man must have land; it is necessary to the rural labourer; he cannot get vegetables without it; the rent they used to pay [in Scobell's home county of Somerset] was £7 or £8 per season'.[12] Nor was even this figure the highest – labourers at Morpeth in Northumberland were paying at a rate of £11 per acre in 1834.[13]

If rents could be high, waiting lists were often long. The situation appears to have been particularly bad in the east Midlands. At Hinckley in

---

9 Statements by Mrs Britton, Mrs Wilshire and Mrs Haynes respectively in *Report on the Employment of Women and Children in Agriculture*, 1843, xii. 66, 69. See also *RC on the Handloom Weavers*, 1840, xxiii. 557.

10 *SC of the House of Lords on the Poor Laws*, 1831, viii. 51–2.

11 *SC on the Labouring Poor*, 1843, vii. 47. Strickland's suggestion that the roots of labourers' attachment to land went deeper than a simple calculation of economic benefits was echoed by G. T. Scobell: 'I have known [a labourer] desire a larger allotment, and yet, when offered it, still retain the ground he had, from an attachment to it, rather than change': *SC on the Labouring Poor*, 1843, vii. 28.

12 Ibid. 25.

13 *RC on the Poor Laws*, 1834, xxvii. 100–8. There are, of course, difficulties in comparing rent levels in the absence of detailed information about soil type, location, use, services provided, etc., but in the context of frequent contemporary statements about the high rents labourers were prepared to pay for land, the figures cited in this paragraph are suggestive.

Leicestershire, there were more than 100 applicants for land in 1843, although no land had yet actually been found. Every able-bodied man in the village apparently wanted land.[14] At Arnold in Nottinghamshire in 1842 there were also more than 100 people on the waiting list, even though 250 of the villagers already had plots.[15] James Orange used regularly to lecture to audiences of several hundreds in the villages between Leicester, Nottingham and Derby.[16] There were also long waiting lists in other parts of the country. At a new site in Ealing, Middlesex, there were over thirty applicants for every plot in 1845, whilst in west Kent in 1839 there were nearly 100 applicants waiting for allotments in Maidstone, over 200 at Tunbridge Wells and more than seventy at Hadlow.[17] At Stroud in Gloucestershire, Francis Pickard (manager of a local allotment site) could 'hardly walk the streets for the number of applicants'.[18]

Labourers would walk long distances to get to their allotments in the 1830s and 1840s. In Kent allotment sites were often as much as one and a half miles from the villages they served.[19] Instances of labourers walking three or even five miles each way were reported from other parts of the country.[20] The average distance between villages and sites appears to have been no more than three-quarters of a mile, but even this represents a return distance of a mile and a half, carrying tools and perhaps produce, not inconsiderable after a long day's field labour.[21]

A further indication of the strength of demand for land among many rural labourers in the era of the second allotment movement is that they were often prepared to rent plots on poor and difficult soils.[22] A few landowners even took advantage of this in order to improve the value of poor land.[23] Labourers

14 SC on the Labouring Poor, 1843, vii. 81.

15 LFM cxxxv (1842), 86.

16 Burchardt, 'The allotment movement', 143–5.

17 LF viii (1845), 154; LFM ciii (1839), 145–6.

18 SC on the Labouring Poor, 1843, vii. 52. It is interesting to note that all three of these examples refer to small towns rather than villages. This does not, however, imply that allotments were more in demand in small towns than in villages. It seems likely that the supply of land for allotments in towns was more constrained by high land values than it was in rural areas; and we would in any case expect, ceteris paribus, to find the longest waiting lists in settlements where the population was higher.

19 SC on the Labouring Poor, 1843, vii. 3.

20 SC of the House of Lords on the Poor Laws, 1831, viii. 294; LFM cxxxvi (1842), 96.

21 Burchardt, 'The allotment movement', 435. Calculations of the distance between villages and sites is, of course, complicated by the fact that a village is an area rather than a point. The figure of just under three-quarters of a mile is derived from seventy-five contemporary statements each relating to single allotment sites.

22 F&I, 23–8, 33, 470; LFM cxliii (1843), 17; cxxxviii (1842), 127–8; SC on the Labouring Poor, 1843, vii. 40, 117; Sir J. Caird, English agriculture in 1850–51, London 1851, 29–30; RC on the Employment of Children, Young Persons, and Women in Agriculture, 1867–8, xvii. 637, 670; Ashby, Joseph Ashby, 38.

23 RC on the Employment of Children, Young Persons, and Women in Agriculture, 1867–8, xvii. 545.

in the first half of the nineteenth century seem rarely to have rejected offers of land because of inadequate soil quality.[24]

Whilst allotments were primarily intended for agricultural labourers, rural artisans and industrial workers were often also eager to rent land.[25] This was particularly marked in the case of the Gloucestershire handloom weavers and the east Midlands framework knitters.[26] The Gloucestershire weavers, faced with ruinous competition from factory production, evidently regarded allotments as their one remaining hope. When William Miles visited the county on behalf of the 1840 royal commission, the weavers presented him with a plan (which he dismissed as 'glaringly injurious') whereby Bisley Common would be enclosed and divided into allotments.[27] The east Midlands framework knitters were, if anything, even more desperate.[28]

Compared with evidence from southern and Midland England, that from the north seems to indicate that labourers may have been less interested in owning or occupying land. The higher level of wages reduced the relative contribution of allotments to living standards, whilst, at least for agricultural workers, the prevalence of annual hiring gave protection against seasonal unemployment. Still more significant may have been the survival on a large scale of living-in (whereby board was provided, making it superfluous for labourers to grow their own food) and payments in kind (which often consisted of foodstuffs).

Turning now to the period between 1850 and 1870, the reports of the 1867–9 Royal Commission on the Employment of Children, Young Persons, and Women in Agriculture provide a useful overview of demand for land. The royal commission's conclusions were emphatic:

> It [i.e. the subject of the provision of allotments] is one of very great importance, both in a physical and in a moral point of view, to the labouring poor. It is, indeed, difficult without opportunities of referring to the great amount of evidence which exists upon the subject [in the evidence appended to the Report], to realize the deep interest which this question possesses for them.[29]

Sub-reports were presented for each area of Britain by assistant commissioners. Some submitted more than one report, often covering non-contiguous areas, and not always stating whether their general comments

---

[24] The rare instances in which labourers did reject offers of land in this period can usually be traced to suspicion of landowners' motives, particularly the anxiety that the offer of land might be conditional on foregoing the right to poor relief.

[25] The occupational characteristics of allotment tenants are assessed in chapter 7.

[26] The Northamptonshire boot- and shoemakers and the black country nailors were also notably keen to obtain allotments: Burchardt, 'The allotment movement', 419–22.

[27] RC on the Handloom Weavers, 1840, xxiii. 550.

[28] Evidence of the intensity of the demand for allotments in the east Midlands is presented in chapter 7.

[29] RC on the Employment of Children, Young Persons, and Women in Agriculture, 1867–8, xvii. p. xxxii.

about the demand for allotments applied to all areas equally or to some areas more than others. The evidence presented below (in an approximate south to north order, report by report) is therefore of most value in the aggregate; it has only limited usefulness in establishing the regional pattern of demand for land.

With respect to allotments in Dorset, Edward Stanhope noted that many were let at as high a rent as £4 an acre: in more half the forty-five parishes submitting returns to him allotments were let at a 'very high rent', while in the Bridport Union rents averaged more that £6 an acre.[30] Such rents presumably indicate strong demand for land.

George Culley's report on Bedfordshire and Buckinghamshire puts the matter more directly:

> that the poor themselves fully appreciate the advantages of having a 'bit of land' is too well known to require any reference to evidence on the subject, the desire is so great that landowners and their agents have used it to overcome the lawless habits of the inhabitants of such villages as are found in the west of Buckinghamshire, by a rule that a conviction before a bench of magistrates carries with it a forfeiture of the allotment. On this subject, Mr Golding, agent for the Dyvenor estate in Bedfordshire, says 'the men would suffer anything, rather than forfeit their allotment'.[31]

In his report on Norfolk, parts of Suffolk, Essex, Sussex and Gloucestershire, the Revd James Fraser wrote that

> I have known cases where labourers, prohibited, by what I think are harsh restrictions, from keeping a pig, have thrown up their allotment, which they found they could no longer cultivate to a profit; but speaking generally allotments are much prized, and on Sir Edward Kerrison's estate [in Suffolk] there is a keen competition for any vacant parcel.[32]

Culley's evidence on Oxfordshire includes an interesting statement by the labourer Jason Ward, of Wardington, on the level of demand for land in his area:

> I have a bit of potato land belonging to Colonel North, about twenty poles. I don't know what I should have done without it. The land is three and a half miles from my house. I can't get any land near. Nobody lets land so cheap as Colonel North. I have had to pay twenty shillings a chain for potato ground, and I pay two shillings to Colonel North. Lots of people would pay twenty shillings a chain. One of our farmers lets land at that rate. . . . I have known £2 given for a chain of potato ground planted.[33]

---

[30] Ibid. 1868–9, xiii. 5–6.
[31] Ibid. 1867–8, xvii. 133.
[32] Ibid. 40. Labourers on the Estcourt estate in Gloucestershire apparently regarded their allotments as equivalent in value to the rent of their cottages: ibid. 145.
[33] Ibid. 1868–9, xiii. 351. Ward's terminology is confusing but since he contrasts the 'potato

F. H. Norman, assistant commissioner for Northamptonshire, offered another strong statement on the demand for allotments: 'Again, the instances are numerous of land let in allotments at rents far beyond the ordinary farming rent; but so great is the value attached by the labourers themselves to the allotments, that they are always ready to pay these extravagant rents rather than not have the allotments at all.'[34]

In Derbyshire Culley found that allotments were much appreciated, although it seems to have been rural industrial workers rather than agricultural labourers who most wanted them: 'Allotments of land are provided near many of the towns and mining villages, and are greatly prized by the miners and mechanics. The Duke of Rutland, for instance, provides allotments of forty poles each in the neighbourhood of Ilkeston, which are in great demand amongst the colliers and framework knitters.'[35]

E. B. Portman's report on Cambridgeshire and Yorkshire noted that allotments were 'usually sought after eagerly'.[36] Stanhope's report on Lincolnshire, Nottinghamshire and Leicestershire provides little useful information about allotments, but a letter appended to the report from Edward Moore of Spalding states that allotments were 'very much prized by the poor' in Spalding itself and 'eagerly sought after' in the nearby village of Weston St Mary, where he also let allotments.[37] In a second letter Moore declared that the poor were 'most thankful' for land and that if he had as much more land to let in the same way it would be gladly taken by them.[38]

The report on Northumberland and Durham contains virtually no information on demand for land, other than a letter stating that tradesmen in the Ewart Park area of Northumberland were eager to accept an offer of allotments.[39]

For the north-west, there is rather more evidence. In Lancashire, Henry Tremenheere found that labourers appreciated allotments but had a marked preference for small plots. Wages were high, and labourers did not want to work long on their allotments after their day's labour was over. At Cartmel,

---

land' belonging to Colonel North (and let at only 2s.) with the 'potato ground' let by farmers at 20s., it seems likely that North was letting allotments whilst the farmers were indeed letting potato ground.

[34] Ibid. 1867–8, xvii. 119.
[35] Ibid. 1868–9, xiii. 120.
[36] Ibid. 1867–8, xvii. 105.
[37] Edward Moore to Edward Stanhope, the Parsonage, Spalding, 26 Jan. 1868, printed ibid. 1868–9, xiii. 146. Other than this letter the main evidence on demand for land in Stanhope's report is his surprising observation that whilst allotments were very common in Lincolnshire, Nottinghamshire and Leicestershire, they were less sought after where they were let without charge. Since allotments were rarely let without charge, it is possible that Stanhope's reference is to potato grounds, which were sometimes included in labour contracts.
[38] Ibid.
[39] Letter from John Bruce, Ewart Park, 9 Feb. 1868, printed ibid. 224.

for example, labourers asked for allotments of only eight poles even though larger plots had been offered.[40]

The situation in Cumberland and Westmorland was different again, and Tremenheere's report deserves quotation because this is the only area of England for which there is clear evidence of little or no interest in allotments:

> The allotment system to which so much importance is justly attached is less applicable to Cumberland and Westmorland than to any other county with which I am acquainted. This is sufficiently accounted for by the prevailing high rate of wages. A man who fairly earns from eighteen shillings to one pound and one shilling a week is seldom disposed for further work at the conclusion of the day . . . I only met with one instance of allotments being in request and appreciated by agricultural labourers, namely, on the property of Lord Kenlis in Westmorland.[41]

This explanation is not wholly satisfactory, since in some other high-wage areas, such as Lincolnshire and Yorkshire, demand for allotments was quite strong. The suggestion made by some of Tremenheere's informants to the effect that where labourers were provided with food as part of their wages they showed less interest in allotments is probably relevant: payment in kind was most common in the northernmost counties where demand for land was consistently weak or confined to urban locations.[42] But even if the distribution of demand for allotments cannot be wholly explained by differential wage levels, agricultural labourers earning high wages do on the whole seem to have valued land less highly.[43] There may have been a significant difference between agricultural and industrial labourers in this respect: whilst for the former, allotment cultivation was a continuation of the same kind of work that they had been doing all day, for the latter, going down to the plot represented fresh air and a change of scene and activity.

Appended to the evidence presented in the reports of the assistant commissioners is an account of a meeting of the London Central Farmers' Club in November 1858, at which the principal subject of discussion was allotments. The main speaker on this occasion was a Mr Trethewy, the agent for the Cowper estate in Bedfordshire. Trethewy's rhetoric disguises a genuine insight – that the demand for allotments was not purely economic in origin:

> Almost every man, whatever may be his pursuit in life, attaches himself more or less to the soil. He feels that he possesses in his garden or paddock at least one spot which he can call his own, and where he can indulge his own peculiar taste. No wonder then that the labourer, whose very existence is identified with vegetable life, should participate in this feeling. No wonder that while

---

[40] Ibid. 154.
[41] Ibid. 147.
[42] Ibid.
[43] This may explain why demand for allotments appears to have been limited in the immediate agricultural hinterland of London: ibid. 120.

the greatest portion of his time is devoted to the cultivation of the crops of his employer he should aspire to the occupation of a small area for himself, independently of its value and convenience to him. And when we consider how influential this feeling often is in diverting his attention from places and objects of demoralisation, surely it is the duty of every one interested in his well-being . . . to promote his wishes.[44]

In the ensuing debate, other speakers echoed the view that labourers felt an intense interest in land provision. Mr Bennett, of Cambridge, declared that he had 'known land let out to labourers at such prices as precluded all hope of the occupier deriving the least profit – poor wretched glebe land, for instance, let at double its value, and irrespective of its distance from the dwellings of the labourers'.[45] Mr Williams, of Baydon, near Hungerford, Wiltshire stated that, in his experience, even where an allotment site was half a mile from a village there were plenty of applicants for any vacancy.[46] Dr Ellis of Sudbrook Park, Richmond, said that he had often felt 'quite ashamed' at the excessive rents sometimes charged for allotments, and that he had heard even of 18d. per pole (i.e. £12 per acre – an extraordinarily high rent).[47] Subsequent remarks underlined the strength of demand for land in Bedfordshire and Northamptonshire.[48]

In summary, the evidence submitted to the 1867–9 royal commission seems to indicated that rural labourers in most parts of the country, but above all in the south Midlands, still felt a strong desire for land in the 1850s and 1860s. Allotments were also highly valued in East Anglia, Lincolnshire, the east Midlands and Yorkshire. Labourers in Lancashire sometimes wanted allotments, but this was very rarely the case in Westmorland and Cumberland.

It would seem, therefore, that in most parts of England, allotments were highly valued by rural labourers in the middle decades of the nineteenth century. Furthermore, the general and severe shortfall of allotments in the 1830s and 1840s had only moderated somewhat by the late 1860s. Indeed, regionally specific deficiencies of rural allotments persisted at least until the First World War. The Land Enquiry Committee of 1913 found that there was much unsatisfied demand for allotments among agricultural labourers, 'amounting in some parts of the country to a veritable land hunger'.[49] There were vacant plots in only 319 of the 1,893 parishes with allotments which returned the questionnaire issued by the committee.[50]

---

[44] Ibid. 1867–8, xvii. 139.
[45] Ibid. 141.
[46] Ibid. 143.
[47] Ibid.
[48] Ibid. 140, 144.
[49] Land Enquiry Committee, The land, i, London 1913, 188–9.
[50] Ibid. 172. Whilst the anti-landlord bias of the Land Enquiry Committee may have led it to overemphasise the intensity and policy significance of 'land hunger', the process by which

If there is such clear evidence of strong demand for allotments, why has this not hitherto been recognised? There are three main reasons. In the first place, demand was far from ubiquitous across the country, and in particular was weak or absent in northern England throughout the nineteenth century. Failure to appreciate the importance of this geographical dimension may have misled historians into supposing that lack of demand was a more significant phenomenon than it actually was. Second, the nature of demand for allotments altered over the course of the nineteenth century. Whilst in the first half of the century labourers were prepared to take land under markedly disadvantageous conditions, in the second the much greater availability of allotments and general improvement in living standards permitted a more discriminating attitude. By the 1890s labourers were often in a position to switch from unattractive plots to better ones on the same or different sites. The third factor is that allotment provision became politicised in the 1870s. This reached a peak in the 1880s but remained at a relatively high level until the First World War. Jesse Collings campaigned for 'three acres and a cow', and Joseph Arch, the leader of the National Agricultural Labourers' Union, entered parliament and demanded legislation to facilitate rural allotment provision.[51] This raised the spectre, if private provision did not succeed in meeting the demand for land adequately, of compulsory purchase. Conservative and Liberal Unionist landowners such as Lord Fortescue, Lady Verney and Lord Onslow wrote articles for the reviews, and in Onslow's case even a book, to prove that there was in fact no unsatisfied demand for land.[52] This literature, which was widely disseminated at the time and almost certainly reached a larger audience than the more thorough and generally less tendentious evidence buried deep within the parliamentary papers, appears to have had a significant and unwarranted influence on subsequent historiography.

The benefits of allotments to labouring families

If, as has been argued, nineteenth-century rural labourers had in general a strong desire for allotments, how can this be explained? A consideration of the contribution made by allotments to material living standards, and also of their non-economic benefits indicates that the advantages of allotments were substantial; in this context the strength of labourers' desire for land is easily understood.

parishes were selected to receive questionnaires appears to have been impartial and the returns received by the committee probably reflect the extent of demand for allotments fairly: ibid. pp. xiv–xvi.

51 Joseph Arch, *The story of his life*, London 1898, 346–8, 359–62.

52 Fortescue, 'Poor men's gardens', 394–402; Verney, 'Allotments', 902–13; the earl of Onslow, *Landlords and allotments: the history and present condition of the allotment system*, London 1886.

The contribution of allotments to material living standards arose in part from the congruence between the changing composition of demand for agricultural labour and the labour input required by allotments. As we saw in chapter 1 rising population, exacerbated by changes in agricultural practice such as conversion to arable, the adoption of labour-saving technology and enclosure, resulted in rapidly rising rural unemployment and underemployment in the late eighteenth and early nineteenth centuries, only temporarily interrupted by the Napoleonic wars.[53] In the predominantly arable south and east, where most agricultural workers lived and where incomes were lowest, these trends affected male winter employment and female harvest employment particularly severely.[54] The seasonal labour requirements of allotment cultivation meshed with this differential gender effect: the heavier tasks, notably digging and manure-spreading, were concentrated during the part of the year when men were most likely to be out of work, whilst the summer tasks of weeding, watering and picking were regarded as particularly suited to women and children.[55] In the second half of the nineteenth century, allotment cultivation continued to be family-based, although changing social attitudes may have reduced adult female participation, and the improved demand–supply situation for male labour increased the importance of hired work.[56]

Allotment cultivation was almost equally well adapted to the labour patterns of rural artisans, whose work was subject to intermittent periods of slack demand. This was especially true of domestic outworkers in the early and mid-nineteenth century. Domestic outwork and allotment tenancy were closely associated for four main reasons: firstly, outworkers were without work for a higher proportion of their time than most other groups of workers; second, outworkers had more control over their hours of work, when they did have work, than most other workers; third, many of the outwork trades were in long-term decline from about the 1830s, due to competition from factory production resulting from the deepening impact of the industrial revolution; and fourth, a large proportion of domestic outworkers lived in the countryside, where allotments were much easier to obtain than in the towns. The first factor meant that the annual incomes of outworkers tended to be low by

---

[53] Alan Armstrong, 'The influence of demographic factors on the position of the agricultural labourer in England and Wales, c. 1750–1914', AgHR xxix (1981), 71–82; E. J. T. Collins, 'Harvest technology and labour supply in Britain, 1790–1870', EcHR 2nd ser. xxii (1969), 453–60; Hobsbawm and Rudé, Captain Swing, 362–5; Snell, Labouring poor, 138–227.

[54] Snell, Labouring poor, 15–66; Humphries, 'Enclosures, common rights, and women', 35–41.

[55] F&I, 27; RC on the Poor Laws, 1834, xxvii. 180; I. Pinchbeck, Women workers and the industrial revolution, 1750–1850, London 1930, 60–1; Moselle, 'Allotments, enclosure and proletarianization', 487–8.

[56] F. Thompson, Lark Rise to Candleford, [1945], London 1973 edn, 114–15; RC on the Employment of Children, Young Persons, and Women in Agriculture, 1867–8, xvii. 179.

comparison with those of regular employees, and so made allotments more important to them, whilst also meaning that they had more time to cultivate them. The second factor was equally important, although less obviously so. Allotments cannot be left entirely alone for long periods, because weeds and pests will destroy or at least severely damage the crops. So at a time when an employee might expect work hours to be twelve hours a day, or even longer, allotments could be more of a commitment than some workers were easily able to take on. But domestic outworkers were able to choose their own hours of work, and so even when trade was at its best they were usually able to find an hour or two to keep their plots in decent order. Furthermore, in most outwork industries there was always at least one day a week on which no work was possible for most members of the household – the day on which the finished product was exchanged for fresh raw material.[57] Even when work was abundant there was, therefore, some time available for the essential regular tasks necessary for allotments, whilst longer but more irregular periods of short work allowed more substantial but less time-specific tasks such as digging, manuring and tool repair to be undertaken.[58] The third factor, the long-term decline of many outwork trades, needs to be interpreted with caution, because the timing of the decline of different trades varied greatly. Whilst framework-knitting, for example, was already experiencing great diffi-culties in the early 1840s, nailmaking as a domestic industry was not to suffer comparably until the 1890s.[59] But although the timing varied, it remains true that most of the outwork trades were at some point or other during the nine-teenth century hard-hit by competition with factory production. The fourth factor, that domestic outworkers tended to live in the countryside, made it much easier for them to obtain allotments than it was for other groups of industrial workers, although, as we shall see, even with this advantage, outworkers still sometimes found it very difficult to obtain land.

To some degree the relationship between domestic outwork and allotments in the nineteenth century is parallel to the 'dual occupationism' particularly associated with eighteenth-century cottage industry. In both cases, a rural location and the freedom to define one's own hours of work made landholding easier. But the differences are rather more significant than the similarities. Allotments were a supplement to income, rather than a prin-cipal source of it. The nineteenth-century domestic outworker's allotment was quite independent of his work, as opposed to the land of the dual occupationist, which was often integral to his work: the West Riding spinners and weavers, for example, needed their land for their tenters, as well as for the

---

[57] In the cotton handloom weaving industry this was known as 'bearing-home day'; D. Bythell, *The handloom weavers: a study in the English cotton industry during the industrial revolution*, Cambridge 1969, 37.

[58] The relationship between domestic outwork and allotment cultivation is considered at greater length in Burchardt, 'The allotment movement', 400–26.

[59] F. E. Green, *A history of the English agricultural labourer, 1870–1920*, London 1920, 137–8.

horse they kept to carry their wool and cloth to and fro.[60] Finally, the importance of allotment-holding to many groups of domestic outworkers in the nineteenth century needs to be seen, not as a feature of these trades when they were in their prime, but as a result of the chronic underemployment and long-term decline brought about by their exposure to competition from factory production.

The labour requirements of allotments were therefore well-matched both to agricultural labourers and to rural artisans and outworkers. So for many rural labouring families, especially in the first half of the nineteenth century, the opportunity cost of cultivating an allotment must have been close to zero. It is true that farm and allotment work schedules tended to converge at harvest time, but differing cropping regimes reduced this potential conflict.[61] The conjunction of abundant underutilised labour and small plots allowed intensive cultivation. Allotments were, for example, almost always dug ('spade husbandry') rather than ploughed, with corresponding benefits for soil aeration and weed destruction.[62] Intensive cultivation also allowed more frequent weeding and hoeing, and more careful harvesting with less waste and spillage. Perhaps the most important aspect of the effectively costless labour which allotment-holding families enjoyed, however, was manuring. The quantity of nitrogen applied to the soil was probably the most important single variable affecting crop yields in nineteenth-century English agriculture.[63] Allotment-holders were able to apply far greater proportionate quantities of nitrogen to their plots than farmers for two reasons. First, allotments were closely associated with pig-keeping.[64] Some allotment-holders kept more than one pig, but even a stocking density of one pig per quarter acre (the average size of a mid nineteenth-century allotment) was well beyond what contemporary farmers normally achieved. Secondly, allotment-holders were able to supplement pig manure with other fertilisers, including vegetable compost, ashes, nightsoil, and, perhaps most important of all, manure collected by their children from the roads.[65] Quite large quantities of dung were deposited on roads, partly because of the movement of stock through lanes from field to farmyard and vice versa, and partly because of horse traffic.

[60] M. J. Daunton, Progress and poverty, Oxford 1995, 148.

[61] Potatoes, the predominant allotment crop, were usually lifted after the main corn harvest was over: T. P. McIntosh, The potato: its history, varieties, culture and diseases, London 1927, 156.

[62] Ploughing did, however, occur on large allotments of half an acre or more, and may have become more common as employment prospects improved for male labourers in the second half of the nineteenth century: RC on the Employment of Children, Young Persons, and Women in Agriculture, 1867–8, xvii.

[63] M. Overton, Agricultural revolution in England: the transformation of the agrarian economy, 1500–1850, Cambridge 1996, 16.

[64] Report on the Employment of Women and Children in Agriculture, 1843, xii. 294–5; SC on the Labouring Poor, 1843, vii. 3; Ashby, Allotments and small holdings in Oxfordshire, 42–3.

[65] SC of the House of Lords on the Poor Laws, 1831, viii. 55; SC on the Labouring Poor, 1843, vii. 2; Report on the Employment of Women and Children in Agriculture, 1843, xii. 248.

Allotment-holders used the unpaid labour of their children to exploit this cost-free supply of fertiliser. It seems that farmers, who of course had to pay their labour, did not find it worthwhile to have manure collected from the roads (although in some instances, perhaps where local roads yielded a particularly abundant supply, labourers did sell road-gathered manure to farmers).

High levels of inputs do not guarantee correspondingly high output because of the problem of diminishing marginal returns. So allotment-holders chose to grow crops which responded well to the impressive quantities of labour and manure which they were able to lavish upon them. Evidence of crops grown on allotments is presented in tables 4, 5 and 6. For a small number of sites, details of all the crops grown in one or more years survive (*see* table 7).

What conclusions can be drawn from the evidence presented in tables 4, 5, 6 and 7? In the first place, it is clear that potatoes were found on all or almost all allotment sites, and that they were also, by some way, the crop which occupied the largest acreage of allotments. This conclusion accords with the observations of contemporary witnesses. Henry Martin, agent of the West Kent Labourer's Friend Society, told the Select Committee on the Labouring Poor that potatoes in general occupied rather more than half of a plot.[66] Alfred Austin, one of the assistant commissioners for the 1843 *Report on the Employment of Women and Children in Agriculture*, felt it necessary to explain that allotments were not always planted only with potatoes.[67] It is not very surprising that the potato was so universally grown, since it was well adapted to allotment cultivation. It benefited from thoroughly dug soil, from careful hoeing and from frequent earthing-up.[68] All these were labour-intensive tasks which could be carried out more easily and thoroughly by allotment tenants than on a farm. Furthermore, land planted with potatoes produced more food per acre than, in Britain, it could in any other way (Salaman's cost-per-calorie calculations indicate that potatoes were normally at least twice as efficient a source of calories as even the best quality white bread).[69] Yet in many areas of rural Britain potatoes were not widely available for sale, because as a field crop their cultivation was restricted to a few parts of the country.[70] The potato was also an easy crop to use: it did not require milling or any other special operation before it could be cooked and eaten, and, if stored correctly, it would keep throughout the winter. Finally, it could be grown in a wide variety of soils. All in all, it was an almost ideal crop for the allotment-holder.

What is much more of a surprise is that so much wheat was grown on allotments. Although less labour-intensive than potatoes, wheat was vulnerable to being eaten by birds, and the allotment tenant, in contrast to the farmer,

66 *SC on the Labouring Poor*, 1843, vii. 3.
67 *Report on the Employment of Women and Children in Agriculture*, 1843, xii. 15.
68 W. E. Shewell-Cooper, *The ABC of vegetable gardening*, London 1948.
69 R. N. Salaman, *The history and social influence of the potato*, Cambridge 1949, 122.
70 R. Morgan, 'Root crops', in Mingay, *Agrarian history of England and Wales*, vi. 303–5.

Table 4
Crops grown on allotments, 1793–1829

Site	County	Date	Crops recorded
Long Newnton	Wilts.	1805	potatoes
Hambleton	Rutland	1808	potatoes, barley
Terrington St Clement	Norfolk	1818	potatoes, peas, beans, cabbage
Byfield	Northants.	1828	potatoes, wheat, barley
Byfield	Northants.	1829	potatoes, wheat, barley
Sarratt	Herts.	1829	potatoes

Note: For the first phase of the allotment movement, between 1793 and 1829, little information about cropping seems to be available. This table is based on the six records (i.e. site-years) in the database which have information about what crops were grown on the sites to which they refer.

Sources: SBCP, *Reports*, v. 71–83; Richard Parkinson, *General view of the agriculture of the county of Rutland*, London 1808 (1813 edn), 103; F&I, 63–4; SC of the House of Lords on the Poor Laws, 1831, viii. 40–7; LFM (1834), 111–12.

Table 5
Crops grown on allotments, 1830–49

Crop	No. of records mentioning	Percentage of all examined records
Potatoes	79	87
Wheat	50*	55*
Beans	23	25
Peas	16	18
Barley	14	15
Cabbage	14	15
Turnips	14	15
Onions	12	13
Carrots	8	9
Parsnips	5	5
Lettuce	4	4
Fruit	3	3
Broccoli	2	2
Flowers	2	2
Leeks	2	2
Oats	2	2
Artichokes	1	1
Clover	1	1

Crop	No. of records mentioning	Percentage of all examined records
Mangel wurzel	1	1
Tares	1	1
All records	**91**	**100**

* The tally for wheat includes eight undifferentiated mentions of 'corn', which were presumed to refer to wheat, since wheat was by so large a margin the commonest grain grown on allotments in this period.

Source: Database.

Table 6
Crops grown on allotments, 1850–73

Crop	No. of records mentioning	Percentage of all examined records
Wheat	21*	72*
Potatoes	16	55
Beans	4	14
Barley	2	7
Cabbage	1	3
Flowers	1	3
Mangel wurzel	1	3
Onions	1	3
Peas	1	3
Turnips	1	3
Total records	**29**	**100**

* Includes ten undifferentiated mentions of 'corn'.

Note: although the table suggests that more wheat than potatoes was grown on allotments in this period, this is unlikely to have been the case. Twelve of the twenty-nine records on which the table was based were taken from the Northamptonshire section of the report of the 1867–8 RC on the *Employment of Children, Young Persons, and Women in Agriculture*. This section devoted particular attention to the question of whether or not corn was grown on allotments, but showed no great interest in whether or not potatoes were grown.

Source: Database.

Table 7
Sites with complete crop records

Site	County	Date	Crops						
			P	W	B	Pe	Bn	C	O
Terrington	Norfolk	1818	x			x	x	x	
Avington	Hants.	1832	x	x	x				
Easton	Hants.	1832	x	x	x	x	x		
Itchin	Hants.	1832	x		x		x		
Gt Missenden	Bucks.	1833	x	x		x	x	x	x
Framlingham	Suffolk	1835	x	x					
Barrow	Rutland	1840	x	x			x		
Cottesmore	Rutland	1840	x	x	x		x		
Exton	Rutland	1840	x	x	x		x		
Ridlington	Rutland	1840	x	x		x			
10 records in total			10	8	5	4	7	2	1
Percentage of records crop occurs in:			100	80	50	40	70	20	10

Key: P = potatoes   W = wheat   B = barley   Pe = peas
         Bn = beans   C = cabbage   O = other

Note: the other crops growing at Great Missenden were parsnips, carrots, french beans, onions, and various unspecified herbs.

Sources: F&I, 63–4, 455–69; LFM (1834), 134–6; (1835), 190–1; Gardener's Chronicle, 4 Jan. 1845, 13, col. 1.

could rarely afford to hire a bird-scarer to protect his plot all day long.[71] Acre for acre, wheat produced considerably less food than potatoes.[72] There were no parts of the country where wheat – or more importantly its main derivative, bread – was not widely and relatively cheaply available. Wheat required grinding or milling, and then baking, before it could be eaten. Grinding was a slow and physically tiring process, requiring ownership of a quern (rare by the early nineteenth century among agricultural labourers), whilst baking depended upon the availability of fuel, which was becoming prohibitively expensive for labourers in most parts of the countryside in this period.[73] Wheat and flour were both more difficult to store in quantity than potatoes.[74] Finally, wheat was less adaptable to different soil and climate conditions than

[71] RC on the Employment of Women and Children in Agriculture, 1867–8, xvii. 180; SC on the Labouring Poor, 1843, vii. 17.
[72] Overton, Agricultural revolution, 102.
[73] W. Cobbett, Cottage economy, [1822], Oxford 1979 edn, 64–8; J. Burnett, Plenty and want: a social history of diet in England from 1815 to the present day, London 1966, 4.
[74] Report on the Employment of Women and Children in Agriculture, 1843, xii. 266.

potatoes, growing well only in the less wet parts of the country, on well-drained soils.

Bearing in mind all these disadvantages, one wonders why nineteenth-century allotment-holders grew so much wheat on their plots. Part of the explanation may be that there were disadvantages to growing potatoes year in, year out, on the same patch of land. It is clear that on some allotments, labourers did actually do just this, but in the long run soil exhaustion was likely to result. In the majority of cases, labourers probably did practise crop rotation, with which, as farmworkers, they would have been quite familiar. Indeed, on many allotment sites regular rotation of crops was required, and on a few sites discretion about what crops they could grow was removed from labourers altogether. Where regulations about rotations existed, they usually specified that labourers cultivate no more than a third, or at most a half, of their plot with potatoes. In so far as labourers either chose, or were forced, to practise crop rotation, it is clear that they had to grow other crops in addition to potatoes. But why did they choose wheat? There were perhaps three main attractions: first, bread could form the mainstay of the labourer's diet, in a way cabbages or carrots could not; second, bread was considered more palatable than potatoes; and third, wheat as a crop had a social significance which went beyond its economic value.

It was important to grow a crop which could form the mainstay of the family's diet because most agricultural labourers in the areas where allotments were commonest had barely enough to eat. In 1850, by which time conditions may have improved somewhat from their nadir in the mid-1830s, Caird found that agricultural labourers in several counties in the south of England subsisted on a diet consisting almost exclusively of bread and potatoes, eating meat (bacon) only once a week.[75] In this situation, the priority was obviously to grow staple foods to fill the hungry mouths of the labourer's family. The two staples in mid nineteenth-century rural England were bread and potatoes, so that if it were not possible to grow only potatoes, some kind of corn might well have seemed the next best option. Bearing in mind the deep-seated attachment of the working population in the south of England to wheaten bread, wheat would have been the corn crop of choice. The suggestion that for some allotment-holders wheat was a second choice is born out by a comment made by Earl Spencer in 1867, to the effect that corn was occasionally necessary on allotments as a change of crop.[76]

But whilst some labourers seem to have grown wheat mainly because they could not grow only potatoes, other labourers may have had more positive reasons for choosing to grow it. The potato had made very little progress in establishing itself as a food crop for human consumption in southern England in the eighteenth century. It was only the grave food shortages of the last years of the eighteenth century that made it a major part of the diet of

75 Caird, *English agriculture*, passim.
76 *RC on the Employment of Children, Young Persons, and Women in Agriculture*, 1867–8, xvii. 667.

labourers in the south.[77] The conversion was an unwilling one; and it is far from clear that even by the 1830s and 1840s agricultural labourers actually liked eating potatoes. If wheat was grown on very many allotments, despite its serious drawbacks, this may well have been because labourers preferred to eat bread rather than potatoes. Some evidence to support this view can be found in the appendixes of the 1843 *Report on the Employment of Women and Children in Agriculture*, which include several statements by labourers or their wives about their allotments. In the case of Mrs Wilshire of Cherill, near Calne in Wiltshire, for example, it is clear that her family wanted to grow wheat on their allotments, but were forced by poverty and lack of land to confine themselves to the higher yielding crop. Mrs Wilshire told the commission that 'We have . . . two small pieces of ground, together sixty-five perches, for which we pay £2 7s. a year, and upon which we grow potatoes. We would like to have an acre more, for then we could raise a little corn, and have more bread than now at a cheaper rate.'[78]

The third factor which probably contributed to the growing of wheat was its social significance. Wheat occupied a unique place among English farm crops. This was partly because it was the most valuable of the common crops, but also because the best bread was made from it and bread, the 'staff of life', was the staple food of the people of England. Even though wheat made up only a third or less of the sown acreage of England in the mid-nineteenth century, the prosperity of farming as a whole was often gauged from wheat prices.[79] It would almost be true to say that growing wheat was the badge of being a farmer. The extent to which farmers were attached to wheat, in a way that was by no means merely a matter of economics, is indicated by their tardiness in shifting away from it when prices fell sharply from the 1870s onwards. It was natural that, when they too had the opportunity, labourers should want to grow wheat themselves. James Marriott, a labourer from Stanwick in Northamptonshire, told Assistant Commissioner F. H. Norman in 1868 that: 'I have half an acre of ground. I can manage that with my regular work; I would not have so much if I could not grow half wheat; I feel a better man for having that.'[80]

It is clear that labourers took great pride in their wheat yields, which as we shall see were often considerably better than those obtained by farmers.[81] There was an element of defiance present in the determination of many labourers to grow a crop which farmers saw as a mark of their identity. It was probably this challenge to their status which lay at the bottom of the attempt by farmers to prevent allotment-holders from growing wheat.[82]

[77] Salaman, *History and social influence of the potato*, 481–503.
[78] *Report on the Employment of Women and Children in Agriculture*, 1843, xii. 69.
[79] Overton, *Agricultural revolution*, 97–8.
[80] *RC on the Employment of Children, Young Persons, and Women in Agriculture*, 1867–8, xvii. 680.
[81] *LFM* cv (1839), 178; *Report on the Employment of Women and Children in Agriculture*, 1843, xii. 68.
[82] Burchardt, 'Rural social relations', 173–4.

The other crops grown on allotments in this period call for less comment. Beans were probably the most important crop after potatoes and wheat, followed by peas and barley. Both beans and peas were known to be good crops for maintaining soil fertility, and complemented rotations involving potatoes and wheat. Beans and peas, and also barley and turnips, were probably used mainly for feeding the pigs that labourers with allotments kept whenever possible. It is striking that green vegetables for human consumption, such as cabbage, broccoli, leeks, sprouts and lettuce made up only a very small part of the total produce of allotments. This must reflect on the one hand the extent to which poverty forced labourers to prioritise staple foods, but may also reflect a lack of appetite amongst labourers for green vegetables. However, a small sub-group of sites, those where prizes were awarded for the best vegetables, or where allotment-holders exhibited at a local horticultural show, did tend to grow a wider range of crops. At Hurstpierrepoint in 1838, for example, prizes were awarded not only for potatoes, but also for turnips, carrots, onions and for the best tray of assorted vegetables.[83] The 1846 show of the East Somerset Labourer's Friend Society, which admittedly drew on the produce of many different sites, included exhibits of onions, turnips, parsnips, leeks, carrots, savoy cabbages, broccoli, potatoes and other, unspecified, vegetables.[84]

The centrality of potatoes to allotment cultivation meant that allotment-holders were highly vulnerable to the effects of the potato blight which attacked Britain in the second half of the 1840s. The disease seems to have been virulent between 1845 and the early 1850s, although even as late as the end of the 1860s there were occasional reports of crops ruined by blight.[85] In the worst years, the late 1840s, there were arrears of rent on some sites because allotment-holders had lost all or nearly all their potatoes, although other sites reported that rent continued to be well paid despite heavy losses to the blight.[86] One of the worst features of the disease was that it could strike the same site several years in a row, and in at least one case an allotment field was abandoned (in the event temporarily) because repeated crop failures had demoralised the tenants.[87] Remissions of rent were widespread.[88] Much concern was expressed in the columns of the *Labourer's Friend* about the devastating consequences of the disease, and an extraordinary variety of exotic remedies were urged upon allotment-holders. These included early planting, covering the potato with lime, growing the potatoes in a conical heap, cutting off the top of the potato once harvested and anaerobic storage.[89] Landowners also made strenuous attempts to encourage their allot-

83 *LFM* xcii (1838), 158–9.
84 Ibid. xxxiii (1847), 18.
85 *RC on the Employment of Children, Young Persons, and Women in Agriculture*, 1868–9, xiii. 27; 1867–8, xvii. 534.
86 *LF* xxxv (1847), 58; xxxviii (1847), 104.
87 Ibid. cviii (1853), 80.
88 Ibid. xix (1845), 356; xxx (1846), 207; xxxi (1846), 219.
89 Ibid. xxx (1846), 206; lii (1848), 159–60; xxi (1846), 20, 22.

ment tenants to grow a wider range of crops.[90] These attempts clearly succeeded in some cases, as for example at Bearsted in Kent, where in 1846 wheat, beans and turnips were apparently fast supplanting potatoes, and at Adlington in Wiltshire where it was not fear of the disease itself but the high price of seed potatoes resulting from the blight that caused the allotment-holders to switch to growing wheat in 1847.[91] However, Bearsted and Adlington may well have been exceptional. To judge by the undiminished frequency with which exhortations to labourers to grow a wider range of crops appeared in the *Labourer's Friend* throughout the late 1840s and early 1850s – and by their increasingly exasperated tone – allotment-holders were reluctant to heed the message.[92] If there was any general shift away from dependence on potatoes, it must have been short-lived, since informants to the 1867–9 Royal Commission on the Employment of Children, Young Persons, and Women in Agriculture indicated that allotment cultivation was still predominantly based on potatoes, despite the risk of disease.[93] A comparison of tables 5 and 6 similarly suggests that there had been no major diversification away from potatoes and wheat over the 1850–73 period.

Potatoes and wheat therefore remained much the most important allotment crops throughout the period 1793 to 1873. For both crops, the intensive cultivation practised on allotments resulted in impressively high yields. Indeed, yields of wheat and potatoes in the first half of the nineteenth century were on average almost double those obtained on farms, as a comparison between table 8 and yield data from farms demonstrates. For potatoes, the national average yield on farmland in the early nineteenth century was about five tons per acre *per annum*.[94] Assuming a conversion ratio of fifty-six pounds to the bushel of potatoes, the comparable figure for allotments (average yield 361 bushels per acre between 1817 and 1846) was just over nine tons. Similarly, the national average yield of wheat on farmland in the mid-1830s was about twenty-one bushels per acre *per annum*.[95] For allotments, over the years 1817 to 1846, yields averaged about forty bushels per acre *per annum*.

The yields data given in table 8 fit well with contemporary opinion. Although estimates varied, they all agreed that allotment yields were significantly higher than farming yields. J. I. Burn, an LFS committee member,

---

[90] Ibid. xxx (1846), 185; xxxiii (1847), 20–3; lii (1848), 159–60; lxxvi (1850), 159.
[91] Ibid. xxx (1846), 206; xlii (1847), 204.
[92] Ibid. xxxiii (1847), 20–3; lii (1848), 159–60.
[93] *RC on the Employment of Children, Young Persons, and Women in Agriculture*, 1868–9, xiii. 27.
[94] Overton, *Agricultural revolution*, 102.
[95] Ibid. 77. However, see Michael E. Turner, John V. Beckett and B. Afton, *Farm Production in England 1700–1914*, Oxford, 2001, 116–49. If this estimate (published too recently to be fully incorporated here) of 26.67 bushels per acre for 1830s farm wheat yields is preferred to Overton's tithe file data, allotment wheat yields would exceed farm yields by 50.0% rather than 90.5%.

thought that the produce of allotments was never less than double and some-times quadruple that of the larger farmers.[96] The estimate of double may be quite accurate, whilst the highest allotment yields both of wheat and of pota-toes were indeed in excess of four times the yields typically obtained by farmers. A somewhat similar estimate was made in 1843 by a Mr Smith, of Gunton in Norfolk. He informed Stephen Denison, the special assistant poor law commis-sioner, that on heavy soils an allotment of a quarter of an acre cultivated by spade husbandry would yield as much as an acre cultivated by the plough.[97] This is a little higher than the figures given in table 8, but it was often said that the difference between the spade and the plough was most apparent on heavy soils, so Smith's estimate may in fact be accurate. The high produc-tivity of allotments was acknowledged at the end of the period covered by this study as well. Thus the marquis of Lansdowne's land agent, Mr J. Spencer, informed the 1867 royal commission that the average yields of allotments in the Calne area exceeded the average yields obtained by farmers in the district.[98]

If we look in more detail at the estimates made by contemporaries of the yields of wheat obtained by allotment-holders, we again find that they corre-spond well with table 8. Mrs Davies Gilbert, in a paper addressed to the British Institution, stated that for years many of her allotment tenants had raised alternately forty bushels of wheat and 400 bushels of potatoes per acre.[99] These figures are virtually identical to those in table 8. Captain H. B. Mason, of Yately in Hampshire, wrote to the Labourer's Friend about two allotment-holders in his parish who had obtained yields of wheat of, respec-tively, twelve and thirteen sacks (thirty-six and thirty-nine bushels) per acre, when in the field on the other side of the hedge the farmer could get six sacks (eighteen bushels) per acre at the very most.[100] The soil in this parish was apparently not thought very good for wheat, as indeed is clear from the yields, but it is interesting that the differential between the allotment and the farm yields is again two-to-one in favour of the allotments.

Contemporary estimates of the yields of potatoes obtained on allotments tell a similar story, although there is slightly more divergence between the figures. D. C. Moylan, one of the 1832–4 assistant poor law commissioners, stated in his report that

> [t]he amount of produce from these small allotments, particularly in the neighbourhood of towns where manure may be had cheap, is quite astonishing – I understand not less than ten or twelve sacks [thirty or thirty-six bushels] of potatoes to the eighth of an acre.[101]

96 LFM cxii (1840), 90.
97 Report on the Employment of Women and Children in Agriculture, 1843, xii. 267.
98 RC on the Employment of Children, Young Persons, and Women in Agriculture, 1868–9. xiii. 475.
99 LFM cxxxvii (1842), 114.
100 LF lxv (1849), 162.
101 RC on the Poor Laws, 1834, xxvii, 268.

Table 8
Crop yields on allotments, 1817–46

Site	County	Date	Yield (bushels/acre)[a]	
			potatoes	wheat
Terrington St Clement	Norfolk	1817	379	30
Byfield	Northants.	1828	480	51
Byfield	Northants.	1829	660	30
Alford	Somerset	1830	300	
Rodbourne	Wiltshire	1830	234	23
Byfield	Northants.	1830	366	39
Alford	Lincs.	1830	350[b]	
Wantage	Berkshire	1831	384	
Kelvedon Hatch	Essex	1831	320	
Tilbury	Essex	1831	328[b]	
Waterbeach	Cambs.	1833		40
Cottesmore[c]	Rutland	1833	570	
Berkswell	Warwicks.	1834	280	36
Cottesmore[c]	Rutland	1834	384	36
Framlingham	Suffolk	1835		26
Barrow	Rutland	1840	418	49
Cottesmore	Rutland	1840	362	27
Exton	Rutland	1840	336	41
Ridlington	Rutland	1840	360	44
West Harptree	Somerset	1841		48
Barrow	Rutland	1841	408	40
Cottesmore	Rutland	1841	360	40
Exton	Rutland	1841	348	40
Ridlington	Rutland	1841	330	42
Barrow	Rutland	1842	512	47
Cottesmore	Rutland	1842	472	44
Exton	Rutland	1842	332	40
Ridlington	Rutland	1842	336	44
Carlton	Notts.	1843	300	
Rothley	Leics.	1843	320	
Rodmarton	Glos.	1844		30
Walsham	Suffolk	1844	300	44[b]
Tingewick	Bucks.	1846		48[b]
Average yields			**361**	**40**

Thirty to thirty-six bushels of potatoes on an eighth of an acre would be between 240 and 288 bushels per acre, which would be within the spectrum of yields given in table 8, although at the lower end of it. A fairly similar estimate came from Robert Hughes, a land agent from Wiltshire, who told the 1837 House of Lords' Select Committee on Agriculture that a labourer could grow twenty sacks of potatoes on a quarter of an acre (240 bushels per acre).[102] Higher estimates came from Alfred Austin, the special assistant poor law commissioner for the south-west in 1843, who stated that the average produce of an acre of allotments was about 300 bushels of potatoes, and from Henry Martin of the West Kent Labourer's Friend Society, who thought that 400 bushels per acre would be below the average figure.[103] *Facts and Illustrations* printed a statement from an unnamed MP to the effect that allotment yields in Leicestershire in the early 1830s averaged 380 bushels of potatoes per acre *per annum*.[104] One of the witnesses to the 1845 Royal Commission on the Framework Knitting gave a somewhat lower estimate, that in a 'good fair average' season, a yield of six to eight strikes a hundred (240 to 320 bushels per acre) would be obtained.[105] At Tilbury in Essex yields ranged from 216 to 440 bushels per acre, depending on manuring, whilst at Pyrton in Oxfordshire 480 bushels per acre was reckoned a good but not exceptional crop.[106] Clearly there is quite a wide variation between these figures, but they are all considerably in excess of the average level of farming yields, and fall either side of the mean value for allotment potato yields given in table 8.

The figures given in the preceding paragraphs were for average yields. But as table 8 demonstrates, allotment-holders who were able to supply more than the average amount of labour, because of having larger families or being

---

[102] *SC of the House of Lords on Agriculture*, 1837, v. 168.

[103] *Report on the Employment of Women and Children in Agriculture*, 1843, xii. 15; *SC on the Labouring Poor*, 1843, vii. 3.

[104] *F&I*, 104.

[105] *RC on the Framework Knitters*, 1845, xv. 532.

[106] *F&I*, 357; *RC on the Poor Laws*, 1834, xxxi. 379.

Key to Table 8

[a] In order as far as possible to exclude atypically high yields recorded on single plots, yield figures have only been included in this table where they were given for the site as a whole, or where it was possible to calculate a figure for the site as a whole.

[b] Range given in original source: mid-point of range given here.

[c] Figures also include yields of Barrow (Rutland) allotments.

Sources: *F&I*, 60, 63–4, 164, 232, 357; *SC of the House of Lords on the Poor Laws*, 1831, viii. 40–7, 198, 349; *LFM* (1834), 39, 79–80; (1835), 190–1; cxxxvi (1842), 96; clvii (1844), 50; *LF* vii (1844), 135–6; xxx (1846), 204–5; *RC on the Poor Laws*, 1834, xxviii. 678; *SC on the Labouring Poor*, 1843, vii. 84, 94; *RC on the Framework Knitters*, 1845, xv; *Gardener's Chronicle*, 4 Jan. 1845, 13, col. 1; *RC on the Employment of Children, Young Persons, and Women in Agriculture*, 1867–8, xvii. 462, 560, 564, 675, 679.

more assiduous, or whose land was particularly fertile, were able to obtain substantially higher yields. At Cottesmore and Barrow in 1833, for example, the mean yield of potatoes for the site as a whole was more than 570 bushels per acre (three times the average farm yields), whilst several allotment-holders at Walsham in Suffolk obtained yields of sixty-four bushels of wheat per acre in 1844 (over three times average farm yields).[107] Exceptional yields on individual plots were of course often even higher.[108] Naturally there were correspondingly low-yielding sites and plots, but the high yields have a particular interest as they indicate what, under good circumstances, allotment-holders might hope to obtain from their plots. As the recent success of the National Lottery appears to demonstrate, the value of an institution may lie at least as much in what participants hope to gain as in what they actually do gain from it.

Calculating nineteenth-century allotment profits is an inexact science, mainly because contemporary statements and estimates rarely specify whether they have costed family labour or not.[109] In general it would seem inappropriate to do so at least for the first half of the nineteenth century, because of the low or even negligible opportunity cost of this labour. So the figures cited in table 9 should be seen as lower-bound calculations unless explicitly excluding the cost of labour.

The average profit for the sites listed in table 9 was £11.37 per acre, or £2.84 for the typical allotment of a quarter of an acre. This is an impressive enough figure. However, it does not fully capture the addition to labourers' incomes provided by allotments, since it was widely accepted that without a sufficient quantity of land it was difficult for labourers to keep pigs.[110] The inadequate number and size of gardens in most parts of arable England probably meant that the majority of southern English labourers fell into this category.[111] Whilst some labourers without land did manage to keep pigs, the introduction of allotments was associated with a sharp rise in the profitability of cottage pig-keeping and in the proportion of labourers who kept them.[112]

---

107 *F&I*, 79; *LF* vii (1844), 136. The Walsham yield figure is not cited in table 8 because it relates to selected plots rather than to the site as a whole.

108 The highest yields I have hitherto encountered for nineteenth-century allotments are one of 18 bushels of wheat on 30 lugs at Wells, Somerset, in 1837 (equivalent to 86 bushels per acre), and another of 11 bushels of potatoes on one rod at Horsmonden, Sussex, in 1840 (1,760 bushels or about 44 tons per acre): *LFM* lxx (1837), 8; cxvi (1840), 166.

109 For a discussion of some of the other difficulties involved in calculating allotment profits see Burchardt, 'The allotment movement', 486–90.

110 *SC on Agriculture*, 1836, viii. 154, q. 3073; *RC on the Handloom Weavers*, 1840, xxiii. 552; *Report on the Employment of Women and Children in Agriculture*, 1843, xii. 15–16, 261, 269, 294–5; *LF* iv (1844), 70; *RC on the Employment of Children, Young Persons, and Women in Agriculture*, 1868–9, xiii. 447. Animals other than pigs were rarely kept on allotments: see appendix 7.

111 J. H. Clapham, *An economic history of modern Britain*, I: *The early railway age, 1820–50*, [1926], Cambridge 1939 edn, 118–21.

112 *F&I*, 334 (after the introduction of allotments, the holders 'all agree in saying this

Table 9
Allotment profits, 1831–45

Site	County	Date	Profit [a] (£/acre)	
Worting St Lawrence	Hampshire	1831	10.00	
Wantage	Berkshire	1831	18.80	b
Kelvedon Hatch	Essex	1831	13.60	b
Byfield	Northants.	1831	10.00	
Avington	Hampshire	1832	11.40	c
Easton	Hampshire	1832	9.55	c
Itchin	Hampshire	1832	9.45	c
Great Missenden	Bucks.	1833	7.71	d
(unspecified)	Essex	1833	13.00	e
Berkswell	Warwickshire	1834	14.00	
Cottesmore and Barrow	Rutland	1834	10.93	f
Nantwich	Cheshire	1845	8.00	
Average profit			**11.37**	

[a] These figures are reported profits per acre averaged over each site.

[b] Does not include labour as a cost.

[c] Includes an aggregate figure for 'labour, carriage and manure'.

[d] Includes an allowance for hired labour (apparently a non-recurrent cost associated with the conversion of the land to allotment use).

[e] Range given in original source: mid-point of range given here.

[f] Includes four days of adult male labour at seed-time as a cost, but not female and child labour.

Sources: F&I, 60, 164, 186, 455–69; LFM (1834), 39, 79–80, 134–6; SC of the House of Lords on the Poor Laws, 1831, viii. 47; William Palin, 'The farming of Cheshire', JRASE v (1844), 97–8.

---

system is the best friend they ever had; they are all better off than they used to be; many, and others who never kept a pig before, keep one or two now for their own consumption, and feed several more which they want themselves for the neighbouring markets': the Revd Lovelace Bigg Wither, 1833); SC on Agriculture, 1833, v. 70, q. 1111 ('they have got their pigs more commonly than I ever remember, but that is very much in consequence of being allowed small portions of land': Robert Hughes, land surveyor, Wiltshire); SC of the House of Lords on Agriculture, 1837, v. 167, qq. 3036–7 (the introduction of allotments had 'very much' increased the agricultural labourers' comforts: 'when I first had management of that estate, there were about 130 cottagers, and there were but very few pigs among them; now there are hardly any without pigs'). G. T. Scobell found that twenty-six of his forty-seven allotment tenants kept pigs; in ten of these cases, the ability to keep a pig was directly attributable to the allotment: LFM (1834), 84.

Allotments provided ample vegetable waste on which one or more pigs could be fed, potatoes or barley to supplement this if necessary, and straw for bedding. The latter was important because farmers, who claimed pig-keeping was associated with theft, often refused to sell straw to labourers, and were sometimes successful in preventing pig-keeping by this means.[113] A large part of the value of an allotment derived from the pig or pigs kept on it. The gross value of the produce of a half-acre allotment at Rodmarton in Gloucestershire in 1844 was, for example, £21 4s. Of this £13 4s. was attributable to the pigs kept on the allotment (a sow worth £2, four pigs sold young at £2 4s. and two fatted pigs at £9).[114] Mid nineteenth-century estimates of the net additional value of a pig to a labourer with an allotment suggest that a single pig was worth at least an additional £1 per annum, and perhaps as much as £2.6.[115] Labourers with allotments were often able to keep two pigs, which would imply an addition to income of between £2 and £5.2.[116] For a labourer able to keep a pig only because of his allotment, the net income derived from an allotment of a quarter of an acre, the most common size of plot, was therefore between £3.84 and £5.44 (or between £4.84 and £8.04 if keeping two pigs). Contemporary estimates of the total financial gain to a labourer fall within this range: the mean of sixteen mid nineteenth-century estimates of the average profit of an allotment is £5.09 per quarter acre.[117]

These high profit figures should cause no surprise given the basis of allotment cultivation. The two main inputs, labour and manure, were in large measure costless. The chief remaining input was seed, which was often obtained by barter with other labourers or saved from the previous year's cultivation, and even if bought was inexpensive.[118] Tools do not appear to have been a major cost: a profit and loss account of a twenty-perch allotment at Horsley in Gloucestershire in 1840 allowed only 6d. for depreciation of tools. If this is representative, it suggests that allotment-holders with plots of the average size of forty perches would have incurred costs for replacing tools of no more than 12d. per year.[119] It was because of the remarkably favourable

---

113 RC on the Employment of Children, Young Persons, and Women in Agriculture, 1867–8, xvii. 534–5, 542.

114 LFM clvii (1844), 55.

115 Report on the Employment of Women and Children in Agriculture, 1843, xii. 15–16 (worth an additional £1.3 per annum); SC on the Labouring Poor, 1843, vii. 341 (worth an additional £1 per annum); W. T. Thornton, Overpopulation and its remedy, London 1846, 347 (worth an additional £2.6 per annum).

116 SC on the Labouring Poor, 1843, vii. 12.

117 LFM lxxxix (1838), 118–19; xciv (1839), 9; cix (1840), 50; cxxii (1842), 41; cxxxvi (1842), 99; SC on the Labouring Poor, 1843, vii. 1, 318; LF xliv (1848), 7; xv (1845), 289; ccxxxi (1870), 22; SC on the Labouring Poor, 1843, vii. 93; RC on the Employment of Children, Young Persons, and Women in Agriculture, 1867–8, xvii. 37, 194; SC on the Inclosure Act, 1868–9, x. 383, q. 506.

118 For a fuller discussion of inputs see Burchardt, 'The allotment movement', 470–2. See also Thompson, Lark Rise, 63.

119 RC on the Handloom Weavers, 1840–1, x. 558.

combination of low input costs and high yields that plots of so small a size could generate such large profits.

To translate profits into living standards presents difficulties, because both wage income and the cost of living were highly variable with respect to time, place, and size and composition of the household. An average is perhaps of more than usually doubtful meaning in this context: all that can be provided is an indication of the approximate contribution allotments may have made to living standards. Broadly speaking, it would seem that, in the second quarter of the nineteenth century, wages for male agricultural labourers across most of arable England south of the Trent, where allotments were most common, were between 9s. and 10s. a week. In parts of Wessex, notably Wiltshire and Dorset, wages were lower than this, but in Kent and some of the other home counties rather higher.[120] Most southern agricultural labourers appear to have suffered winter unemployment (at least in the first half of the nineteenth century), but on the other hand harvest wages were higher than in the rest of the year, and we need also to make allowance for the earnings of women and children.[121] The latter were, however, by the 1830s generally both intermittent and low in value in arable southern England.[122] A rough approximation would be to assume that the value of harvest wages and of women's and children's earnings compensated for winter unemployment, but did no more than this. We would then have a weekly average income of about 10s. per family, or £26 per annum.[123] Using the figures for profits cited above, an allotment of a quarter of an acre, with no pig, would increase annual income by 11 per cent, and, with a pig, by between 15 per cent and 21 per cent. In the second quarter of the nineteenth century an allotment of average size and profitability would therefore have formed an important part of the annual income of most of those agricultural labouring families in southern England fortunate enough to possess one.[124]

By the end of the nineteenth century, the significance of allotments for material living standards would have been less, because of the fall in food prices from the 1870s. Family incomes probably rose a little too: higher male wages and more regular employment seem likely to have more than offset the

---

120 John, 'Statistical appendix', in Mingay, Agrarian history of England and Wales, vi. 1089–1107.
121 Snell, Labouring poor, 28; Reay, Last rising, 43.
122 Snell, Labouring poor, 22, 29–35, 38, 51–6.
123 This figure takes no account of poor relief. Allotments only became common after 1830, i.e. they were essentially a feature of the era of the New Poor Law. Under the New Poor Law relief became more stigmatising and its availability increasingly restricted, rather than being a normal part of family income as it had often been before 1834.
124 Although most rural allotments were rented by agricultural labourers, industrial workers and artisans were a significant minority presence on many sites. However, their incomes varied so widely, both occupationally and over time, that any attempt to calculate an average comparable to that given for the contribution of allotments to the living standards of agricultural labourers would be misleading.

continuing decline in the earnings available to women and children.[125] Nevertheless, as late as 1913–14 Arthur Ashby's authoritative study of rural allotments in Oxfordshire found that in a low-wage county an allotment of only twenty poles (0.125 acres) could contribute as much as 12.5 per cent of total family income.[126] Ashby concluded that 'by the cultivation of vegetables and corn [on an allotment], and by feeding a pig, the labourer is enabled in a low-wage county to keep from his growing family the insistent pangs of hunger, and sometimes put a considerable barrier between himself and the poor-house'.[127]

Valuable as allotments might be, however, from an economic point of view, it was probably their non-material benefits which were of greatest importance to their holders (although the two were, of course, intimately connected). Once again, it seems likely that it was in the first half of the nineteenth century that the benefits were greatest. We need to remember the bleak situation in which most southern agricultural labouring families found themselves at this time. The influences which did so much to undermine rural living standards prior to 1830, notably seasonal unemployment, low wages, deindustrialisation and enclosure (see chapter 1), remained powerful during the following twenty years, albeit on a more intermittent basis.[128] If the excess supply of male labour began to dry up in some areas after 1835, the recovery was patchy and incomplete. Wages remained very low, especially in the south: in 1850 James Caird found that in part of Wiltshire male agricultural labourers were earning only 6s. a week.[129] Women continued to be displaced from activities such as dairying and hay-making by the shift from pasture to arable in the south and east.[130] Changing harvest technology had similar effects: the widespread adoption of the bagging-hook and the scythe, and later the horse-drawn reaper, compressed the high-earnings harvest period and displaced women in the primary operations.[131] Women's and children's work opportunities were reduced still further in much of the south and east by the decline of cottage industry, particularly the textile industry in parts of East Anglia, the west country and Gloucestershire.[132] In addition there were adverse changes in the administration of the poor law. Even before 1834, relief policies became markedly less generous under pressure from rising poor rates, and even though the practice of the new poor law fell a long way short of its theory, there is little doubt that after 1834 many labouring families who would otherwise have sought poor relief were deterred from doing so.

---

[125] Armstrong, Farmworkers, 120–1, 123–4, 132.

[126] Ashby, Allotments and small holdings in Oxfordshire, 60.

[127] Ibid. 78.

[128] Snell, Labouring poor, 138–227.

[129] Caird, English agriculture, 84.

[130] Snell, Labouring poor, 40–5.

[131] Collins, 'Harvest technology', 453–60.

[132] E. J. T. Collins, introduction to chapter v, 'The agricultural servicing and processing industries', in Mingay, Agrarian history of England and Wales, vi. 384–6.

Snell's evidence that the introduction of the new poor law was associated with a subsequent fall in wages suggests that the effects of the act may have been more insidious than was previously realised.[133] For most agricultural workers, male or female, the 1834 act added the prospect of the workhouse to the near-certainty of penury in old age. It was probably also at this time that social relations between labourers and their employers reached their eighteenth- and nineteenth-century low-point. During the early nineteenth century, the social gap between labourers and farmers widened, not only because of the immiseration of southern labourers, but also because of the rise of larger farms and the decline of living-in and annual hiring.[134] Agricultural labourers in early nineteenth-century southern England lived in an environment which was, to an extraordinary extent, dominated in an immediate sense by their employers, and more remotely by the great landowners. In such an environment, and in the context of these economic and social conditions, the likelihood that hard work and self-denial would lead to an escape from poverty and dependency was slight. A chance illness, the birth of an additional child or loss of employment could all unpredictably eliminate any meagre savings that a labouring family had been able to scrape together.

What, other than land provision, was there which could be set against these negative trends? Most obviously, during the Napoleonic wars the prosperity of agriculture and demand for labour created directly and indirectly by the war did something to cushion the longer-term downwards pressure on wages and employment. Some areas and specific localities saw an expansion rather than a contraction of rural industry. The growth of urban employment opportunities, especially in industry, made seasonal migration possible for some groups of agricultural workers, such as those East Anglian labourers who migrated to Lancashire each winter. There was also some expansion of paternalistic charity in the 1830s and 1840s, again affecting some places much more than others.[135] However, especially after 1815 it seems clear that these positive trends were far outweighed by adverse ones.[136] The situation of labourers in the first half of the nineteenth century therefore had little to redeem it, and it is unsurprising that the mood of agricultural labourers and their families appears often to have been one of bitter despair – as exemplified by the riots, threatening letters, arson and animal maiming which characterise rural protest in this, but not in preceding or succeeding periods.

In this context, perhaps the most important contribution made by an allotment to a labouring family was that it provided a source of hope. Obtaining employment was, in the main, not within the control of a labouring family – it depended on economic forces and decisions made by

---

133 Snell, *Labouring poor*, 125–30.
134 A. S. Kussmaul, *Servants in husbandry in early modern England*, Cambridge 1981, 120–5.
135 Roberts, *Paternalism*, 25, 145.
136 Armstrong, *Farmworkers*, 85.

farmers and landowners over which labourers had little influence. But an allotment would produce food, barring exceptional events such as severe droughts or outbreaks of plant disease, so long as the family paid the rent, kept to the conditions of the tenancy and provided adequate labour, manure or other fertiliser and seed. Allotments therefore gave back an area of control over their own lives to labouring families, an area which was admittedly limited, but which offered the prospect of living in modest comfort rather than indigence, and with less fear of the workhouse. Ashby's early twentieth-century observation that an allotment allowed labourers in low-wage counties to put a considerable distance between themselves and the workhouse must have been even more true in the first half of the nineteenth century.[137] Furthermore, there was in general a direct relationship between the time and energy expended on an allotment, and the quantity of produce subsequently obtained. Time which could not otherwise have been put to remunerative use could be 'invested' in allotments, which was why contemporaries frequently described them as 'savings banks for labour'.[138] Allotments could be seen as a form of saving in a financial sense too: allotment-holding labourers were likely to spend a proportion of any spare cash on their plots (for example by buying new seed, tools or additional fertiliser). Because an allotment had a physical, tangible presence, and because the opportunities and benefits of allocating resources to it were likely to be evident to its holder in a way in which the benefits of saving in the abstract were not, allotments encouraged labourers to shift any temporarily spare financial resources from consumption in the present to investment for the future.[139]

A second, valuable, non-economic benefit of an allotment was the mental stimulus it provided. In watching their crops grow, and tending them to ensure that they flourished, labouring families had an absorbing and benign focus for their thoughts.[140] The immense popularity that gardening has enjoyed in many societies widely separated in time and space seems partly to be due to this. Gardening is an intrinsically creative pursuit, where the end result is visibly latent in almost every stage of the process. A related aspect is the contentment and peace that gardening can bring. The pace of plant growth is slow and unhurried in comparison with human activity: there are few garden tasks which require to be done at short notice or over a very constricted time period.[141]

---

137 Ashby, Allotments and small holdings in Oxfordshire, 78.
138 RC on the Employment of Children, Young Persons, and Women in Agriculture, 1868–9, xiii. 450; LFM lxvi (1836), 146; Gardener's Chronicle, 21 Sept. 1844, 642, cols 1–2; F. Clifford, The agricultural lockout of 1874, with notes upon farming and farm-labour in the eastern counties, Edinburgh 1875, 37.
139 C. W. Stubbs, The land and the labourers: a record of facts and experiments in cottage farming and co-operative agriculture, 2nd edn, London 1885, 29.
140 RC on the Employment of Children, Young Persons, and Women in Agriculture, 1868–9, xiii. 155.
141 A. Huxley, An illustrated history of gardening, London 1978, 6–7, 338–40.

Allotments provided not only hope, interest and contentment, but also did much to restore a sense of self-respect to labouring families. Their effects in alleviating poverty were of course important from this point of view but at least equally significant was the relationship between land and social status. The economy of nineteenth-century rural England was overwhelmingly land-based. The three most important social classes in the countryside were defined in large part by their relationship to land. The aristocracy and gentry owned land (the term 'landowner' was used almost synonymously); farmers occupied it; and agricultural labourers, in the main, neither owned nor rented it, but simply cultivated it on behalf of others. In obtaining an allotment, a labouring family therefore achieved a marked rise in terms of the predominant rural status category. Even if an allotment was small, it nevertheless represented land which was as much the labourer's own as a tenant farmer's land was his. W. F. Cowper expressed this aspect of allotment-holding with great clarity:

> The feelings of possession which are given to labouring men [by possessing an allotment] have sometimes produced most remarkable changes in their whole character; the sense of their responsibility, and the delight that arises from being able to speak of a bit of land as belonging to themselves, when they can talk of 'my potatoes' and 'my peas', and 'my beans', – it gives a new current to their thoughts, and is often the commencement of that self-respect which one likes to see in their character.[142] [italics in original]

There was a resemblance between an allotment-holding labourer and a farmer in another respect too. Just as farmers employed labour, so an allotment-holder might himself, if only occasionally and at times of peak requirement, become an employer of labour.[143] This happened increasingly in the second half of the nineteenth century: whilst, in a tighter labour market, labourers of prime working age usually preferred to work for wages, they would employ old men or young boys to harvest their allotment crops or even dig their plots over.[144] The developing labour shortage in agriculture in the second half of the nineteenth century also gave the labourer with an allotment more freedom to turn down low wages and work on his plot instead. In an increasingly weak position, farmers faced with this refusal to work were likely to make a better offer. But without some alternative means of subsistence and profitable occupation, it is doubtful whether such a tactic on the part of a labourer would have been credible, sustainable or effective.

If allotments could provide self-respect and even a measure of independence, they were also a source of pride, as is indicated in the frequent use by

---

142 *LF* lxxxvi (1851), 113.
143 Archer, 'The nineteenth-century allotment', 35.
144 This appears to have been especially common in Northamptonshire: *RC on the Employment of Children, Young Persons, and Women in Agriculture*, 1867–8, xvii. 673, 675, 680, 683, 686, 689–90, 694, 696.

early and mid nineteenth-century labourers of the term 'little farms' to refer to allotments.[145] As we have seen, the yields of allotments normally far surpassed those obtained by most farmers. Especially significant in this respect was the widespread growing of wheat, with its powerful symbolic significance, on allotment sites. Farmers were so hostile to this that some landowners were induced to prohibit it.[146] If labourers with allotments saw themselves as 'little farmers', their employers often resented their presumptuousness in growing wheat and derided their efforts to do so.[147] However, in the second half of the nineteenth century there seems to have been some reduction in farmers' opposition to corn-growing by labourers. This may have been because the falling price of corn made it a less attractive crop for labourers to grow and a less important source of income for farmers. Furthermore, even before the 1850s some farmers had recognised the beneficial effects of allotments in fostering pride amongst labourers. This applied particularly to small farmers with close work and family relationships with labourers and to very large farmers who moved in the same social circles as the gentry and imbibed some of the same cultural influences. Especially significant was the endorsement of allotments by the farming press, including the *Mark Lane Express*, the *Farmers Magazine* and the *Gardeners Chronicle*.[148]

It is indicative of the effects of allotments in fostering pride that they were so closely linked with the rise of local horticultural societies and shows.[149] In the nineteenth century, as now, allotment-holders cherished their fine and carefully nurtured potatoes, cabbages and other vegetables (and in the nineteenth century of course also their corn). Flora Thompson's *Lark Rise* contains a magnificent description of the effect of allotments in this respect – demonstrating that the significance of pride in fine crops was so great in late nineteenth-century Oxfordshire that it could lead labourers to select varieties which actually resulted in a smaller and less appetising food output:

Allotment plots were divided into two, and one half planted with potatoes and the other half with wheat or barley. The garden was reserved for green vegetables, currant and gooseberry bushes, and a few old fashioned flowers. Proud as they were of their celery, peas and beans, cauliflowers and marrows, and fine as were the specimens they could show of these, their potatoes were their special care, for they had to grow enough of these to last the year round. They grew all the old-fashioned varieties – ashleaf kidney, early rose, American rose, magnum bonum, and the huge misshaped white elephant. Everybody knew the elephant was an unsatisfactory potato, that it was awkward to handle when paring, and that it boiled down to a white pulp in cooking; but it produced tubers of such astonishing size that none of the men could resist the temptation to plant it. Every year specimens were taken to the inn to be

145 *LFM* lviii (1836), 2; lxxviii (1837), 121; lxxxi (1837), 180.
146 *RC on the Poor Laws*, 1834, xxviii. 124–6.
147 Archer, 'The nineteenth-century allotment', 35.
148 *LFM* cxi (1840), 81–4.
149 E. Hyams, *English cottage gardens*, London 1970, 116.

weighed on the only pair of scales in the hamlet, then handed round for
guesses to be made of the weight. As the men said, when a patch of elephants
was dug up and spread out, 'You'd got summat to put in your eye and look
at.'[150]

The preference of the men of *Lark Rise* for the elephant potato presumably
did not meet with undiluted enthusiasm from their wives. But in general
allotments made a large contribution to intra-family relationships. One of the
most widely reported consequences of allotment provision was that it made
men less likely to drink to excess.[151] James Brooks, one of the witnesses to the
1843 Select Committee on the Labouring Poor, cited the following case:

> An individual that I know myself, the first time that I spoke to him was when
> he was in a state of intoxication, and that man has become a sober man from
> his allotment. His wife, before I came up, thanked me very much; she was so
> glad because her husband had become acquainted with me; she said he had left
> off drinking and abusing her and her children; she said that if he only kept
> sober (and I have heard since that he has kept sober), they should do tolerably
> well.[152]

There is an echo here of Arthur Young's famous comment about the consequences of depriving the poor of their cows:

> Go to an alehouse kitchen of an old enclosed county, and there you will see
> the origins of poverty and poor rates. For whom are they to be sober? For
> whom are they to save? (Such are their questions). For the parish? If I am dili-
> gent, shall I have leave to build a cottage? If I am sober, shall I have land for a
> cow? If I am frugal, shall I have half an acre of potatoes? You offer no motives;
> you have nothing but a parish officer and a workhouse! – Bring me another
> pot.[153]

Allotments had a double effect from this point of view. In the first place, not
the least of the social deficiencies of the nineteenth-century village was its
dearth of leisure opportunities. Enclosure and a more restrictive attitude on
the part of the gentry to rural leisure pursuits undermined many of the more
robust leisure elements of traditional popular culture, and the invented or
sanitised substitutes did not go far in replacing them. In particular, there was a
lack of 'day-to-day' leisure provision; and in the absence of anything else to
do, village men often turned to the beerhouse, which at least offered warmth,
comfort and company.[154] Allotments, however, provided an interesting and

---

150 Thompson, *Lark Rise*, 63.
151 Clifford, *The agricultural lockout*, 187.
152 *SC on the Labouring Poor*, 1843, vii. 84.
153 Young, *An inquiry*, 13.
154 R. W. Malcolmson, 'Leisure', in Mingay, *Victorian countryside*, ii. 613–14; Hugh
Cunningham, 'Leisure and culture', in F. M. L. Thompson (ed.), *The Cambridge social history
of Britain, 1750–1950*, II: *People and their environment*, Cambridge 1990, 305–6.

rewarding alternative occupation for much of the year (and one which mirrored the pub in terms of providing companionship as well as being out of the house). Secondly, however, allotments were more than merely an alternative venue for leisure. They had a distinct attraction and holding power of their own. All forms of gardening are continuous processes: one task leads into another, and there is almost always something which has been started but not completed, or is obviously waiting to be done. It might be the earthing-up of the potatoes which had been begun but left incomplete, the picking of ripe lettuce, or digging-in of some freshly-gathered manure. Once there on the plot, the activity would have a certain holding-power: the wish to finish what had been begun might keep the labourer working on the plot until dark (and, according to many reports, sometimes even by moonlight).[155]

If a labourer spent less time in the beerhouse, his family was likely to gain in three respects at least. First, less would be spent on alcohol and more would be available for general family purposes. Secondly, a sober labourer with a clear conscience was likely to behave more considerately than a drunken one. Thirdly, the first two factors meant that there was likely to be less conflict and resentment within the family.

The benefits of allotment cultivation for family life, however, extended beyond the issue of drink. Equally important was the fact that for most of the nineteenth century allotment cultivation was a family matter. Much of the work was done by women and children, although men were clearly fully involved as well. The value of shared work for family unity and in militating towards greater equality within the family is obvious, but it is worth noting that Snell's evidence from the letters written by emigrant agricultural labourers indicates that being able to work together was a particularly high priority of nineteenth-century agricultural labouring families.[156] Sensitive contemporary commentators, such as Hardy in *Far from the madding crowd*, echoed this point.[157]

There may have been a decline in the extent to which allotments provided the experience of shared family labour in the last few decades of the nineteenth century, as there is some evidence that women came to regard the allotment as tainted by the grime of field work.[158] In so far as the prejudice against field work came to be held by labouring women themselves, this may have reduced the extent of female participation in allotment cultivation. This may indeed represent the origins of the twentieth-century tradition of the allotment as the place where a man went to get away from his family. However, late nineteenth-century and early twentieth-century accounts show that, even if some women did distance themselves from the allotment,

155 *SC on the Labouring Poor*, 1843, vii. 93.
156 Snell, *Labouring poor*, 9–12, 399–410.
157 T. Hardy, *Far from the madding crowd*, [1874], London 1985 edn, 458–9.
158 Thompson, *Lark Rise*, 114.

there were many others who felt no such inhibitions.[159] Even where women did withdraw from allotment cultivation, this appears to have been a phenomenon limited to the very end of the period we are considering, and children would still have continued to help their fathers on the plot.

If allotments were good for family relationships, they were also good for community relationships – at least amongst the poor themselves. In terms of the social relationships which subsist on them, allotments are a remarkable hybrid of private and public. Each plot is let and cultivated privately and there is often intense competition between plot-holders to produce the largest and finest crops. Yet the plots are not divided from each other by fences, and are bound together collectively by a common external fence. There is typically a single common point of entry to the site, and other facilities, especially water, are often shared. In some respects it is easy to see that allotments correspond to the 'participative competitiveness' which was so marked a feature of much self-generated nineteenth-century working-class leisure.[160] The committee of the Blything Poor Law Union in West Suffolk reported in 1843 that allotments created a 'spirit of emulation, which is felt even by the young of the family, and also by the women, who are much employed on the allotments, each endeavouring to excel his neighbour in the quantity and quality of the produce'.[161] But allotments went beyond 'participant competitiveness' in the extent to which competition was interwoven with co-operation. It appears to have been common, and possibly even normal practice, for allotment-holders to cultivate the plot of someone who was incapacitated by undeserved ill-fortune (for example in the case of injury, illness or recent widowhood).[162] Furthermore, allotment-holders commonly gave each other, and other villagers, gifts of vegetables.[163] This served a double purpose. On the one hand, it was an innocent expression of pride in the skilful cultivation which had produced so fine a specimen. On the other, it was an important part of an 'economy of regard', based on the gift relationship. Allotments provided the material substrate and social matrix in which such an economy could flourish. Without the vegetables obtained from the allotment or the social interchange facilitated by working alongside neighbours on an allotment site, the gift relationship was less easily sustained and developed. In this context, an interesting question is whether allotments breathed new life into the sort of communal interchange which many historians have attributed to common land and the open-field system, or whether the communality of allotments operated in a different way.

159 RC on the Employment of Children, Young Persons, and Women in Agriculture, 1868–9, xiii. 701; H. Levy, Large and small holdings: a study of agricultural economics, Cambridge 1911, 90; Green, A history of the English agricultural labourer, 138–9; Ashby, Joseph Ashby, 111–12.
160 Cunningham, 'Leisure and culture', 316.
161 Report on the Employment of Women and Children in Agriculture, 1843, xii. 259.
162 LFM lxx (1837), 10; Ashby, Joseph Ashby, 134.
163 SC on the Labouring Poor, 1843, vii. 17; Crouch and Ward, The allotment, 94–7.

It is not unreasonable to suggest that the non-economic benefits of allotment provision may have been even more significant than the contribution it made to material living standards. The distinction is, however, artificial: on the one hand, allotments would have had little capacity to generate hope, for example, if they had not increased living standards; and on the other, part of the reason allotment yields were so high was because of the assiduity with which they were cultivated, which in turn was a direct reflection of the hope and pride allotments inspired in their holders.[164] Perhaps the most telling indication of how much more allotments were to the labouring poor than simply a means of supplying food is the names given to allotment sites: names such as 'The Promised Land' and 'Made for Ever'.[165]

The rise of allotments in the nineteenth century needs therefore to be explained as much in terms of why allotment tenants wanted to rent them as why allotment landlords wanted to let them. But although the letting of an allotment depended on the participation of both landlord and tenant, the question of where the impetus for allotment provision came from remains. Were the rural poor passive, reactive recipients of landlords' unprompted initiative? Or did they play a more active role in stimulating allotment provision?

In some parts of the country, and among some occupational groups, prospective tenants played a prominent role in securing allotments. This was most obviously true in the east Midlands. Here the allotment movement had a very different character than in southern England. The aristocracy, gentry and clergy unsurprisingly remained the most important providers of land: of ninety-one allotment sites listed in the *Report of the Royal Commission on the Framework Knitters* of 1845, at least sixty-one were let by peers, baronets or clergymen.[166] However, these social groups played a less active part in promoting allotments than they did in southern England. Prospective tenants took matters into their own hands in many villages in the east Midlands: they formed committees and societies, which collected subscriptions from an often extensive membership, and lobbied local landowners to offer land for allotments. Whilst landowners and clergymen often featured as honorary members of these allotment societies, their direction and day-to-day running was in the hands of the working men: as Orange noted, the main reason for having the gentry on the committees was to give security for the payment of rent.[167] In the east Midlands it was, therefore, prospective

[164] It is of course largely because of their non-economic benefits that allotments have survived as an important feature of the contemporary landscape. A survey in the late 1960s suggested that only 17% of allotment holders rented their plots primarily for economic reasons: Moran, 'Origin and status', 165–6.

[165] 'The Promised Land': Tysoe (Warwickshire); 'Made for Ever': Colerne (Wiltshire): *F&I*, 33; Ashby, *Joseph Ashby*, 133.

[166] *RC on the Framework Knitters*, 1845, xv. 138–9.

[167] *SC on the Labouring Poor*, 1843, vii. 95.

tenants who were the active force; landlords did little other than provide land, and that often tardily.

One of the important aspects of the allotment movement in the east Midlands was its different social constituency from the movement in southern England. In Leicestershire, Nottinghamshire and Derbyshire, it was framework knitters rather than agricultural labourers who made up the majority of allotment tenants. It seems likely that this occupational contrast partly explains the more energetic, active character of the demand for allotments in the east Midlands. This seems to be borne out by evidence relating to another group of impoverished outworkers, the handloom weavers of Gloucestershire. Whilst not demonstrating as impressive or persistent a degree of organisation as the framework knitters, the Gloucestershire handloom weavers also actively lobbied local landowners for allotments. One of the most striking examples of this can be found in the minutes of evidence of the *Royal Commission on the Handloom Weavers* of 1840. These describe how a delegation of weavers presented a proposal to W. A. Miles, the assistant commissioner, for the division of Bisley Commons into allotments. The wording of the proposal, as recorded by Miles, was:

> The common should be portioned out in 'lotments [sic] to families in proportion to their number, and to descend, by right of inheritance, from heir to heir, and that every possessor should pay a penny per lug [i.e. perch] annually, to assist in maintaining the workhouse poor; and in default of heirs, that the minister should let the land to some other family.[168]

Across most of southern England, it was quite different. There are very few recorded instances of rural labourers making formal requests for land provision. Furthermore, although the rural poor in most parts of England seem to have valued allotments highly once they had had direct experience of them, the initial reaction to the establishment of an allotment site was not always so favourable. Quite commonly, it was only after one or two years that the tenants came to prize their allotments.[169] This initial suspicion can probably best be understood as a measure of the depth of distrust existing between labourers and their social superiors in the 1830s and 1840s. Understandably, labourers were inclined to suspect that darker intentions lay behind the smiling face of landowner benevolence. In the case of allotments, there was some specific justification for this. Some early allotments, for example, were

---

168 *RC on the Handloom Weavers*, 1840, xxiv. 550.
169 Amongst the villages where this pattern was reported were Littlebury, Tilbury and Wenden in Essex, Eynsham Hall and Studley in Oxfordshire, Cranborne in Dorset, Cheshunt in Hertfordshire, Hessle in the East Riding, Northallerton in the North Riding, Tingewick in Buckinghamshire and Hitcham in Cambridgeshire: *F&I*, 19–20, 224, 357, 443; *LFM* (1834), 14; lxx (1837), 6; lxii (1836), 84; clix (1844), 88; *Report on the Employment of Women and Children in Agriculture*, 1843, xii. 128, 331–2; *LF* xxxx (1846), 204–5; (1852), 66–73.

let on condition that labourers forgo eligibility to poor relief. By the 1830s, this condition was very rarely made, but the link between landowner allotments and the loss of entitlement to poor relief may have remained in labourers' minds.

However, although labourers may have been suspicious of the intentions of landowners, this does not foreclose the possibility that they put pressure on landowners to let land to them. It remains quite possible that southern agricultural labourers were not as passive as they appear to have been with respect to allotment provision. We need to remember that we face an intractable problem of source bias in attempting to understand whether allotment provision was granted freely from on high, or was prompted by pressure from below. Almost all the surviving information about allotment provision emanates from those who belonged to what we might describe as the allotment-letting rather than the allotment-renting class. The reports of the SBCP, the magazines and papers of the LFS and SICLC, parliamentary reports and papers, newspaper articles – none of these directly report the words of the rural poor. Initiatives taken by the poor at a local level to secure allotment provision will almost certainly be under-represented. This applies with even more force to the less literate labourers of agricultural southern England than it does to the better-educated textile outworkers of the Cotswolds and east Midlands.

A small number of incidents in which southern English agricultural labourers took active steps to obtain allotments in the 1830s and 1840s is recorded in the evidence. One early example was at Bozeat in Northamptonshire, from where a letter addressed by labourers to a local landowner has survived.[170] There may have been many other cases where labourers made their feelings known to local landowners in less formal ways – either by waiting on the landowner in person, or through other channels of communication such as the incumbent of the parish, rent-collectors or domestic servants. The social equilibrium of rural parishes was delicate, and many landowners would have responded negatively to an outright, formal request for land provision. But that need not imply that landowners were unresponsive to more indirectly-stated requests. On the contrary, the implicit bargain on which landowner benevolence rested was precisely that requests for assistance made within the language and framework of deference would be received sympathetically. It is, therefore, quite possible that the apparent passivity of southern agricultural labourers in the first half of the nineteenth century is at least in part an illusion. Allotments may sometimes have been prompted by pressure from below rather than merely being handed down from on high. This, however, must remain but an attractive and plausible hypothesis unless more evidence of active initiative on the part of southern agricultural labourers can be found.

[170] LFM lix (1836), 36.

7

The Social Consequences of Allotments

Once we are aware of the strength of demand for allotments among rural workers for most of the nineteenth century, and of the very good reasons they had for wanting them, the importance of allotments to the individuals who rented them is manifest. But to assess the social consequences of allotment provision we need to know more about who these tenants actually were, and how adequate the provision of allotments was in proportion to the number of those who wanted to rent them.

In the mid-nineteenth century, allotments were generally seen as being provided for, and occupied by, agricultural labourers. It was no accident that the main organisation promoting allotments was entitled the Labourer's Friend Society; and even a cursory reading of any one of the society's publications is enough to make it clear that the labourer referred to was a field worker. Parliamentary committees and commissions from the great poor law inquiry of 1832–4 onwards similarly saw allotments as being essentially connected with agricultural labourers. Even as late as 1913, when the Land Enquiry Committee published its report on *The land*, political discussion of allotments was still focused almost entirely on the needs of the agricultural labourer.[1] But as we saw in the last chapter, rural artisans and industrial workers also sometimes wanted to rent allotments, and on many sites – perhaps even a majority – agricultural labourers were not the only occupational group represented. Of fifty-five sites for which evidence from this period about the occupations of allotment tenants survives, on only four was 'agricultural labourer' the sole occupation represented. On the remaining fifty-one sites, some of the allotment-holders were not agricultural labourers. Admittedly, contemporaries seem generally only to have found the occupation of an allotment-holder worthy of comment if he were not an agricultural labourer, so these figures undoubtedly give an inflated impression of the extent to which those who were not agricultural labourers held plots. But even allowing for this, it is clear that on a significant number of sites, agricultural labourers were not the only tenants.

Those allotment-holders who were not agricultural labourers seem to have come from a fairly wide range of occupations. On the fifty-five sites mentioned above, twenty-five different occupations were recorded, ranging from fishermen on a site in Hampshire to college servants on an Oxford site. This may even be an underestimate, because on some of these sites general

---

1   Land Enquiry Committee, *The land*, i.

Table 10
Occupations of allotment holders on four sites, 1793–1873

Site	Falmer, Sussex	Upton, Hunts.	Timsbury, Somerset	Horsley, Glos.	All sites
Date	1831	1833	1834	1840	
Agricultural labourers	20 80%	3 50%	11 19%	31 47%	65 42%
Miners	–	–	48 81%	–	48 31%
Weavers	–	–	–	19 29%	19 12%
Widows	–	–	–	6 9%	6 4%
Masons	3 12%	–	–	1 2%	4 3%
Plasterers	–	–	–	4 7%	4 3%
Shoemakers	–	–	–	2 3%	2 1%
Blacksmiths	1 4%	–	–	1 2%	2 1%
Odd-job	–	2 33%	–	–	2 1%
General labourer	1 4%	–	–	–	1 1%
Carpenters	–	–	–	1 2%	1 1%
Gardeners	–	1 17%	–	–	1 1%
Shopkeepers	–	–	–	1 2%	1 1%
Total	**25**	**6**	**59**	**66**	**156 100%**

Sources: *F&I*, 210; *RC on the Poor Laws*, 1834, xxviii. 677; *LFM* (1834), 85; *RC on the Handloom Weavers*, 1840, x. 557–8

descriptive terms such as 'tradesman' or 'artisan' were used. The most commonly mentioned occupations, other than agricultural labourer, artisan/mechanic and tradesman (thirty-six, fourteen, and eleven mentions respectively), were cloth-workers (nine mentions), shoemakers (six mentions), bricklayers and masons (five mentions), miners (four mentions) and general labourers (four mentions). For four sites, complete lists of the occupations of the allotment-holders survive (see table 10).

Whilst it would be hazardous to make generalisations on the basis of only four cases, table 10 does highlight the diversity of occupations which might be found among allotment-holders, and in particular the fact that on many sites a few artisans and small tradesmen seem to have rented plots. However, whilst the sites described in table 10 are probably typical in terms of the range of occupations represented on them, they are almost certainly less so when it comes to the proportion of tenants who belonged to the different occupations listed. In particular, the figure of 42 per cent for the proportion of tenants on the four sites combined who were agricultural labourers seems very low, whilst the figures of 31 per cent for miners and 12 per cent for cloth-workers seem correspondingly too high. As can be seen from table 10, the latter two figures each derive from a single site. Neither site is typical: Timsbury was one of a small group of mining villages in East Somerset, whilst Horsley was part of the clothing district centred on Stroud in Gloucestershire. Of the four sites in table 10, Falmer, being purely agricultural, is probably the most representative.

Other than agricultural labourers, the group of workers for whom allotments were of most importance was probably domestic outworkers. It is true that there were few outworkers across much of the region in which the allotment movement was most active, i.e. rural southern England, and that both in terms of number of plots rented and of the proportion of sites on which they rented plots, domestic outworkers were, to judge by frequency of mentions, probably of relatively limited significance at a national level. But in areas where there were concentrations of outworkers, they often outnumbered agricultural labourers on allotment sites. There are five main identifiable areas where this was the case. The first was the woollen cloth district around Trowbridge, Bradford-on-Avon, Westbury, Warminster, Frome and Shepton Mallet in Wiltshire and Somerset. The second was the Gloucestershire clothing district, particularly around Stroud (Horsley was in this area). Third was the framework-knitting district of the east Midlands, stretching roughly in a triangle between Leicester, Nottingham and Derby. Fourth was the shoemaking area of Northamptonshire. Finally, there was the north Worcestershire and south Staffordshire ironware district. Nailmakers, and to a lesser extent other ironworkers, were particularly often found on allotment sites in this area.[2] The work patterns of rural industrial workers

2 For a fuller account of the relationship between allotment provision and domestic

often matched the labour requirements of allotment cultivation well, but from the point of view of understanding the social implications of allotment provision, what is more important is that all five of these categories of outworkers suffered sharp declines in real incomes in the mid-nineteenth century as a result of competition from the more highly mechanised urban sector, to the point where their living standards were little, if at all, higher than those of agricultural labourers in their regions.

Allotments were, therefore, mainly let to the most impoverished occupational groups within rural society, especially to labourers. However, the consequences of allotment provision were affected by their intra-occupational as well as inter-occupational distribution. Whether or not a given individual was able to rent a plot, even assuming the existence of an accessible allotment site, depended on whether the individual met the eligibility criteria governing the site and whether there were vacant plots available to rent.

One of the most frequent eligibility criteria used by landlords to limit demand was to restrict allotment tenancy to inhabitants of the parish in which the site was located, and sometimes to those with a legal settlement in the parish.[3] In some parishes, this was the only hurdle that would-be tenants had to overcome, as when allotments were provided they were offered to all labourers who wanted them, and enough land was set out to provide for all applicants. This was the case, for example, at the earliest three known allotment sites, Long Newnton, Ashley and Shipton Moyne.[4] But it was rare that enough land was available for this to be possible, and some method of selecting applicants had to be devised. The commonest, especially in the 1830s, seems to have been to give priority to those with the largest families.[5] However, applicants were also commonly selected by lot, or simply on a first-come-first-served basis.[6] There was disagreement over whether applicants should be selected on the basis of their moral character. On the one hand, it was felt that applicants of good moral character were more deserving, would make better tenants and would reflect more credit on the allotment system, and – most important – if allotments were made available only to those of good character, this would act as a potentially strong incentive to labourers to gain and maintain a good character.[7] But on the other hand, the

outwork in Somerset, Gloucestershire, the east Midlands, Northamptonshire and the black country see Burchardt, 'The allotment movement', 404–25.

3   Under the provisions of 59 Geo III c 12 and 1 and 2 Will IV c 42, eligibility to allotment tenancy under the acts was explicitly limited to parishioners, whilst 2 Will IV c 42 made allotments available only to those with a legal settlement in the parish. Such restrictions seem also to have been common for sites let privately (see, for example, SC on the Labouring Poor, 1843, vii. 98).

4   SBCP, Reports, v. 71–83.

5   Report on the Employment of Women and Children in Agriculture, 1843, xii. 15.

6   F&I, 171.

7   SC of the House of Lords on the Poor Laws, 1830–1, viii. 292; LF xxxiv (1847), 41–2.

more ardent advocates of allotments argued that the great virtue of allotments was precisely that they were capable of reclaiming those labourers thought to be of bad character. It was then argued, logically enough, that the system would only have a chance to realise its full benefits if bad characters just as much as good were admitted to it. Many of these more enthusiastic advocates of allotments took pride in pointing to examples from their own sites of bad characters reclaimed by working an allotment.[8] At Hadlow, in Kent, for example, the *Labourer's Friend Magazine* reported that

> in receiving the tenants but little regard is paid to character, as the object of the [West Kent Labourer's Friend] society is to reclaim the indolent and reward the industrious; and the propriety of this plan was made apparent at the last meeting, when one of the tenants received a prize for good conduct who had been previously one of the worst characters in the parish.[9]

A related but distinct issue was how easy it should be to get a plot. In general it was thought desirable for plots to be available to all who wanted them, but there was a minority current of opinion which urged that there should be a certain shortfall, so that there would be competition for plots. This, it was thought, would increase the value placed upon the plots by those who had them, and cause those who did not to behave impeccably in an attempt to ensure that if a plot did fall vacant they would be favoured with it.[10]

An important question in this context is whether there was a threshold income below which the labouring poor could not afford to rent allotments. Conceivably, if the start-up costs of renting a plot had been sufficiently high, those labourers who most needed allotments might not have been able to afford to rent them. What, then, were the main costs to labourers of becoming an allotment tenant? Much the most significant expense was the rent itself. This was usually paid annually in arrears, although occasionally quarterly payments were preferred.[11] A lump sum annual payment of 10s. – the average rent of a quarter-acre plot – represented a substantial sum for an agricultural labourer – more than the typical weekly wage of a male agricultural labourer in southern England.

However, there were several respects in which the burden of the rent was in

---

8 *SC on the Labouring Poor*, 1843, vii. 92, 110–11; *LF* xxix (1846), 185.
9 *LFM* cxxxiii (1838), 25.
10 *SC of the House of Lords on the Poor Laws*, 1830–1, viii. 292. John Archer has suggested that allotments created a line of division within villages between the 'respectable', who had allotments, and the 'rough', who had no hope of obtaining them. The most important component of the latter category were single young men. This may have been the case in some villages but the important unit with respect to allotment cultivation was the household rather than the individual. Those single young men who lived on their own in any case stood to gain less from allotments than other villagers because they did not have under-utilised female and child labour to call upon: Archer, 'The nineteenth-century allotment', 31–2.
11 Burchardt, 'The allotment movement', 341–2.

fact less than it appeared. First, rent was usually paid on Michaelmas day, by which time part at least of the harvest had already been taken in. These crops could have been sold to raise the cash required for the rent; alternatively, the sum required to pay the rent could have been borrowed against the security of crops which had not yet been harvested, or (for allotment-holders in their second or subsequent year of tenancy) financed out of the savings achieved by the previous year's crop. Secondly, Michaelmas fell at the height of the farm harvest period, when employment was at its peak and wages at their highest. Almost all areas of southern England, especially the more arable areas where allotments were most widespread, experienced an excess of demand for labour over supply during harvest, as is evident from the frequent use of migratory labour, the high level of harvest wages and the seasonal pattern of poor relief payments apparent from settlement examination data. Demand for female and child labour was also high during harvest in arable areas. So almost all the rural labouring poor capable of working would have been in receipt of good wages at the time the rent for allotments was due. Indeed, one of the difficulties faced by agricultural labourers in the nineteenth century was to spread their extremely uneven income flow over the year. Income-smoothing mechanisms were inadequately developed in the nineteenth-century English village, especially in the first half of the century. Village-based friendly societies and savings banks were neither sufficiently universal nor actuarially sound to provide an effective solution, whilst the large county and national friendly societies which established so many branches in the countryside in the second half of the century had a less significant presence prior to the 1860s. The uneven incidence of allotment rent was in this respect actually an advantage: allotments served, amongst their other purposes, an income-smoothing function.[12]

The one group amongst the rural poor that would not have been able to afford allotment rent is that which would have been unable to save, borrow or raise the equivalent of a year's rent by the sale of crops. But there can have been few labouring households unable to accumulate a sum of 10s. by Michaelmas in the course of a year's work. Even those whose incomes were likely to be lowest – widows and old men – are recorded as allotment tenants.

It is therefore unlikely that the level and incidence of allotment rent was high enough to prevent any large group amongst the rural poor from renting allotments. What about other costs? As we saw in the last chapter, these were usually low. Hired labour was rarely used, at least in the first half of the century. Seed was cheap and was sometimes provided free by allotment landlords. From the second year of tenancy onwards seed could also be obtained by exchange with other

---

[12] Rural artisans and industrial workers did not experience such regular seasonal income fluctuations and would have benefited less from the income-smoothing function of allotment rent. Because they were unlikely to have as much disposable income at Michaelmas as agricultural labourers, they may have found the incidence of allotment rent more burdensome. For evidence that framework knitters sometimes had difficulties in paying allotment rents (and that labourers did not) see RC on the Framework Knitters, 1845, xv. 842, q. 3003.

allotment tenants. The tools required for allotment cultivation were also cheap and simple: nothing more than a wooden spade was essential, although without a hoe weeding would be laborious and preparation of the seed-bed more difficult. The main difficulty other than rent for an incoming allotment tenant with low household earnings and entitlements was likely to be finding enough manure. Whilst pigs were not expensive, there may have been some labouring families who could not afford to buy them, and in this case the best potential source of manure for an allotment would be debarred. However, there were other sources of manure, notably that gathered from the roads. Any household with underutilised labour resources – which probably included most households with children or elderly people – could exploit this. Families with no underutilised labour resources would be likely to have a high enough level of wage income to be able to afford to buy a pig or, less efficiently, to buy manure directly. Very few of the rural poor can have been unable for financial reasons to take advantage of allotments.

The main limitation on the uptake of allotments was probably therefore their availability rather than their affordability, or indeed restrictions on eligibility. So what was the ratio between the supply of allotments and the potential demand? Table 11, based on data from the 1873 return and from the 1871 census, gives some indication. It shows, on a county-by-county basis, the number of allotments per male agricultural labourer (outdoor labourer and shepherd) aged ten and over.[13]

Table 11 shows that by 1873 there was one allotment for every three male agricultural labourers in England: allotments were widely but not universally available. Significantly, however, the ratio between the number of allotments and the number of male agricultural labourers was better than average in many of the counties in which wages were lowest. In Wiltshire, the lowest wage county of all according to Caird's 1851 survey, there was one allotment for every 1.6 male agricultural labourer, and in Dorset, probably next after Wiltshire in the league table of low-wage counties, there was one allotment for every 2.2 male agricultural labourers. The most obvious exceptions were the East Anglian counties of Essex and Norfolk, with ratios of 5.3 and 6.6 male agricultural labourers respectively per allotment, and Sussex, with a ratio of 11.4 to 1. The three counties with the best ratios were Leicestershire, Derbyshire and Nottinghamshire, but these figures are inflated by the large number of allotments rented by framework knitters in the east Midlands.

13 The most relevant measure of the adequacy of allotment provision would be the number of rural labouring households per allotment rather than the number of male agricultural labourers aged ten and over. The problems of definition and data collection involved in calculating a household measure are, however, considerable and must await further research. That being said, the number of male agricultural labourers aged ten and over per allotment may in fact not be very far removed from the number of rural labouring households per allotment. Many rural labouring households contained more than one male agricultural labourer aged over ten but this is counterbalanced by the fact that others contained none and that not all allotments were let to agricultural labourers.

Table 11
Number of male agricultural labourers aged ten and over per allotment in 1873

County	No. of allotments	Male agricultural labourers aged ten and over per allotment
Leics.	17,168	0.7
Derby	5,628	0.9
Notts.	11,317	1.0
Northants.	16,447	1.4
Warks.	12,794	1.4
Wilts.	15,445	1.6
Rutland	1,252	1.8
Bucks.	8,632	1.9
Yorks. (N.R.)	4,731	1.9
Beds.	8,364	2.0
Oxon	9,088	2.1
Dorset	7,322	2.2
Cambs.	9,596	2.3
Hunts.	3,376	2.5
Glos.	7,552	2.6
Staffs.	5,444	2.6
Somerset	9,503	2.7
Worcs.	4,919	2.7
Yorks. (W.R.)	6,876	3.1
Suffolk	11,664	3.4
Herts.	5,197	3.6
Devon	7,063	3.7
Berks.	5,007	4.2
Hants.	6,712	4.5
Durham	1,000	5.1
Lincs.	7,430	5.2
Northumb.	968	5.2
Essex	8,269	5.3
Yorks. (E.R.)	1,781	5.6
Norfolk	6,400	6.6
Cornwall	1,762	7.0
M'sex	689	9.0
Kent	4,150	9.5
Hereford	997	9.7
Cumb.	410	11.3

County	No. of allotments	Male agricultural labourers aged ten and over per allotment
Sussex	2,782	11.4
Surrey	1,263	11.9
Salop	1,002	14.5
Ches.	929	14.7
Lancs.	992	20.9
Westmor.	52	29.7
England	**241,973**	**3.1**

Sources: Calculated from *Agricultural Returns of Great Britain for 1873*, 1873 lxix. 301–74, and B. Afton and M. Turner, 'The statistical base of agricultural performance in England and Wales, 1850–1914', in E. J. T. Collins (ed.), *The agrarian history of England and Wales*, VII/2: *1859–1914*, Cambridge 2000, 1986, 1992.

Allotments therefore not only made an impressive contribution to the living standards of those who rented them but were available in quite large numbers in proportion to the size of their primary occupational constituency by 1873. It seems *prima facie* likely that something which had such important effects on the lives of so many agricultural labourers would also have had a significant impact on rural social relations in this period. Contemporaries were, indeed, in little doubt that this was the case, above all in the second quarter of the nineteenth century, when many amongst the rural ruling class believed that allotments were the best, or even the only, way of averting social breakdown in the countryside.[14] In the late nineteenth and early twentieth centuries the social effects of allotments were still seen as important: they could slow the 'rural exodus' and provide a vital first step on an 'agricultural ladder' by means of which the aspiring young labourer could achieve upward social mobility.[15] For most of the twentieth century, however, historians have failed to recognise the importance which contemporaries attributed to the social effects of allotments. The general consensus has been that allotments were no more than a footnote in the history of the nineteenth-century countryside. The Hammonds, whilst acknowledging that allotments could bring benefits where introduced, believed that 'experiments in the provision of allotments of any kind were few', and regarded the allotments legislation of 1831 as the 'merest mockery' of Lord Suffield's hopes for a generous policy of land provision.[16] Mingay's assessment of the significance of allotments in mitigating the

14 Edwards, 'The influence of free trade', 567; *Oxford Herald*, 7 Nov. 1835, cited in *LFM* lxii (1836), 85.
15 J. Frome Wilkinson, 'Pages in the history of allotments', *Contemporary Review* lxv/340 (Apr. 1894), 537; Earl Carrington, 'The land and the labourers', *Nineteenth Century* xl/265 (Mar. 1899), 368, 373; H. Rider Haggard, *Rural England*, London 1902, 239–42.
16 Hammond and Hammond, *Village labourer*, 134, 300.

hardships of rural life is scarcely more favourable: 'However much allotments or gardens became available to farm labourers in the first half of the nine-teenth century, such access could effect only a marginal improvement in family living standards and do little to provide any real independence.'[17]

No full-scale academic treatment of the history of the allotment move-ment has ever been published, and until recently the only available account of any substance was Barnett's article of 1967.[18] Since 1995, Moselle, Archer and Burchardt have all published articles on allotments, but in each case focusing on the opposition to allotments rather than on their significance in themselves.[19] Nor are there any signs of a re-evaluation of the importance of allotments in the broader historiography of nineteenth-century society. One of the most ambitious and well-received recent textbooks, Martin Daunton's *Progress and poverty: an economic and social history of Britain, 1700–1850*, does not contain a single reference to allotments in the index.[20]

But there are good reasons – aside from intrinsic likelihood – for believing that nineteenth-century contemporaries understood better than twen-tieth-century historians the importance of allotments within the social struc-ture. The remainder of this chapter substantiates the views of contemporaries firstly through a general overview of the effects of allotment provision on three key sets of relationships (between labourers and farmers, farmers and landowners and landowners and labourers). Secondly, it considers in more detail the consequences of allotment provision for criminality, protest, poli-tics and trade unionism.

Relations between farmers and agricultural labourers in the south of England were already bad in the 1820s. But allotments were a significant new source of friction and antagonism. The ultimate cause of this may have been the threat to the clarity of existing status divisions: as we have seen, labourers who had land often liked to refer to themselves as 'little farmers' and to grow their own corn. Farmers reacted with surprising bitterness to this infringe-ment of their monopoly as landholders and corn-growers. But there were also economic reasons underlying farmers' opposition. It has been argued, for example, that allotments increased the efficiency wage farmers had to pay labourers to secure their labour or at least their effort.[21] This was probably more true in the second half of the century than in the first (when labourers were not usually in a sufficiently strong position to refuse work, or to displease an employer through slacking). Perhaps equally significant was the fact that

[17] G. E. Mingay, 'Conclusion: the progress of agriculture, 1750–1850', in Mingay, *Agrarian history of England and Wales*, vi. 967.
[18] Barnett, 'Allotments and the problem of rural poverty'.
[19] Moselle, 'Allotments, enclosure, and proletarianization', 482–500; Archer, 'The nine-teenth-century allotment', 21–36; Burchardt, 'Rural social relations', 165–75.
[20] Daunton, *Progress and poverty*.
[21] Moselle, 'Allotments, enclosure, and proletarianization', 495–8.

allotments tended to drive out potato grounds. Both the terms on which potato grounds were let and the benefits they could yield were far inferior to those typical of allotments. But for farmers potato grounds offered corresponding advantages, and they were not pleased when they were upstaged by the landowners' allotment movement. Farmers further complained that allotments led to theft (if the labourer was growing crops, he could supposedly easily steal crops from the farmer and, if caught, claim they were his own), and that labourers working long hours on their allotments were too exhausted to work effectively for their employers the next day.[22] Whilst not all farmers were hostile to allotments (there is some evidence that small farmers employing labour only intermittently may have had a more favourable attitude, for example), many were extremely antipathetic, their antagonism finding expression in jibes, refusals to lend equipment, and in some instances refusing to employ labourers who had allotments.[23]

An interesting social consequence of allotments which has received little attention is their effect on relations between farmers and landowners. Farmers bitterly resented allotments, and thus by implication the landlords who provided them. An aspect which caused particular bad feeling was the allocation of land for allotments. 'Spare', uncultivated, land very rarely existed close to English villages in the nineteenth century, so if allotments were to be provided the land had usually to be removed from some existing use. Often this meant a landowner persuading or coercing a farmer into giving up a piece of land which the farmer might naturally regard as 'his', and which might indeed be an integral part of his farm operation. Whilst farmers reacted grudgingly or even bitterly to the efforts of landowners to promote allotments, landowners for their part were dismayed by what they saw as the narrow or even downright selfish attitude of farmers.

The difficulties over allotments came at a particularly sensitive time in relations between farmers and landowners: the second quarter of the nineteenth century saw farmers increasingly unhappy at the way in which landowners were representing their views and interests in parliament. Their problems mainly related to the corn laws, and to a lesser extent concerned subsidiary issues such as tithes and the malt tax, and led to a flirtation with Cobbetite political radicalism in the 1820s, and in the 1840s contributed to the split in the Conservative Party over the repeal of the corn laws. Whilst landowners took a rather broader and more political view, farmers were less likely to see beyond their immediate economic horizons. Landowners were more conscious of the need to conciliate urban middle-class opinion, which might involve modifying or even repealing the corn laws. Differences of opinion over allotments damagingly mirrored the tensions over the corn laws, in that once again landowners could see themselves taking a more

22 Anne Digby, 'Social institutions', in Collins, *Agrarian history of England and Wales*, vii/1, 1471.
23 Burchardt, 'Rural social relations', 169–74.

generous and politically far-sighted stance in the face of apparently bigoted and mean-spirited resistance from farmers.[24]

Relations between labourers and landowners seem, in contrast, to have improved as a result of allotments. It was the intention of the landowners who advocated and let allotments that they should bring about a marked change in this respect, and certainly there is much evidence that labourers were grateful for allotments, not all of which can easily be dismissed as wishful thinking on the part of landowners. Many allotment-holders, for example, brought their landlords gifts of produce.[25] Nor should we be surprised by gratitude in the context of what we now know about the benefits brought by allotments. Some support for the view that the allotment movement was a significant chapter in the history of relations between labourers and landowners is lent by Archer's work on East Anglia, which suggests that after 1830 landowners were more rarely the victims of arson attacks (whilst tenant farmers found their stackyards alight more often).[26]

We can gauge the social implications of allotments more accurately by assessing their effects on four central aspects of the relationship between the labouring poor and rural society: criminality, protest, political activism and trade unionism. It will be argued that allotments made labourers more 'respectable', and in so doing diminished criminality and riotousness; but that they had no general tendency to suppress political or economic conflict, and in some respects promoted them.

The effect of allotments on rural crime

In the 1830s and 1840s landowners were desperate to find a way of reducing the level of rural crime. It is not therefore surprising to find them looking hopefully towards allotments as the means by which this might be achieved, and equally unsurprising that proponents of allotments sought to underpin their arguments by claiming that allotments did reduce crime. A character-istic statement – taken almost at random from hundreds of similar examples – made by a contributor to the *Labourer's Friend Magazine* was that 'burglary, poaching and intemperance, together with incendiarism, fly from every neighbourhood into which [the allotment system] has once entered'.[27] But although the elements of wishful thinking in the landowners who hoped that allotments would reduce crime and of bias in the evidence cited by advocates of allotments are easy to detect, there are nevertheless good reasons for believing that allotments did reduce rural crime. First, crime in the country-side was closely associated with poverty. Theft of food (notably vegetables) or

[24] Ibid. 174.
[25] F&I, 173.
[26] Archer, By a flash and a scare, 147–8, and 'The nineteenth-century allotment', 26–7.
[27] LFM lxi (1836), 72.

fuel (mainly wood) were amongst the commonest rural crimes. Crimes of protest, such as rick burning and animal maiming, were also associated with areas, such as East Anglia, and periods, such as the 1830s and early 1840s, in which the living standards of agricultural labourers were especially low. Allotments significantly raised living standards, so it would be surprising if they had no effect on rural crime.

A second consideration is that the rules of perhaps as many as half of all allotment sites specified that any tenant found guilty of a criminal offence would be evicted.[28] Since allotments were both highly valuable and highly valued, it is reasonable to suppose that fear of losing a plot would have been a deterrent. How effective a deterrent this would have been presumably depended on the increment to income provided by the allotment; land-owners who let allotments on good soil, close to the tenants' houses, at low rents, may have achieved better results with respect to crime reduction than those who were less generous.

Even on the approximately 50 per cent of sites where the rules did not specify that a criminal conviction would end the tenancy, it is possible that fear of eviction operated to reduce crime. Allotments were let on an annual basis, so whatever the rules stated, an allotment landlord could normally get rid of a tenant who had incurred his displeasure within a few months, simply by refusing to renew his tenancy. Some allotment landlords believed so firmly in the reformative powers of allotments that they may have been unwilling to deprive tenants who committed crimes of their plots, whilst other landowners probably exercised lax supervision and failed to evict lawbreakers through inefficiency or indifference. The latter category no doubt embraced some allotment sites where the rules stipulated eviction for lawbreakers. Neverthe-less, it seems likely that more than half of all rural allotment tenants had good reason to fear that being convicted of a crime might result in the loss of their plot.

A third respect in which allotment provision may have tended to reduce rural crime is through the attitudinal changes wrought by allotments. Allot-ments encouraged 'respectable' behaviour, notably thrift, sobriety and indus-triousness, all qualities which militated against criminality. Furthermore, obtaining an allotment could have a significant effect on the allotment-holder's sense of identity. Although allotment-holders rented rather than owned their land, the 'ramparts of property' strategy which Conservative governments were to pursue with such success in the late nineteenth and

---

28 *F&I*, 21–2, 30, 115, 170–1, 188, 279–80, 348–9, 396–8, 400–1, 408–10, 432–3, 499–500; *Useful Hints* xxxiii. 129–30; *SC on the Labouring Poor*, 1843, vii. 1–11, 112, 122, 128, 346, 347; *Report on the Employment of Women and Children in Agriculture*, 1843, xii. 263–4, 271, 273, 332; *RC on the Framework Knitters*, 1845, xv. 531; *Gardener's Chronicle*, 1 Jan. 1845, 27, cols 1–2; 31 May 1845, 372, col. 1; *LF* xi (1845), 200–4; xlvi (1848), 46–7; xlviii (1848), 66–7.

twentieth centuries neverthless applied. James Brooks told the 1843 select committee that before allotments were provided in Hinckley,

> the greater part of the people had sympathy with an individual who broke the laws; they felt sorry for him and felt as if he was wronged; but now the case of those individuals is very different; if anything happens to their crops, or an individual robs them, they feel that there is some injury done to them, and that if it were not for the laws, the property they have laboured hard for would not be secure.

Brooks described a particular court in Hinckley 'where many men of bad character resided'. When the introduction of a new county police force was discussed, they disliked the idea. Brooks remonstrated with them, but they apparently said 'no, we have nothing to lose; what do we care about whose property is robbed?' However, 'as soon as they had a prospect of having land, many of those individuals ceased to have any sympathy with such persons'. Brooks added that 'most of the individuals who have land now act in a certain sense as policemen; in fact, every man is the guardian of his neighbour's property'.[29]

Brooks doubtless exaggerated the effects of allotment provision on attitudes to property, since he was attempting to convince a select committee of MPs very much concerned with property rights that allotments were beneficial. But even allowing for the inflated claims made by advocates of allotments, the attitudinal changes associated with allotment provision, particularly with respect to the rights of property, tended to reduce the incidence of rural crime.

There are, therefore, good reasons for supposing that allotments reduced crime. Direct evidence to support this assumption is impressive in quantity but deficient in quality. For this reason table 12 only includes statements supported by evidence; the literally hundreds of unsupported assertions made by contemporaries to the effect that allotments reduced crime have not been listed.[30]

Not all contemporaries were wholly convinced that allotments reduced crime, but the number who believed that they actually increased it was strikingly small. Table 13 lists all such instances encountered in the course of research for this book (including unsubstantiated claims as well as evidence). Claims that allotments raised crime levels were sufficiently rare that the evidence given in table 13 merits individual consideration.

---

[29] *SC on the Labouring Poor*, 1843, vii. 84–5.

[30] Further evidence can be derived from the allotments database. Thirty-three allotment sites in the database provide information about whether crime was thought to have decreased or not as a result of the provision of the allotments. In thirty of these cases, the allotments were thought to have had a positive effect on crime; in the remaining three they were thought either to have had no effect or a negative effect.

Table 12
Evidence that allotments reduced crime

Place	County	Evidence	Authority	Source	Date
'An estate' belonging 'I believe' to Mr Heneage	Wiltshire	Has put a stop to poaching and other crimes	Montague Gore	F&I, 175	(c. 1831)
Saffron Walden	Essex	Up to last Midsummer, five sessions were held in the town consecutively without a single prisoner being brought to trial (and this was implicitly attributed to the allotment system). One occupier did, however, forgo his allotment for an offence against the game laws.	Committee of Saffron Walden LFS	F&I, 223	(c. 1831)
Wells (and elsewhere?)	Somerset	Not a single act of spoliation (i.e. theft by one allotment tenant of another's property) had occurred among the bishop's several hundred allotment tenants.	G. H. Law, bishop of Bath and Wells	F&I, 33	(c. 1831)
High Littleton and Midsomer Norton	Somerset	No criminal convictions among 179 allotment tenants over three years.	G. T. Scobell	LFM (1834), 84	1834
(West Somerset)	Somerset	Only one eviction for crime or dishonesty among a hundred allotment tenants over several years.	Sir T. B. Lethbridge	LFM xciv (1839), 7	1839
(An unspecified village)	Wiltshire	No crimes committed since introduction of allotments nine years ago by any of the allotment tenants.	Ludlow Bruges	LFM xcvii (1840), 19	1840
(42 parishes in West Kent)	Kent	Only five criminal convictions in four years among nearly 2,000 allotment tenants.	West Kent JPs	LFM cvii (1840), 23	1840
(West Kent)	Kent	A man who had been in prison seven times and begged pardon for fourteen other offences had given no cause of complaint since renting land two years ago.	West Kent JPs	LFM cvii (1840), 23	1840

Place	County	Evidence	Authority	Source	Date
A parish of c. 2,000 inhabitants	West Kent	In 1833/4, the year before the allotments were first provided, there were thirty-four commitments to prison from the village; last year there were only four. Only one criminal conviction among the eighty allotment tenants over six years.	'An old officer'	*LFM* cviii (1840), 47–8	1840
(An unspecified village)	Kent	'G.S.' used to be seen every sessions, but had not been seen since 1838, when he had got an allotment	Attributed to a Kentish JP	*LFM* cxvi (1840), 164	1840
East Somerset	Somerset	An allotment tenant at Batheaston had been ejected from his plot recently for a felony. The committee of the East Somerset LFS recorded their 'painful satisfaction' in noting this sole instance which has come before them of an allotment tenant committing an offence.	Committee of the East Somerset Labourer's Friend Society	*LF* cviii (1840), 36	1840
West Kent	Kent	Only one commitment to prison known among all West Kent allotment tenants last year	John Ilderton Burn	*LFM* cxxii (1841), 67	1841
West Kent	Kent	No offences committed in this parish (in which allotments had been introduced) in 1840	John Ilderton Burn	*LFM* cxxii (1841), 67	1841
High Littleton, Midsomer Norton, North Bruham	Somerset	Amongst Scobell's over 200 allotment tenants only two had been convicted of a crime in eleven years.	G. T. Scobell	*LFM* cxxvii (1841), 144	1841
'A populous town'	West Kent	Thefts from gardens, orchards and of poultry had been very common, but since the introduction of allotments had become very rare.	The chief constable	*LFM* cxlvii (1843), 83	1843

Place	County	Evidence	Authority	Source	Date
West Kent	Kent	'Another year has passed in which not a single allotment tenant has been committed.'	Henry Martin, secretary of the West Kent Labourer's Friend Society	*LFM* cliii (1843), 186	1843
Cranworth	Norfolk	'I don't recollect an instance of a holder of an allotment having been brought to trial for any crime.'	Mr Howman	*Report on the Employment of Women and Children in Agriculture,* 1843, vii. 261	1843
	Kent	No commitments in 1841 and 1842 among the *c.* 3,000 families holding allotments in Kent.	Henry Martin	*SC on the Labouring Poor* , 1843, vii. 5	1843
Hempsted	Glos.	'Among my very numerous allotment tenants, not one has been brought before a court on any charge.'	Samuel Lysons	*LFM* clvii (1844), 54	1844
	Kent	No commitments in 1843 among Kent's 3,000 allotment tenants.	John Labouchere	*LFM,* 13th Report of LFS, May 1844	1844
	Somerset	No commitments in 1843 among Somerset's allotment tenants.	John Labouchere	*LFM,* 13th Report of LFS, May 1844	1844
West Kent	Kent	Crime has fallen sharply. Many current allotment tenants were previously prisoners. One baronet saw 200 men armed in riot and two years later gave prizes to some of them for good conduct and outstanding plots.	LFS Annual Report	*LFM,* 13th Report of the LFS, 1844, 5–7	1844
(East Somerset)	Somerset	Only one felony committed in fourteen years by Scobell's approximately 230 allotment tenants.	G. T. Scobell	*LF* xv (1845), 287	1845

Place	County	Evidence	Authority	Source	Date
'A village not thirty miles from London'		Seventeen of c. eighty allotment tenants had been imprisoned in 1836/7, but since taking allotments had been honest, industrious and respectable.		*LF* xxx (1846), 205–6	1846
Sir Edward Kerrison's estate	Suffolk	Had reclaimed poachers.	Revd J. F. Whitty	*LF* xxx (1846), 186	1846
Hadlow	Kent	About twenty former convicts were now steady and respectable allotment tenants.	Reported by Henry Martin	*LF* lxxix (1850), 193–4	1850
Dover	Kent	No convictions this year among the fifty allotment tenants at Dover.	Henry Martin	*LF* lxxx (1851), 1	1851
Margate	Kent	Two former convicts have now been allotment tenants for three years and are entirely redeemed.	Henry Martin	*LF* lxxxi (1851), 17	1851
	England as a whole	In the past year, no instance of any of the SICLC's 1,264 allotment tenants breaking the law.	Report of the SICLC	*LF* cx (1853), 104	1853
	Kent	After careful enquiry Henry Martin had not heard of any instance of misconduct in Kent during the late 'severe and trying winter'; this was attributable to the fact that the majority of labourers in Kent were allotment tenants.	Henry Martin	*LF* cxxxi (1855), 50	1855
Methley	West Riding	'Among the large number of allotment tenants I have there has not been a single case, during the 12 years they have had allotments, of an allotment tenant being brought before the magistrates.'	W. B. Ferrand	*LF* cxxviii (1855), 14	1855

Table 13
Evidence and claims that allotments increased crime

Place	County	Evidence	Authority	Source	Date
Banbury area	Oxon/ Northants.	'The allotment system tended to make labourers a set of thieves. Practical farmers had confirmed his own observations of last winter. They [i.e. allotment tenants] trebled farmers' crops – but that produce did not come off poor lots – it came off the land of the farmer. He could prove it.' Dryden's comments were attacked by the chair of the Banbury Agricultural Association, W. R. Cartwright, MP; by Col. Miller, Revd W. C. Risley, Revd J. R. Rushton and by the editor of the *Northampton Herald*. Subsequently also by Samuel Catton of Plaistow.	Sir Henry Dryden	*Northampton Herald*, reprinted *LFM* cxxviii (1841), 157–61; *LFM* cxxix (1841), 177.	1841
Brackley Petty Sessional Division	Northants.	A woman was convicted of robbing her neighbour of sprouts (Eydon); a chimney sweep named Shepherd set a snare for hares in the allotments (Evenley). 'Clearly allotments give great opportunities to stealing and poaching . . . if the poor continue in this behaviour, they will lose their plots.'	*Northampton Herald*	*LFM* cxli (1842), 184	1842
Stradbrooke	Suffolk	'They [the allotments] are all planted with fruit trees, which is a great objection; it makes boys trespass after the fruit, and injure the corn to get at it; they secrete themselves in it.'	Mr Gissin	*Report on the Employment of Women and Children in Agriculture*, 1843, xii. 265	1843
	(England)	The conditions on which they (allotments) are given cause discontent, starvation, despair and crime in all who don't get them.	Alexander Somerville	*Morning Chronicle*, 17 June 1844, reprinted *LF* ii (1844), 42	1844

The important point about Sir Henry Dryden's suggestion that allotments increased the frequency of theft is that it was so unsympathetically received by his peers (*see* chapter 3).

The *Northampton Herald* report of the convictions for theft and poaching at the Brackley Petty Sessions in 1842 is interesting, in that the question of theft by allotment-holders from each other was raised on several occasions in the columns of the *Labourer's Friend Magazine*. Clearly some allotment-holders, then as now, did suffer theft. But in the main the point made by Brooks to the 1843 select committee probably holds: allotment tenants acted as 'policemen' for each other to prevent theft from their plots. With respect to poaching, allotments again presented opportunities which had not existed in the same form previously. On the other hand, some allotment site rules made explicit stipulations against poaching, and some landowners provided allotments specifically because they believed that they would diminish the level of poaching.

The Stradbrooke example is of only minor significance, in so far as fruit trees were permitted on only a few allotment sites, whilst fruit-stealing by boys was hardly the sort of crime about which landowners were most concerned. Of more interest is Alexander Somerville's criticism of allotments. Because Somerville's letter was printed in the *Morning Chronicle*, it received considerable publicity. But the accusations made were rather wild ones. It is difficult to see how allotments could have caused 'starvation' or even, for that matter, despair. Whilst it is possible to think of ways in which allotments could have increased crime, Somerville provides no evidence that they did so, trading merely on his authority as 'one who has whistled at the plough' to support his statement. Probably Somerville's attack on allotment provision is best understood as being politically motivated. At this point Somerville was working for the Anti-Corn Law League. Because allotment provision was associated with landowners, and represented an alternative approach to the relief of rural poverty to that advocated by the league, allotments became tarred with the brush of protectionism in the eyes of some of the league's supporters. The same process can be seen at work within parliament: allotments commanded cross-party support except for a small group of radical corn law repealers who, in the heat of the conflict over the corn laws, were inclined to interpret everything through this prism, and began to denounce allotments as an aristocratic plot dreamed up to divert attention from the iniquity of the corn laws.

The question of whether allotments encouraged labourers to steal from farmers – one which is related to but distinct from the larger question of whether they reduced crime *in toto* – deserves some further discussion. Concern about this issue derived, unsurprisingly, largely from farmers, but the question exercised the minds of some landowners too. The point generally made was that labourers with allotments would both have more incentive to steal from farmers (because they were likely to keep a pig, which they would need to feed) and be more easily able to conceal that they had done so,

Table 14
Evidence and claims that allotment tenants stole from farmers

Place	County	Evidence	Authority	Source	Date
	Somerset	'There is an evil sometimes arises from allotments, where they have not the straw the labourers thieve a good deal from their masters.'	John Hancock, farmer	*SC on Agriculture*, 1836, viii. 110, q. 11398	1836
		'Of land allotments, encouraging as they do activity, care and happy homes, with consequent sobriety and value of character, almost as much might be said in praise, but for the painful consciousness that the cottager's pig, which the possession of land certainly invites him to keep, is not always or altogether so honestly fed and fattened as it should be.'	Revd Francis Litchfield	*LFM* cvii (1840), 16	1840
		Note added by editor of *LFM*: 'we think our own knowledge of the moral effect of allotments quite sufficient to justify us in stating that such an imputation is an exception only to a general rule'.			
Banbury area	Oxon/ Northants.	'The allotment system tended to make labourers a set of thieves. Practical farmers had confirmed his own observations of last winter. They [i.e. allotment tenants] trebled farmers' crops – but that produce did not come off poor lots – it came off the land of the farmer. He could prove it.'	Sir Henry Dryden	*Northampton Herald*, reprinted *LFM* cxxviii (1841), 157–61; *LFM* cxxix (1841), 177	1841

Place	County	Evidence	Authority	Source	Date
	Dorset	Allotments larger than about twenty perches lead to thieving: 'a labourer will grow a little corn, which gives him a reason for having straw in his possession, and then he will sometimes take his master's, who can't identify it, for his pig; he will also steal seed etc. I have known such cases.'	Mr Tarver of Blandford, tallow-chandler and farmer	*Report on the Employment of Women and Children in Agriculture*, 1843, xii, appendix 22, p. 88	1843

because their allotments would give them an 'excuse' for having field crops, particularly corn, in their possession. Statements to the effect that labourers with allotments were more likely to steal from their employers are listed in table 14.

Evidence that labourers with allotments did not steal from their employers is, by its very nature, impossible to obtain. However, many contemporaries took it upon themselves to deny the charges made by some farmers (*see* table 15). The claims that allotments led labourers to steal more from their employers are difficult to evaluate. On the one hand, almost all such claims were either made by, or clearly originated with, farmers, and farmers were often violently prejudiced against allotments. Furthermore, on examination almost all the claims turn out to be based on what farmers supposed was happening, rather than on evidence about what actually was happening. On the other hand, it may well have been easier for allotment-holders to conceal a theft of field crops than for other labourers and no doubt some allotment-renting labourers did steal barley or even wheat from farmers to feed to their pig.

Taken together, the evidence that allotments decreased rural crime is much more extensive and on the whole persuasive than the evidence that they increased crime, as a comparison of tables 12 and 13 indicates. Although allotments may have facilitated and even encouraged some kinds of minor theft, notably of corn from farmers and of crops from other allotment tenants, this was probably on a small scale, and was almost certainly outweighed by the effects of higher incomes, greater respect for the law and fear of losing the allotment. But although there seems little doubt that allotments did reduce rural crime, the extent of this reduction remains unclear. This is a question which deserves further research. What is required is detailed and painstaking work comparing the rate of committals or convictions from an adequately large sample of parishes with and without allotments, and then regressing these against other potential influences on crime rates. This would be an ambitious and time-consuming project, but only in this way will it be possible to gauge the dimensions, rather than merely the direction, of the effect of allotment provision on rural crime.

Table 15
Claims that allotment tenants did not steal from farmers

Place	County	Evidence	Authority	Source	Date
Cranworth, Southburgh and Reymerston	Norfolk	'I am not aware of a single instance of dishonesty . . . having occurred, that can be considered as arising out of the allotment system.'	Revd Philip Gurdon	*LF* xxxiv (1847), 42	1847
Sywell	Northants.	'I don't think they steal seed.'	George Robinson, farmer	*RC on the Employment of Children, Young Persons, and Women in Agriculture, 1867–8,* xvii. 685	1867
Harpole	Northants.	'I don't think a grain crop is likely to make a man dishonest; if he wants to take corn he will take it whether he has an allotment or not.'	Revd R. B. Dundas	*RC on the Employment of Children, Young Persons, and Women in Agriculture, 1867–8,* xvii. 690	1867
	(England)	'It was of course possible that the labourer might, by the production of such an article as wheat, be tempted to turn rogue, and to increase his stock by robbing his employer; but he did not think they ought to stand in the way of the agricultural labourer by supposing he must of necessity be a rogue.'	W. Bennett of Cambridge	*RC on the Employment of Children, Young Persons, and Women in Agriculture,* 1867–8, xvii. 203	1867

Allotments and rural protest

It was very often claimed that where labourers had allotments, they did not participate in the Captain Swing riots in 1830 and 1831.[31] The *Proceedings* of the LFS for 1833 stated that 'the almost invariable testimony of those who adopted the allotment system prior to 1830/1 is that the allotment tenants not only abstained from riot but usually came forward voluntarily' to defend

---

[31] *LFM* cliv (1844), 3; *Proceedings of Labourer's Friend Society* (1832), 10; *F&I*, 124; *SC on the Labouring Poor*, 1843, vii. 12. The Hammonds believed that had the riots continued longer, they might have forced the government to accept Suffield's ambitious home colonisation scheme: *Village labourer*, 300.

the property of the local landowners.[32] Amongst the parishes in which it was claimed rioting did not occur as a result of the existence of allotments were Great Somerford, Malmesbury, Rodbourne, Worton and West Lavington (Wiltshire), Crondall (Hampshire) and Saffron Walden (Essex).[33] In many places allotments were provided in or shortly after 1830 as a direct and explicit response to the riots. Amongst the allotment sites causally linked with the riots in this way by contemporary statements were Alconbury (Huntingdonshire), Fordingbridge (Hampshire) and an unnamed site in Somerset.[34] Presumably where such a link can be demonstrated it implies a belief that parishes where labourers had land were less likely to be riotous.

As always, some exceptions can be identified. One of the witnesses to the House of Lords Select Committee on the Poor Laws in 1831, asked whether there had been any disturbances in parishes where labourers had land, replied 'I think not in any parish where the labourers had land', but then immediately went on to contradict himself by stating that 'there was a fire in the parish of Coton [Cambridgeshire], but . . . it [i.e. land provision] was not considered a boon by the labourers; they had it upon too cheap terms'.[35] Another instance in which allotments, or at least support for allotments, did not appear to have protected against incendiarism was Westwell, 'more famed for fires than any other parish in East Kent'. Here the victim of one of the fires was 'one of the most respectable farmers in the place, a strong advocate for cottage allotments and a kind and liberal man'.[36] However, it is not clear that allotments were actually in existence in Westwell at the time of the incident. Other than the partial exception of Coton and the possible exception of Westwell, no cases have been identified of parishes where allotments existed in 1830 and rioting occurred.

Contemporaries certainly believed that rioting did not occur in parishes with allotments, as the interest in this question of both the House of Lords Select Committee on the Poor Laws and the Royal Commission on the Poor Laws demonstrates. But in fact even if it could be demonstrated that no one from a parish with allotments took part in the Swing riots, the conclusions which could legitimately be drawn from this would be limited. Very few parishes had allotments in 1830, possibly no more than a hundred across the country as a whole. Some of these were in areas where the Swing riots made little impact, such as Northamptonshire, although admittedly most were in Wiltshire and the adjacent counties and so did lie in the direct path of Swing.

---

32 *Proceedings of the Labourer's Friend Society* (1833), 7–8.
33 SC of the House of Lords on the Poor Laws, 1830–1, viii. 29, 53–4; *F&I*, 281–3, 424–31; RC on the Poor Laws, 1834, xxviii. 226–7.
34 *F&I*, 331, 394; RC on the Employment of Children, Young Persons, and Women in Agriculture, 1867–8, xvii. 264.
35 SC of the House of Lords on the Poor Laws, 1830–1, viii. 311. The claim that where labourers had land on cheap terms they appreciated it less, which was made by other observers too, is paradoxical but not psychologically implausible.
36 RC on the Poor Laws, 1834, xxviii. 213.

It is possible that it was due as much to chance as to the effects of land provision that parishes with allotments often seem to have remained unscathed by the riots.

The allotment system was in its infancy when the Swing riots swept through southern England. A better test of the relationship between land provision and agricultural unrest would be an event which occurred, for example, in the mid-1840s, by which time allotments were numerous and well established. But since there were no major non-localised outbreaks of agricultural rioting after 1831, such a test is unavailable. The prospects of developing a more complete understanding of the relationship between allotment provision and episodes of localised, covert protest (such as local episodes of incendiarism) are better but, as with the connection between allotments and crime reduction, depend upon establishing data series from crime records for a large number of individual parishes, and linking these with data on allotment provision.

The allotment movement and Chartism

Some supporters of the LFS claimed that allotment provision deflected the rural poor from radical political activity, the most salient manifestation of which in the years between 1830 and 1873 was Chartism. Such claims came particularly from areas in which industrial workers or miners formed a high proportion of allotment tenants. A letter written by Charles Parry to the editor of the *Bath Herald* in December 1839 urged the adoption of the allotment system on the grounds that it created a 'peaceful, loyal population'. The letter claimed that 'all the efforts of the Chartists have failed to sway the Somerset miners, who have become attached to the soil through the new allotment system . . . in those districts of the collieries, as at Timsbury, Radstock etc., where miners had allotments, such allotment tenants had generally withstood all the allurements of the Chartists, and in several cases driven them out'. Parry contrasted the behaviour of the Somerset miners in this respect with that of the miners of South Wales, who were without allotments and had given active support to Chartism.[37] However, Parry appears to have exaggerated the resistance of the miners to Chartism. A Chartist meeting at Radstock on 9 March 1839 was attended by 700 or 800 people and caused unrest over the next few days at the Tining coal works and in the

---

[37] Charles H. Parry to the editor of the *Bath Herald*, 12 Dec. 1839, reprinted *LFM* cviii (1840), 43–4. An almost identical claim was made by the Revd G. A. Baker at the 1839 annual general meeting of the East Somerset Labourer's Friend Society. Baker noted that 'there was no field garden system in the districts across the Severn . . . where disturbances had occurred' and asserted that if the allotment system had existed there, these 'disgraceful outrages' would never have occurred: *LFM* cviii (1840), 38.

village.[38] There was another Chartist meeting in the village on 9 April, whilst in early August the Radstock miners were apparently sympathetic to the 'sacred month' (general strike) proposed by the national convention.[39] Subsequently, Chartist activity does appear to have subsided on the Somerset coalfield (although continuing quite vigorously in the nearby towns of Bath and Trowbridge).

There were also contemporary claims that allotment provision militated against Chartism in the east Midlands. In his evidence to the 1843 select committee, James Orange described the effects of the introduction of allotments in the Nottinghamshire village of Lambley, where previously 'the inhabitants generally talked politics and neglected their Sabbath duties', but 'after the rector granted 17½ acres in allotments, the church became well filled spontaneously. The parishioners stopped talking about politics.'[40] John Brooks, one of the leading figures in the allotment movement in Hinckley, informed the same committee that the Hinckley operatives had been more contented since the introduction of allotments in the town and that

> as a proof of that . . . one of the lecturers of the Chartists, from Leicester, came there [i.e. Hinckley] a week or two ago, and made a great noise, but none of the allotment tenants visited him; instead of going to the meeting, they went with their spades on their shoulders to their gardens

whilst the men without allotments went to the meeting.[41] A similar claim was made by William Brooke Stevens, the assistant curate of Sutton-in-Ashfield, also in Nottinghamshire. In a letter to the *Labourer's Friend*, Stevens wrote that he believed the allotments at Sutton-in-Ashfield had been 'productive of a great deal of good, to a population heretofore considered the hotbed of Chartism and every disorder'. Stevens enclosed a copy of an address from nearly 450 of the allotment-holders to the duke of Portland, the local allotment landlord, evincing 'deep veneration and respect' for the duke.[42]

These claims receive some support from the fact that on a number of occasions east Midlands Chartists tried energetically and persistently to hinder James Orange's efforts to promote the allotment movement. At Ilkeston, for example, after an apparently successful meeting in January 1842, Orange found on his return in February that the enthusiasm for allotments had, mysteriously, entirely vanished and the committee had not carried out a single one of its duties. He discovered that the committee had been packed by Chartists intent on frustrating his plans.[43] There were other examples. At

---

[38] R. B. Pugh, 'Chartism in Somerset and Wiltshire', in Asa Briggs (ed.), *Chartist studies*, London 1967, 181.
[39] Ibid. 182, 189.
[40] *SC on the Labouring Poor*, 1843, vii. 93.
[41] Ibid. 87.
[42] *LF* cxi (1853), 141–2.
[43] *LFM* cxxxiii (1842), 54.

Lambley on 29 November 1841 Orange gave a lecture on the advantages of allotments that was initially interrupted by Chartists.[44] Similarly at Hyson Green on 3 December 1841 Chartists attempted to disrupt one of Orange's lectures, having failed to obtain a hall in which to hold a meeting of their own.[45] Another of Orange's meetings, held in Leicester town hall on 15 June 1842, was interrupted by the secretary of a local Chartist association.[46] In an interesting entry in his journal for 23 March 1842, Orange recorded his belief that 'often I have been suspected of being in the pay of the government, since the effect of my addresses has been to divert attention from politics'.[47] Unfortunately, the *Labourer's Friend Magazine* only printed Orange's journal until mid-1843 (whether because the journal was no longer being kept, no longer being submitted or no longer being accepted for publication is unclear). As a result, information about the relationship between Chartism and the allotment movement after this time is scanty. However, it seems unlikely that the rivalry between the two movements ceased abruptly after the Chartist wave peaked in 1842. A straw in the wind which supports this interpretation is that as late as 1850 the annual general meeting of the SICLC was disrupted by Chartists, although this may have been as much because of the presence of Lord John Russell, the prime minister, as because of Chartist opposition to the SICLC or its aims *per se*.[48]

However, the relationship between Chartism and the allotment movement was more complex than these examples might suggest. Although there was a strong element of rivalry, part of the reason that Chartists feared the allotment movement was because it was in many ways so congruent with the ideology of Chartism. For both movements, independence was the central value. The Chartist version of independence tended, of course, to be more conflictual and politically-orientated than that proposed by the allotment movement. But there was a real overlap of ideals as well as a coincidence of words: for both Chartism and the allotment movement, independence meant relying on one's own efforts and having a least a modicum of economic self-sufficiency. Chartism was the inheritor of a powerful and long-standing radical tradition to which agrarian solutions had been central; so the allotment movement's identification of land as the solution to the problem of poverty seemed readily comprehensible and worthy of sympathy to many Chartists. In urging self-respect, temperance and 'respectable' behaviour, the allotment movement was also at one with important strands within Chartism. Nor in practice was the Chartist emphasis on mutuality alien to the allotment movement. On the contrary, mutuality was a central component of the culture of allotments: seeds and produce were exchanged and, in

44 Ibid. cxxx (1842), 8.
45 Ibid. cxxxi (1842), 19–20.
46 Ibid. cxxxvii (1842), 121.
47 Ibid. cxxxv (1842), 87.
48 *LF* lcciv (1850), 106–19.

cases of illness or bereavement, allotment-holders not uncommonly cultivated each other's plots. Furthermore, in the east Midlands would-be allotment tenants played a leading, active role in establishing allotment sites,
organising themselves into societies and lobbying local landowners to
provide allotments. The process of obtaining land was one which depended
upon and militated towards collective popular action.

The objectives and the values informing the two movements were, therefore, in many respects very close; and it was in no small part for this reason
that allotments appealed so strongly to the Chartist constituency. The framework knitters who put their names to the national petition in their thousands
were the same people who subscribed to the local branches of the Northern
and Midlands Artisans and Labourer's Friend Society set up by Orange in the
hope of obtaining land. If the relationship between Chartism and the
allotment movement was often a difficult one, this was probably due more to
institutional competition than to ideological incompatibility. On the ground,
indeed, the allotment movement was not necessarily contradictory to
Chartism at all. Many Chartists enrolled in allotment societies, even at
places such as Lambley and Hyson Green where direct conflict between the
two movements had taken place.[49] In fact, some Chartist sympathisers were
even instrumental in establishing allotments. The lace manufacturer Henry
Frearson was a signatory of a petition for a Chartist meeting in Nottingham
Forest in 1838.[50] Yet Frearson also let 100 acres of forty-perch allotments in
nearby Arnold.[51] The allotment system could as easily be seen by Chartists as
emancipatory rather than repressive. The *Northern Star* printed a lengthy
two-column account of the benefits of allotments and of the Labourer's
Friend Society, written by the Leeds manufacturer James Garth Marshall, on
25 June 1842.[52] Just over a year later William Hill, the editor of the *Northern
Star*, made a visit to Arnold and gave a glowing report of the sick-club allotments, which indicates the extent to which allotments could be congruent
with Chartist political thought:

> I met with one thing at Arnold that pleased me to the very soul: a sure
> evidence that daylight is dawning upon 'the workies'. The sick club have
> drawn out their money from the savings bank and rag shops and invested it in
> land. Whole fields have been purchased and divided into small garden plots
> among their members, for which a light rental is paid to the club. The advan-
> tages of this, to the institutions, are many. Their funds are secure. The bank
> will not break; their money will be used always for their benefit, and not for

[49] *LFM* cxxxi (1842), 20; cxlv (1843), 53.

[50] *Nottingham Review*, 9 Nov. 1838, list of signatories reprinted in Peter Wyncoll, *Nottingham Chartism: Nottingham workers in revolt during the nineteenth century*, Nottingham 1967,
57.

[51] William Felkin, *History of the machine-wrought hosiery and lace manufactures*, [1867],
Newton Abbot 1967, 461.

[52] *Northern Star* v/256, 25 June 1842, 6. I am grateful to Jamie Bronstein for this reference.

their oppression; their funds pay better interest than before; while they derive individually a great advantage from their application of them. Thus are they better able to pay their contributions than they would be if the money were banked with government for their oppression as before; and this 'banking' of it in mother earth, by the additional interest it pays, gives a drawback to each member of some pound a year already, which will, of course, increase as the funds accumulate, and they acquire more land. This is glorious! A beginning of good things! Oh, it did my heart good to walk over those gardens, and to see the savings of the poor man thus sensibly disposed of. All honour to the Arnold sick clubs. Let all clubs follow their example.[53]

Other east Midlands sick and benefit clubs appear also to have invested their funds in land which they then divided into allotments.[54]

To some extent, the opposition between Chartism and allotment provision was more sharply defined and hard-edged when under discussion by a parliamentary select committee in London, or in the columns of the *Labourer's Friend Magazine*, than it was on the ground in the east Midlands. Orange, who hoped to obtain a position as full-time paid agent of the LFS, was well aware of the cautious, establishment values of the MPs who were members of the 1843 select committee and, to a lesser extent, of the LFS leadership. Orange cited the example of the effects of the Lambley allotments to the 1843 committee and noted in his journal (which he later sent to the *Labourer's Friend Magazine* for publication) that the effect of his lectures had been 'to withdraw attention from politics'.[55] Orange's lectures were addressed to a quite contrasting audience – mainly framework knitters, many with Chartist sympathies. When lecturing, Orange took a rather different line than he did when writing or speaking to the landowners of the LFS or the select committee. In his lectures, Orange insisted that the allotment movement was in fact non-political in character. At Hyson Green on 3 December 1841, for example, Orange quieted a turbulent audience of Chartists by explaining that the LFS was 'an entirely non-political association', a claim he repeated when a meeting at Ratcliffe-upon-Trent was threatened with interruption by corn law repealers.[56] At Lambley on 29 November 1841 and at Snenton on 3 March 1842 Orange noted with approval that men of all religious and political persuasions were in attendance, whilst a report of a lecture given by Orange at Beeston on 13 July 1842 praised him for 'cautiously abstaining from all observations which might tend to promote dissension amongst the humble orders'.[57] Clearly, allotment provision, as Orange presented it to potential allotment tenants in the east Midlands, was differ-

---

53 Reprinted in the *Nottingham Review*, 4 Aug. 1843, 2, col. 1.
54 *LFM* cxlv (1843) 53; Julie O'Neill, 'Self-help in Nottinghamshire: the Woodborough Male Friendly Society, 1826–1954', *Transactions of the Thoroton Society of Nottinghamshire* xc (1986), 57, 63.
55 *SC on the Labouring Poor*, 1843, vii. 94; *LFM* cxxxv (1842), 87.
56 *LFM* cxxxi (1842), 20.
57 Ibid. cxxx (1842), 8; *Nottingham Review*, 22 July 1842, 4, col. 5.

ently inflected from the version which he offered to MPs and the landowners of the LFS.

A similar tension exists between the claims made to the 1843 select committee by John Brooks, to the effect that allotments had pacified the town of Hinckley, diverting the inhabitants away from politics, and the actual behaviour of the leader of the allotment movement in Hinckley, Amos Foxon. It was Foxon who asked Orange to come to Hinckley to set the allotment system in motion in the town, who orchestrated the subsequent campaign to get allotments provided, and who became secretary of the ensuing Hinckley Artisans and Labourer's Friend Society. But Foxon was no tame apologist for the establishment and was scarcely a model of deferential submission to adversity. On the contrary, he led a struggle against the truck system in Hinckley, and was able to do so without losing his job because 'I am rather a public character in the town, and had I been turned off of work for resisting the trucking system, there would have been a bit of an oration [sic] about it, and the employers would not have liked it.'[58] The implications of the allotment movement as put into practice in the east Midlands were, therefore, politically more uncertain than the reassuring statements made to politicians and landowners gave reason to believe.

Indeed, it is possible that the effects of the allotment movement in the east Midlands actually strengthened rather than undermined Chartism in the area. Orange's advocacy of allotment provision evoked a powerful response from the framework knitters, and certainly contributed largely to, if it was not indeed responsible for, a deep entrenched demand for land in the east Midlands. The number of people who attended Orange's lectures in the framework-knitting villages speaks for itself, especially in view of the fact that Orange often spoke repeatedly in the same villages. At Ratcliffe-upon-Trent on 16 December 1841 more than 250 people (most of the householders) were present and 100 enrolled in the branch allotment association Orange formed.[59] A 'crowded' lecture in Carlton on 3 January 1842, lasting for an hour and a half, resulted in more than 100 new members for the local association, even though land had as yet not been obtained. A second large meeting at Ratcliffe-upon-Trent on 10 January led to a further 100 people joining the local association; at Ilkeston on the following day a two-hour lecture persuaded ninety people to join the branch association.[60] At Kegworth on 31 March 1842 there were 'great crowds', despite the rain; another well-attended meeting in the village was held on 28 April in the national school.[61] At Carlton on 5 April there was 'feverish excitement' at a meeting, whilst

58 RC on the Framework Knitters, 1845, xv. 395.
59 LFM cxxxi (1842), 20.
60 Ibid. cxxxii (1842), 43–5.
61 Ibid. cxxxv (1842), 88–9; cxxxvi (1842), 101. At yet another lecture given by Orange in Kegworth (his fourth) on 20 June 1842, there were 'hearty cheers' during and after the lecture: ibid. cxxxvii (1842), 121.

Orange's lecture at Sawley on 4 May was attended with 'lively interest' and 115 people were enrolled.[62] A further lecture at Sawley on 7 June 1842 obtained a 'very large attendance' and a memorandum requesting land for allotments was signed by 'nearly all the male inhabitants'.[63] In Long Eaton on 8 June a crowded meeting, including mothers with their babies, resulted in seventy-four enrolments, whilst 200 people were enrolled after a lecture by Orange given in a 'well-filled' Hinckley Town Hall on 27 June 1842.[64] There were 'great crowds' at Castle Down on 18 July, and again at a third meeting in Long Eaton on 20 July; on the following day the church bells were rung in Long Eaton in celebration of the apparent decision of local landowners to provide land for allotments.[65]

At Nuneaton in early August Orange obtained one of his largest audiences ever, when 1,000 people gathered to hear him speak in the town hall.[66] Further meetings at Earl Shilton on 15 August, Beeston and Market Harborough probably in early September, Nuneaton on 12 September and Hinckley on 14 September were all described as 'crowded' in Orange's journal.[67] There was a large crowd when Orange lectured at Mowsley on 12 June 1842, and a few days later again at Arnsby, where he gave three subsequent lectures and where almost all the male villagers joined the allotments association.[68] Orange was in high demand in summer 1843, having received invitations to give lectures at Great Peatling, Willoughby, Dunton Bassett, Saddington, Kibworth, Smeeton, Great Glenn, Cosby, Blaby, Great Wigston, Whetstone and Sutton Bassett.[69] On 14 and 15 August he lectured at Willoughby Waterless (population c. 600). 'Almost all' the labouring poor attended the first meeting and about 150 joined the allotments association.[70] On 17, 18 and 21 August Orange lectured to a 'large audience' at Dunton Bassett and more than 100 people joined the allotments association.[71] There were 'very large crowds' at four lectures given in the parish of Kibworth Harcourt in August and on 3 August between 700 and 800 people attended Orange's lecture at Great Glenn.[72]

Of course not every lecture Orange gave was thronged. At Old Radford on 2 December 1841, for example, few attended the meeting in the Primitive Methodist Chapel because of bad weather and poor publicity, and the

---

62 Ibid. 100–1.
63 Ibid. 119.
64 Ibid. 122.
65 Ibid. cxxxviii (1842), 136–7.
66 Ibid. cxxxix (1842), 141.
67 Ibid. 142; cxl (1842), 165–6.
68 Ibid. cli (1843), 147–8.
69 Ibid. 149.
70 Ibid. cliii, 179.
71 Ibid.
72 Ibid. 180–1.

meeting was adjourned, whilst attendance at a lecture at Snenton on 21 March 1842 was 'a little thin'.[73] But such occasions were exceptional.

Independent reports of Orange's meetings in the Nottingham press confirm the impression given by his journal. According to the *Nottingham Review* a meeting addressed by Orange at Castle Donnington on 18 July 1842 was 'excessively crowded', and a clue to Orange's ability to sustain audience interest for as long as two hours at a stretch is given by the reporter's supplementary comment that 'we do not remember ever to have heard a more clear and comprehensive lecture on any subject'.[74] The *Nottingham Journal* report of the meeting in the national school at Kegworth on 28 April 1842 recorded that 'every part of this spacious room was crowded to excess'.[75] The same newspaper expressed the view that Orange's plan was extremely popular in a report of a meeting at Castle Donnington on 23 June 1842 and that Orange was repeatedly cheered when he spoke at Kegworth on 20 June 1842.[76]

Nor was the excitement evident in the response to Orange's lectures an evanescent phenomenon. In many respects, Orange created a demand for land which was far in excess of anything the Northern and Midland Artisans and Labourer's Friend Society could satisfy. Orange was, in short, almost too successful. In many villages where he had established branches of the society it proved impossible to obtain land even after months of effort. In Hinckley, for example, there were over 100 applicants for plots, with no prospect of obtaining land. According to James Brooks, when the allotment association was established in Hinckley, 'it seemed to fill the people with hope; it was about the last thing that could inspire hope; and so anxious were the people to secure land that even those in the stone-yard, the greater part of them, were members of the society and paid their penny in order to share the benefits of it'. At the same time, 150 people at Oadby were paying a penny a week to the allotment association but without any real prospect of success.[77] Inevitably, in some cases discouragement eventually resulted and the local allotment association was abandoned. According to Orange this happened to many local societies in the east Midlands, including at Beeston, Hyson Green, Lenton, Ratcliffe-upon-Trent, Radford and Snenton.[78]

The effect of Orange's energetic proselytising was therefore to foster a pent-up demand for land, which was more likely to contribute to political discontent than to placate it. The following statements, given in evidence to Richard Muggeridge for the Royal Commission on the Framework Knitters in 1844–5, indicate that the framework knitters were still gripped by land hunger two years after Orange's activities in the area reached their peak:

[73] Ibid. cxxxi (1842), 19; cxxxv (1842), 86.
[74] *Nottingham Review*, 22 July 1842, 8, col. 2.
[75] *Nottingham Journal*, 6 May 1842.
[76] Ibid. 1 July 1842.
[77] *SC on the Labouring Poor*, 1843, vii. 82, 89.
[78] Ibid. 90.

Two things, and only two, would in my opinion remedy the trade – one, a restriction of hours of labour; the other, the allotment system. – George Eyre, framework knitter, Belper.[79]

[Reply to the question 'is there any general desire on the part of the work people to have small pieces of land?'] – Certainly, a very great desire: whereever there is a chance, they embrace that chance, though they give too much for it. – Joseph Turney, framework knitter, Chilwell.[80]

It would be a great benefit if we had them; there is not a vegetable in the place, only what is brought from Nottingham and other places . . . there is a very great desire for them [i.e. allotments]. – James Clarke, framework knitter, Ruddington.[81]

The framework knitters would be very thankful to get a piece of ground; it would be a great assistance to them indeed. – Samuel Parker, framework knitter, Ruddington.[82]

[The allotment system] is a thing that is very much desired, I believe, generally throughout the parish, and I believe it would benefit the condition of the framework knitters throughout the three counties, if they had small allotments of ground at a low price, as it would enable them to grow a few potatoes for themselves. – Thomas Hallard, framework knitter, Horsley Woodhouse.[83]

We have struggled very hard to get a little potato ground, but we cannot get a yard in our parish. – William Robinson, framework knitter, Sawley.[84]

[Reply to the question 'are the people anxious to get land?'] Yes, we have tried for a long time, and paid 1d a week for a long time to try and get a bit; and when we had done all, we could not prevail upon the farmers to let us have a bit anywhere. – Thomas Wilcox, framework knitter, Sawley.[85]

[The introduction of the allotment system] would be a thing that would be very acceptable and useful. – S. Taylor, framework knitter, South Wingfield.[86]

The hands very much want allotments. – George Walters, framework knitter, Swanwick.[87]

I believe it would be a very good thing if they were adopted. – Joseph Morley, framework knitter, Tibshelf.[88]

---

[79] *RC on the Framework Knitters*, 1845, xv. 927.
[80] Ibid. 790.
[81] Ibid. 818.
[82] Ibid. 822.
[83] Ibid. 958.
[84] Ibid. 903.
[85] Ibid. 904.
[86] Ibid. 914.
[87] Ibid. 916.
[88] Ibid. 918.

My son was secretary to a club which endeavoured by subscription to get some land for allotments, but we were unable to do so. I believe it would be very beneficial to have some, because in slack times and when out of work men would have plenty of time to work it, instead of standing at the corners of the streets. – Samuel Appleton, framework knitter, Belgrave, Leicester.[89]

This eagerness, almost desperation, for land must have provided a highly favourable environment for the Chartist land plan. It is true that some historians have argued that the land plan was only poorly supported in the east Midlands. Joy MacAskill noted that Nottingham and its surrounding district was 'only just beginning to contribute trifling amounts' of subscription money by December 1845 and that 'recruitment in the centres of Midland industry was definitely slower than in Lancashire'.[90] Peter Wyncoll makes even more disparaging remarks about the success of the land plan in Nottingham, arguing that the land plan 'never succeeded in generating much more than a limited support amongst the workpeople of Nottingham. When O'Connor's Land Company finally came to be wound up, Sweet, the Nottingham collector, claimed for £1,200; which since it was divided among nine hundred people, made the average Nottingham contribution very small indeed'.[91]

Other historians, however, offer a different view. Alice Hadfield suggests that the land plan was greeted with great enthusiasm in the framework-knitting villages between Leicester and Loughborough, and describes a four-hour mass meeting held on the banks of the Soar at which the land plan was explained amid 'breathless attention'.[92] Temple Patterson cites the land plan as 'a factor which had done something to keep Chartism alive in Leicester' in spite of the difficulties and dissension which affected the movement in the town in the mid-1840s.[93] Similarly, J. F. C. Harrison noted that 'the land scheme found enthusiastic supporters in the town [i.e. Leicester] who contributed regularly to its funds and became shareholders in it'.[94] The suggestion that the land plan was popular in Nottingham, and that this was in part because of the prior success of the allotment movement locally, is endorsed by an anonymous teaching pack prepared for Nottingham University Manuscripts Department:

The Nottingham Chartists were keen supporters of the [land] scheme and in 1845 had contributed as much as £200 per week towards it. The reason for their enthusiasm lay in the success of a similar scheme which had been started in 1842 when the Nottingham [Independent Cottage] Garden Society was founded to provide allotments for working men. Many framework knitters

89 Ibid. 336.
90 Joy MacAskill, 'The Chartist land plan', in Briggs, Chartist studies, 316–17.
91 Wyncoll, Nottingham Chartism.
92 Alice Hadfield, The Chartist Land Company, Newton Abbot 1970, 41.
93 A. Temple Patterson, Radical Leicester: a history of Leicester, 1780–1850, Leicester 1954, 355.
94 J. F. C. Harrison, 'Chartism in Leicester', in Briggs, Chartist studies, 115.

took allotments and managed to grow much needed additional food for their homes.[95]

On balance the evidence that the land plan evoked an enthusiastic response from the framework knitters seems stronger than that which points in the contrary direction. MacAskill acknowledges that after 1845 subscriptions to the land plan from the Midlands picked up, so that there were forty-eight districts of the land company in the Midlands by August 1847 (as compared to eighty-six in the north).[96] 'The Midlands' is of course a large area and MacAskill's data is compatible with an over-representation of east Midlands framework knitters as subscribers to the Chartist Land Company. However, we should also remember that subscriptions, or even numbers of districts or delegates, are not necessarily a good guide to the intensity of support for the land plan. The income of the framework knitters was notoriously low and as a group they would have found contributions to the Land Company far more burdensome than the more highly paid and secure factory workers of the north. Careful consideration of MacAskill's evidence therefore suggests that it provides no reason to believe that the land plan was unpopular amongst the east Midlands framework knitters. Wyncoll's suggestion that the Chartist land plan had little support in Nottingham at any time seems inherently unlikely in view of the fact that O'Connor was elected MP for the town in 1847, when he was closely identified with the land plan and when the land plan was at the height of its popularity nationally. Furthermore, other than a disparaging comment about the merits of the land plan from the *Nottingham Mercury*, the only evidence that Wyncoll provides of the land plan's unpopularity is the limited size of the claim made by the Nottingham Chartists when the land company was wound up. This is open to the same objection as that applied to the evidence of contributions: financial contributions measure ability to pay rather than political support.

If it is accepted that the east Midlands framework knitters probably were enthusiastic supporters of the land plan, and that the allotment movement played an important role in creating the demand for land on which this enthusiasm was based, the effects of the allotment movement in the east Midlands are more likely to be seen as politically radicalising rather than conservative.

It is tempting to go further than this, and suggest that the success of the allotment movement among the framework knitters may have contributed

[95] Nottingham University Manuscripts Department, *Working-class unrest in Nottingham 1800–50*, IV: *Chartism*, teaching pack, Nottingham 1965 [no pagination]. The claim that the Nottingham Chartists contributed 'as much as £200 per week' to the land plan in 1845 appears to contradict MacAskill's statement about the negligible scale of contributions from Nottingham throughout 1845 cited above. Unfortunately the teaching pack is unreferenced, so it is not possible to pursue the contradiction by checking the original source.

[96] MacAskill, 'Chartist land plan', 319, 321.

significantly to the genesis of the land plan. One would imagine that the Chartist leadership would have been concerned to find so many of its supporters being drawn into enthusiastic involvement with another move-ment, and the evidence from Orange's journal of repeated Chartist attempts to disrupt the promotion of allotments confirms that at a local level this was probably the case. Presumably the news that the prospect of obtaining land had created such excitement amongst a core element of the Chartist constit-uency found its way through to the national leadership. Orange's journal and the 1845 *Report* demonstrate that enthusiasm for allotments was still running at a high level in the east Midlands in the period when the Chartist tide was ebbing rapidly, after the failure of the 1842 national petition and 'sacred month'. It was in the years between 1842 and 1845 that the land plan became established as a central plank of Chartism, largely in response to the need for a new direction. Is it not possible that the land plan was adopted partly because Chartist leaders had taken good note of the effectiveness of the promise of land in mobilising popular support, as demonstrated by the success of the allotment movement with the framework knitters?

Attractive as this hypothesis is, however, very little evidence exists to support it. The only direct connection I have found is in the comments of William Hill on the Arnold sick-club allotments. Hill had obviously been deeply impressed by what he had seen, and furthermore had become convinced that purchasing and cultivating land was one, if not the, way ahead for Chartism. As editor of the *Northern Star*, he had contacts with senior figures in the Chartist movement, including O'Connor, but there is no evidence that O'Connor, or any of the other leading Chartists, was directly influenced by the success of the allotment movement in the east Midlands. Malcolm Chase identifies 'provincial support' as the crucial factor deter-mining approval for the land plan at the Birmingham Convention in 1843, but although he mentions activists from Cirencester, Cheltenham, Manchester, north Lancashire, Bradford, Leeds and London as early advo-cates of the land plan, he lists no east Midlands leaders.[97] It could also be argued that the depth of attachment within the radical tradition to agrarian solutions which Chase documented so tellingly in *The people's farm* makes other explanations for the emergence of the land plan in the mid-1840s superfluous.[98] However, despite Chase's work and that of MacAskill and Hadfield we still lack a comprehensive modern history of the land plan. It is possible that such a history would demonstrate that the allotment movement, especially in the east Midlands, did indeed make a distinctive contribution to its genesis.

---

[97] Malcolm Chase, ' "We wish only to work for ourselves": the Chartist land plan', in Malcolm Chase and Ian Dyck (eds), *Learning and living: essays in honour of J. F. C. Harrison*, Aldershot 1996, 138–9.
[98] Idem, *The people's farm*.

Allotments and trade unionism

Whether or not the allotment movement stimulated Chartism, in at least one other respect the longer-term consequences of allotment provision were not quite what landowners had anticipated, or what most would have desired. For allotments both fostered and helped to sustain agricultural trade unionism. The 'revolt of the field' is conventionally dated to 1872, at the very end of the period covered in this book. Certainly it is true that the institutions of rural trade unionism were mostly created after 1873. But strikes and incipient trade-union activity were features of English agriculture from much earlier than this, and not only in the celebrated example of Tolpuddle. An early instance of an agricultural strike which was facilitated, if not made possible, because the labourers had allotments was at Berkswell, Warwickshire, in 1833. C. P. Villiers described the incident as follows:

> An instance was mentioned to me by Mr Illedge, in the parish of Berkswell, where the allotment system has been adopted, which though perhaps alarming to farmers, is certainly indicative of its effect upon the character of the labourer. He states, that during the harvest of this year, he had engaged some Irishmen to assist in getting in the crops; upon which every one of his own labourers struck work, and said that if the Irish were suffered to come upon the land that they would not do a stroke of work again for him. Mr Illedge said that he was obliged to submit, and sent away the Irish. These men had each allotments.[99]

Villiers was perceptive in pointing to the 'effect upon the character of the labourer' of allotment provision in this context. For ironically, allotments contributed to the conditions which made agricultural trade unionism possible partly because of their effectiveness in promoting the respectability which landowners so hoped they would inculcate. Agricultural trade unionism, perhaps even more than most forms of trade unionism in late nineteenth-century England, was imbued with a quasi-religious determination to regenerate its membership – in Joseph Arch's words, to bring 'redemption from bondage, beer, ignorance, and tyranny'.[100] Labourers who had a higher sense of their self-worth, and who wanted to 'raise' themselves and their fellow labourers, were more likely to be attracted to what was essentially a form of self-improvement. In other ways, too, allotment provision made agricultural labourers more amenable to trade unionism. As we have seen, allotments stimulated horizontal solidarity whilst emphasising vertical divi-

---

[99] *RC on the Poor Laws*, 1834, xxix. 75. A strike by about fifty agricultural labourers in 1831–2 at West Lavington, Wiltshire, precipitated by a wage cut from 9s. per week to 8s., may also have been facilitated by allotments. In 1833 there were 134 allotment tenants in West Lavington holding large plots of between a quarter and three-quarters of an acre. These allotments had been in existence for the previous eight years: *F&I*, 73–4, 426–7.
[100] Arch, *Autobiography*, 109.

sions (at least as regards employee–employer relationships). But probably the most important way in which allotments contributed to agricultural trade unionism was through providing a food supply on which labourers could draw during a strike. This aspect of allotments was well described by F. E. Green, author of one of the standard early twentieth-century histories of agricultural labourers, in terms which echo Villiers's account of the strike at Berkswell:

> The allotment, indeed, becomes a base 'to fly to', as labourers say, when times are hard and labour troubles have to be fought out. To the labourer the allotment is his castle behind the walls of which he can bargain more manfully with his heavily armed foe – the farmer.[101]

Allotments therefore both provided an economic resource which made it easier for labourers to undertake strike action and fostered social relationships and values which contributed to the growth of trade unionism. It was no doubt partly for these reasons, as well as because of strong demand for land from their members, that agricultural trade-union leaders later attributed so much importance to allotment provision. Joseph Arch argued strongly for land to be made more easily available to labourers and believed that compulsory measures were necessary.[102] He gave energetic support to Jesse Collings's allotments extension bill in the early 1880s, and continued to argue for allotment provision when elected to parliament in 1885. When Arch stood for the Wellesbourne division of Warwickshire County Council in 1889, the need for more allotments was the main focus of his campaign.[103] George Edwards, the great Norfolk labourers' leader, was equally committed to the struggle for allotments. Allotment provision was one of the main aims of the Norfolk and Norwich Amalgamated Labour Union, formed by him in 1889. After his election to the Aylmerston-cum-Felbrigg parish council in the mid-1890s, one of the first things Edwards did was to obtain allotments for the local labourers. In the discussions leading up to the formation of the Eastern Counties Agricultural Labourers' and Small Holders' Union in 1906 Edwards again argued that allotment provision should be one of the principal

---

101 F. E. Green, 'The allotment movement', *Contemporary Review* cxiv (1918), 91. See also Green, *A history of the English agricultural labourer*, 139 ('there is no doubt that the allotment is a standby in a time of stress such as lock-outs or strikes'). Hasbach noted that labourers found that allotments 'created a reserve-fund similar to that of a trade union': *A history of the English agricultural labourer*, London 1908, 349. However, most rural allotments were still let by landowners in the late nineteenth century. Trade unionist allotment holders were therefore often vulnerable to victimisation, as striking labourers on the duke of Marlborough's Oxfordshire estate found in 1872: Pamela Horn, 'Agricultural labourers' trade unionism in four Midland counties (1860–1900) (Leicestershire, Northamptonshire, Oxfordshire and Warwickshire)', unpubl. PhD diss. Leicester 1968, 63.

102 Arch, *Autobiography*, 129–32, 138. Despite this, Arch's maiden speech in the House of Commons was to oppose Chaplin's allotments bill, essentially on party grounds.

103 Pamela Horn, *Joseph Arch*, Kineton 1971, 159, 179, 192.

aims of an agricultural trade union.[104] Indeed, virtually all the agricultural trade unions formed in the late nineteenth century strongly advocated allotments, including J. Matthew Vincent's National Farm Labourers' Union (the main objective of which was the acquisition of land for allotments or co-operative farms), the Dock, Wharf, Riverside and General Workers' Union (which had fifty-eight agricultural branches in 1891) and the short-lived Oxfordshire and Lincolnshire Agricultural Labourers' Union.[105] Local agricultural trade-union leaders such as Joseph Ashby, who led the labourers of Tysoe, Warwickshire, in a seven-year campaign for land, were equally committed to obtaining allotments.[106]

In the first half of the nineteenth century rural protest had typically been spontaneous, episodic and illegal – characteristic manifestations included rioting, arson, machine breaking and animal maiming. The organised, disciplined and legal trade unionism of the last three decades of the century indicates that an immense and impressive cultural shift had taken place. The symbiotic relationship of allotments and agricultural trade unionism, and the close connection between the attitudes, values and forms of sociality encouraged by allotments and those which sustained rural trade unions, suggest that allotments should be seen alongside Methodism, education and fuller employment as one of the causes of this remarkable change in the nature of rural protest. Nor, in view of the effects of allotments in promoting self-respect, solidarity and the hope of a better future, and in giving labourers a stronger bargaining position *vis-à-vis* their employers, is there any reason to believe that allotment provision was the least of these causes.

104 George Edwards, *From crow scaring to Westminster*, London 1922, 55, 68, 101.
105 Pamela Horn, 'Agricultural trade unionism in Oxfordshire', in J. P. D. Dunbabin (ed.), *Rural discontent in nineteenth-century Britain*, London 1974, 101, 122–3, 125.
106 Ashby, *Joseph Ashby*, 122–34.

PART IV

TOWARDS THE THIRD ALLOTMENT MOVEMENT

8

Allotment Promotion and Provision,
c. 1845–1873

The organised allotment movement suffered a severe decline in the third quarter of the nineteenth century, but despite this the number of allotments continued to rise. In explaining this paradox, this chapter also attempts to account for the brief revival of parliamentary interest in allotments at the end of the period and to indicate the ways in which developments during these years foreshadowed the emergence of the third allotment movement in the 1880s.

The decline of the organised allotment movement

The decline of the organised allotment movement after 1845 was rapid. By the mid-1850s collective activity to promote allotments had been reduced to almost negligible proportions. The LFS, newly reincarnated as the SICLC, concentrated increasingly on the provision of housing. Parliament paid no significant attention to the allotments issue between the passing of the 1845 General Enclosure Act and the 1867 Royal Commission on the Employment of Children, Young Persons, and Women in Agriculture, in striking contrast to the welter of bills, acts and reports relating to allotments between 1830 and 1845. There are clear indications that the level of activity of the organised allotment movement on the local level also declined precipitately. Thus, for example, the Stewpony Allotment Society, founded in 1844, expanded rapidly in its first three years of life and was letting 190 acres, 1 rood, 35 perches in allotments by 1847.[1] But at this point expansion came virtually to a standstill, so that twenty years later, in 1867, the society was letting only just over an acre more than it had in 1847.[2] General public interest in allotments seems to have fallen quite drastically too, a point which can be illustrated by the number of references to allotments in the annual index to the *Gardener's Chronicle*. Between 1841 and 1850 there were a total of 105 references, but between 1851 and 1860 there were only seventeen and between 1861 and 1870 only four.[3] There is, therefore, ample evidence that the allot-

---

1   *LF* xlvi (1848), 45.
2   *RC on the Employment of Children, Young Persons, and Women in Agriculture*, 1868–9, xiii. 492.
3   *Gardener's Chronicle*, 1841–70, passim.

ment movement went into severe decline in the second half of the 1840s and the early 1850s. But why?

In the case of the LFS, the obvious explanation is the take-over of the society by Lord Ashley and his friends in 1844. The background to this event is a little obscure. In particular, it is not clear whether the existing leadership of the LFS welcomed Ashley's involvement, or whether they were more or less coerced. According to the 'Thirteenth report' of the LFS, the committee had for some while felt that the aims of the society should become broader, and was therefore glad to receive Ashley's proposal.[4] However, the first issue of the relaunched *Labourer's Friend Magazine* (now known simply as the *Labourer's Friend*) to appear after the formation of the new society stated that it was not the committee of the LFS but 'a body of gentlemen, not hitherto connected with that society [i.e. the LFS]' that decided that the LFS should be 'extended and invigorated'.[5] After the conversion of the LFS into the SICLC, Ashley showed little interest in allotments and it seems likely that he and his friends had always intended that the society should not merely be 'extended and invigorated' but redirected as well. In short, it looks very much as if the LFS was taken over, if not necessarily against its will, then at least without having much say in the matter.

Whatever the antecedents of the take-over, its results are clear: the new society from the first focused its attention on housing, rather than allotments. Although the formal declaration of the aims of the SICLC placed allotments at the head of its list of goals, even at the launch meeting of the new society the emphasis of the speeches fell firmly on housing. The main address, by Lord Ashley himself, discussed housing first, and at length, and mentioned allotments only very briefly.[6] This initial public meeting set the pattern for the future. The annual reports of the SICLC always devoted many pages to housing, and treated allotments in an increasingly cursory fashion.[7] The society soon became involved in heavy expenditure on its London model-housing projects, and it was these which came to dominate the energies and time of both the important finance committee, and the general committee which had overall executive responsibility for the SICLC's work.[8]

In one respect, the influx of capital and influence which Lord Ashley brought with him allowed the SICLC to go beyond what the LFS had dared to attempt: the new society began to let allotments on its own account. This was in accordance with the 'model' philosophy at the heart of the SICLC: just as model housing would demonstrate how good-quality housing for the poor could be constructed at low cost and let at low rents, so model allotments would demonstrate to landowners that allotments could be provided

---

4 'Thirteenth report of the LFS', *LFM* (1844), 4.
5 *LF* (1844), 1.
6 Ibid. 1–26.
7 Ibid. (1844–73), passim.
8 SICLC, general committee minute books, 1844–9, 1849–54, GLRO, 7/1/618–19.

cheaply, easily and advantageously. But the allotments sub-committee of the SICLC was small and marginalised, and it is hard to avoid the suspicion that the decision to let model allotments was more a sop to malcontent elements of the old LFS than an expression of commitment to allotments. Indeed, the society's new allotments were soon under threat, and although some degree of involvement with allotments continued into the mid-1850s, this was residual. Eventually, at a meeting of the sub-committee on finance on 9 June 1856, it was resolved that the SICLC should cease to hold any allotments; the end of the line for the society and allotments had been reached.[9]

How should the take-over of the LFS, and the eventual cessation of the new society's interest in allotments be interpreted? To some extent these events should be seen as representing the defeat of the old rural perspective on Britain's social problems that had informed the LFS by a new urban perspective. The society's advocacy of allotments had constituted a rural perspective in two main respects. On the one hand the LFS certainly placed much more emphasis on the problems of the countryside than on the problems of the towns; on the other, in turning to allotments as the solution to social problems, the LFS was looking to the land and to landowners, rather than to industry, for a way of dealing with the tensions which wracked British society in the 1830s and 1840s. As we saw in chapter 3, it was not merely the social problems of agriculture but also those of industry which the LFS believed could be resolved by looking to the land: the rural perspective of the LFS was an attempt to address the problems of British society as a whole, rather than merely those of the countryside.[10] The over-riding concern of the SICLC with the provision of model housing equally clearly represented an urban perspective on Britain's social problems. All their model-housing projects were located in cities, and whilst the high-density nature of the tenements it built made them well-adapted to urban locations with their high ground rents, they were not suitable for, and were never intended to be built in, the countryside.

However, a second and equally valid perspective on the supercession of the LFS by the SICLC would be to see it as a victory for the centre over the periphery, and hence as an early example of that general shift in the locus of social concern from the provinces to the metropolis which was apparent in the mid and late Victorian period. It is true that the LFS had always had many London subscribers, but the *Labourer's Friend Magazine* had hardly ever mentioned London, except as the venue for its annual general meetings. The SICLC, in contrast, came to be every bit as focused on London as the LFS had been on the provinces. For many years all its model housing was located within the capital, and even after this ceased to be the case the sum of money invested in London dwellings dwarfed that invested in the society's other properties. The *Labourer's Friend* also came to have a predominantly metro-

---

9   SICLC, finance sub-committee minute book, 1856–7, GLRO, 7/16/629, fo. 30.
10 LFS, *Proceedings*, 1832, 24; LFS, *Cottage husbandry*, 1835, 236; LFM cxlvii (1843), 82–3.

politan focus. Even the limited amount of attention the SICLC did pay to allotments was concentrated heavily on ones within a short distance of London: in 1849, for example, nine of the society's twelve sites were in the home counties.[11]

But whether the conversion of the LFS into the SICLC is seen as a victory for an urban perspective over a rural one, or a victory for London over the provinces, one thing is clear: it only came about because those whose commitment was primarily to the promotion of allotments were too weak to prevent them being removed from the top of the society's agenda. So whilst Ashley's coup in 1844 was undoubtedly a key moment in the decline of the organised allotment movement, it was more a symptom than a cause of that decline. Indeed the organised allotment movement was in decline not only at the national level, but at the local level too, even though none of the local societies were directly affected by the events within the 'parent' society. So in order to understand the decline of the organised allotment movement in the late 1840s and early 1850s we need to look beyond the internal politics of the LFS for an explanation which has a more general applicability.

One part of such an explanation may be that many within the allotment movement seem to have felt that their task had been essentially accomplished. At the annual general meetings of the SICLC, and even at some of the meetings of the local societies, the opinion was repeatedly advanced that it had become unnecessary to reiterate the arguments in favour of allotments and that other issues were now more pressing.[12] At the third annual meeting of the SICLC in 1846, for example, Ashley declared that

> it is not necessary that I should go into any detail on that subject [i.e. allotments], because I believe that question is beyond dispute. I find very few persons who now declare that the system of allotments, under proper regulations, will not materially contribute to better the condition of working men in our rural districts. I believe that is a matter so fully established that very few persons would attempt to gainsay it.[13]

There was certainly something to be said for the claim that the principal goals of the LFS had been broadly achieved. Whether one looked at the number of allotments, at the legislative position or at public opinion, much had been accomplished by 1845. As regards the number of allotments in existence, by the mid-1840s there may have been something like 100,000 plots in England, and these were, by and large, concentrated in the areas where rural poverty was at its worst and where they were therefore most needed. With respect to legislation, in 1845, more than three years of cumulative effort on the part of the allotment movement to secure the passing of a comprehensive act to

---

[11] *LF* lxiii (1849), 120.
[12] Ibid. 114; lxxiv (1850), 98–9; lxxxvi (1851), 119; xcviii (1852), 102; cxcii (1854), 102; cliii (1857), 27–8; ccxxxi (1870), 26–7.
[13] Ibid. xxv (1846), 82.

promote allotments was rewarded with the General Enclosure Act.[14] Whilst the act may not have been all that some advocates of allotments had hoped, it seems generally to have been felt that it was good enough to make pressure for further legislation unnecessary.[15] The success of the allotment movement in winning the public debate was described in chapter 3. It is clear that by the second half of the 1840s allotments were almost universally accepted within the landed elite as being socially beneficial. So those within the allotment movement who felt that the movement's task had been basically completed undoubtedly had evidence to justify their viewpoint.

But whilst the allotment movement had certainly achieved some impressive successes between 1830 and 1845, its decline after 1845 cannot simply be seen as a measure of its success. It is true that there was little influential opposition to, and much sympathy for, the aims of the allotment movement in the late 1840s, but this was not an entirely new development. The acts of 1831 and 1832, and the favourable discussion of allotments in the great *Poor law report* of 1834, were as much endorsements of the allotment movement as was the report of the 1843 select committee and the 1845 General Enclosure Act. Although there is little doubt that opinion within landed society was even more favourable to allotments in the mid-1840s than it had been in the mid-1830s, even in the earlier period few landowners actually opposed them. So advocates of allotments might with almost as much justification have said in 1835 that there was no need to repeat arguments which were already well-known and widely accepted. Yet, of course, they did not do so. Again, whilst it was true that the number of allotments had grown enormously since 1830, this did not necessarily mean that enough allotments had been provided. By the early 1880s the number of allotments had increased at least threefold, whilst standards of living for agricultural labourers had risen considerably, and yet the inadequate provision of allotments in rural districts was considered an issue of major political concern. The claim that the allotment movement had achieved its objectives by the late 1840s is, therefore, only partially correct, and reflects at least as much a decreased sense of urgency about allotments as it does the reality of the situation on provision.

A decreased sense of urgency can best be explained as resulting from the marked slackening in social tension in the late 1840s in both rural and urban England. In the countryside, the main causes of instability in the 1830s and early 1840s had been unemployment and low wages.[16] From the late 1840s, the labour surplus began to dry up quite rapidly, and employment became correspondingly fuller and more stable. Wages increased, and if these increases were relatively slow, they nevertheless made an important differ-

14 8 and 9 Vict c 118. See chapter 3 for a discussion of the genesis of the act.
15 *LF* xvi (1845), 305.
16 W. A. Armstrong and J. P. Huzel, 'Food, shelter and self-help, the poor law and the position of the labourer in rural society', in Mingay, *Agrarian history of England and Wales*, vi. 824–35.

ence to agricultural labourers, many of whose incomes were barely above subsistence level. The effect of rising wages on living standards was made greater by the fact that food prices were in most cases rising more slowly than wages, and were in some cases actually falling. With declining unemployment and rising real wages, living standards improved significantly in the country-side between the late 1840s and the early 1870s. Whilst rural crime remained a serious problem, much of it could now be attributed to vagrants or discontented individuals – it no longer signified the pervasive class alienation signalled by the incendiarism of the 1830s and 1840s. Archer notes that, whereas labourers in East Anglia in the 1830s and 1840s had often taken pleasure in arson attacks on ricks and farmyards, 'after 1851 labourers' attitudes dramatically altered and they invariably helped in fighting the fires'.[17]

Looking beyond rural England, the anxieties and conflicts of the 1830s and early 1840s were also sharply on the wane. The repeal of the corn laws in 1846 was a climactic moment, which gave a clear signal that whilst the political system might remain aristocratic, it would henceforth be worked with the interests of the middle class, and of consumers generally, borne clearly in mind. Chartism had its final fling in 1848, and when it became clear that the British political system had survived that year of European revolution virtually unscathed, there seems to have been a general sense that the moment of danger had passed and that calmer waters lay ahead. With the renewed economic growth of the 1850s and 1860s, calmer waters had been reached. The lessening of discontent and of the fear of social disorder, or even of revolution, to which it gave rise, go far towards explaining why, even though the majority of agricultural labourers had yet to be provided with allotments, there was so marked a slackening of energies in the allotment movement in the late 1840s and thereafter. The allotment movement, like so many other features of early Victorian society, bears witness to the onset of an 'age of equipoise' in the second half of the 1840s, an equipoise to which it had itself contributed significantly through its effects on rural living standards and on the values and behaviour of agricultural labourers. Ironically, in the longer term, these same consequences were to facilitate the rise of a force which did more than anything else to bring the rural age of equipoise to a close – agricultural trade unionism.[18]

The continued growth in the number of allotments

Sources for the number of allotments are extremely sparse for this period, but fortunately the first official 'census' of allotments, collected in 1873 as an

[17] Jones, 'The agricultural labour market', 322–38; Archer, *By a flash and a scare*, 7, 121, 161–2.
[18] G. M. Young, *Portrait of an age*, London 1936, Oxford 1977 edn, 41, 68–9, 76, 88–9; W. L. Burn, *The age of equipoise*, London 1968, passim.

appendix to the crop returns of that year, can be used to measure the extent of change over these years. It contains no information about the number of sites, but was intended to be comprehensive as regards the number of plots and the total allotment acreage in each county. However, in practice the 1873 survey falls short of completeness. There are two main reasons for this. In the first place, because information about the number of allotments was collected with the agricultural returns, the survey covers only rural parishes. The allotment movement was increasingly important in towns in the last part of the nineteenth century, so in this respect the 1873 figures understate the total number of allotments then in existence, perhaps significantly. However, in so far as the rural and urban movements had different causes, chronologies and geographical patterns of growth, it is perhaps fortunate that the 1873 returns are purely rural in character, since this allows for a more valid and informative comparison with the position estimated for 1845.

The second respect in which the 1873 returns are deficient is that it seems likely that they do not include allotments of more than an acre. The genesis of the 1873 returns was an appendix to the agricultural returns of 1872, which provided information about the number of allotments of between a quarter of an acre and one acre. It was pointed out that since a great many allotments were of less than a quarter of an acre, the 1872 figures were of limited value. The 1873 returns were collected in order to remedy this defect. So whilst the preamble to the returns does not explicitly state this, it seems likely that the figures do not include allotments of more than an acre.[19] In this respect too, therefore, the returns understate the true number of allotment plots in existence in 1873. However, the effect on total allotment numbers of omitting all plots of more than an acre is by this date likely to be small, since only about 3 per cent of all plots in the 1850–73 period were of that size.[20] Table 16 summarises the information about plot numbers and acreages provided by the 1873 returns: the caveats about urban allotments and allotments of more than an acre should be borne in mind.

The figures imply that the total number of allotment plots in England more than doubled between 1845 and 1873. Indeed, since there is little doubt that the 1873 returns were an understatement, it may well be that the number of allotment plots in England increased as much as three times between the mid-1840s and the mid-1870s. During the same period the proportion of parishes with allotments probably increased from under a quarter to about a third of all English parishes.[21] Thus the number of

19 *Agricultural Returns of Great Britain for 1873*, 1873, lxix. 301–5.
20 This figure is derived from the allotments database (see appendix 1). Of 160 sites for which the mean plot sizes for a date between 1850 and 1873 were recorded in the database, only five had a mean plot size of more than an acre.
21 The mean number of plots per site for the 154 sites for which information on this point was available from the database for the 1850–73 period was 58.42. On the basis of the figure of 242,542 plots given by the 1873 returns, this implies a total of about 4,150 sites in 1873, as compared to about 2,000 sites in the mid-1840s (see previous section).

Table 16
Total number and acreage of allotments in England, 1873

County	Total plots	Total acres
South-west		
Cornwall	1,762	288
Devon	7,063	1,814
Dorset	7,322	1,701
Somerset	9,503	2,015
Wilts.	15,445	4,310
Glos.	7,552	2,802
South		
Hants.	6,712	1,571
Berks.	5,007	1,146
Sussex	2,782	519
Kent	4,150	741
Middx	689	107
Surrey	1,263	345
East Anglia		
Essex	8,269	1,468
Cambs.	9,596	2,501
Hunts.	3,376	1,035
Suffolk	11,664	3,442
Norfolk	6,400	1,628
Lincs.	7,430	2,181
South Midlands		
Oxon	9,088	2,360
Bucks.	8,632	2,203
Herts.	5,197	727
Beds.	8,364	3,206
Northants.	16,447	4,294
West Midlands		
Worcs.	4,919	1,908
Warks.	12,794	2,734
Staffs.	5,444	1,116
East Midlands		
Derby	5,628	798
Notts.	11,317	2,104
Leics.	17,168	2,829
Rutland	1,252	327

County	Total plots	Total acres
Welsh borders		
Mon.	569	251
Hereford	997	192
Salop	1,002	230
Ches.	929	248
North		
Lancs.	992	102
Westmor.	52	6
Cumb.	410	46
Yorks. (E.R.)	1,781	759
Yorks. (W.R.)	6,876	1,385
Yorks. (N.R.)	4,731	1,240
Durham	1,000	139
Northumb.	968	148
Total	**242,542**	**58,966**

Source: *Agricultural returns of Great Britain for 1873*, 1873. lxix. 301–74.

allotments continued to grow at an equal or perhaps even greater rate between 1845 and 1873 than it had between 1830 and 1845.

As regards the regional distribution of allotments the south Midlands are newly significant – not only Northamptonshire, but also Oxfordshire, Buckinghamshire and Bedfordshire. The importance of this period for allotment provision in Oxfordshire is confirmed by Arthur Ashby, who noted in 1917 that '[t]here was a considerable extension of the amount of land under allotments from 1850 onwards'.[22] As a result of this, and of the continuing importance of the east Midlands, the centre of gravity of the allotment movement moved between 1845 and 1873 from the south to the Midlands. However, the extent of continuity between 1845 and 1873 is also striking. This is particularly so with respect to the areas in which allotments were very rare: still Cornwall, the Welsh borders and the north (although 'very rare' in 1873 meant something different from 'very rare' in 1845: only for Westmorland could it still be said that allotments were essentially unknown). It is also apparent that those counties in which allotments were most common in the 1830s and 1840s remained in the lead in 1873. The overriding feature, of course, is that almost everywhere experienced large increases in allotment numbers and acreage. How, then, can we explain the paradox that whilst the organised allotment movement became almost completely moribund, the number of allotments continued to grow healthily?

The 1845 act certainly played a part: by 1886, 2,113 acres of allotment

[22] Ashby, *Allotments and small holdings in Oxfordshire*, 17–18.

land had been provided under its auspices.[23] But if we assume that the average size of these sites was the same as it had been for all sites over the 1850–73 period, i.e. 15.5 acres, this implies that only 136 new sites had been created under the 1845 legislation. This would represent about 8,000 plots. Bearing in mind that this figure would be for 1886, it is clear that whilst the contribution of the 1845 act to the increase in the number of allotments between 1845 and 1873 was not entirely negligible, it was nevertheless small. If the estimates made above are not misleading, rather under 5 per cent of all new plots between 1845 and 1873 were created under the General Enclosure Act.

A more plausible explanation for the continued strong growth in the number of allotments is that whilst activists were no longer making a major contribution to allotment provision after the early 1850s, ordinary, non-activist landowners were. It was indeed to sympathetic non-activists that the SICLC itself attributed the continuing rise in the number of allotments.[24] Whilst the society did not specify why it was that non-activists were still making a significant contribution, it seems likely that the advantages of allotments to landowners described in chapter 5 had by this time become so well known that allotments continued to spread of their own accord. Some of the reasons landowners had for providing allotments may indeed have operated more strongly in the 1850s and 1860s. Contemporary testimony – notably the minutes of evidence of the 1867–9 Royal Commission on the Employment of Children, Young Persons, and Women in Agriculture – suggests, for example, that landlords felt less inhibited about using allotments as a means of increasing their rental income in these years.[25] The average level of allotment rent certainly rose in comparison to the earlier period, averaging 44s. per acre between 1830 and 1849, but 51s. per acre between 1850 and 1873, although this rise (of 13.1 per cent) was in fact less than the 18.5 per cent increase in the level of assessed agricultural rent in the second as compared with the first of these periods.[26] Another consideration which may have affected potential allotment landlords more strongly in the 1850s and 1860s than before is the pressure of expectations. The success of the LFS in achieving a moral ascendancy for allotments over their detractors by the early 1840s meant that landowners and clergymen increasingly took it for granted that allotments were desirable and should be provided where possible. At the same time, as allotments became more widespread, those parishes in which they were not provided became more conspicuous, both to neighbouring gentry and clergy and to their labouring inhabitants.

---

[23] Hall, *Law of allotments*, 37–8.

[24] *LF* lxxiv (1850), 99.

[25] *RC on the Employment of Children, Young Persons, and Women in Agriculture*, 1867–8, xvii; 1868–9, xiii, esp. 1867–8, xvii. 659–700.

[26] It is not, however, clear that the rise of allotment rents reflects a steady increase during the 1850s and 1860s: Burchardt, 'The allotment movement', 286–7. The figures for assessed agricultural rent were calculated from Turner, Beckett and Afton, *Agricultural rent*, 316.

Admittedly, some of the reasons that had induced landowners to provide allotments in the 1830s and 1840s became less pressing in the 1850s and 1860s. Neither fear of rural unrest nor dismay at the level of the poor rates were as prominent in 1870, for example, as they had been forty years earlier. Crime, particularly poaching, still concerned landowners in the third quarter of the nineteenth century, but less acutely than in the 1830s and 1840s. Most marked of all was a diminished interest in the old LFS project of across-the-board transformation in the moral character of rural labourers achieved by means of allotment provision. Whilst some landowners retained their belief in the efficacy of allotments in this regard, by the 1870s few allotment sites were established with such high hopes in mind. There had been a general retreat from the intensity of the second allotment movement; but this was partly because allotments had become a normal, if still by no means universal, feature of the rural landscape, their advantages well understood and accepted. This does not, of course, imply that they would not have spread at a faster rate had the organised allotment movement remained in being.

The revival of parliamentary interest in allotments in the late 1860s and early 1870s

In the late 1860s and early 1870s there was a temporary revival of parliamentary interest in allotments. This seems to have resulted directly from the 1867–8 and 1868–9 reports of the Royal Commission on the Employment of Children, Young Persons, and Women in Agriculture. The commission's task of investigating rural living standards made the question of the effects of allotment provision an important one, and, unsurprisingly, many of the assistant commissioners stressed the beneficial effects that allotments could have.[27] The report gave rise to the question of why there were not more allotments, if their effects were as beneficial as maintained, and, following a suggestion by H. S. Tremenheere that the attitude of the enclosure commissioners had prevented the 1845 act from operating as effectively as it was intended to, a select committee was set up to investigate how well the 1845 act had worked.[28] This reported in the 1868–9 session, and urged that a return be made of the acreage of allotments with the annual agricultural returns of the Board of Trade.[29] This return duly appeared in 1873. However, after 1873 there seems to have been a lull for a number of years, and whilst there were several amendments to the 1845 act, most of them were primarily concerned with enclosure and with commons preservation and touched on the question of allotment provision only in passing. It was only in the early

---

[27] RC on the Employment of Children, Young Persons, and Women in Agriculture, 1867–8, xvii, passim; 1868–9, xiii, passim.
[28] Ibid. 1868–9, xiii. 29–32.
[29] SC on the Inclosure Act, 1868–9, x. 332.

1880s that allotments again became a matter of pressing parliamentary concern in their own right.

The revival of parliamentary interest in allotments in the late 1860s and early 1870s does not seem to have led to any more general revival of public interest in the subject. The SICLC still survived, if only a shadow of its former self, but it showed no sign of a re-awakened enthusiasm for allotments in this period.[30] The regional societies seem to have been similarly unaffected by the attention that allotments were receiving in parliament.[31] Nor does it seem that new organisations dedicated to allotment provision emerged until the 1880s.[32] The lack of any strong public response to the revived parliamentary interest in allotments is also evident in the annual indexes to the *Gardener's Chronicle*, which for the period 1867–73 contain in total only two references for the seven-year span, as compared to five over the previous seven-year period.

After 1873, the number of allotments continued to rise. By 1887 there were, according to the parliamentary return of that year, 344,712 allotment plots of an acre or less in England, a marked increase on the 242,542 reported in 1873, whilst on the eve of the First World War there were probably somewhere between 450,000 and 600,000 plots.[33] In 1913, the Land Enquiry Committee estimated, on the basis of a survey of 2,685 parishes, that about two-thirds of rural parishes had allotments; since they had never been much wanted or provided in the northern counties, this suggests that allotments must have been available in the great majority of parishes in the southern half of England.[34] By this date it was indeed probably the case that virtually all agricultural labourers who wanted an allotment were able to obtain one. Certainly this was the case in Oxfordshire, the one county for which we have a detailed study from this date, and one in which, fortunately from our point of view, there had been considerable unsatisfied demand for land even as late as the 1870s and 1880s. According to Arthur Ashby, whose study was published in 1917, 'it has been possible for nearly every labourer in the county to obtain one or more allotments during the last twenty-five, perhaps thirty, years'.[35]

However, whilst the pattern of expanding allotment numbers represented continuity with the pre-1873 period, in almost all other ways the allotment movement entered a new era after 1873, in which, for the first time, most of the characteristic features of twentieth-century allotments emerge. In two

---

30 *LF* (1867–73), passim.

31 *LF* ccxxxi (1870), 26–7.

32 Peter C. Gould, *Early Green politics: back to nature, back to the land, and socialism in Britain, 1880–1900*, Brighton 1988, 105–23.

33 Unfortunately, the lack of acreage statistics from either the 1887 return or the Land Enquiry Committee frustrates attempts to calculate national acreage figures (and, consequently, average plot sizes) in the current state of knowledge.

34 Land Enquiry Committee, *The land*, i. 174, 188.

35 Ashby, *Allotments and small holdings in Oxfordshire*, 9.

respects, hints of the shape of things to come were already apparent in the late 1860s and early 1870s. In the first place, in their evaluation of the importance of allotments, the assistant commissioners of the Royal Commission on the Employment of Children, Young Persons, and Women in Agriculture placed the weight of their emphasis on the material benefits of allotments, and touched on their moral benefits in passing, if at all.[36] This marked a complete reversal of the attitudes that had prevailed towards allotments twenty years before. It was this new attitude, which saw allotments as important almost solely because of their impact on living standards, that was to be characteristic of the debate over allotment provision in the 1880s. The second important pointer towards the future was the advocacy of allotment provision by the new agricultural trade unions. Whilst it was only with the formation of the National Farm Labourers' Union in 1875 that allotments became an object of primary concern to agricultural trade unionism, even in 1872 there had been calls from within the National Agricultural Labourers' Union for more allotments for labourers.[37] Pressure from agricultural trade unions and their leaders was to contribute significantly to the passing of legislation on allotments in the 1880s. This again marks a distinctive break with the landowner-dominated allotment movement of the past (even if, as argued in chapter 6, labourers may have played a more important role in stimulating allotment provision than the bias of our sources might lead us to believe). So even though it was only in the 1880s that a vigorous allotment movement was to be reborn, there were already indications in the late 1860s and early 1870s of how radically different from its past the future of allotments would be. A new era, in which the pressure for allotment provision came from labourers rather than from landowners, and the grounds of provision were material rather than moral improvement, was about to begin.

Whilst the harbingers of this new era can be detected in developments in the allotment movement in the 1850s, 1860s and early 1870s, other major characteristics of the third allotment movement could less easily be read in the sands in 1873. It was only in the 1880s, for example, that the rising political awareness of agricultural labourers, in combination with the passing of the Third Reform Act, turned allotments into a subject of intense party-political controversy, with Liberals and Conservatives vying for the rural vote by trying to outbid each other over allotment provision. It was largely as a result of legislation passed in the wake of the high political profile that allotments enjoyed in the 1880s (and, more intermittently, down to 1914) that another great change in the nature of the allotment movement came about: the shift from the typical provider of allotments being a private landowner, to the typical provider being a public authority. There were also in 1873 as yet few indications of a further decisive change: that, whilst allotments were to

---

36 *RC on the Employment of Children, Young Persons, and Women in Agriculture*, 1867–8, xvii, passim; 1868–9, xiii, passim.
37 Horn, 'Agricultural trade unionism', 111–13.

maintain or even increase their popularity, they would in the future be significant more as a form of leisure and for the intrinsic pleasure they afforded, than as a means of eking out an inadequate income. Finally, in 1873 allotments were still, and were still perceived as being, overwhelmingly a phenomenon of rural life. Yet in the last quarter of the nineteenth century and in the twentieth century the growth in the number of allotments was to be primarily in the towns, so that in a surprisingly short space of time allotments would come to be seen as an archetypal feature of urban life. As living standards rose, agricultural labourers found that they no longer needed to use their few hours of freedom to toil on the land; whilst in the towns the reduction in the length of the working day and the availability of municipally-provided sites at affordable rents led to the allotment becoming an increasingly important element in urban working-class culture.[38]

[38] Crouch and Ward, *The allotment*, 61–3, 240–1, 25–6.

Conclusion

The allotment movement came into being at the cusp of the transition from the old 'organic' economy of pre-industrial England to the new mineral-based economy created by the industrial revolution. Whilst, in the long run, the development of capitalism led to an across-the-board rise in living standards, in the last decade of the eighteenth and the first half of the nineteenth centuries this hung in the balance as a result of the conjunction of very rapid population growth with increased exposure to market forces. In the countryside, the check to living standards was particularly sharp, because the demand for labour grew more slowly than in the towns, whilst the proletarianising effects of enclosure intensified dependence on the labour market. Severe underemployment and a fall in wages almost to subsistence level ensued, the economic conditions in which allotments could flourish. Underemployment and the loss of common rights reduced almost to zero the opportunity cost to rural workers (especially women and children) of the time spent working on an allotment, whilst near-subsistence wages made it possible for small plots of land cultivated by spade husbandry to offer a significant increment to income.[1]

The combination of Malthusian population crisis and proletarianisation brought rural society close to breaking point twice in the late eighteenth and early nineteenth centuries. The first occasion was the harvest failures of 1794–6 and 1799–1801, whilst the second was the Swing riots of 1830–1. Each occasion generated an interest in land provision for labourers amongst the rural elite. In the 1790s, both population growth and proletarianisation were still in their early stages, the crises proved temporary and landowners quickly lost interest in land provision; but they rightly recognised the Swing riots as symptomatic of a much deeper crisis. Indeed, the riots prompted a broad recognition among landowners that, in the context of the high rate of population increase, the policy of proletarianisation had proved socially unworkable; and they decided to reverse it by providing allotments.[2]

It is important to emphasise that allotments were a substantial, not merely

---

[1] The reason why in twenty-first-century Britain allotments no longer make a significant contribution to living standards, even for the unemployed, is that the value of the produce of an allotment has fallen to negligible levels in relation to the much higher incomes of even the poorest households.

[2] Reversing the policy of complete proletarianisation did not, of course, mean reversing the policy of enclosure; on the contrary, allotments were amongst other things a means by which landowners could continue to enclose without incurring the high social costs which had contributed to the Swing riots.

a token replacement for common right. If the value of an allotment is compared with the value of common right, we find that whilst a common right was usually worth more than an allotment of average size, the difference between the two is not as large as appears previously to have been supposed. Humphries cites contemporary estimates which imply that the net annual income yielded by the right to keep a cow (the most valuable element of common right) was probably between £7 and £9 *per annum*.[3] As chapter 6 demonstrated, an allotment-holder keeping a pig on the produce of an allotment of a quarter of an acre may have derived a net income of £4 or £5 from the allotment. Thus, if a quarter-acre allotment was not an adequate replacement for the right to keep a cow, neither was it negligible by comparison. Furthermore, it is doubtful whether many of the labouring poor possessed common right.[4] The majority without common right of course also gained from commons, but to a lesser extent. The main economic benefits which those without common right were normally able to obtain from commons were the gathering of fuel, food and materials, and the keeping of poultry.[5] Of these, the most valuable was usually considered to be fuel-gathering, but Humphries suggests that this may not have been worth much more than £1 per year. The value of commons to those without common right can scarcely have been much more, if as much, as that of a quarter-acre allotment.

Allotments not only raised family incomes substantially – perhaps by as much as a fifth – but were also available to a high proportion of agricultural labourers in southern England by the third quarter of the nineteenth century. They formed an important component of the rural socio-economic regime, making what might otherwise have been an unsustainably exploitative economic basis socially viable. In some respects, the revised significance of rural popular landholding this implies adds weight to the revisionist attack on the exaggerated contrast between the 'peasant'-type societies predominant in continental Europe and the proletarian character of agricultural labour in England.[6] In recent years revisionists have argued that, certainly in the nineteenth century and in some areas even in the twentieth, characteristic attributes of peasant societies can be found in rural England.[7] In particular, by no

[3] Humphries, 'Enclosures, common rights, and women', 25–7. Humphries makes no allowance for the cost of hay, on the grounds that it was either unnecessary to labourers with common right or available to them at a low price. Including the cost of hay would significantly reduce the estimated net annual income derived from a cow-keep.

[4] Shaw-Taylor, 'Labourers, cows, common rights'.

[5] Neeson, *Commoners*, 158–84; Humphries, 'Enclosures, common rights, and women', 31–4. On very large, poorly regulated, commons cottagers without right of pasture may have been allowed *de facto* to keep a few sheep or pigs but there were few commons of this kind.

[6] Macfarlane, *The origins of English individualism*, was the influential expression of this view.

[7] Reed, 'The peasantry of nineteenth-century rural England', and 'Nineteenth-century rural England'; Mills, 'Peasants and conflict'; Donajgrodzki, 'Twentieth-century rural England'; Hall, 'Fenland worker-peasants'; Howkins, 'Peasants, servants and labourers'.

means all rural labourers had been reduced to a proletariat dependent on a single source of waged income. Many continued to be hired annually, which gave greater security, and to be paid at least partly in kind.[8] Nor was the division between labourers and farmers a stark one in all parts of the country. Where, as in many areas, small farms remained common, a real prospect of social mobility existed. Labourers might themselves be the sons of small farmers, or even part-time farmers themselves.[9] Multiple occupationism, involving a mix of labouring, small farming, artisan production and trade, was widespread in these areas.[10]

The evidence presented in this book adds a new dimension to this emergent view. One of the crucial components of the 'peasant' mentality has usually been considered to be a high valuation set on land.[11] Some previous studies have suggested that, at least by the nineteenth century, English agricultural labourers had little interest in land.[12] However, the evidence presented in chapter 6 suggests that this was no more a characteristic of English agricultural labourers than it was of the continental peasantry.

But whilst reinforcing the central contention of revisionists who argue that English rural society contained more peasant elements than has hitherto been acknowledged, the evidence provided in this book suggests that the revisionists may in one respect have misdirected their arguments. One of the major premises of the revisionist case has been that previous scholars concentrated unduly on southern and eastern England, where a proletarianised, non-peasant labour force did indeed exist. Had more attention been paid to the north and west, where peasant elements were more obviously present, a more accurate conception of rural society might have been formed.[13] But as we have seen even in the supposedly proletarianised south and east of England, landholding by labourers formed an important part of the socio-economic regime. To see labourers with allotments as wholly proletarianised is simplistic and inadequate, and rests upon a failure to appreciate how significant a contribution to family incomes allotments actually made. Furthermore, if we fail to recognise the place occupied by land-holding by labourers in the political economy of rural society we misconceptualise the nature and workings of that society *in toto*.[14]

8 Howkins, 'Peasants, servants and labourers'.
9 Mutch, 'The "farming ladder" ', 162–83.
10 Reed, 'Nineteenth-century rural England', 85–8; Hall, 'Fenland worker-peasants', 5–6, 9–13; D. Mills, 'The peasant tradition', *Local History* xi/4 (1974), 200–6.
11 T. Shanin, *Defining peasants: essays concerning rural societies, expolary economies, and learning from them in the contemporary world*, Oxford 1990, 24–5.
12 Hobsbawm and Rudé, *Captain Swing*, 16, 66.
13 Hall, 'Fenland worker-peasants', 60; Howkins, 'Peasants, servants and labourers', 51, 60–1.
14 I am not, of course, arguing that we should use the term 'peasant' to describe southern agricultural labourers. My point is that, contrary to received wisdom, one of the most important facets of peasant societies – i.e. landholding – was also an important component of the social and cultural regime for southern agricultural labourers. On the whole it seems

If allotment provision restored a substantial role to plebeian landholding in rural society, did it represent a regression to a pre-capitalist, neo-feudal form of society? Some historians have seen allotments in this way, but their arguments are misleading: neither in its intentions nor in its effects was the mainstream allotment movement backwards-looking. On the contrary, the allotment movement was a persistently modernising force. This can be seen particularly clearly in the case of the first allotment movement. The SBCP, which together with the Board of Agriculture played the leading role in the movement, was an evangelical organisation founded by William Wilberforce and some of his friends. The remarkable constitutive influence of Wilberforce's evangelicalism on early and mid nineteenth-century thought and values is widely acknowledged. A number of historians, including A. M. C. Waterman and Boyd Hilton, have linked the 'moderate evangelicalism' of Wilberforce and the SBCP with the diffusion and acceptance of classical political economy amongst the landed elite and, correspondingly, with the making of liberal Toryism. It was the liberal Toryism of Huskisson, Peel and Gladstone that established the policy framework (especially through the reduction of import duties and retrenchment of expenditure), and much of the personnel, for the High Victorian Liberal Party. The allotment movement therefore emerged at the same time and from the same small group as did one of the most important strands of nineteenth-century liberalism.

The second allotment movement was also dominated politically by liberal elements. Of the twenty-six MPs subscribing to the LFS in 1833, all but two described themselves as Reformers, Whigs or Liberals, and although in the 1840s the bias within the society shifted towards Conservatism, even in 1850 there were twenty-three Whig, Liberal or Peelite MPs in the SICLC and only thirteen Protectionists. Admittedly, the ideological complexion of the second allotment movement differed from that of the first in that it was much more broadly based and correspondingly less closely identified with moderate evangelicalism. Indeed, if the Christian political economics of Whately and Copleston represented the authentic expression of moderate evangelical social thought, then a certain tension had developed between it and the more pragmatic and terrestrially optimistic economic tendencies of the allotment movement. This tension was perhaps most evident in the differing perspectives over the new poor law. Recent work by Peter Mandler has demonstrated how large a share Christian political economy played in the making of the new poor law. The LFS, by contrast, responded with ambivalence or even outright hostility to the restriction on relief entitlements which the 1834 Act sought to impose. But although many within the LFS rejected the methods proposed by the poor law commissioners, they were almost entirely in agreement with their objectives. The LFS correctly recognised that the commis-

unhelpful in the English context to classify one social group as 'peasant' as opposed to another social group which was not. More appropriate to English conditions is the concept of a continuum from proletarian to peasant.

sion's aim was an immense project of social engineering, whereby the poor would be taught to depend on their own exertions rather than on institutional charity. This was very similar to the LFS's own drive to promote independence, industriousness and prudence.

The second allotment movement did not, therefore, abandon the liberal ideology of the first; on the contrary, it was permeated with it. So although allotment provision did constitute an admission that the policy of proletarianisation through enclosure was socially unsustainable, it was also the continuation of similar ideological objectives by other means. In this respect, the response of landowners to the Swing riots was a surprisingly confident one, comparable to the similarly self-assured reaction of the political elite to Chartism in the next decade. Just as Chartism elicited a more active attempt to bridge the gap between the 'two nations' through class-integrative measures such as the reform of taxation, but no direct political concessions, so the Swing riots prompted the restoration of land but on a new basis which militated towards the attitudinal changes landowners wished to encourage.

The modernising character of allotment provision is also apparent in its form. Although allotments involved some collective elements, they differed from common land in that they were tenanted and cultivated individually or on a family basis. Secondly, valuable as allotments were to their tenants, they were not held by customary right but let through a market contract. Although land was restored to the labourers, it was on a new basis and pointed towards the individual enterprise and cash nexus of a fully marketised economy.

If allotments were modernising both in the intentions of those who sought to promote them and in the form in which they were provided, they appear also to have been so in their attitudinal and behavioural consequences. Allotments brought the values of the rural labouring poor more closely into line with characteristic elements of urban working-class culture, notably respectability, independence, self-help and mutuality. In the context of rural society, in which status was based on property and the most prestigious form of property was land, providing labourers with land had the effect of enhancing their self-respect. Allotments also gave back to their tenants a small area of control over their lives, which could be, and sometimes was, used to resist farmers' attempts to set wages at low levels. There were also close links between allotments and the related virtues of sobriety, thrift and self-help, because allotments gave labourers an incentive to stay away from the beerhouse on summer evenings and provided a tangible outlet for spare cash, which could be used to buy seed, manure or tools. There is also evidence of the symbiosis between allotments and the development of horticultural shows, fostering individual competitiveness. At the same time, mutuality was an important feature of allotment sites, which by their form and through the exigencies of their cultivation promoted the exchange of seed, crops and on occasion labour. Finally, allotments reduced criminality and, at least in the view of most contemporary authorities, encouraged industrious habits.

The combined effect of these changes was to make villages less 'rough' and more 'respectable' and to control and channel social conflict into more regularised, peaceable and legal channels, such as agricultural trade unionism. Whilst 'rough' and criminal features persisted in the late nineteenth-century countryside, few would dispute that a remarkable transformation in the character of rural protest had occurred between the riots and incendiarism of the 1830s and the trade unionism of the 1870s. Several forces, amongst them improved elementary education, the spread of Methodism and more regular employment, contributed to this transformation; but at least in rural southern England, where the change was most marked, allotments may have made as large a contribution as any of these.

Allotment provision was therefore a vector of rural modernisation. It was a recognition that enclosure had proved socially unviable, but rather than representing an anachronistic reversion to feudal social ties or to a pre-capitalist subsistence agriculture, should be seen as a half-way house on the road to the division of labour: allotments restored land to labourers, but in a marketised form. The final stage of the process, however, could only occur when rising wages and the development of more effective forms of social insurance allowed agricultural workers to forgo the security provided by land: a process that was not complete, in many villages, until the second decade of the twentieth century.

APPENDIX 1

The Allotments Database

Much of the statistical evidence used in this book derives from the allotments database, a dataset compiled by the author for this purpose. The database consists of 1,971 records from 1,641 different allotment sites between the years 1795 and 1873. Each record is for a particular site in a particular year. As many primary sources as possible containing information about allotments in the relevant period were located and all information contained in them about specifically-named allotment sites noted on filing cards. It was then necessary to establish criteria for inclusion in the computer database. The first criterion was that the record should genuinely be for an allotment site, rather than some other form of landholding. In particular, it was important to exclude all records which were actually for potato grounds. Potato grounds differed in many important respects from allotments, but especially in the early years of the nineteenth century were not always sharply differentiated from them by contemporaries (see chapters 1 and 2 and appendix 2). In constructing the database, it was usually easy to identify potato grounds because they were let, on a temporary basis, by farmers to their own labourers rather than by landowners to the inhabitants of the parish in general. Doubtful cases (including many from the 1834 poor law commissioners' 'Rural queries') were excluded from the database. The second criterion for inclusion was that the record must be unique, in that it did not duplicate any other record in the database. Many records were excluded for this reason: often, nineteenth-century sources do not identify the particular site involved in a clear and unambiguous way, and where it was possible, but not certain, that a record was for the same site as another record of the same date, one of the records was excluded. Thirdly, because it was intended to use the database to assess changes affecting individual sites over time, it was considered essential to exclude all records where it was not clear whether they were for the same site as another database record from a different year. Many records from the reports of the Royal Commission on the Employment of Women and Children in Agriculture were excluded for this reason. Where it was necessary to exclude a record from the database for one of the last two reasons mentioned, the record which contained the greater quantity of relevant information was retained.

As a result of these selection criteria a substantial number of sites for which information had been recorded had to be excluded from the database. Even so, the number of records which could be included remained very large.

The question of how representative the database sites are of all allotment sites in this period cannot be answered with absolute conclusiveness. Since we cannot know anything about those sites for which information does not survive, we cannot, by the same token, know anything about how like, or unlike, the sites in the database they were. However, because the database sites were drawn from as wide a range of sources as possible, it seems unlikely that they differ significantly from others. Furthermore, the characteristics of records derived from the different sources seem in general to be quite similar to each other which, unless all the main sources providing records for the database are biased in the same direction, again suggests that the database sites are quite representative of all sites.

It is also reassuring to note that, bearing in mind the fragmentary nature of the surviving evidence, a remarkably high proportion of all existing contemporary sites appear to be included in the database, especially for the 1830 to 1849 period. According to estimates made by Lord Ashley and by J. I. Burn in the mid-1840s, there were then about 2,000 allotment sites in existence (see chapter 2). The database includes records from 988 sites for the 1830 to 1849 period. In other words, if we make the plausible assumption that few sites became extinct in this comparatively brief period – one in which a very high proportion of all sites had recently been established – almost half of all sites in existence in the mid-1840s appear to be included within the database. For the pre-1830 period, only thirty-five eligible records (for twenty-six sites) were found. This number partly reflects the much smaller quantity of source material relating to allotments before 1830, but is mainly a consequence of the fact that very few allotment sites were established before 1830. Indeed, since there may actually have been no more than about 100 sites in existence before 1830, the twenty-six sites in the database are a significant proportion of the whole. For the post-1850 period, 627 sites are included in the database. Whilst this represents a decrease from the 1830–49 period, again reflecting the more limited quantity of source material available, the actual number of sites is still a large one, if less significant as a proportion of all allotments in existence in this third period.

The database covers the whole of England, with every English county apart from Westmorland (where allotments were very rare) being represented. Whilst some counties, such as Wiltshire, Leicestershire, Northamptonshire and Somerset supply many records, and others, in particular those in the north and along the Welsh border, supply few, this appears broadly to reflect the regional distribution of allotment sites.

It should be emphasised that the chronological and geographical distribution of the sites included in the database has not been determined in any way by a process of selection on the part of the author. On the contrary, every record found in the sources used for this study was included in the database, if it met the minimal criteria set out above.

Nevertheless, even though great care has been taken to make the database as comprehensive and representative as possible, the imperfections of the surviving evidence are such that it can only approximate to such ideals. In using it, the possibility of bias must always be borne in mind, particularly where the number of records on which a particular conclusion rests is small. For this reason, where database evidence has been used in the book, the number of records involved in each case has always been given. Care has also been taken to establish whether records deriving from different sources yield similar conclusions. In most respects, differences between records deriving from different sources appear to be slight. It should, however, be emphasised that, so long as they can be isolated and identified, such differences can actually be valuable, in that they may throw light on variations within the allotment movement in this period.

The software package on which the database was built was Microsoft Access 97. The database can be inspected on application to the author.

The Origins and Definition of Allotments

When was the first allotment site established? We will never be able to answer this question with complete certainty. Many allotments which the research for this study has not identified must have existed. More detailed local research would bring to light a number of these sites. To be sure of having identified the first allotment site we would need either a comprehensive national survey of allotments or of land use, neither of which exists for the late eighteenth or early nineteenth centuries. However, even if the ideal of perfect knowledge evades us, we can still draw some interesting conclusions about the probable origins of allotments in England. One interesting starting point is the history of the word itself. We may be able to catch a glimpse of the way in which the word came to be used in the modern sense by looking at the third *Report* of the SBCP, in which the earl of Winchilsea describes fourteen acres of ground at Whelford which were to be 'alloted in gardens, for the labouring poor'.[1] However, the word 'allotment' does not itself appear at all in the *Reports*, nor evidently had any other phrase come into general use, since the SBCP writers resort to a variety of unsatisfactory terms such as 'potato gardens' and even just plain 'land' for what we would now refer to as allotments. Sturges Bourne's Select Vestries Act of 1819, which amongst other things enabled parochial officers to let allotments, did not use the term either. But by the 1830s and 1840s compound forms of the word, such as 'cottage garden allotment' or 'allotment of land', were in common use. Thus the full title of the *Labourer's Friend Magazine* was *The Labourer's Friend Magazine: for disseminating information on the advantages of allotments of land to the labouring classes, and on other means of improving their condition.* Similarly, the 1843 select committee on allotments was officially known as the Select Committee on the Labouring Poor (Allotments of Land). In the 1840s the word was coming to be used more frequently on its own: presumably people had begun to find 'allotments of land' too cumbersome a phrase. It was also acquiring a more settled meaning: up until this time it had sometimes been used in quite eccentric ways, to refer for example to gardens or to cow pastures.

The word 'allotment' and its derivatives was by no means the only term used in the early nineteenth century to describe the phenomenon with which we are concerned. Other phrases in common use before 1850 were 'field gardens', 'garden ground' and 'cottage gardens'. Phrases involving the word

---

1 SBCP, *Reports*, iii. 118.

'potato' were also frequently used, especially 'potato ground', but this phrase was generally used for the quite different arrangement described under that name in chapter 1 and appendix 3. Interestingly, the variation in names was to some extent a regional matter: in east Somerset, for example, the term 'field garden' was the usual one.[2] From the 1840s these alternative phrases were becoming rarer, and by 1867 the word 'allotment' on its own had become standard.

What can be learnt from the history of the word 'allotment' and its various synonyms? The fact that several words were in common use to describe allotments in the first half of the nineteenth century suggests that they were not a long-established national phenomenon. That the word which eventually became the standard term seems not even to have existed in the first decade of the century points in the same direction. Finally, that the meaning of the word 'allotment' had not settled in the first half of the century is another indicator that the phenomenon was not yet a clearly recognised one.

We turn now to archaeological and documentary evidence. In the nave of the parish church of Great Somerford, Wiltshire, is a notice recording that the Revd Stephen Demainbray, rector from 1799 to 1854, 'originated the allotment system in England by giving part of his glebe to the poor cottagers of the parish'. The notice further informs its readers that the grant was made in 1809. Stephen Demainbray can be traced: he was one of the witnesses to the 1843 Select Committee on the Labouring Poor (Allotments of Land). Since he had also been summoned to the House of Lords Select Committee on the Poor Laws of 1831 to give evidence on allotments, and was not infrequently referred to by other advocates of allotments, Demainbray was evidently regarded as an authority on the subject. He, however, did not claim to be the founder of the allotment system: 'it was begun by the father of the present member for Oxford, Mr Estcourt; he began it in his parish of Newnton, near Tetbury, in Gloucestershire'.[3]

The father of 'the present member for Oxford' was Thomas Estcourt, a considerable landowner on the Gloucestershire/Wiltshire border and a frequent contributor to the *Reports* of the SBCP. Estcourt's allotments were described in the 86th *Report* of the SBCP by Sir Thomas Bernard, who stated that 'the plan itself is new'.[4] This was in 1801.

Bernard was not the only well-informed individual to state that the allotment system was begun in the early years of the nineteenth century. George William Gent, another witness to the 1843 select committee, made the following statement: 'I began it about 1840; I afterwards heard the Bishop of London say, that he was the first who suggested it, and that he adopted it when he was rector of Chesterford.'[5] This was in about 1820. A different

---

2   LFM cxxxiv (1842), 70–2.
3   SC on the Labouring Poor, 1843, vii. 11.
4   SBCP, Reports, iii. 163.
5   SC on the Labouring Poor, 1843, vii. 40.

suggestion was made by the Revd Richard Warner of Castle Cary. In an article he wrote for the LFS in the early 1830s, he asserted that the allotment system was 'brought into operation' by the bishop of Bath and Wells, then merely a rector, at Willingham in Cambridgeshire in 1807.[6] Independent evidence confirms that allotments were established in Willingham by the future bishop at about this time.[7] The SICLC's obituary of the bishop also claimed that Law's Willingham site was the original allotment site: 'His Lordship, we believe, had the honour of being the first individual who let out small portions of land upon that plan which is now universally known by the name of the Field Garden or Allotment system.' The obituary noted that there were several prior accounts of 'detached parts of the subject' in the *Reports* of the SBCP (it listed amongst others the description of Estcourt's allotments at Long Newnton), 'but in all these cases, and in fact in every other that has come under our notice, there was not the Field Garden system in that simplicity, disinterestedness and regularity which have since distinguished it'.[8]

Neither the SICLC's obituary writer, nor Gent, nor Warner was correct in his beliefs. But it is interesting to find four presumably independent sources (the SICLC, Gent, Warner, Demainbray and Bernard) stating that the allotment system was begun in the early years of the nineteenth century.

However, the history of allotment provision can in fact be traced back a little earlier than this. The first description of Thomas Estcourt's allotments in fact appears in the first of the two 1796 volumes of Arthur Young's *Annals*. Young notes that 'in the parishes of Ashley and Newnton, in the county of Wiltshire, and Shipton Moyne, in Gloucestershire, the landlord gave every cottager fifteen perches of ground, enclosed in one large piece, containing acres sufficient in that proportion for every cottage; thus thrown together in one piece to save the expense of separate enclosures'. No date is given for the establishment of these allotments, but from the context 1795 seems probable.

Perhaps it is unhelpful to think in terms of allotments originating in a single locality. The fact that people in the mid-nineteenth century attributed the origins of the movement to at least three different individuals in three different places may indicate that it was begun independently by several different people in the late eighteenth and early nineteenth centuries. If we are to rely on Gent's statement, the bishop of London believed that he was the first to think of the idea of allotments. Presumably the bishop would not have said that unless he believed he was speaking the truth. Yet we know that other allotments predated his by up to twenty years. The fact that at first different terms were in use in different regions for what we now call allotments lends support to the suggestion that the allotment movement may

6   *F&I*, 8.
7   *SC of the House of Lords on the Poor Laws*, 1831, viii. 170.
8   *LF* xviii (1845), 330–3.

have had multiple points of origin. It is not hard to believe that several people could have had the idea autonomously at about the same time: since it was widely believed that enclosure had, by depriving the poor of land and of access to land, been the cause of rising poor rates and immiseration, the idea of restoring land to the poor in some form was a relatively obvious course of action. Furthermore, as we have seen, many people had argued that the poor should be provided with land, even if they had not specifically proposed the division of fields into plots for this purpose.

So the notion of the allotment movement having a single point of origin is probably analytically unhelpful. Nevertheless, it cannot be denied that a certain perhaps antiquarian interest attaches to the question of where and when the first allotment site was established. The answer depends on how an allotment is defined. The most straightforward and encompassing definition is simply 'a small plot of land used for food production'. If this definition is adopted, allotments have presumably existed since agriculture began. But an allotment is surely more than merely a small piece of land. A crucial element of an allotment plot is the relationship between it and the other plots on the site – the collective dimension of allotments is as important as the private. Perhaps the most precise definition of an allotment as a physical entity is 'a plot of land, not attached to a house, in a field divided into similar plots, surrounded by a common external fence but without internal partitions'. The last clause is necessary to differentiate between genuine plots on the one hand and small fields on the other. An interesting consequence of this definition is that it excludes the Birmingham 'guinea gardens', which were separated from each other by tall hedges.

If this definition is accepted there would probably be a few English sites which would qualify as allotments from before the late eighteenth century, although it is often difficult to establish whether plots adjoined houses and whether they were individually fenced. But the danger with purely physical definitions like this is that whilst they may be logically precise, they can be arbitrary and meaningless when applied historically. It might, for example, be quite possible to find a site from (for example) ancient Assyria which would qualify as an 'allotment' according to the definition given above. But clearly there is absolutely no real connection between the hypothetical Assyrian site and the allotments of nineteenth- and twentieth-century Britain. If demonstrable historical continuity with what we know as allotments today is added to the definition, the Estcourt allotments, dating probably from 1795, have the strongest claim to be the first true allotment sites. The Estcourt sites appear to be the earliest which not only meet all the criteria of the physical definition but also have a traceable historical continuity with modern allotments (in that they were known to, and influenced, later allotment providers).

APPENDIX 3

Allotments and Potato Grounds

Two articles on allotments in nineteenth-century England appeared in the *Economic History Review* in the late 1990s – the first by Boaz Moselle, and the second by John Archer.[1] Both make some valuable observations, which are considered in the relevant sections of the main text of this book. However, Moselle and Archer differ sharply on several important points. The aim of this appendix is to demonstrate that these differences are attributable to the fact that neither author distinguishes between allotments and potato grounds, causing unnecessary historiographical confusion as a result.

The first major disagreement between the two authors is over the question of who let allotments. Moselle contends that

> based on the testimony collected (and a certain degree of cynicism as to the frequency of philanthropy as a motive force) it seems that, at the least, subletting by farmers must have been the dominant source of allotments in a significant proportion of parishes, while in many others it would have co-existed with landlord and/or parish provision.[2]

Archer, on the other hand, refers to the 'misleading impression that is given [by Moselle] of the farmers being the main lessors of allotments'.[3]

Secondly, Moselle and Archer disagree about the chronology of allotment provision. Moselle is rather vague about the dating of the rise of allotments. He states that '[a]lthough it is impossible to obtain exact figures, contemporary accounts make it clear that allotments, which were little known or used in the eighteenth century, did indeed spread rapidly in the first half of the nineteenth century'.[4] The link he makes between rising allotment numbers and falling relative wheat prices (illustrated by a graph showing the relative price movements of wheat and potatoes between 1790 and 1826) implies an earliest date of about 1811, when, according to his figures, the fall in the price of wheat relative to potatoes began (though the emphasis which, as we shall see, Moselle places on unemployment elsewhere in his article would suggest an earliest date three or four years later than this).[5] Archer again takes a different view: while accepting that there were a few earlier instances of allot-

---

[1] Moselle, 'Allotments, enclosure, and proletarianization', 482–500; Archer, 'The nineteenth-century allotment', 21–36.
[2] Moselle, 'Allotments, enclosure and proletarianization', 486.
[3] Archer, 'The nineteenth-century allotment', 21.
[4] Moselle, 'Allotments, enclosure and proletarianization', 488.
[5] Ibid.

ment provision, he states that in East Anglia, the area covered by his study, interest in allotments 'only really began to gather momentum with the onset of the Captain Swing riots in 1830'.[6]

Thirdly, Moselle and Archer also disagree about what was grown on allotments. One of the central claims of Moselle's article is that allotment holders primarily grew potatoes on their plots, and that whilst they might sometimes grow a small proportion of other vegetables, they very rarely grew corn.[7] Archer, by contrast, states that many labourers in East Anglia grew wheat as well as potatoes on their plots.[8] Finally, Moselle and Archer adopt different views about whether allotment provision should be understood as an economic phenomenon, or whether allotments were provided for primarily social reasons.[9]

The main reason for these major differences of opinion it that neither author makes the crucial terminological distinction between potato grounds and allotments proper. The differences between potato grounds and allotments have already been outlined (*see* chapter 1). However, since these differences are of such importance to clarifying the disagreement between Moselle and Archer, a fuller discussion of them seems warranted here.

The contrasts between allotments and potato grounds were numerous and significant. Potato grounds were let by farmers, whilst allotments were let by landowners or others, but only exceptionally by farmers. Potato grounds were let to the labourer on a temporary basis, normally for the duration of the summer potato-growing season only, whilst allotments were let on an annual basis and were intended to have a quasi-permanent character (which meant that most farmers, being mere tenants rather than owners, were not in a position to let allotments even had they wished to). Potato grounds seem to have become common from about the 1790s, whereas allotments only became common after 1830. Potato grounds were let at a market rent, or formed part of a labour contract, whereas allotments were generally let at a 'fair' rent (which meant in practice the rent that a farmer would have paid for the same parcel of land – not at all the same thing as a market rent, since allotments were considerably more profitable than farmland). Potato grounds were nearly always ploughed, and were often manured, by the farmer whose land they were on, whereas spade husbandry was almost universal on allot-

---

6   Archer, 'The nineteenth-century allotment', 23.
7   Moselle, 'Allotments, enclosure and proletarianization', 486, 488.
8   Archer, 'The nineteenth-century allotment', 29.
9   Moselle, 'Allotments, enclosure and proletarianization', 498–9; Archer, 'The nineteenth-century allotment', 25. Moselle and Archer also disagree over the separate but related issue of why farmers were so often hostile to allotments. This question is discussed at some length in Burchardt, 'Rural social relations', 165–75, which endorses Archer's criticisms of Moselle's economically reductionist approach. The bitterness with which many farmers opposed allotments can only be explained if we take into account the less tangible aspects of the impact of allotments on the relationship between farmers and labourers, in particular with respect to social status.

ments, ploughing being very rare on all but the small number of very large allotments. The labourer's unexhausted inputs from potato grounds (labour, and in some instances manure) went to the farmer, benefiting his next year's crop, whilst on allotments, because of their quasi-permanent character, the labourer gained the full value of his inputs. Potato grounds seem normally to have been let only to the farmer's own employees, whereas eligibility for an allotment was only in a tiny minority of exceptional cases restricted to the landowner's own employees (the main category of exception in the first half of the nineteenth century being the handful of sites let by industrialists to their workers). On potato grounds, only potatoes seem to have been grown, whereas on allotments, although potatoes were the most important crop, wheat also occupied a significant share of the total acreage, while a small share was devoted to a wide variety of additional vegetables and grains. The benefit derived by labourers from potato grounds seems, unsurprisingly in view of the contrasts described above, generally to have been very much less than that derived by labourers from allotments, and may indeed have been so small as to be of limited significance. The benefits derived by labourers from allotments were normally substantial, and sometimes very substantial (*see* chapter 6). Finally, potato grounds were let almost purely for economic reasons, whereas allotments were let for overwhelmingly social and moral purposes.[10]

The reason that Moselle does not distinguish between allotments and potato grounds is that his article is almost completely dependent for its information about allotments on no more than two contemporary sources, the 1834 poor law inquiry and the report of the 1843 Select Committee on the Labouring Poor, neither of which makes a clear distinction between allotments and potato grounds. In other contemporary sources, notably the *Labourer's Friend Magazine* but also other parliamentary reports such as the 1843 and 1867 reports on women's and children's employment in Agriculture, the distinction is made more explicitly. The reason that Archer does not distinguish sharply between potato grounds and allotments is again because of the nature of the sources used. He relies primarily on newspaper evidence. Allotment provision was a public act with important social implications; there was an organised allotment movement and the subject of allotments generated much public interest. Consequently, allotments were much reported and discussed in the press. Potato grounds, however, were a purely commercial arrangement between farmers and labourers, and had only limited social implications. There was no such thing as a 'potato grounds movement' and, unsurprisingly, potato grounds seem rarely to have been mentioned in the press. In order to find out about potato grounds it is necessary to look at sources such as parliamentary reports and, again, the *Labourer's Friend Magazine*. A further reason for Archer failing to distinguish clearly

---

[10] For further discussion of the contrasts between potato grounds and allotments see Burchardt, 'Land and the laborer', 667–84.

between allotments and potato grounds may be that potato grounds seem to have been considerably less common in Norfolk, Suffolk and Essex (though not in Cambridgeshire or Huntingdonshire) than they generally were in the rest of the country.

The fact that Archer does not distinguish between allotments and potato grounds does not on the whole undermine his arguments, although it does prevent him from realising why Moselle reaches such different conclusions. The sources Archer uses provide information almost exclusively about allotments, and Archer writes almost exclusively about allotments. Moselle's failure to distinguish between allotments and potato grounds, however, causes several serious confusions. The three most important of these concern rent, crops and plot size respectively.

As regards rent, Moselle explains that his figures, derived from the answers to question twenty of the 'Rural queries' of the 1834 poor law commissioners, exclude 'all figures where the answer suggested either that the allotment was provided as a form of charity/relief, or that the figure included services such as ploughing or manuring as well as pure rent'.[11] It is almost impossible to know what the figures arrived at as a result of this procedure represent. Depending on the degree to which Moselle was successful in identifying rents including 'services', he will have excluded many or most potato grounds, since potato grounds were always ploughed and often manured too by the farmer. Had Moselle succeeded in eliminating all cases where rents included such services, he would have been left with rents for allotments only (although the fact that a significant proportion of the rents in his dataset are very high, i.e. characteristic of potato grounds rather than allotments, suggests that he has been less than completely successful in this). However, by excluding all cases where the answer 'suggested . . . that the allotment was provided as a form of charity/relief', Moselle leaves us with figures which would be meaningless even if uncontaminated by potato ground rents. Many, perhaps even most, allotments were not let at a market but at a 'fair' rent.[12] Allotments let at 'fair' rents could well be considered a form of charity, since the landowner was foregoing potential profit by not letting them at a market rent. Any attempt to demarcate sharply between 'fair' and 'charitable' rents runs into the problem that the decision about just how much potential profit has to be forgone for the letting to be called charitable rather than fair is inevitably entirely arbitrary. The effect of Moselle's attempt to weed out allotments provided as a form of charity/relief will therefore merely have been to exclude the lower-rented allotments. So the figures we are left with are presumably in the main those for allotments let at medium and high rents, mixed in with some for potato grounds which have slipped through the net. It is clear that any average of such a set of figures will be virtually meaningless, and that it most certainly cannot be taken as indicative of average allotment rents.

---

11 Moselle, 'Allotments, enclosure and proletarianization', 500.
12 See chapter 5.

Moselle's main purpose in attempting to establish allotment rents is so that they may serve as a proxy for pre-rent profits. The rents of allotments proper are not actually very suitable for this, since, as explained above, many allotments were let at 'fair' rents which were a long way below the maximum rents that the profits of their holders would have allowed. However, it is true that (as Moselle suggests) they do at least set a lower bound for profits. But again, it must be pointed out that it is not legitimate to assume that pre-rent profits on allotments and on potato grounds would have been similar. There were numerous differences in the cultivation of allotments and potato grounds which make it seem likely that pre-rent profits on the two would have differed. Potato grounds were almost always ploughed, whereas allotments were almost always dug. It was widely agreed that on all but very light soils digging led to much higher yields than ploughing. Furthermore, it was very often the farmer who provided the manure for potato grounds. But one of the main reasons for the high yields of allotments proper was that they were generally very heavily manured: the labourer was able to use his children as free labour to go round the parish roads collecting up manure for the allotment (in addition to manure from the pig which the labourer often kept). So allotments may well have been more heavily manured than potato grounds. Even in the case of those potato grounds manured by the labourer manuring may have been less heavy, because whilst on an allotment all the benefit of the raised soil fertility went to the labourer, with a potato ground it was the farmer who would reap the benefit of the improved soil in subsequent seasons. So labourers would have had much less incentive to manure a potato ground heavily. Bearing these considerations in mind, it seems quite likely that yields and similarly pre-rent profits would have been substantially higher on allotments than on potato grounds. So even had Moselle's calculation of rent been a valid method of assessing allotment rent, it would still not be very useful as a measure of potato ground pre-rent profits. Yet Moselle's subsequent argument builds on the evidence he thinks he has assembled that 'allotments let by farmers' [i.e. potato grounds] were highly profitable in order to explain why farmers sometimes let land to labourers but nevertheless opposed allotments.

Moselle's failure to distinguish between allotments and potato grounds also leads him into confusion on the question of the crops grown on allotments. He states that 'allotments were not in general used to grow corn'.[13] His evidence for this view is (1) that sixty-four of the sixty-six replies from southern parishes to question twenty of the 'Rural queries' which 'discuss' the crops grown by local labourers mention only potatoes; (2) that the authors of the 1834 report mention only potatoes; (3) that 'of the nineteen witnesses who spoke before the 1843 select committee, six specified the crops grown on allotments to be potatoes and/or other vegetables, while with one exception the growing of corn was associated only with holdings of a few acres'; (4) that

---

13 Moselle, 'Allotments, enclosure and proletarianization', 486.

ten of the witnesses to the 1843 select committee mention the use of spade culture, while none mention the ploughing of allotments; and (5) that '[t]he repeated insistence that allotment holders could not cultivate more than a very small area of land also suggests that they were engaged in a heavily labour intensive activity, that is spade culture and vegetable growing rather than ploughing and cultivation of corn'.[14]

But Moselle has misread the evidence here. It can scarcely be said that the replies to question twenty of the 'Rural queries' discuss anything, since they are brief responses of no more than a few words which had to be fitted into a small space on a large questionnaire. Certainly they do not, with very few exceptions, discuss what crops labourers grew on their land. What Moselle has read as a discussion of cropping is in fact merely the use of a descriptive term to identify the type of land let. The only terms available for potato grounds were terms which incorporated the word 'potatoes' (the main terms in use at this time were 'potato grounds' and 'land, to grow potatoes'), whereas allotments were generally referred to as 'small allotments of land', 'allotments of land', or 'field gardens' (there are actually relatively few references to allotments in the 'Rural queries', which is not surprising as they were still rare in most counties in 1833). This means that where a source, such as the 'Rural queries', contains information about whether land (of either sort) was let to labourers, but does not actually discuss the question of what was grown on the land, the source will, merely in referring to the land, mention the word 'potatoes' frequently, and corn or indeed anything else grown on the land only in the very limited number of instances where the response actually discusses what was grown on the land, rather than merely mentions that land was let to labourers. In short, the sixty-six replies to question twenty mentioned by Moselle do not, in the overwhelming majority of cases, discuss what crops were grown on the land at all. The great majority of these sixty-six replies are merely mentions of potato grounds. Since the 'Rural queries' were carried out in the infancy of the allotment movement (no more than two or three years after its real onset), it is not surprising that the 'land' being referred to is predominantly potato grounds.

Moselle's second piece of evidence, that the 'authors' of the 1834 report mention only potatoes, is not very convincing either. It is not clear what Moselle is referring to – does he mean the section on 'occupation of land by labourers' in the report itself, or does he also include the appended reports and evidence of the assistant commissioners? It is not very surprising that the former does not specifically mention corn as a crop grown on allotments, since the section is brief and does not include a discussion of what crops were grown on allotments.[15] If Moselle means to include the appended reports too, his assertion is not correct, since the growing of corn is in fact mentioned several times, even though the question of what was grown on allotments was

14 Ibid.
15 *RC on the Poor Laws*, 1834, xxvii. 100–8.

not amongst the topics the assistant commissioners had been asked to investi-gate with respect to the occupation of land by labourers.[16] Nor is Moselle's third piece of evidence, that only one of the witnesses to the 1843 select committee spoke of the growing of corn, strictly accurate.[17] Moselle's fourth and fifth grounds for believing that corn was only very rarely grown on allot-ments both rest on the mistaken assumption that corn was only grown on land which had been ploughed, and so are also of little weight. This error results from the limited range of sources Moselle uses: had he read the *Labourer's Friend Magazine*, for example, he would have been aware that land cultivated by the spade was often used for growing corn.

There is, indeed, conclusive evidence that corn was often grown on allot-ments. This is discussed at some length in chapter 6 of this book. Briefly, after an examination of a wide range of sources, records were available for the 1830–73 period for 120 sites with at least some information about what crops were grown. Of the 120 sites, corn was grown on at least seventy-one. For ten of the 120 sites, information about not just the most commonly grown crops but about all crops grown on the site was available. Of these ten sites, corn was grown on nine. The growing of corn on allotments was also widely discussed in the contemporary literature; there is, for example, an interesting discussion of this issue in the 1867–8 *Report of the Royal Commission on the Employment of Children, Young Persons, and Women in Agriculture*.[18]

So, once again, Moselle has been led astray by missing the distinction between allotments and potato grounds. Whilst it is quite correct to suggest that corn was not grown on potato grounds, it is wholly misleading to claim that the same is true of allotments. The fact that corn was commonly grown on allotments seriously undermines Moselle's central argument, that the spread of allotments in the first half of the nineteenth century 'represented an alternative technology, the use of labour intensive techniques to produce vegetables, in contrast to the capital intensive methods used on large, corn-producing farms'.[19] Whilst this may help to explain the rise of potato grounds, it is at best only partially relevant to the history of allotments proper.

A third respect in which Moselle's lack of awareness of the distinction between allotments and potato grounds leads him into confusion is when he comes to discuss plot size. Moselle again uses the 'Rural queries' to establish plot size; but it must be said that an average figure for plot size of two types of landholding which were so different from each other seems of limited useful-ness.[20]

The fact that corn was in fact commonly grown on allotments means that Moselle's explanation for the spread of what he calls allotments is not actu-

16 Ibid. xxviii. 669, 677–8; xxix. 74.

17 *SC on the Labouring Poor*, 1843, vii. 9, 17.

18 *RC on the Employment of Children, Young Persons, and Women in Agriculture*, 1867–8, xvii. 180.

19 Moselle, 'Allotments, enclosure and proletarianization', 488.

20 Ibid. 484–5.

ally applicable to allotments proper. However, most of Moselle's argument is about 'allotments' let by farmers (i.e. potato grounds), and his flawed procedures for calculating rents and plot sizes and his erroneous assumptions about cropping do not significantly undermine his account of potato grounds. But whilst Moselle's account of potato grounds may be broadly internally consistent, there is nevertheless a serious difficulty with it: it is not compatible with the actual chronology of the spread of potato grounds in early nineteenth-century England. Moselle argues that 'allotments' spread in the early nineteenth century firstly because labourers and their families were, in an era of high unemployment and underemployment, more efficient producers of labour-intensive crops such as potatoes, and secondly, because the early nineteenth century saw a decline in the price of wheat relative to that of potatoes, making potato cultivation more profitable than it had been. Unemployment and underemployment only became a major feature of nineteenth-century English rural life after the demobilisation that came with the ending of the Napoleonic wars.[21] The relative price of wheat to potatoes fell from about 1811 onwards, three or four years earlier.[22] But, as a reading of the Board of Agriculture county surveys conclusively demonstrates, the rise in the number of potato grounds, far from following these events, in fact preceded them by many years. Indeed, in several counties potato grounds were already common in the 1790s.[23]

On almost all the points on which he disagrees with Archer, therefore, Moselle is incorrect if his article is taken as an account of allotments, but at least partially accurate as an account of potato grounds. Far from being 'the dominant source of allotments in a significant proportion of parishes', farmers hardly ever let allotments; but they let thousands of potato grounds. The steep rise in the rate of allotment provision can be dated not to 1811 or thereabouts but to 1830; potato grounds, on the other hand, were common long before 1830 (although actually from at least a decade earlier than Moselle suggests). Potatoes were not the only important crop on allotments – on the contrary, corn was very often grown too – but they were on potato grounds. Finally, allotments were provided by landowners more for moral, social and political than for economic reasons, but potato grounds were let almost entirely for economic purposes. The seemingly wide interpretative differences between Archer and Moselle therefore largely resolve themselves once the significance of the distinction between the two forms of landholding is fully appreciated.

[21] Norman Gash, 'Rural unemployment, 1815–34', *EcHR* vi (1935), 91; Jones, 'The agricultural labour market in England, 1793–1872', 337–8.
[22] Moselle, 'Allotments, enclosure and proletarianization', 488.
[23] For evidence of the county-by-county incidence of potato grounds see Burchardt, 'Land and the laborer', 671–4.

APPENDIX 4

Legislative Limits on Plot Size

Legislation affected the maximum permitted plot size of allotments let under act of parliament. Under 2 Will IV c 42 ('for the conversion of fuel allotments into gardens for the poor'), allotments could be no larger than an acre and no smaller than a quarter of an acre. The provision that allotments let under the act were not to be smaller than a quarter of an acre was repealed in 1873 by 36 Vict c 19. Under the General Enclosure Act of 1845 (8 and 9 Vict c 118), allotments provided as a result of enclosure under the act were not to be larger than a quarter of an acre. This was partially repealed by 39 and 40 Vict c 56 which allowed allotments created under the 1845 Act to be let in plots of up to an acre where it proved impossible to let them in plots of a quarter of an acre or less. Subsequent allotments acts also set limits to the size of plots that could be provided by public authorities under their provisions, but these fall outside the time period covered by this study.

However, the limitations on the size of allotments let under 2 Will IV c 42 and 8 and 9 Vict c 118 should be put into context. Allotments provided by public authorities formed a small proportion of the total in the period 1793 to 1873. Of 565 sites included in the database, and for which information about who let the site is available, only 74 sites (13.1 per cent) were let by public authorities. Even this may be an overestimate of the proportion of allotments let publicly in the period as a whole, since the database suffers from an over-representation of sites from the period 1830–5, and it was widely thought that the three acts of 1831 and 1832 fell into disuse after 1835. Certainly by 1886 the proportion of sites let publicly seems to have fallen to a level distinctly below 13 per cent, since Hall, writing in that year, claims that 'allotments let voluntarily by private landowners are probably twenty times as numerous as those let under special acts of Parliament'.[1] It is difficult to imagine, therefore, that limitations on the size of allotments let under act of parliament could have had anything other than a very small effect on the average plot size of all allotments in this period. In any case, the upper limit set by 2 Will IV c 42 was fairly generous, and there were two further acts (1 and 2 Will IV c 42 and 1 and 2 Will IV c 59) passed in the early 1830s which set no limit (beyond that specified for sites as a whole) on plot size.

---

[1] Hall, *Law of allotments*, p. vi.

APPENDIX 5

Allotment Plot Size

Table 17
Plot size (national averages)

The dataset used for this study provides the following information for the mean plot size of allotment sites in England (excluding Monmouthshire):

1793–1829:	91.37 perches	(19 records)
1830–49:	61.49 perches	(479 records)
1850–73:	45.25 perches	(160 records)

Source: Database

Notes:

1. There are 160 perches in an acre, and forty in a rood (quarter of an acre).
2. The modern norm is 10 perches.[1]
3. A 'record' means the average plot size for a given site in a given year.
4. For further discussion of the data on which this table is based see Burchardt, 'The allotment movement'.

The special return of allotments included with the 1873 *Agricultural Returns* allows a figure for national mean plot size to be calculated (again, after Monmouth has been excluded) at 38.82 perches. This figure, however, cannot be directly compared with the database figure for 1850–73, because it seems likely that the 1873 return excluded all allotments of over an acre.[2] If the database figure is recalculated on the same basis (i.e. excluding all allotments of over an acre), the result is 36.99 perches (155 sites), very close to the 1873 return figure of 38.82 perches.

[1] Moran, 'Origin and status', 12.
[2] *Agricultural Returns of Great Britain for 1873*, 1873, lxix. 304–5.

Table 18
Mean plot size by region

Region	Period	Mean plot size (perches)	No. of records
South-west	1830–49	61.85	140
	1850–73	37.89	27
South	1830–49	54.52	81
	1850–73	21.37	22
East Anglia	1830–49	58.94	83
	1850–73	36.11	12
South Midlands	1830–49	62.41	37
	1850–73	59.49	43
West Midlands	1830–49	70.49	29
	1850–73	34.00	5
East Midlands	1830–49	45.80	89
	1850–73	24.44	6
Welsh borders	1830–49	72.14	7
	1850–73	80.00	4
North	1830–49	66.24	13
	1850–73	55.13	37

Source: Database

Notes:
South-west = Cornwall, Devon, Dorset, Somerset, Wiltshire, Gloucestershire
South = Hampshire, Berkshire, Sussex, Kent, Surrey, Middlesex
East Anglia = Essex, Cambridgeshire, Huntingdonshire, Suffolk, Norfolk, Lincolnshire
South Midlands = Oxfordshire, Buckinghamshire, Hertfordshire, Bedfordshire, Northamptonshire
West Midlands = Worcestershire, Warwickshire, Staffordshire
East Midlands = Derbyshire, Nottinghamshire, Leicestershire, Rutland
Welsh borders = Monmouthshire, Herefordshire, Shropshire, Cheshire
North = Lancashire, Westmorland, Cumberland, East Riding, North Riding, West Riding, Durham, Northumberland

Table 19
Mean plot size by quinquennium, 1830–49

1830–4:	75.92 perches
1835–9:	50.87 perches
1840–4:	49.22 perches
1845–9:	36.26 perches

Source: Database

Note: Figures weighted to allow for changing regional distribution of records.

Table 20
Mean plot size by year, 1830–49

Year	Mean plot size (perches)	No. of records
1830	89.67	9
1831	87.87	27
1832	94.24	14
1833	72.44	162
1834	72.06	36
1835	57.34	14
1836	40.00	6
1837	59.56	3
1838	46.06	8
1839	43.13	8
1840	51.35	16
1841	47.96	13
1842	58.00	15
1843	37.11	24
1844	57.26	10
1845	43.42	73
1846	41.42	18
1847	44.28	7
1848	43.56	13
1849	40.00	3

Source: Database

APPENDIX 6

Allotment Rent

Table 21
Mean rent by quinquennium, 1830–49

Year	Rent (s.)	No. of records
1830–4	41.36	241 records
1835–9	43.54	22 records
1840–4	49.53	60 records
1845–9	58.44	32 records

Source: Database

Table 22
Mean rent by region, 1830–49

Region	Rent (s.)	No. of records
South-west	48.73	129
South	37.12	54
East Anglia	35.43	72
South Midlands	32.50	26
West Midlands	53.63	36
East Midlands	60.50	24
Welsh borders	32.25	4
North	57.13	10

Source: Database

Table 23
Mean rent by region, 1850–73

Region	Rent (s.)	No. of records
South-west	48.50	72
South	62.78	14
East Anglia	46.79	16
South Midlands	52.13	36
West Midlands	62.45	26
East Midlands	37.67	6
Welsh borders	115.99	1
North	41.18	22

Source: Database

Table 24
Mean rent by county

County	Period	Rent (s.)	No. of records
Somerset	1830–49	46.34	24
Dorset	1830–49	47.15	20
	1850–73	55.61	41
Wiltshire	1830–49	50.23	56
Gloucestershire	1830–49	49.09	26
	1850–73	43.93	20
Hampshire	1830–49	31.09	13
Berkshire	1830–49	47.69	13
Sussex	1830–49	29.60	10
Essex	1830–49	54.27	17
Cambridgeshire	1830–49	29.57	14
Suffolk	1830–49	31.58	15
Lincolnshire	1830–49	25.10	13
Hertfordshire	1830–49	28.93	10
Worcestershire	1830–49	54.76	12
	1850–73	67.63	15
Warwickshire	1830–49	53.00	13
Staffordshire	1830–49	53.14	11
	1850–73	56.93	10
Nottinghamshire	1830–49	56.00	12

Source: Database

Note: Only for a few counties does the database contain sufficient records to make it worth disaggregating the data to this level.

257

Table 25
Mean rent: publicly and privately let sites

Period	Landlord	Rent (s.)	No. of records
1830–49	public	27.20	31
	private	49.10	211
1850–73	public	23.11	14
	private	53.32	179

Source: Database

APPENDIX 7

Animal-Keeping on Allotments

Whilst animals were very rarely actually reared on the allotment plot itself, they could be fed from the products of the allotment. Many animals were, it is true, unsuitable. For example, the economic value and the food-producing capacity of sheep and goats were too low ever to make them attractive to allotment-holders. Horses and even ponies were expensive to buy and to feed, although sometimes labourers with allotments bought ponies and used them either to run a carrying service, or let them out to other allotment-holders for carting or even ploughing. Bearing in mind the difficulties allotment-holders often had in getting farmers to plough or cart for them, and the expense this often entailed, letting out a pony in this way could be a profitable business where allotments were large.[1]

It was not possible for labourers to keep a cow on an allotment, nor to use the produce of an allotment as fodder for a cow. Even if the cow was entirely stall-fed, a minimum of about three acres of land would be needed. Most allotments were of about a quarter of an acre, and they were very rarely of more than an acre. Providing labourers with cow pastures required a much greater acreage, and tended only to occur on the estates of great landowners, almost exclusively in the north, where land was more plentiful.

Poultry seem to have been kept by some labourers, but there is no indication that this was on a large scale. Neither eggs nor poultry itself seem to have featured largely in the diets of labourers in the mid-nineteenth century, despite the fact that some of the crops grown on allotments, particularly barley, were well suited to poultry-feeding. It is possible that poultry simply took too much feeding to be economically viable from the labourer's point of view.

By far the most important animal to the labourer was, of course, the pig. Without an allotment or large garden, pig-keeping was expensive, perhaps prohibitively so, because of the cost of feed. But with an allotment, large quantities of beans, barley, peas or turnips could be grown for the pig, whilst the pig would also dispose of the waste from the allotment, such as bad potatoes and wheat, the outer leaves of cabbages, and so forth. The pig could also be given the straw from corn crops, again otherwise useless, and, mixed with the pig's dung, providing large amounts of free manure. Allotment cultivation was far more intensive than farm cultivation, using extremely exhausting rotations such as wheat and potatoes in alternation. The system depended to

---

1 G. E. Evans, *Ask the fellows who cut the hay*, London 1965, 116–17.

some extent on thorough digging and high standards of weeding and hoeing, but above all on heavy manuring. Without the pig to act as a manure-producing engine, a severe limitation would have been placed on the capacity of the allotment to achieve high yields. In this way, pig and allotment formed a complementary system.

Quite aside from its vital role in maintaining soil fertility, the pig had, of course, a very significant economic value of its own. On an allotment of half an acre at Rodmarton in Gloucestershire in 1844, the total value of the produce and the labourer's pigs was £21 4s. Of this, the produce made up only £8; the remaining £13 4s. was attributable to a sow (value £2), four pigs sold young (value £2 4s.) and two fatted pigs (value £9).[2]

The psychological importance of the pig was every bit as great as its economic importance (although the two were inextricably interconnected). The pig, as we know from numerous autobiographical accounts, most famously of course Flora Thompson's *Lark Rise to Candleford*, played a central role in the family life of nineteenth-century rural labourers.[3] Sir Francis Doyle, one of the special assistant poor law commissioners for the 1843 inquiry into women and children's employment in agriculture, had this to say about the importance of the pig, and its essential connection with the allotment:

> Of . . . [the labourer's] pig, the first product of allotment, garden, or potato-land, it is the fashion among political economists to speak disrespectfully. Now, whatever might be the superior profit to the cottager of saving the money which he spends upon his pigs, and buying his bacon in the market, this, as it never has been and never will be so saved, we may dismiss. In the meantime, his pig, besides its usefulness, is also a real pleasure to him – it is one of his principal interests in life – he makes sacrifices to it; he exercises self-control for its sake; it prevents him living from hand to mouth, stupidly careless of the future. I am persuaded that a greater act of cruelty could hardly be perpetrated than the discountenancing this practice, or rather amusement and enjoyment, among the poor.[4]

A similar view was taken by Samuel Sevill, who made a brief study of allotments in the Stroud area for the 1840 Royal Commission on the Handloom Weavers. Sevill observed that the pig was 'the poor man's best friend. I have often observed that nothing contributes so much towards smiling happy countenances in a cottage family as a pig in their stye; the pig becomes their household god whilst alive, and their sheet-anchor when dead'.[5]

---

[2] *LFM* clvii (1844), 55.
[3] Thompson, *Lark Rise*, 24–7. See also Robert Malcolmson and Stephanos Mastoris, *The English pig: a history*, London 1998, esp. pp. 51–6.
[4] *Report on the Employment of Women and Children in Agriculture*, 1843, xii. 294–5.
[5] *RC on the Handloom Weavers*, 1840, xxiv. 552.

APPENDIX 8

*Allotment Site Rules**

Rule	Frequency (no. of sites)
No underletting	27
Spade husbandry only	27
Good cultivation	20[a]
Cropping restrictions	18[b]
Criminal conviction ends tenancy	17[c]
No trespass on other's plots	17
No work on Sundays	17[d]
Maintaining fences, etc.	17
No theft	16
Breach of rules ends tenancy	15
Failure to pay rent ends tenancy	14[e]
Disputes between tenants	11
No drunkenness	10
Sunday worship	8
No daytime working on plots	8
Prevent depredations	7
Good conduct	7
Educate family	7[f]
No poaching	7
Compensation for crops	7
Hiring assistance	5[g]
Restrictions on animals	3
Theft from allotments	3
Swearing	3
Restrictions on other land held	2

Notes:
a. Including eleven requiring adequate manuring
b. Including two forbidding the growing of corn
c. Including one where the tenancy ended only if the tenant was convicted of a felony
d. Three of these allowed gathering
e. Including three where rent had to be paid on the exact day due
f. Including one requiring school attendance
g. One forbade this; the other four specified that only parishioners were to be hired

Rule	Frequency (no. of sites)
No breach of the peace	1
No gross immorality	1
Industry	1
Lose plot if leave parish	1
Use of water supply	1
No buildings	1

* This table lists the rules governing thirty-three mid nineteenth-century allotment sites for which complete rulesheets survive.

Sources: *F&I*, 21–2, 30, 115, 170–1, 188, 279–80, 348–9, 396–8, 400–1, 408–10, 432–3, 499–500; *Useful Hints* xxxiii. 129–30; *SC on the Labouring Poor*, 1843, vii. 1–11, 112, 122, 128, 346, 347; *Report on the Employment of Women and Children in Agriculture*, 1843, xii. 263–4, 271, 273, 332; *RC on the Framework Knitters*, 1845, xv. 531; *Gardener's Chronicle*, 1 Jan. 1845, 27, cols 1–2; 31 May 1845, 372, col. 1; *LF* xi (1845), 200–4; xlvi (1848), 46–7; xlviii (1848), 66–7.

Bibliography

Unpublished primary sources

Gloucester, Gloucestershire Record Office
D1571 Estcourt family papers

London, Greater London Record Office
Peabody Trust, 1830 Housing Society
7/1/617 Labourer's Friend Society, general committee minute book, 1832–9
7/1/618–20, 7/8/621–2, 7/5/623–4 Society for Improving the Condition of the Labouring Classes, general committee minute books, 1844–9, 1849–54, 1854–61, 1862–9, 1869–77, 1877–88, 1888–1905
7/6/226 SICLC – a survey, 1830–1939
7/6/706 Summary of the achievements and objects of the 1830 Housing Society [n.d]
7/6/714 Bundle of twenty letters from various correspondents concerning the annual meeting of the Labourer's Friend Society, 1831
7/6/720–6 Labourer's Friend Society, local committee of the district of Long Acre, reports, June, August, September, October, December 1832, February 1833
7/6/726 Labourer's Friend Society, local committee of the district of Long Acre, Friendly Loan Society rules, 1836
7/6/734 Bundle of miscellaneous letters, 1831–67
7/7/604 Proceedings of the Labourer's Friend Society, 1832
7/9/735 Registry book of the real property of the Society for Improving the Condition of the Labouring Classes, 1850–77
7/11/630–702 Society for Improving the Condition of the Labouring Classes, annual reports, 1850–62/3, 1857–63/4, 1865–6, 1866–7, 1872–1935
7/16/629 Society for Improving the Condition of the Labouring Classes, finance sub-committee, minute book, 1856–7

London, Public Record Office
BT41/136/790 Return of name, business, and promoters of Chartist Land Company
BT41/474/2659 Chartist Land Company broadsheets
HO45/OS2665 Petition from Nottingham members of the National Land Company
MH12/11992/1839 Letters from Walton Kent to the board of guardians of the Stow union and to the poor law commissioners on the allotment system, 6 Feb. 1839

Published primary sources

Official documents and publications (in chronological order)

Report of the Select Committee on the Cultivation and Improvement of the Waste, Uninclosed, and Unproductive Lands of the Kingdom, 1795, ix

Report of the Select Committee on the Poor Laws, 1817, vi

Report of the Select Committee on the Poor Laws, 1818, v

Report of the Select Committee on the Poor Laws, 1818, v

Report of the Select Committee on the Poor Laws, 1819, ii

Report of the Select Committee on Agricultural Labourers' Wages, and the Condition and Morals of Labourers in that Employment, 1824, vi

Abstract of Returns on Labourers' Wages, 1825, xix

Report of the Select Committee on Emigration, 1826, iv

Report of the Select Committee on Emigration, 1826–7, v

Report of the Select Committee on the Relief of Able-bodied Persons from the Poor Rates, 1828, iv

Report of the Select Committee of the House of Lords on the Poor Laws, 1830–1, viii

Report of the Select Committee on Agriculture, 1833, v

Report of the Royal Commission on the Poor Laws, 1834, xxvii–xxxviii

Report of the Select Committee on the Handloom Weavers, 1834, x

Report of the Select Committee on the Causes and Extent of Agricultural Distress, 1836, viii

Report of the Select Committee of the House of Lords on Agriculture, 1837, v

Report of the Royal Commission on the Handloom Weavers, 1840, xxiii

Report of the Special Assistant Poor Law Commissioners on the Employment of Women and Children in Agriculture, 1843, xii

Report of the Select Committee on the Labouring Poor (Allotments of Land), 1843, vii

Report of the Royal Commission on the Framework Knitters, 1845, xv

Report of the Royal Commission on the Employment of Children, Young Persons, and Women in Agriculture, 1867–8, xvii

Report of the Royal Commission on the Employment of Children, Young Persons, and Women in Agriculture, 1868–9, xiii

Report of the Select Committee on the Inclosure Act, 1868–9, x

Agricultural Returns of Great Britain for 1873, 1873, lxix

Return of Number of Allotments and Agricultural Holdings in Great Britain, 1886, lxx

Return of Allotments Detached from and Attached to Cottages, in England and Wales, and Scotland, 1886, 1887, lxxxviii

Newspapers and periodicals

Annals of Agriculture
Blackwood's Magazine
Christian Observer
Contemporary Review
Edinburgh Review
Facts and Illustrations
Farmer's Magazine
Gardener's Chronicle

Journal of the Royal Agricultural Society of England
Journal of the Royal Horticultural Society
Labourer's Friend
Labourer's Friend Magazine
Mark Lane Express
Nineteenth Century
Northern Star
Nottingham Journal
Nottingham Review
Proceedings of the Labourer's Friend Society
Quarterly Review
The Times
Transactions of the Society of Arts, Manufactures, and Commerce
Useful Hints for Labourers

Contemporary books, articles and pamphlets

Allen, W., *Colonies at home*, Lindfield 1827
Anon, letter dated 17 Dec. 1795, *Annals* xxvi (1796), 215
——— *Essays on the principles of charitable institutions*, London 1836
Arch, J., *The autobiography of Joseph Arch*, [1898], London 1966 edn
——— *The story of his life*, London 1898
Ashby, J., and B. King, 'Statistics of some Midlands villages', *Economic Journal* iii
    (1893), 1–22
Bailey, J., *General view of the agriculture of the county of Durham*, London 1810
——— and G. Culley, *General view of the agriculture of Cumberland*, London 1805
——— and G. Culley, *General view of the agriculture of Northumberland*, London
    1805
Baird, T., *General view of the agriculture of the county of Middlesex*, London 1793
Baker, J., *Life of Sir Thomas Bernard*, London 1819
Barclay, R., 'On labourers in husbandry renting land', in Board of Agriculture,
    Communications, I/2: *Cottages*, 91–2
Barton, J., 'Successful industry of a labourer', *JRASE* iv (1843–4), 577–8
Batchelor, T., *General view of the agriculture of the county of Bedford*, London 1808
Bearn, W., 'On the farming of Northamptonshire', *JRASE* xiii (1852–3), 44–113
Billingsley, J., *General view of the agriculture of the county of Somerset*, London 1797
Bishton, J., *General view of the agriculture of the county of Salop*, London 1794
Board of Agriculture, *Report of the committee of the Board of Agriculture concerning
    the cultivation and use of potatoes*, n.d. [c. 1796]
——— *Communications to the Board of Agriculture on subjects relative to the
    husbandry and internal improvement of the country*, I/2: *Cottages*, London 1797
——— *General report on enclosures*, London 1808
——— *The agricultural state of the kingdom*, London 1816
Booth, C., *The aged poor in England and Wales*, London 1894
Boys, J., *General view of the agriculture of the county of Kent*, London 1796
Bray, C., *Essay upon the union of agriculture and manufactures*, London 1844
Brenton, Sir J., *Memoir of Captain Edward Pelham Brenton, RN*, London 1842
Brodrick, G., *English land and English landlords*, London 1881

Brown, T., *General view of the agriculture of the county of Derby*, London 1794

Brownlow, Lord, 'Answers to queries', in Board of Agriculture, *Communications*, I/2: *Cottages*, 85–90

Burn, J. I., *Familiar letters on population*, London 1832

Burne, J. B., *Parson and peasant*, London 1891

Caird, J., *English agriculture in 1850–51*, London 1851

Carrington, earl of, 'The land and the labourers', *Nineteenth Century* xl/265 (1899), 368–77

[Chalmers, T.], 'The report of the Select Committee on the Poor Laws', *Edinburgh Review* lviii (1817–18), 261–301

Claridge, J., *General view of the agriculture of the county of Dorset*, London 1793

Clark, J., *General view of the agriculture of the county of Hereford*, Hereford 1794

Clifford, F., *The agricultural lockout of 1874, with notes upon farming and farm-labour in the eastern counties*, Edinburgh 1875

Cobbett, W., *Cottage economy*, [1822], Oxford 1979 edn

—————— *Rural rides*, [1830], Nelson Classics edn, n.d. n.p.

Copleston, E., *A second letter to the Right Honourable Robert Peel*, Oxford 1819

Crutchley, J., *General view of the agriculture of the county of Rutland*, London 1794

—————— 'Answers to queries', in Board of Agriculture, *Communications*, I/2: *Cottages*, 93–6

Davies, D., *The case of the labourers in husbandry stated and considered*, London 1795

Davies, M., *Life in an English village*, London 1909

Davis, R., *General view of the agriculture of the county of Oxford*, London 1794

Davis, T., *General view of the agriculture of the county of Wiltshire*, London 1794

—————— *General view of the agriculture of the county of Wiltshire*, London 1811

Demainbray, S., *The poor man's best friend, or land to cultivate for his own benefit*, London 1831

Dickson, R. W., *General view of the agriculture of the county of Lancashire*, London 1815

Disraeli, B., *Sybil, or the two nations*, Harmondsworth 1985

Donaldson, J., *General view of the agriculture of the county of Northampton*, London 1794

Driver, A. and W. Driver, *General view of the agriculture of the county of Hampshire*, London 1794

Duncumb, J., *General view of the agriculture of the county of Hereford*, London 1805

Eden, F. M., *The state of the poor*, London 1797

Edwards, E., 'The influence of free trade upon the condition of the labouring classes', *Blackwood's Magazine* xxvii (1830)

Edwards, G., *From crow scaring to Westminster*, London 1922

Ensor, G., *The poor and their relief*, London 1823

Estcourt, T. G. B., *Substance of the charge delivered to the grand jury at the quarter sessions held at Michaelmas 1827 for the county of Wiltshire*, London 1827

Farey, J., *General view of the agriculture of the county of Derby*, London 1811

Felkin, William, *History of the machine-wrought hosiery and lace manufactures*, [1867], Newton Abbot 1967 edn

Foot, P., *General view of the agriculture of the county of Middlesex*, London 1794

Fortescue, Earl, 'Poor men's gardens', *Nineteenth Century* xxiii (1888), 394–402

Fox, J., *General view of the agriculture of the county of Monmouth*, London 1794

Fraser, R., *General view of the agriculture of the county of Devon*, London 1794

Gooch, W., *General view of the agriculture of the county of Cambridge*, London 1811

Gourlay, R., 'An inquiry into the state of cottagers in the counties of Lincoln and Rutland', *Annals* xxxvii (1801), 514–49, 577–99

———— *The village system*, London 1817

Graham, P. A., *The rural exodus*, London 1892

Granville, A. B., *The spas of England, and principal sea-bathing places*, II: *Midland and southern spas*, London 1841

Griffith, T., 'Support of the poor in south Wales', *Annals* xxxv (1800), 5–10

Grigg, Messrs, *General view of the agriculture of the county of Essex*, London 1794

Haggard, H. R., *Rural England*, London 1902

Hall, J., *A plan for the abolition of the present poor rates*, London 1824

Hall, T. H., *The law of allotments*, London 1886

———— *The allotments acts, 1887*, London 1888

Hardy, T., *Far from the madding crowd*, [1874], London 1985 edn

Hassall, C., *General view of the agriculture of the county of Monmouth*, London 1812

Hinton, Revd Dr, 'On land for cottages', *Annals* xxxvi (1801), 265–8

Hodder, E., *The life and works of the seventh earl of Shaftesbury, KG*, London 1886

Hole, J., *The homes of the working classes*, London 1866

Holland, H., *General view of the agriculture of Cheshire*, London 1808

Holt, J., *General view of the agriculture of the county of Lancashire*, London 1794

Howitt, W., *The rural life of England*, London 1840

Jacob, J., 'Crops in Kent', *Annals* xxiv (1800), 601–7

James, W. and J. Malcolm, *General view of the agriculture of the county of Buckingham*, London 1794

———— *General view of the agriculture of the county of Surrey*, London 1794

Jefferies, R., *Hodge and his masters*, London 1890

Jennings, L. J. (ed.), *The Croker papers*, London 1884

Kebbel, T. E., *The agricultural labourer: a short summary of his position*, London 1870, 1887

Kent, N., *Hints to gentlemen of landed property*, London 1775

———— *General view of the agriculture of the county of Norfolk*, London 1796

Labourer's Friend Society, *Proceedings of the Labourer's Friend Society*, London 1832

————, *Cottage husbandry*, London 1835

———— *The labourer's friend: a selection from the publications of the Labourer's Friend Society*, London 1835

Land Enquiry Committee, *The land*, i, ii, London 1913, 1914

Lawrence, C., *Practical directions for the cultivation and general management of cottage gardens*, London 1831

Leatham, I., *General view of the agriculture of the East Riding of Yorkshire, and the ainsty of the city of York*, London 1794

Legard, G., 'On the farming of the East Riding of Yorkshire', *JRASE* ix (1848–9), 85–136

Little, J. Brooke, *The law of allotments*, London 1887, 1895

Lowe, R., *General view of the agriculture of the county of Nottingham*, London 1798

Marriage, J., *Letters on the distressed state of the agricultural labourers*, Chelmsford 1830

Marshall, W., *Reviews and abstract of the county reports to the Board of Agriculture, 1808–17*, London 1808–17

Mavor, W., *General view of the agriculture of the county of Berkshire*, London 1809, 1813 edn

Maxwell, G., *General view of the agriculture of the county of Huntingdon*, London 1793

Mill, J. S., 'The claims of labour: an essay on the duties of the employers to the employed', *Edinburgh Review* clxiv (1845), 498–525

Mitford, M. R., *Our village*, London 1824

Monk, J., *General view of the agriculture of the county of Leicester*, London 1794

Murray, A., *General view of the agriculture of the county of Warwick*, London 1813

Nicholls, G., 'On the condition of the agricultural labourer, with suggestions for its improvement', *JRASE* vii (1846), 1–30

Onslow, earl of, *Landlords and allotments: the history and present condition of the allotment system*, London 1886

Orange, J., *History and antiquities of Nottingham*, London 1840

Owen, R., *A new view of society*, [1813], London 1927 edn

—— *Report to the county of New Lanark*, London 1820

Palin, W., 'The farming of Cheshire', *JRASE* v (1844), 57–111

Parkinson, J., 'Cottagers land – crops in fallow open fields – Asgarby, Lincolnshire', *Annals* xxxvi (1801), 360–3

Parkinson, R., *General view of the agriculture of the county of Rutland*, London 1808

—— *General view of the agriculture of the county of Huntingdon*, London 1811

Parliamentary debates

Pearce, W., *General view of the agriculture of the county of Berkshire*, London 1795

Pitt, W., *General view of the agriculture of the county of Stafford*, London 1794, new edn 1796

—— *General view of the agriculture of the county of Northampton*, London 1809

—— *General view of the agriculture of the county of Worcester*, London 1810

—— *General view of the agriculture of the county of Leicester*, London 1813

Plymley, J., *General view of the agriculture of the county of Shropshire*, 2nd edn, London 1803

Priest, Revd St John, *General view of the agriculture of the county of Buckingham*, London 1813

Pringle, A., *General view of the agriculture of the county of Westmoreland*, London 1805

Pulteney, W., 'Culture of potatoes', *Annals* xxxvii (1801), 77–86

Rowntree, B. S. and M. Kendall, *How the labourer lives*, London 1913

Rudge, T., *General view of the agriculture of the county of Gloucester*, London 1807, 1813 edn

Ruggles, T., 'Land for the poor: Clare, Suffolk, 15 Dec. 1800', *Annals* xxxvi (1801), 354–5

Scott, Joseph, 'Crops, markets, poor: Chatteris, 30 Dec. 1899', *Annals* xxxvi (1801), 377–8

Skinner, J., *Journal of a Somerset rector, 1803–34*, Bath 1971

Society for Bettering the Conditions and Increasing the Comforts of the Poor, *Reports*, i–vii, London 1797–1818

Somerville, A., *Autobiography of a working man*, London 1848

Spearing, J. B., 'On the agriculture of Berkshire', *JRASE* xxi (1860), 1–46

Stevenson, W., *General view of the agriculture of the county of Surrey*, London 1809

———— *General view of the agriculture of the county of Dorset*, London 1812

Stone, T., *General view of the agriculture of the county of Huntingdon*, London 1793

———— *General view of the agriculture of the county of Bedford*, London 1794

———— *General view of the agriculture of the county of Lincoln*, London 1794

———— *A review of the corrected agricultural survey of Lincolnshire*, by Arthur Young, London 1800

Strickland, H. E., *General view of the agriculture of the East Riding of Yorkshire*, London 1812

Stubbs, C. W., *The land and the labourers: a record of facts and experiments in cottage farming and co-operative agriculture*, 2nd edn, London 1885

Sturt, G., *Change in the village*, London 1912

———— *William Smith, potter and farmer, 1790–1858*, London 1920

Sussex Association for Improving the Condition of the Labouring Classes, *Quarterly report, number one*, Lindfield 1831

Thornton, W. T., *Overpopulation and its remedy*, London 1846

Tuke, J., *General view of the agriculture of the North Riding of Yorkshire*, London 1794

Turner, G., *General view of the agriculture of the county of Gloucester*, London 1794

Vancouver, C., *General view of the agriculture of the county of Cambridge*, London 1794

———— *General view of the agriculture of the county of Essex*, London 1795

———— *General view of the agriculture of the county of Devon*, London 1808

———— *General view of the agriculture of the county of Hampshire*, London 1810

Verney, Lady F. P., 'Allotments', *Nineteenth Century* xix (1886), 902–13

Walker, D., *General view of the agriculture of the county of Hertford*, London 1795

Wallington Labourer's Friend Society, *Prospectus*, n.d. [c. 1835]

Wedge, T., *General view of the agriculture of the county of Chester*, London 1794

———— *General view of the agriculture of the county of Warwick*, London 1794

Wickens, J., 'Cottage gardens', *Annals* xxxv (1800), 205–8

Wilberforce, R. I. and S. Wilberforce, *Life of William Wilberforce*, London 1838

Wilbraham, G., 'System in which potatoes are rendered beneficial to the poor in Cheshire', *Annals* xxxv (1800), 11–14

Wilkinson, J. F., 'Pages in the history of allotments', *Contemporary Review*, lxv/340 (1894), 532–44

Willis, J., 'On cows for cottagers', *Annals* xl (1803), 544–63

Worgan, G. B., *General view of the agriculture of the county of Cornwall*, London 1811

Wylie, W., *Old and new Nottingham*, London 1853

Young, A., *A farmer's letters to the people of England*, London 1767

———— *Observations on the present state of the waste lands of Great Britain*, London 1773

———— 'A farming tour to the south and west of England, London 1796', *Annals* xxviii (1797), 113–28, 225–40, 353–79, 460–83, 620–40

———— *General view of the agriculture of the county of Suffolk*, London 1797

———— *General view of the agriculture of the county of Lincoln*, London 1799

———— *The question of scarcity plainly stated, and remedies considered, with observations on permanent measures to keep wheat at a more regular price*, London 1800

———— *General view of the agriculture of the county of Hertford*, London 1804

—————— *General view of the agriculture of the county of Norfolk*, London 1804

—————— *General view of the agriculture of the county of Essex*, London 1807

—————— *General view of the agriculture of Oxfordshire*, London 1813

—————— *Autobiography*, ed. M. Betham-Edwards, London 1898

Young, Revd A., *General view of the agriculture of the county of Sussex*, London 1793

—————— *General view of the agriculture of the county of Sussex*, London 1808

Secondary sources

Afton, B. and M. Turner, 'The statistical base of agricultural performance in England and Wales, 1850–1914', in E. J. T. Collins (ed.), *The agrarian history of England and Wales*, VII/2: *1850–1914*, Cambridge 2000, 1955–92

Allison, K. J., 'The provision of allotment gardens in East Yorkshire', *Northern History* xxxvii (2000), 275–92

Archer, J. E., *By a flash and a scare: incendiarism, animal maiming and poaching in East Anglia, 1815–70*, Oxford 1990

—————— 'The nineteenth-century allotment: half an acre and a row', *EcHR* 2nd ser. l (1997), 21–36

Armstrong, W. A., 'The influence of demographic factors on the position of the agricultural labourer in England and Wales, c. 1750–1914', *AgHR* xxix (1981), 71–82

—————— *Farmworkers: a social and economic history, 1770–1980*, London 1988

—————— 'Rural population growth, systems of employment, and incomes', in Mingay, *Agrarian history of England and Wales*, vi. 641–728

—————— and J. P. Huzel, 'Food, shelter and self-help, the poor law and the position of the labourer in rural society', in Mingay, *Agrarian history of England and Wales*, vi. 729–835

Ashby, A. W., *Allotments and small holdings in Oxfordshire*, Oxford 1917

Ashby, M. K., *Joseph Ashby of Tysoe, 1859–1919*, Cambridge 1961

—————— *The changing English village*, Kineton 1974

Baker, M., 'Aspects of the life of the Wiltshire agricultural labourer, c. 1850', *Wiltshire Archaeological Magazine* (1981), 74–5

Barnett, D. C., 'Allotments and the problem of rural poverty, 1780–1840', in E. L. Jones and G. E. Mingay (eds), *Land, labour, and population in the industrial revolution: essays presented to J. D. Chambers*, London 1967, 162–83

Beckett, J. V., 'The disappearance of the cottager and the squatter from the English countryside: the Hammonds revisited', in Holderness and Turner, *Land, labour, and agriculture*, 49–68

Bennett, E. N., *Problems of village life*, London 1914

Benson, J. (ed.), *The working class in England, 1875–1914*, London 1983

Bensusan, S. L., *Latter-day rural England 1927*, London 1927

Bowley, A. L. and B. S. Burnett-Hurst, *Livelihood and poverty*, London 1915

Boyer, G., *An economic history of the English poor law, 1750–1850*, Cambridge 1990

Briggs, Asa (ed.), *Chartist studies*, London 1967

Bronstein, J. L., *Land reform and working-class experience in Britain and the United States 1800–1862*, Stanford, CA 1999

Burchardt, J. F. S., 'Rural social relations, 1830–50: opposition to allotments for labourers', *AgHR* xlv/2 (1997), 165–75

———— 'Land, labour and politics: parliament and allotment provision, 1830–1870', in J. R. Wordie (ed.), *Agriculture and politics in England, 1815–1939*, London 2000, 98–127

———— 'Land and the laborer: potato grounds and allotments in nineteenth-century southern England', *Agricultural History* lxxiv/2 (2000), 667–84

Burn, W. L., *The age of equipoise*, London 1968

Burnett, J., *Plenty and want: a social history of diet in England from 1815 to the present day*, London 1966

Bythell, D., *The handloom weavers: a study in the English cotton industry during the industrial revolution*, Cambridge 1969

Chambers, J. D., 'Enclosure and labour supply in the industrial revolution', *EcHR* 2nd ser. v (1953), 319–43

———— *Population, economy, and society in pre-industrial England*, London 1972

———— and G. E. Mingay, *The agricultural revolution, 1750–1880*, London 1966

Charlesworth, A., *An atlas of rural protest in Britain, 1548–1900*, London 1983

———— 'An agenda for historical studies of rural protest in Britain, 1750–1850', *Rural History* ii (1990), 231–40

———— 'The spatial diffusion of riots: popular disturbances in England and Wales, 1750–1850', *Rural History* v (1994), 1–22

Chase, M., *The people's farm: English radical agrarianism, 1775–1840*, Oxford 1988

———— ' "We wish only to work for ourselves": the Chartist land plan', in M. Chase and I. Dyck (eds), *Learning and living: essays in honour of J. F. C. Harrison*, Aldershot 1996

Checkland, S., *British public policy*, London 1985

Christie, I. R., *Wars and revolutions: Britain 1760–1815*, London 1982

Church, R. A., 'James Orange and the allotment system in Nottingham', *Transactions of the Thoroton Society of Nottingham* (1960), 74–80

Clapham, J. H., *An economic history of modern Britain, I: The early railway age, 1820–50*, [1926], Cambridge 1939 edn

Clark, G. Kitson, *Churchmen and the condition of England, 1832–85*, London 1973

Clemenson, H., *English country houses and landed estates*, London 1982

Collins, E. J. T., 'Harvest technology and labour supply in Britain, 1790–1870', *EcHR* 2nd ser. xxii (1969), 453–73

———— 'Dietary change and cereal consumption in the nineteenth century', *AgHR* xxiii (1975), 97–115

———— 'Migrant labour in British agriculture in the nineteenth century', *EcHR* 2nd ser. xxix (1976), 38–59

———— Introduction to chapter v, 'The agricultural servicing and processing industries', in Mingay, *Agrarian history of England and Wales*, vi. 384–6

Crafts, N. F. R., *British economic growth during the industrial revolution*, London 1985

Crouch, D. and C. Ward, *The allotment: its landscape and culture*, London 1988

Cunningham, Hugh, 'Leisure and culture', in Thompson, *Cambridge social history of Britain*, ii. 279–340

Daunton, M., *Progress and poverty*, Oxford 1995

Denman, D. R. and V. F. Stewart, *Farm rents: a comparison of current and past farm rents in England and Wales*, London 1959

Digby, A., 'Social institutions', in E. J. T. Collins (ed.), *The agrarian history of England and Wales*, VII/1: *1850–1914*, Cambridge 2000, 1465–1500

Donajgrodzki, A. P., 'Twentieth-century rural England: a case for "peasant studies"?', *Journal of Peasant Studies* xvi/3 (1989), 425–42

Douglas, R., *Land, people, and politics*, London 1976

Dunbabin, J. P. D., 'Labourers and farmers in the late nineteenth century', *Bulletin of the Society for the Study of Labour History* xi (1965), 6–9

—— (ed.), *Rural discontent in nineteenth-century Britain*, London 1974

Evans, E. J., 'Some reasons for the growth of rural anti-clericalism, *c*. 1750–*c*. 1830', *Past and Present* lxvi (1975), 84–109

Evans, G. E., *Ask the fellows who cut the hay*, London 1956, 1965 edn

—— *Where beards wag all*, London 1970

Everitt, A., 'Country carriers in the nineteenth century', *Journal of Transport History* 2nd ser. iii (1976), 179–202

Fay, C. R. and H. C. Fay, *The allotment movement in England and Wales*, London 1942

Fitzgerald, R., *British labour management and industrial welfare*, Beckenham 1988

Freeman, M., 'The agricultural labourer and the "Hodge" stereotype, *c*. 1850–1914', *AgHR*, xlix (2001), 172–86

Fussell, G. E., *The English rural labourer*, London 1949

—— *The English dairy farmer, 1500–1900*, London 1966

—— and K. R. Fussell, *The English countryman*, London 1955, 1981 edn

Gash, N., 'Rural unemployment, 1815–34', *EcHR* vi (1935), 90–3

Ginter, D. E., 'Measuring the decline of the small landowner', in Holderness and Turner, *Land, labour, and agriculture*, 27–48

Girouard, M., 'Victorian values and the upper classes', in T. C. Smout (ed.), *Victorian values*, Oxford 1992, 49–60

Goddard, N., 'The development and influence of agricultural periodicals and newspapers, 1780–1870', *AgHR* xxxi (1963), 116–31

—— 'Agricultural literature and societies', in Mingay, *Agrarian history of England and Wales*, vi. 361–83

—— 'Information and innovation in early-Victorian farming systems', in Holderness and Turner, *Land, labour, and agriculture*, 165–90

Gosden, P. H. J. H., *The friendly societies in England, 1815–75*, London 1961

Gould, P. C., *Early Green politics: back to nature, back to the land, and socialism in Britain, 1880–1900*, Brighton 1988

Green, F. E., 'The allotment movement', *Contemporary Review* cxiv (1918), 90–6

—— *A history of the English agricultural labourer, 1870–1920*, London 1920

Groves, R., *Sharpen the sickle!*, London 1949

Hadfield, Alice, *The Chartist Land Company*, Newton Abbot 1970

Hall, A., 'Fenland worker-peasants: the economy of smallholders at Rippingale, Lincolnshire, 1791–1871', *AgHR* supplement ser. i (1992), 1–61

Hammond, J. L. and B. Hammond, *The village labourer, 1760–1832*, London 1911, 4th edn, London 1927

Haresign, S. R., 'Small farms and allotments as a cure for rural depopulation on the Lincolnshire fenland, 1870–1914', *Lincolnshire History and Archaeology* xviii (1983), 27–36

Harrison, J. F. C., 'Chartism in Leicester', in Briggs, *Chartist studies*, 99–146

Hasbach, W., *A history of the English agricultural labourer*, London 1908

Havinden, M. A., *Estate villages: a study of the Berkshire villages of Ardington and Lockhinge*, London 1966

Hennell, M., *John Venn and the Clapham sect*, London 1958

Hilton, B., *The age of atonement: the influence of evangelicalism on social and economic thought, 1785–1865*, Oxford 1988

Hobbs, P., *Somerford Magna*, Gloucester 1982

Hobsbawm, E. and G. Rudé, *Captain Swing*, London 1970

Holderness, B. A., 'Prices, productivity, and output', in Mingay, *Agrarian history of England and Wales*, vi. 84–189

— and M. Turner, *Land, labour, and agriculture, 1700–1920: essays for Gordon Mingay*, London 1991

Horn, P., *Joseph Arch*, Kineton 1971

——— *The Victorian country child*, Kineton 1974

——— 'Agricultural trade unionism in Oxfordshire', in Dunbabin, *Rural discontent*, 85–129

——— *Labouring life in the Victorian countryside*, Dublin 1976

——— *The rural world, 1780–1850*, London 1980

——— *Victorian countrywomen*, Oxford 1991

Hoskins, W. G., *The Midland peasant*, London 1957

Howkins, A., *Poor labouring men*, London 1985

——— 'Labour history and the rural poor, 1850–1980', *Rural History* i (1990), 113–22

——— *Reshaping rural England, 1850–1925*, London 1991

——— 'Peasants, servants and labourers: the marginal workforce in British agriculture, c. 1870–1914', *AgHR* xlii/1 (1994), 49–62

Hueckel, G., 'War and the British economy, 1793–1815: a general equilibrium analysis', *Explorations in Economic History* x (1972–3), 365–96

——— 'English farming profits during the Napoleonic wars, 1793–1815', *Explorations in Economic History* xiii (1976), 331–45

Humphries, J., 'Enclosures, common rights, and women: the proletarianization of families in the late eighteenth and early nineteenth centuries', *Journal of Economic History* i (1990), 17–42

Hunt, E. H., 'Labour productivity in English agriculture, 1850–1914', *EcHR* 2nd ser. xx (1967), 280–92

——— and S. J. Pam, 'Essex agriculture in the "golden age", 1850–73', *AgHR* xliii (1995), 160–77

Huxley, A., *An illustrated history of gardening*, London 1978

Hyams, E., *English cottage gardens*, London 1970

Jebb, L., *Smallholdings*, London 1901

Jenkins, G., *The craft industries*, London 1972

John, A. H., 'Statistical appendix', in Mingay, *Agrarian history of England and Wales*, vi. 972–1155

Johnson, A. H., *The disappearance of the small landowner*, London 1909

Jones, D., 'Thomas Campbell Foster and the rural labourer: incendiarism in East Anglia in the 1840s', *Social History* i (1976), 5–43

——— 'Rural crime and protest', in Mingay, *Victorian countryside*, ii. 566–79

——— *Crime, protest, and the police in nineteenth-century Britain*, London 1982

Jones, E. L., 'The agricultural labour market in England, 1793–1872', *EcHR* 2nd ser. xvii (1964), 322–8

Joyce, P., *Work, society and politics: the culture of the factory in later Victorian England*, Hassocks 1980

Kain, R. J. P. and H. C. Prince, *The tithe surveys of England and Wales*, Cambridge 1985

Kitchen, F., *Brother to the ox*, London 1940

────── *Life on the land*, London 1941

Kussmaul, A. S. *Servants in husbandry in early modern England*, Cambridge 1981

Landau, N., 'The laws of settlement and the surveillance of immigration in eighteenth-century Kent', *Continuity and Change* iii (1988), 391–420

────── 'Who was subjected to the laws of settlement? Procedure under the settlement laws in eighteenth-century England', *AgHR* xliii (1995), 139–59

Levy, H., *Large and small holdings: a study of agricultural economics*, Cambridge 1911

Leyland, N. L. and J. E. Troughton, *Glovemaking in West Oxfordshire*, Oxford 1974

Lister, R. P., *Allotments*, Cambridge 1991

MacAskill, Joy, 'The Chartist land plan', in Briggs, *Chartist studies*, 304–41

Macfarlane, A., *The origins of English individualism*, Oxford 1978

McIntosh, T. P., *The potato: its history, varieties, culture and diseases*, London 1927

Malcolmson, R. W., *Popular recreations in English society, 1700–1850*, Cambridge 1973

────── 'Leisure', in Mingay, *Victorian countryside*, ii. 603–15

────── and Stephanos Mastoris, *The English pig: a history*, London 1998

Mandler, P., *Aristocratic government in the age of reform*, Oxford 1990

Marlow, J., *The Tolpuddle martyrs*, London 1971

Martin, D., 'Land reform', in P. Hollis (ed.), *Pressure from without in early Victorian England*, London 1974, 131–58

Martin, E. W., *The secret people*, London 1954

Martins, S. W., *A great estate at work: the Holkham estate and its inhabitants in the nineteenth century*, Cambridge 1980

Mills, D., 'The peasant tradition', *Local History* xi/4 (1974), 200–6

────── *Lord and peasant in nineteenth-century Britain*, London 1980

────── 'Peasants and conflict in nineteenth-century rural England: a comment on two recent articles', *Journal of Peasant Studies* xv/3 (1988), 395–400

Minchinton, W. E. (ed.), *Essays in agrarian history*, Newton Abbot 1968

Mingay, G. E., *The gentry: the rise and fall of a ruling class*, London 1976

────── *Rural life in Victorian England*, London 1977

────── 'Conclusion: the progress of agriculture, 1750–1850', in Mingay, *Agrarian history of England and Wales*, vi. 938–71

────── *The unquiet countryside*, London 1989

────── *A social history of the English countryside*, London 1990

────── 'Agricultural taxation', in E. J. T. Collins (ed.), *The agrarian history of England and Wales*, VII/1: *1850–1914*, Cambridge 2000, 936–44

────── (ed.), *The Victorian countryside*, London 1981

────── (ed.), *The agrarian history of England and Wales*, VI: *1750–1850*, Cambridge 1989

Mitchell, E. L., *The law of allotments*, 3rd edn, London 1926

Mitchison, R., *Agricultural Sir John: the life of Sir John Sinclair of Ulster, 1754–1835*, London 1962

Morgan, D. H., *Harvesters and harvesting, 1840–1900*, London 1982

Morgan, R., 'Root crops', in Mingay, *Agrarian history of England and Wales*, vi. 296–304

Moselle, B., 'Allotments, enclosure, and proletarianization in early nineteenth-century southern England', *EcHR* 2nd ser. xlviii (1995), 482–500

Mutch, A., 'The "farming ladder" in north Lancashire, 1840–1914: myth or reality?', *Northern History* xxvii (1991), 162–83

Neeson, J. M., *Commoners: common right, enclosure and social change in England, 1700–1820*, Cambridge 1993

Newby, H., *The deferential worker*, London 1977

Noiriel, G., *Longwy – immigrés et prolétaires, 1880–1980*, Paris 1984

Nottingham University Manuscripts Department, *Working-class unrest in Nottingham 1800–50, IV: Chartism*, teaching pack, Nottingham 1965

O'Neill, J., 'Self-help in Nottinghamshire: the Woodborough Male Friendly Society, 1826–1954', *Transactions of the Thoroton Society of Nottinghamshire* xc (1986), 57–63

Olney, R. J., *Lincolnshire politics, 1832–85*, Oxford 1973

Orwin, C. S. and E. H. Whetham, *History of British agriculture, 1846–1914*, London 1964

Overton, M., *Agricultural revolution in England: the transformation of the agrarian economy, 1500–1850*, Cambridge 1996

Patterson, A. Temple, *Radical Leicester: a history of Leicester, 1780–1850*, Leicester 1954

Peacock, A. J., *Bread or blood: a study of the agrarian riots in East Anglia in 1816*, London 1965

Pelling, H., *Popular politics and society in late Victorian Britain*, London 1968

Perkin, H., *The origins of modern English society, 1780–1880*, London 1969

Perkins, J. A., 'Allotments in nineteenth-century Lincolnshire', *Lincolnshire History and Archaeology* xviii (1983), 21–5

Pinchbeck, I., *Women workers and the industrial revolution, 1750–1850*, London 1930

Plummer, A., 'Spade husbandry during the industrial revolution', *Journal of the South-West Essex Technical College and School of Art* i (1942), 84–96

Porter, J. H., 'The development of rural society', in Mingay, *Agrarian history of England and Wales*, vi. 836–65

Poynter, J. R., *Society and pauperism: English ideas on poor relief, 1795–1834*, London 1969

Pugh, R. B., 'Chartism in Somerset and Wiltshire', in Briggs, *Chartist studies*, 174–219

Randall, A. and E. Newman, 'Protest, proletarians and paternalists: social conflict in rural Wiltshire, 1830–50', *Rural History* vi (1995), 205–8

Rawding, C., 'Society and place in nineteenth-century Lincolnshire', *Rural History* iii (1992), 59–85

Reay, B., *The last rising of the agricultural labourers: rural life and protest in nineteenth-century England*, Oxford 1990

Redford, A., *Labour migration in England, 1800–50*, London 1926

Reed, M., 'The peasantry of nineteenth-century rural England: a neglected class?', *History Workshop* xviii (1984), 53–76

———— 'Nineteenth-century rural England: a case for "peasant studies"?', *Journal of Peasant Studies* xiv/1 (1986), 78–99

———— 'Gnawing it out: a new look at economic relations in nineteenth-century rural England', *Rural History* i (1990), 83–94

Richardson, T. L., 'Agricultural labourers' wages and the cost of living: a contribution to the standard of living debate', in Holderness and Turner, *Land, labour, and agriculture*, 69–90

Roberts, D., *Paternalism in early Victorian England*, London 1979

Rose, M. E., *The English poor law, 1780–1930*, Newton Abbot 1971

Russell, R. C., *The revolt of the field in Lincolnshire*, London 1956

———— *Cottagers and cows, 1800–1892*, London 1987

Salaman, R. N., *The history and social influence of the potato*, Cambridge 1949

Samuel, R. (ed.), *Village life and labour*, London 1975

Saville, J., *Rural depopulation in England and Wales, 1851–1951*, London 1957

Scotland, N., *Methodism and the revolt of the field*, Gloucester 1981

Seeley, E., *Village trade unions in two centuries*, London 1919

Shanin, T., *Defining peasants: essays concerning rural societies, expolary economies, and learning from them in the contemporary world*, Oxford 1990

Shaw-Taylor, L., 'Labourers, cows, common rights and parliamentary enclosure: the evidence of contemporary comment, c. 1760–1810', *Past and Present* clxxi (2001), 95–126

Shewell-Cooper, W. E., *The ABC of vegetable gardening*, London 1948

Slater, G., *The English peasantry and the enclosure of the common fields*, London 1907

Snell, K. D. M., *Annals of the labouring poor: social change and agrarian England, 1660–1900*, Cambridge 1985

———— 'Pauper settlement and the right to poor relief in England and Wales', *Continuity and Change* vi (1991), 375–415

———— 'Agricultural seasonal unemployment, the standard of living, and women's work, 1690–1860', in Pamela Sharpe (ed.), *Women's work: the English experience, 1650–1914*, London 1998

Soloway, R. A., *Prelates and people*, London 1969

Springall, L. M., *Labouring life in Norfolk villages, 1834–1914*, London 1936

Thirsk, J., *English peasant farming*, London 1957

Thompson, E. P., *The making of the English working class*, London 1963, London 1980 edn

———— 'Patrician society, plebeian culture', *Journal of Social History* vii (1974), 382–403

———— 'Time, work-discipline and industrial capitalism', in E. P. Thompson (ed.), *Customs in common*, London 1991, 352–403

Thompson, F., *Lark Rise to Candleford*, [1945], London 1973 edn

Thompson, F. M. L., *English landed society in the nineteenth century*, London 1963, 1971

———— *The rise of respectable society: a social history of Victorian Britain, 1830–1900*, London 1988

———— *The Cambridge social history of Britain, 1750–1850*, II: *People and their environment*, Cambridge 1990

Turner, M., *Enclosures in Britain, 1750–1830*, London 1984

Turner, M. E., J. V. Beckett and B. Afton, *Agricultural rent in England, 1690–1914*, Cambridge 1997

Valentine, A., *The British establishment, 1760–1784*, Oklahoma 1970

Walvin, J., *Victorian values*, London 1987

Wells, R., *Wretched faces: famine in wartime England, 1793–1803*, Gloucester 1988

Wordie, J. R., 'The chronology of English enclosure, 1500–1914', *EcHR* 2nd ser. xxxvi (1983), 483–505

Wrigley, E. A., and R. S. Schofield, *The population history of England, 1541–1871: a reconstruction*, London 1981

Wyncoll, P., *Nottingham Chartism: Nottingham workers in revolt during the nineteenth century*, Nottingham 1967

Young, G. M., *Portrait of an age*, London 1936, Oxford 1977 edn

Unpublished works

Barnett, D. C., 'Ideas on social welfare 1780–1834, with special reference to friendly societies and allotment schemes', MA diss. Nottingham 1961

Burchardt, J. F. S., 'The allotment movement in England, 1793–1873', PhD diss. Reading 1997

Haresign, S. R., 'Agricultural change and rural society in the Lincolnshire fenlands and the Isle of Axholme, 1870–1914', PhD diss. East Anglia 1980

Horn, P., 'Agricultural labourers' trade unionism in four Midland counties (1860–1900) (Leicestershire, Northamptonshire, Oxfordshire and Warwickshire)', PhD diss. Leicester 1968

Martin, D., 'Economic and social attitudes to landed property in England, 1790–1850, with particular reference to J. S. Mill', PhD diss. Hull 1972

Moran, D. M., 'The origin and status of the allotment movement in Britain, with particular reference to Swindon, Wiltshire', PhD diss. Oregon 1976

Morgan, R., 'The root crop in English agriculture, 1650–1870', PhD diss. Reading 1978

Rowton, J., 'Rented gardens in Birmingham 1823–1837', undergraduate diss. Birmingham 1975

Shaw-Taylor, L., 'Did labourers have common right?', unpubl. paper, British Agricultural History Society spring conference, London 1999

Index

Lightning Source UK Ltd.
Milton Keynes UK

177762UK00001B/26/P